LAND OF MANY FRONTIERS

LAND OF MANY FRONTIERS

A HISTORY OF THE AMERICAN SOUTHWEST

Odie B. Faulk

NEW YORK

OXFORD UNIVERSITY PRESS

1968

FOR LAURA

PREFACE

The Southwest has a long history, for Spanish explorers were crossing the region less than four decades after Columbus discovered America, many decades before the east coast of the United States was opened. The Spanish empire had planted permanent outposts here well before Jamestown and Plymouth Bay were colonized. Yet the Southwest has only recently been developed. Just one century ago only a few hardy pioneers inhabited West Texas, while Arizona boasted not a single school, jail, courthouse, stageline, or clergyman. The Southwest contains great geographical contrasts, from barren deserts to lofty mountains, from swift-flowing rivers to arid stretches, from endless varieties of cacti to aspens and towering pines. The area is still a land of many frontiers.

The Southwest has a proud legacy. Its original inhabitants, the Indian tribes, still survive; and the Spanish heritage of *conquistadores* and missionaries can be detected in place names, architecture, food, music, dress—even in methods of handling cattle, extracting metals, and irrigating farms. There are Mexican, French, English, and distinctly American elements as well. Above all, the region has unlimited sunshine and great open spaces where a man can stretch out and feel at one with his surroundings. It is my hope that, in the pages that follow, the reader will sense the excitement of this land,

and will see it as both General William T. Sherman, who hated it, and William S. Oury, who loved it, saw it; for it is a land both to love and to hate, one that defines a man's strengths and his weaknesses.

In the writing of this work I have received help and advice from a number of people. Professors David M. Vigness, Seymour V. Connor, and Ernest Wallace, all of Texas Technological College, early challenged me in this area, and many of the concepts here I borrowed from them. I discussed the book on many occasions with Professor John Alexander Carroll, of the University of Arizona, and have benefited greatly from his suggestions. Professor W. Eugene Hollon, now at the University of Toledo, gave generously of his wide knowledge of the Southwest, as did Dr. Billy Mac Jones, head of the Department of History at Angelo State College. Professor Michael Thurman, of Southern Methodist University, kindly read portions of the manuscript, and I am indebted to him for his knowledgeable comments. The directors of numerous libraries and historical societies, and particularly the staff of the Arizona Pioneers' Historical Society, generously made available their time and their collections.

Beyond these many scholars and librarians, I owe much to the editors of Oxford University Press, especially to Mr. Sheldon Meyer. Finally, my dedication of this book to my wife reflects only a small portion of my thanks to her for years of help and encouragement.

ODIE B. FAULK

Arizona Western College
January 1968

CONTENTS

LAND OF MANY FRONTIERS

1

INTRODUCTION

What distinguishes the Southwest as a region? Other parts of the United States have deserts, mountains, and plains; these are not unique to it. Some parts of the Southwest even receive large amounts of precipitation. Yet the overriding geographic feature of the Southwest *is* aridity. The economy of the region, the outlook of individuals, and the philosophy of the state governments are based on the limited availability of water and the fight to secure more of it. Its economy is based on ranching, farming, and mining. Its cultural heritage derives from a Spanish, Indian, and American past. Finally, everything is big in the Southwest—big mountains, big deserts, big lava beds, big droughts, and, when it does rain, big floods. It is nature on a grand scale, which has forced its settlers to think in terms of large, rapid changes in order to survive. The Southwesterner has had great pride in his accomplishments, and in fact the bragging Texan—long an object of national humor—is far

3

more Southwestern in his overbearing pride than he is a Southerner looking to the past.

These factors of aridity, Spanish-Indian influence, farming-ranching-mining industry, and an expansive attitude appear dominant in West Texas, New Mexico, Arizona, and Southern California, with the addition of a portion of southern Nevada, Utah, and Colorado. If a semicircle were drawn from Santa Barbara, California, to Corpus Christi, Texas, the Southwest would lie between that line and the Mexican border. Obviously this is an arbitrary line and not precisely accurate; but drive from Abilene, Texas, to San Diego, California, and you pass through the heart of the Southwest. You will notice more similarities than differences along this route, and together they will add up to something that tourist agencies would label the "atmosphere" of the Southwest.

2

THE SPANISH ERA

1519–1821

THE GOLDEN AGE OF DISCOVERY AND CONQUEST

Álvar Nuñez Cabeza de Vaca hardly resembled a man of destiny on the cold and clear dawn of November 6, 1528, off the coast of Texas. His beard was coarse and matted, his clothing hung in tatters, and he was suffering from exposure, thirst, and near-starvation. Yet he stood at the helm of a crude, flat-bottomed raft containing approximately fifty Spanish *conquistadores*. He alone had sufficient strength to man the tiller. All looked "the perfect figures of death," Cabeza de Vaca later wrote of that morning. Suddenly the booming of surf on a nearby beach roused him, and he instinctively steered toward it. As the craft approached land, a huge wave suddenly threw it several feet into the air. The violent shock when it hit the water again awakened the sleeping members of the party, who, seeing land nearby, flopped overboard and swam ashore. The barge was safely beached, and the stronger members of the troop quickly gathered wood, kindled a fire, and cooked the meager remains of their store of food. Their landing on Texas soil marked the true beginning of Southwestern history.

These men were survivors of the expedition led by Pánfilo de Narváez into Tampa Bay in Florida in February 1528. From there they had moved northward in search of treasure, but found only hostile Indians. The ships that were supposed to meet them on the northwest coast of the Florida peninsula failed to arrive, and a council of officers—which included Cabeza de Vaca as treasurer and high sheriff—decided to construct small boats and sail westward along the Gulf coast until they reached Spanish settlements in New Spain (Mexico). "None of us knew how to construct ships," Cabeza de Vaca recalled years later. "We had no tools, no iron, no smithery, no oakum, no pitch, no tackling. . . . There was nobody to instruct us in shipbuilding, and above all, there was nothing to eat." Despite these handicaps, they began to build five rafts. They killed the horses and converted their hides into waterbags and twisted the hair from their manes and tails into ropes for rigging. The men's shirts became improvised sails, and stones were used for anchors and ballast. Cabeza de Vaca declared, "So great is the power of need that it brought us to venture out into . . . a troublesome sea in this manner, and without any one among us having the least knowledge of the art of navigation."

As they drifted westward the horseskin waterbags rotted, their food supplies dwindled, and natives along the coast attacked every time they tried to land to secure more supplies. Then, after five weeks of drifting, a hurricane scattered the boats. Cabeza de Vaca and his companions in the one boat drifted until they made their landfall. They eventually beached their craft at a place they called Malhado—the Isle of Misfortune—which was probably Galveston Island.

Actually other Europeans had seen the island before them, for in 1519 four ships under the command of Alonso Álvarez de Piñeda had sailed on a mapping and reconnaissance journey around the Gulf of Mexico, from Florida to the Pánuco River in Mexico. Piñeda had stopped briefly at the mouth of the Rio Grande, which he named the "River of Palms," but he had not penetrated the region.

Within an hour of the landing, Cabeza de Vaca and his men were being watched silently by three natives standing on a nearby hill. Half an hour later, a hundred companions, all armed with bows and arrows, joined the first three. The Spaniards represented an easy mark, for they were too weak to resist an Indian attack. The natives were members of the Karankawa tribe, a nation that lived mainly on cactus fruit, shellfish, roots, berries, and small game (and later would be accused of cannibalism, although the charge was never proved). Of course Cabeza de Vaca knew nothing of this at the time. Bravely he stepped forward to offer the natives gifts from his supply of bells and beads. The Karankawas accepted the trinkets, and in return each offered the Spaniard an arrow as a token of friendship. They even promised to return the following morning with food, a promise they kept not once but several times. Cabeza de Vaca carefully rewarded them with more trinkets each time they came.

After a few days' rest the Spaniards attempted to resume their trip, but a wave overturned the boat. In this disaster three soldiers were drowned, and all their supplies, along with most of their clothing, were lost. The survivors were forced to cast themselves on the hospitality and mercy of the Karankawas. Within a week another of the five boats was washed ashore on the island with approximately thirty men aboard. The Spaniards from both groups tried to continue in this boat, but it too was sunk by a wave. Shortly after, the weather turned much colder, food became scarce, and the Indians and the Spaniards began to starve. An epidemic carried off more than half the Karankawas and many of the Spaniards. When spring finally arrived, only fifteen of the eighty soldiers still lived, and the Indians made them slaves. In fact, the Spaniards were forced to become medicine men, a demand which Cabeza de Vaca said was made "without any examination or asking for our diplomas."

Cabeza de Vaca soon gained a reputation as a healer and so was allowed some freedom of movement, since his services were in wide demand. Like the others, however, he was subject to the capricious whims of his masters, who often beat and mistreated him cruelly. He determined to escape. But it took six long years before an attempt was possible. Eventually Cabeza de Vaca, Alonso de Castillo, Andrés Dorantes, and a Moorish slave named Estevanico (Steven) "recommended themselves to God," and fled.

They walked westward, reached the Rio Grande, and turned upstream. Cabeza de Vaca's fame as a medicine man had preceded the party, and near the present El Paso area it almost caused trouble. The Spaniard was called upon to cure an Indian who had an arrow embedded near his heart, an operation of great delicacy. He stated, "With a knife, I cut open the breast as far as the place. . . . By cutting deeper, and inserting the point of the knife, with great difficulty I got it out; it was very long. Then, with a deerbone, according to my knowledge of surgery, I made two stitches." Had the Indian died, the natives might have turned on the Spaniards; but within a short time the patient was well again, and Cabeza de Vaca's fame spread even wider.

Cabeza de Vaca's party probably did not enter present-day New Mexico or Arizona. Turning due west, they crossed the Rio Grande and proceeded across Chihuahua and Sonora, and then southward to the Gulf of California. In the southern part of Sonora they encountered Indians who told them about a party of men with beards who were riding horses. On May 8, 1536—seven and a half years after being shipwrecked off the coast of Texas—the party, four Spaniards, found them near the settlement of Culiacán.

Cabeza de Vaca and his three companions soon hurried to Mexico City where they made a report to Viceroy Antonio de Mendoza. The viceroy wanted to know particularly about the wealth of the unknown north country. Had the man seen any gold? silver? turquoise? Cabeza de Vaca truthfully reported that he had seen no precious metal or stones, but that he had heard of the Seven Cities of Cíbola, an area where gold and silver abounded. Cabeza de Vaca's report greatly interested the viceroy, for it seemed to support long-standing rumor and legend. The Spaniards had a legend, dating from the days of the Moorish conquest, of seven Christian bishops who had fled westward across the ocean to escape the heathen invaders, and who had established seven cities; and Nuño de Guzmán, a rival of Cortés during the conquest of Mexico, had found an Indian named Tejo near Culiacán who swore that in his youth he had visited seven golden cities in the north.

Viceroy Mendoza tried to persuade Cabeza de Vaca to lead an expedition back to the north country, but the newly rescued *conquistador* declined. Instead, he soon returned to Spain to tell his story to the king and to request permission to lead another expedition into Florida. But only six weeks before, the king had granted permission for such an expedition to Hernando De Soto. So Cabeza de Vaca was made governor of what is now Paraguay; he never returned to the American Southwest.

Having failed to persuade Cabeza de Vaca to lead an expedition to the north, Viceroy Mendoza offered it to Cabeza de Vaca's companions, Castillo and Dorantes. When they also declined, the viceroy purchased Steven, the Moorish slave, to help guide the expedition when a leader was found. The viceroy decided on a small exploratory party first. A major expedition would follow, as soon as gold and silver had been discovered. Soon a man appeared to lead the party, a Franciscan missionary who had been in Peru during the conquest by Pizarro, Fray Marcos de Niza. This remarkable Franciscan had gone to Guatemala from Peru, then had walked overland to Mexico City to report to the archbishop. Courageous, resourceful, and capable, he was just the man for the viceroy's task.

Guided by Steven and accompanied by a few friendly Indians and a European, Father Onorato, Fray Marcos started north from Culiacán on March 7, 1539. Father Onorato became ill and was left on the way to get better. On March 23, Fray Marcos sent Steven and a few of the friendly Indians in advance of the main party with instructions to report back, especially about any signs of gold or silver. Steven was to send back a wooden cross, whose size would be in direct relation to the wealth he found. Four days later, Steven's Indian messengers returned, burdened with a cross as tall as a man, and bearing news that Steven had found people who had actually visited the country of the Seven Cities. Steven was hurrying on to the Seven Cities, and Fray Marcos was to follow as fast as possible. Accompanying the messengers was an Indian who reported the Seven Cities lay thirty days' journey to the north and that turquoise abounded there.

Fray Marcos entered what is now Arizona by way of the San Pedro Valley, journeyed down that stream to the vicinity of present-day Benson, pushed across the White Mountains, and came into the country of the Zuñi Indians. On May 21 he received word that Steven had been killed at the Seven Cities. A survivor reported that Steven had reached the first of these cities and had sent his cala-bash (a rattle adorned with feathers) to the chief of the city with a request to be allowed to enter. Steven was told not to enter on pain of death; nevertheless, he entered. He and his men were stripped of their possessions, locked in a room on the outskirts of the city, and given nothing to eat or drink. The next morning the inhabitants of the city fell on the party with clubs and killed almost every one of them.

Since the Indians accompanying Fray Marcos were related to those massacred with Steven, the Franciscan feared for his life. To protect himself he gave presents and trinkets to his followers, whereupon they deserted him. But this did not daunt Fray Marcos, who went forward alone until he reached a hill overlooking the city where Steven was killed. Later he wrote:

> The houses are built in order, according as the Indians told me, all made of stone several stories in height, as far as I could discern from a mountain, whither I climbed to view the city. The people are nearly white, they wear clothes, and lie in beds, their weapons are bows. . . .

On the spot where he stood, Fray Marcos erected a small cross, "not having materials to make a larger one," and claimed all that country for Spain. "Then," he said, "I returned with much more fear than food in order that I might report."

Fray Marcos reached Mexico City in August 1539, and de-scribed his journey to the viceroy; but he embroidered it with tales of the great wealth, including emeralds and turquoise, he had sup-posedly seen. His story was soon spread throughout the streets and taverns. Men rushed to join an expedition that promised to surpass Pizarro's in Peru in its opportunity for personal riches. More vol-unteered than could possibly go. Franciscan missionaries, anxious to convert the natives of the region, preached that the expedition was a holy obligation. Fray Marcos's report came at an opportune time. The conquest of central Mexico was virtually accomplished, so the soldiers and noblemen were looking for new adventures. Here was a grand opportunity for wealth and for salvation as well.

Mendoza first thought of leading the expedition personally, but was persuaded that he was needed in the capital. He then chose as leader of the expedition Francisco Vásquez de Coronado, governor of Nueva Galicia, in the northwest corner of New Spain. Coronado, then thirty years old, had come to the New World with Mendoza in 1535, had performed several tasks well, and had married into one of the wealthiest families of Mexico. Mendoza, Coronado, and Coronado's men themselves raised the nearly one million pesos needed to launch the expedition, so they could reap all the profits from it rather than having them go to the royal treasury, as would have happened if the crown had provided the money.

On February 23, 1540, Mendoza personally inspected Coronado's expedition as it set out from Compostela. It was the largest land expedition yet assembled in Mexico. At the head of the column rode Coronado, resplendent in gilded armor. Behind him came 336 Spaniards, followed by several hundred Indian allies. Fifteen hundred horses and mules and numberless sheep and cattle followed. Two vessels under the command of Hernando de Alarcón, supporting the expedition, were already moving up the coast. Alarcón was to keep a parallel course with Coronado, search for a water route to the Seven Cities, and provide naval support for their conquest.

The first stage from Compostela to Culiacán toughened the men, and it weeded out the weak, who turned back along the way. On April 22 the expedition left Culiacán, the last Spanish outpost in the northwest, and the march began in earnest. Although Fray Marcos served the party as a guide, Coronado sent one hundred men ahead as an advance guard. Following Fray Marcos's route, Coronado entered Arizona after leaving a small party behind in Sonora under Captain Melchior Díaz.

As Coronado neared his goal, he took special precautions to avoid a surprise attack. Perhaps remembering the treacherous death of Steven at the hands of the natives at Cíbola, he kept fifteen horsemen ahead of the main column as scouts. This small party was soon met by four natives from Cíbola, who said that they had been sent to welcome the Spaniards and that on the following day the army would be supplied with food—no doubt extremely welcome news to the footsore travelers. Two of the Indians were seized as hostages, the other two sent back to Cíbola with a cross and news that the Spaniards were coming to defend and aid them. Even after this seeming welcome, Coronado insisted on caution, with justification, for the next night the advance guard was attacked just outside Cíbola. The guard repulsed the attack and then informed Coronado, who called his men together. The young *conquistador* knew that the men were more hungry than afraid, so he urged them to tighten their belts and he moved them forward.

On July 7, 1540, the army reached its goal—the golden city viewed by Fray Marcos. But "Cíbola" proved to be only a Zuñi pueblo named Hawikúh, whose inhabitants were bristling for a fight. In fact, the pueblo's women and children, together with most movable possessions, had already been sent to a place of safety in the cliffs. Outside the pueblo two to three hundred defenders stood in military formation, while inside an equal number were poised for a surprise attack. Those Indians in sight threatened the Spaniards, and their medicine man drew a line on the ground with sacred cornmeal and warned the invaders not to cross it.

Halting his men at a safe distance, Coronado told the pueblo dwellers through an Ópata interpreter that he came not to injure them but to defend them in the name of the Spanish king. The defenders answered by rushing forward and trying to kill the interpreter. Thereupon Coronado issued the traditional Spanish battle cry, *"Santiago y a ellos"* (St. James and at them). The battle raged furiously for nearly an hour, and the Spaniards suffered heavily. Coronado himself had two or three wounds in his face, an arrow in his foot, and many bruises on his arms, legs, and shoulders. But Spanish armor and weapons finally overwhelmed the Indians. When the Spaniards hurried into the pueblo, they found no precious metals or gems, but as one soldier later declared, "There we found something we prized more than gold or silver; namely, plentiful maize and beans, turkeys larger than those . . . in New Spain, and salt better and whiter than any I have ever seen in my life."

After food and rest Coronado informed the Zuñi council that

they had done wrong in not surrendering peacefully, and now they must render obedience to Spain, after which they would be well treated. The Indians at Hawikúh pledged allegiance, and so did the chiefs of the outlying pueblos, who also declared they would become Christians. From these leaders Coronado solved the mystery of the Seven Cities. Actually there were only six pueblos comprising the "province" of Cíbola, not seven; all had the same culture and architecture, and none was the El Dorado the Spaniards had been seeking. In his report to Viceroy Mendoza of August 3, Coronado commented sadly, "Fray Marcos has not told the truth in a single thing that he said, except the name of the cities and the large stone houses. . . ." With the bearer of this message went Fray Marcos himself, for the friar was no longer welcome in the disappointed expedition.

Coronado had no intention of turning back, even though he had found no precious metals. Instead he began questioning the Zuñi Indians about the surrounding country. He learned of the Kingdom of Tontonteac, reportedly containing a hot lake, and of the Kingdom of Tusayán, which supposedly had great wealth. Coronado sent Captain Pedro de Tovar with seventeen mounted men to investigate the latter area. Led by Zuñi guides, Tovar soon reached his goal—which proved to be Hopi Indian villages (in his report he spelled their name "Moqui," and Spanish documents usually refer to them by this name). At the first village the same sequence of events occurred as at Hawikúh. Tovar called for obedience; the Spaniards were ordered not to cross a line the Indians had drawn. But one charge carried the battle that followed, for the Hopis had heard of the conquest of Hawikúh by men "riding about on animals that devoured people." The other villages surrendered shortly afterward, but Tovar found no great wealth. He did report back to Coronado that "notice was had of a great river, and that downstream several days there were some very tall people with large bodies."

Coronado immediately equipped another small expedition to explore for this "great river," placing it under the command of Captain García López de Cárdenas. With twenty-five men the captain set out late in August, followed Tovar's trail to Tusayán, and proceeded westward. He finally came to the gorge of a river "from whose brink it looked as if to the opposite side it must be more than three or four leagues by air line." They had found the Grand Canyon, one of the world's great natural wonders—but they were not looking for natural wonders. Still they found neither gold nor silver. Desperately in need of water, and unable to find a way to descend to the river, they turned and hurried back to Hawikúh.

Alarcón meanwhile had sailed northward up the Gulf of California to the mouth of the Colorado, and during August and September of 1540 made two trips up the great river. Possibly he reached the junction of the Gila and Colorado rivers, thus actually penetrating what is now the American Southwest, but he made no mention of this in his report. From the Indians along the river he heard reports of Cíbola, of Fray Marcos de Niza's adventures, and even of Coronado's arrival at Hawikúh. Tiring of waiting for word from Coronado, he buried letters at the base of a tree, on which was carved, "Alarcón came this far. There are letters at the foot of this tree." Then he sailed for home.

Late in September, Melchior Díaz, who had remained behind in Sonora, set out to make contact with Alarcón, in order to secure food from Alarcón's vessels. He hurried northwestward from San Gerónimo in the Sonora Valley with twenty-five men. Passing through Pima and Papago Indian territory, up el Camino del Diablo (the Devil's Highway), along what is now the international boundary line of southern Arizona, he and his men reached the Colorado River about thirty leagues (one league = 2.6 miles) above its mouth. The Yuma Indians told him of Alarcón's visit, and he found the letters the naval commander had left. When his company crossed the Colorado and explored the western side, Díaz accidentally impaled himself on his own lance while chasing a greyhound that was bothering their sheep. The men of his expedition hurriedly returned to San Gerónimo and dispatched messengers to Coronado.

These messengers found that Coronado was no longer at Hawikúh. A few days after the Cárdenas party had returned from the Grand Canyon area, a delegation of Indians had arrived from Cícuye, a pueblo about thirty miles southeast of modern Santa Fe, with an invitation for the Spaniards to visit their country. Coronado had sent a small party of twenty men to Cícuye with these

Indians, and their report was so glowing that the Spanish commander decided to winter in that area, which he designated Tiguex. He moved his main body of men there during the fall of 1540 and maintained his headquarters there for the next two years.

The natives of Tiguex at first welcomed their Spanish visitors, but soon they grew hostile when they discovered the Spaniards requisitioned their food—and the Spaniards had hearty appetites. During this winter "the Turk" appeared. He was not a Pueblo Indian, but had come from the plains country to the east. He was called the Turk by the Spaniards because, as one of them said, "he looked like one." Into willing listeners' ears he poured a wondrous tale of a fabulous land called the Gran Quivira, a place on a river five miles wide with fish as large as horses, where the canoes had sails, and the chief of the land took an afternoon nap under a tree adorned with golden bells that tinkled musically as the breeze blew among them. In Quivira, the Turk declared, even the humblest peasant ate from golden dishes, and all manner of precious metals and jewels were the property of all. And he said he would gladly lead the Spaniards there.

By March 1541 all revolts in New Mexico had been suppressed, and Coronado set out in search of Quivira. Leaving a small force at Tiguex, he marched eastward, guided by the Turk. Reaching the Pecos River, his force turned south for three days before again heading eastward. On the high plains of West Texas, they found and killed many buffalo. But day after weary day the plains were unchanging. This was the Llano Estacado—the Staked Plains— "so level and smooth that if one looked at the (buffalo) the sky could be seen between their legs, so that if some of them were at a distance they looked like smooth-trunked pines whose tops were joined," according to the chronicler of the expedition.

When they at last reached a large canyon (probably Palo Duro Canyon, near present-day Amarillo, Texas), Coronado began to doubt the Turk's word. Besides, his men and horses were showing signs of weariness. He stopped there and ordered the Turk to be put in irons, then called a conference with his captains. It was decided that all except thirty of the best horsemen would return to Tiguex with Captain Tristan de Arellano; the thirty, mounted on the best horses of the expedition, would push on to Quivira. For forty days Coronado led his small group to the northeast, and finally reached his goal. He found Quivira to be an Indian village consisting of mud and straw huts (located near present-day Wichita, Kansas). The Indians there were miserably poor—they had no golden plates, no golden bells, no large canoes with sails, in short, none of the wonders described by the Turk. Under torture, the Indian said that he had made up the tale of Quivira at the insistence of the Pueblo Indians, who promised him a rich reward for leading the Spaniards out on the plains and losing them. He was garroted.

During the dejected return to Tiguex, Coronado fell from his horse and broke his arm. And the following winter in New Mexico, the Spanish commander was seriously injured in a horse race when his saddle girth broke and he was trampled by the horse of his competitor. However, the winter at Tiguex was not as hard as the first one had been. There were no uprisings, and the men who had returned in July under Captain Arellano had gathered enough supplies to keep the men from hunger. But the men were discontented since no precious metals or gems had been discovered, and some of them began plotting to return to the comforts of Mexico. Because of his painful injuries, Coronado supported them and summarily announced that the majority had decided to go home. In the spring of 1542 the dejected army set out on the long trek to Culiacán; painfully, wearily, and hungrily they retraced their route.

Coronado went directly to Mexico City, where he made his report to Viceroy Mendoza. Then, after resting for several months, he resumed his post as governor of Nueva Galicia. He was no longer a promising young man on the rise, however, for his health was broken and the money he had invested in the ill-fated expedition was gone. And he faced a trial, for discontented members of the expedition, who likewise had lost money, brought charges against him—charges of mismanagement, excessive cruelty to the natives, even charges that he had found wealth at Quivira but had concealed it for his own purse. The commission appointed to investigate these charges found him guilty on several counts of cruelty and mismanagement, and he was fined 650 pesos and removed from the governorship of Nueva Galicia. A reviewing board in

Spain completely absolved him in 1546, but by then he was a broken man. He died at the age of forty-four.

Coronado's report on his expedition completely discouraged further explorations in the American Southwest. The year after his return, survivors of the De Soto-Moscoso expedition safely reached the mouth of the Pánuco River, and their report reinforced Coronado's findings. Hernando De Soto had been made governor of Cuba in 1536 and had permission to explore and conquer in Florida. Landing in Tampa Bay on May 25, 1539, with six hundred men, he had trekked through present-day Florida, Georgia, South Carolina, North Carolina, Tennessee, Alabama, Mississippi, Arkansas, and out onto the plains of Oklahoma before returning to the Mississippi River. There he died on May 21, 1542, and was buried in "The Father of Waters." His successor, Luís de Moscoso de Alvarado, led the expedition into East Texas, penetrating to the fringes of the Southwest. The Indians proved hostile, food became scarce, and scouts reported that nothing but desert lay ahead; so Moscoso de Alvarado led his men back to the Mississippi River, where they constructed seven crude boats. On these they drifted down the river to the Gulf, turned west, and finally reached a Spanish settlement in 1543. Only three hundred twenty of the original six hundred men were still alive, and no treasure had been found. Moscoso's report paralleled Coronado's in many respects—there was no gold, no silver, nothing but hostile Indians to the north of New Spain, and thus no reason why any other expedition should explore the region.

THE SETTLEMENT OF NEW MEXICO

In 1578 the English seadog Francis Drake piloted his ship, the *Golden Hind*, through the Straits of Magellan at the southern tip of South America, then boldly dashed up the west coast of that continent, along Central America, and New Spain, raiding the seaports and looting the ships he encountered. He paused on the coast of California near present-day San Francisco to rest and to refit his ship, then struck out across the Pacific, rounded Africa, and returned to a royal welcome in England. His daring feat not only won him a knighthood and great treasure for his country, but it changed the course of Southwestern history. Spanish New World officials watched and waited for Drake to return to England by way of the Straits of Magellan, not believing the seadog would venture across the vast Pacific. When Drake arrived in England—a fact reported to them by their diplomats in that country—they concluded that he had discovered the long-sought Northwest Passage, a water route around the top of North America.

So certain were these Spanish officials that the Northwest Passage existed that they gave it a name: the Strait of Anián. Furthermore, these same officials were determined that Spain must control the strait. The north country would once more be explored, but this time not for gold or silver, not even for natives who could be exploited; instead, there would be a search for a strategic site to hold off foreign encroachment of the region.

Father Agustín Rodríguez, a Franciscan missionary, made a preliminary reconnaissance. In 1581 he led a small party of two other missionaries, nine soldiers, and sixteen Indian servants from San Bartolomé, Coahuila, down the Conchos River of Mexico to its juncture with the Rio Grande, turned up that river, and followed it to the pueblo country of New Mexico. Although his party found the Indians apparently friendly, they did not discover the Northwest Passage nor did they hear word of it. One priest thereupon elected to return to San Bartolomé to make a report. He went alone and was murdered by the Indians once they had got him away from his companions. The rest of the Rodríguez party, after exploring the pueblo region, separated into two groups. The two missionaries insisted on remaining in New Mexico to attempt to convert the natives; the soldiers voted to return home.

The report turned in by these soldiers was forwarded to Mexico City, and from there it went to Madrid. In due time the king reached a decision—a contract was to be awarded to any deserving citizen who conquered, colonized, and civilized the New Mexico area. While the viceroy and his advisers were discussing ways to effect the king's wishes, Franciscan missionaries were worried about their two brethren still in the land of pueblos. Father Bernadino Beltrán volunteered to lead a rescue party to New Mexico, and secured the necessary permission from the viceroy. A wealthy private citizen, Antonio de Espejo, heard of the project and offered to equip and lead an escort of fourteen soldiers for Beltrán. The Franciscans welcomed Espejo's offer, and the expedition quickly readied itself.

On November 10, 1582, the Beltrán-Espejo expedition set out from San Bartolomé, following the same route used by Rodríguez the previous year. They reached the pueblo country without incident, only to learn that Rodríguez and his companion had been killed. Espejo decided to explore in the vicinity. First he went eastward, but he decided the plains country held little attraction. Returning to the Rio Grande, he proceeded westward to the Zuñi pueblo of Hawikúh, where he and his men were well received. He was especially interested in the cotton blankets these natives made, and he listened eagerly to stories of the Coronado expedition. Leaving Father Beltrán there, Espejo and nine men went on to the Hopi country where they heard of rich mines farther to the west. He took four men to investigate and sent the other five back to Hawikúh. He arrived at a stream he named El Rio de los Reyes (doubtless the Verde River in north-central Arizona), and found mines of debatable value.

Returning to Hawikúh, Espejo found Beltrán anxious to return to Mexico. But Espejo wanted to continue his explorations, so the expedition split, Beltrán returning home and the commander and his soldiers proceeding east to the pueblos on the Rio Grande. After a brief skirmish with the natives, Espejo journeyed north to the vicinity of present-day Sante Fe, turned east to the Pecos River, which he followed partway to the Rio Grande, then proceeded overland to the junction of the Rio Grande with the Conchos, and up that river to San Bartolomé. He arrived there on September 10, 1583. Espejo in effect had almost duplicated the feat of Coronado with only fourteen soldiers; he reported that he had visited seventy-four pueblos containing an estimated 250,000 Indians. This report did much to interest the high Spanish officials in New Mexico: there were rumors of silver mines; cotton blankets meant trade items; and there were a quarter of a million souls to be saved. Soon wealthy men of Mexico, men of high social and financial standing, were vying with one another for the royal patent to oversee this settlement. On March 11, 1589, Juan Bautista de Lomas y Colmenares was actually awarded a contract by the viceroy, but the patent was not approved by the king.

While wealthy men contended with each other to secure exclusive concessions in New Mexico, more impulsive Spaniards hurried into the area, perhaps hoping to find sufficient riches to buy a royal pardon for their rashness. Gaspar Castaño de Sosa, the lieutenant governor of Nueva León, gathered 170 colonists and in 1590 set out for New Mexico. He reached his goal by way of the Conchos, the Rio Grande, and the Pecos, and led several successful assaults against hostile pueblos. He reached as far north as the vicinity of Taos Pueblo before being arrested by an army sent expressly for that purpose under Captain Juan Morlete. Later Castaño was brought to trial and convicted, but the decision was reversed in Spain; Castaño was to be returned to the place where he had been arrested and all his goods and possessions restored to him. He never went back to New Mexico, however.

The contract for Spanish settlement of New Mexico was finally awarded in 1595 to Juan de Oñate, the son of a silver magnate. Oñate was named governor, captain general, and *adelantado* of the province. After long and wearisome delays, he set out on February 7, 1598, with one hundred twenty-nine soldiers, many of them with their families, eighty-three cartloads of baggage, seven thousand animals, and several Franciscan missionaries. Oñate's nephew, Captain Vicente de Zaldívar, considerably shortened the distance to be traveled by pioneering a route directly north from the headwaters of the Conchos River to the Rio Grande near El Paso del Norte (present-day Juárez, Chihuahua). Oñate and his colonists followed this trail, then proceeded up the Rio Grande to their destination. On April 30 he formally took possession of New Mexico in the name of the king of Spain; the Indians submitted peacefully, and a capital city, named San Juan de los Caballeros, was laid out. This was located approximately twenty-five miles north of present-day Sante Fe, at a pueblo named Caypa. Three years later the capital was moved to a site named San Gabriel, located on the west side of the Rio Grande where that river is joined by the Chama River.

With the civil settlement laid out and the natives submissive,

Oñate turned his attention to exploration, looking, so he said, for the Strait of Anián. On October 8, 1598, he set out with a small force toward the east; however, he found the plains country uninviting and reversed his direction, intending to view the South Seas. On October 23 he reached the pueblo of Ácoma, the "city in the sky." There he was received as a friend and given food and water. Journeying westward, he reached the Zuñi and Hopi pueblos, stopping at the latter point and sending Captain Marcos Farfán on to the west to investigate rumors of mines. Farfán's party reached north-central Arizona and staked out what appeared to be rich deposits, then returned to report. Before these deposits could be investigated, word reached Oñate of an Indian uprising. The natives of Ácoma had attacked a party trekking westward under Oñate's nephew, Zaldívar, and Zaldívar and twelve of his men had been killed.

Oñate hurried back to his capital, gathered an army, and set out to punish the Indians at Ácoma. The governor knew that if Spaniards were to be safe in New Mexico this first attempt at rebellion must be severely punished. The Indians showered Oñate's army with rocks and arrows when it arrived at Ácoma, hurling insults and taunts of defiance down from the safety of their fortress home atop the mesa. Oñate offered them peace, but this was spurned. Thereupon the Spaniards feigned an attack on one side of the mesa while another part of the army scaled the opposite side. After two days of hard fighting, the Indians surrendered; seventy-five men and approximately five hundred women and children were marched to the village of Santo Domingo for trial. Oñate sentenced all males over twenty-five years of age to have one foot cut off and to serve twenty years of personal service—that is, as slaves. The women and the boys and girls over twelve were also to serve for twenty years; the children under twelve were turned over to the mission fathers for raising and instruction. These brutal measures had the desired effect, for more than eight decades passed before another uprising occurred in New Mexico.

In 1601 Oñate made a full-scale expedition to the east in search of Coronado's Gran Quivira, but found the same miserable village that had been visited in 1541. After this failure, only one hope of mineral wealth was left to the governor—the area to the west.

However, three years passed before he could make the attempt. Dissension broke out among the colonists of New Mexico, and some of them fled southward to New Spain and the relative comforts to be found there. Oñate attempted to bring back the deserters by force, but they eluded him.

On October 7, 1604, Oñate, thirty soldiers, and two missionaries left San Gabriel, taking the traditional route westward: to Ácoma, the Zuñi pueblos, and the land of the Hopi. Crossing the Verde north of present-day Prescott, he came to an attractive country where the natives told him of a great river to the west. Oñate followed their directions, and soon came to a river he called Rio Grande de Buena Esperanza, which was the Colorado. He followed it to the country of the Yuma Indians, who were described as "very friendly and of good disposition, tall of stature and well proportioned." The Spaniards showed them silver buttons and samples of gold, and in return were informed that such metals were to be had five days' journey toward the west. Oñate then followed the Colorado to the Gulf of California; there he learned that pearls were to be had in the vicinity, but Father Francisco de Escobar, the chronicler of this expedition, declared: "We could not find a single one among the Indians, even though the governor did his best."

The entries in Escobar's journal reveal the credulity of the age. He carefully reported stories of "monstrosities" in the vicinity: people "with so large and long ears that they dragged on the ground, and . . . five or six persons could stand under each one." A near-by nation of people had only one foot, while another tribe in the vicinity slept underwater at night (this was the same tribe that had knowledge of gold). Near them was a nation that supported itself solely "on the odor of their food. They prepared it only for this purpose, not eating anything at all." Father Escobar declared personal doubt as to the existence of such people, but he declared, "I would be wrong in not telling of such things which, if discovered, would, I believe, redound to the glory of God and the service of the King our lord."

Oñate chose not to explore farther in search of mines. His horses were jaded and his men tired and anxious to return to their homes. So he retraced his route, and arrived at his capital of San Gabriel on April 25, 1605. Again the geography of the Southwest had been traced, and again no great mineral wealth had been found.

Three years later, in 1608, Oñate was removed from his post of governor and captain general of New Mexico. Continued dissatisfaction with his administration had resulted in a host of charges against him; he was accused of cruelty to the Indians, with having found riches that he had concealed, and with general unfitness. In 1614 he was convicted on twelve charges and fined six thousand ducats, exiled from Mexico City for four years, and stripped of his title as governor of New Mexico. Evidence indicates that he was pardoned by the king at a later date because of the enormous expense he had incurred in exploring and settling New Mexico. The date of his death is unknown.

The Franciscans still hoped to make many converts in New Mexico. Pedro de Peralta was appointed governor in the spring of 1609 and came north with new soldiers and missionaries. Peralta, following instructions, removed the capital to a new site, and a city was laid out in 1610 bearing the name Villa Real de la Santa Fé de San Francisco de Asis—present Santa Fe. For the next two decades the colony slowly grew. Indian allies of the Spaniards were brought from Mexico and settled near Santa Fe, and hardy pioneers joined those already in the province. The Franciscans pushed on with their work of conversion, reaching north to Taos in 1621 and west to the land of the Hopi, where a mission named San Bernardino was constructed in 1629. Despite the fact that several of these missionaries were murdered, among them Father Francisco de Porras at San Bernardino, the work continued. These missionaries were self-supporting, although they did receive an annual stipend from the royal treasury. The soldiers who were frequently stationed near by were in theory obligated to protect the pueblos and the padres and to provide an escort service for the supply caravans; in return they were to receive an annual tribute from the head of each Indian household, consisting of one and a half bushels of corn and a piece of cloth. According to law, all other services performed by the Indians were to be paid for. This was not the custom, however, and a deep resentment gradually developed among the natives against their Spanish conquerors.

The chief deterrent to progress in the province came from the nomadic Navajo and Apache. At first the Spaniards clearly had the advantage in battle, for they possessed horses, firearms, and cross-bows. However, the Apache quickly adapted themselves to the horse culture and the employment of guerilla tactics, and they secured European weapons from French and English traders to the east. As the Indians began to win more battles, the Spaniards took measures for better defense. New Mexico was divided into two administrative districts; Rio Arriba (literally, "upriver") included the area north of Santa Fe, while Rio Abajo ("downriver") encompassed the territory south of the capital. Juan Domínguez de Mendoza, an outstanding soldier, was placed in charge of the southern district, and he conducted several noteworthy campaigns against the eastern Apache. But the raiding continued until the mid-seventeenth century and steadily increased in intensity.

The governors during this period for the most part considered their office to be a means of enrichment rather than a public trust. They monopolized commerce, bringing trade goods to the province for sale to the civilians, soldiers, and Indians at exorbitant prices, and they appropriated the bounty of nature, piñon nuts and salt, and sold it for personal gain. Indians captured in battle were frequently set to work for the governor, weaving woolen goods and preparing hides for export. These burdens, in addition to those imposed by the other Spaniards in the province, caused great unrest among the natives. From the European point of view, the pueblo Indians were receiving Christianity and civilization, and these considerations far outweighed the taxes and labor exacted from them. But from the Indian point of view, they were being exploited, some of their best lands had been taken, and their culture was being subverted to an alien way of life.

Discontent in the pueblo lands reached a head in 1680. A resident of San Juan Pueblo named Popé assumed the leadership, and over a number of months he planned and schemed to rid New Mexico of the Spanish yoke. Making Taos his headquarters, Popé began sending runners to the other pueblos seeking support; he made appeals to Indian patriotism and exploited native superstition in recruiting entire pueblos. Apparently the rebellion was set for August 13, but some missionaries were warned by certain of their converts of the impending uprising. Governor Antonio Otermín sent messengers to outlying settlements and missions, warning the inhabitants to flee southward. Popé thereupon precipitated the revolt on August 10, three days prematurely. In the massacre that followed, it was apparent that the Indians intended nothing less than the total extermination of all Spaniards, for soldiers, settlers, and missionaries all were killed wherever possible. In the Rio Arriba district, the survivors fled to Santa Fe, bringing with them all their readily transportable goods and their livestock. All were gathered within the royal building and guards posted.

On the morning of August 15 the insurgents entered the city. They sent a messenger to the royal building for a conference. He said the Indians had killed God and Saint Mary, and that the king must yield. He offered Otermín two crosses, one red, and one white. The red meant that the Spaniards would fight, the white that they would immediately quit the country. Otermín chose the red cross, and soon ventured out to do battle. Just at the point when it seemed his force would defeat the rebels, Indian reinforcements arrived from Taos, Picurís, and Tehuas, forcing the Spaniards back inside their fortress. The siege lasted until August 21, when the governor decided the situation was hopeless. One thousand people in the capital fled southward. On their trek down the Rio Grande they found that the survivors of Rio Abajo had gathered under Alonso García at the pueblo of Isleta. They marched down a ruined cordon of missions, outposts, and settlements, finally reaching El Paso del Norte by the end of September. This town, the site of a Franciscan mission, became their new home—and the headquarters of the reconquest of New Mexico. More than four hundred lives had been lost, along with a province.

Officials in Mexico City quickly decided that the lost province must be reconquered and the Indians punished. But Governor Otermín was not enthusiastic, and his efforts were halfhearted. On November 5 he went north with 146 soldiers and 112 Indian allies, beyond Isleta, but then he turned back. He found churches burned and religious objects smashed everywhere, and at Cochití an Indian army gathered and prepared to fight. Returning to El Paso, Otermín reported on conditions as he had found them, and asked for a leave of absence to visit Parral for medical attention. The viceroy refused this leave, and Otermín remained as governor until 1683, when he was replaced by Domingo Jironza Petriz de Cruzate.

The settlements near El Paso became permanent villages in the years that followed. A presidio was built in the vicinity, and all former residents of New Mexico who had fled to the interior of New Spain were ordered to return to El Paso. The Christian natives of New Mexico who had journeyed southward with the refugees were given a mission across the Rio Grande from the new settlement; it was founded in 1682 and named San Antonio de la Isleta, later changed to Corpus Christi de la Isleta. The mission became a permanent one, and was thus the first Spanish settlement in the present state of Texas.

In September 1683 the king ordered that every effort to reconquer New Mexico should be made, but decreed that the reconquest should be accomplished at the slightest possible expense. Cruzate's four years in office were marked by a few sorties northward, but mostly he had to concern himself with returning fugitives from the El Paso settlement who had fled southward. His successor, Pedro Reneros de Posada, also did little to recapture the lost province.

Then in June 1688 a real military figure was appointed, a man capable of carrying the war to Santa Fe and beyond—Don Diego de Vargas Zapata y Luján Ponce de Leon y Contreras. Vargas had had years of service in the Spanish army, both in Europe and the New World, and he had proved himself a capable administrator as well. Vargas was hindered in his efforts to march northward by the scarcity of soldiers and the timidity of the civilian militia. But by August 21, 1692, he was ready, and he set out with sixty soldiers, one hundred Indian allies, and three padres. By September 13 they were at Santa Fe. Vargas found the former capital occupied by defiant pueblo Indians who said they would perish before surrendering. Rather than attack, Vargas simply cut off the city's water supply and waited. The natives soon came out, begging for pardon. Vargas accepted the Indians' request. The royal standard was raised in the plaza, and the natives ordered to wear crosses and attend morning and evening prayers.

The outlying pueblos were also induced to return to their former submissiveness without bloodshed, for they had not found their twelve years under Popé to their liking. Popé, upon the successful conclusion of the revolt in 1680, had declared himself supreme authority of all New Mexico. After an orgy of destruction of Spanish property and religious symbols, Popé tightened his hold on the natives by cruel and excessive measures. He killed many of his enemies, and his taxes and levies were far more onerous than those of the Spanish governor. Civil war broke out, followed by plague and famine and an increase in Apache and Navajo raiding. So in 1692 the natives seemingly welcomed the return of the Spaniards.

Vargas's reconquest of New Mexico without bloodshed was hailed throughout New Spain, and the governor found himself a popular hero. But the celebration was premature. Vargas marched his army back to El Paso and began gathering colonists. On October 13, 1693, he led one hundred soldiers, approximately seventy families, and a number of missionaries, totaling about eight hundred people, out toward Santa Fe. Winter cold caught them in transit, and thirty persons died from hunger and exposure before the column reached the capital. On December 16 Vargas led them into the plaza at Santa Fe. They established camp outside the town, waiting for the Indians to move out.

The natives refused to go, so on December 29 the question of ownership of Santa Fe was settled by battle. Vargas and his troops rushed the town, but met determined resistance. The following day the natives surrendered; their seventy surviving warriors were shot immediately and the four hundred women and children were divided among the colonists as "hostages," a term that meant slaves. In February 1694, Vargas led his hundred soldiers out from the capital to reduce other pueblos, but this task took not two or three months, but three years. By 1696, when Vargas's term as governor was due to expire, the reconquest had at last been accomplished, and as a reward the king offered him his choice of becoming a marqués or a count. The local citizens were not as vocal in his praise, however, for Vargas had restored the enslaved natives to their pueblos as a gesture of good will. Pedro Rodríguez Cubero, the new governor, sided with the local citizens, and Vargas was illegally imprisoned for almost three years in Santa Fe, where he was harshly treated, and was fined four thousand pesos. In July 1700 he secured his release and journeyed to Mexico City, where an investigation was held. He was completely exonerated. In 1703 Vargas was reappointed governor of New Mexico, and Cubero fled the country before Vargas arrived. With the title Marqués de la Nave de Brazinas, Vargas reassumed the office on November 10, 1703, and remained there until his death on April 4, 1704.

THE SETTLEMENT OF TEXAS

During the seventeenth century, the governors of New Mexico, in addition to their other duties and private endeavors, carried on the work of exploration to the east. Usually the pretext for such activity was religious, but actually they hoped to discover the wealth which Coronado or Oñate might have overlooked. They still hoped to find the Gran Quivira or even the Seven Cities of Gold. Dreams of quick wealth die slowly, even in the face of overwhelming evidence to the contrary. While these expeditions did not find gold or silver, they did acquire much information about the geography and the people native to the region that came to be known as Texas.

The first of these expeditions to trek eastward was led by Father Juan de Salas. In 1629, with a small party of soldiers, he journeyed to the banks of the Concho Rivers and the Colorado River of Texas (near present day San Angelo). The Indian tribe of the region, the Jumano, was friendly, and three years later, in 1632, he returned to proselyte further. In his reports of the two trips, he stressed that the tribe could easily be converted permanently to Christianity, and that the entire region could readily be brought under Spanish domination.

Despite Salas's optimism, it was not until 1650 that more Spaniards returned. Perhaps this was because Salas's report had mentioned Indian souls and not mineral wealth. In the middle of the seventeenth century Captains Hernando Martín and Diego del Castillo led a detachment of soldiers to the region of the Jumano and stayed there some six months. They found supplies plentiful, the Indians friendly, and buffalo hides easily procurable. In addition, they discovered mussels in the nearby rivers which contained pearls with an appearance of value. Naming the rivers the Perlas, they gathered a large quantity of the pearls and returned to New

Mexico, where they reported their discovery to Governor Hernando de Ugarte y la Concha. The governor in turn forwarded their account and the pearls to Mexico City. Experts at the capital of New Spain said that the pearls were inferior, but the viceroy was sufficiently impressed to order another expedition to the region of the Jumano.

This new expedition to West Texas set out in 1654 under the command of Captain Diego de Guadalajara, and consisted of thirty soldiers and two hundred Indian allies. At the Perlas River, however, they found few pearls, and they became involved in a quarrel with a tribe of Indians they called the Cuitaos. In the battle that resulted, Guadalajara and his men emerged victorious, confiscated many buffalo hides, and took several prisoners. Then without further exploration they returned to New Mexico, where Guadalajara reported he had been unable to find many pearls. Afterward the Perlas River was renamed the Concho River.

The next penetration of West Texas came in 1683, while New Mexico was under the rule of Popé and the New Mexicans were at El Paso. Delegates from the Jumano came to the new settlement at El Paso that year and asked Governor Cruzate for missionaries. The governor agreed to the request because he had heard that to the east of the Jumano lived the Tejas Indians, a nation which was reportedly ruled by a king and grew grain in great abundance. And, according to Cruzate's information, the Gran Quivira of Coronado was just beyond the Tejas. Cruzate sent a report about the Jumano request and about their neighbors, the Tejas, to the viceroy, but without awaiting a reply he readied an expedition. Captain Juan Domínguez de Mendoza was chosen to command this party because he had accompanied Guadalajara thirty years earlier to the Jumano region. Accompanying him, but for different reasons, was Father Nicolás López, custodian of the New Mexico missions; he saw the Jumano request as an opportunity to open a new mission field and win many converts.

Leaving El Paso on December 15, 1683, with a large escort of soldiers, Mendoza and López went down the Rio Grande to the mouth of the Conchos River (site of present-day Presidio, Texas) then turned to the northeast. They crossed the Pecos River at Horsehead Crossing, marched eastward to the Middle Concho

River, and arrived at that point in late February 1684. From there they moved down the Concho and came to its junction with the Colorado River of Texas, where they found an area that Mendoza thought very beautiful. There at the confluence of the Concho and Colorado rivers they built a combined fort and chapel which became their headquarters for the next six weeks. While López preached to and baptized the Jumano, Mendoza and his soldiers busied themselves collecting the hides of the four thousand buffalo they killed. Then, promising the Jumano they would return shortly to found a permanent mission, the Spaniards returned to El Paso. Governor Cruzate had little sympathy for such a return, however, for the report of the expedition made no mention of the Tejas Indians living near by and no pearls had been discovered.

Suddenly news came that the hated French were in East Texas along the Gulf Coast, and official attention shifted to this threat. Word came from diplomatic sources in Paris and from a Spanish buccaneer in the Caribbean that a French fort had been built in Texas. Such a settlement had to be found and destroyed; West Texas could wait.

The report of French activity in Texas was true, for French colonists had indeed arrived under the command of René Robert Cavelier, Sieur de La Salle. Born in Rouen in 1643, La Salle had been educated for the teaching profession. His was a restless spirit, however, one that could not be confined to the endless monotony of a classroom, and as a young man he went to Canada. There he became legendary as an expert woodsman, a remarkable Indian fighter, and a leader of men. Gradually he became obsessed with the desire to be the discoverer of the mouth of the Mississippi River. This dream was realized on April 9, 1682, when he stood at the mouth of "The Father of Waters" and intoned the ritual formula of possession: "In the name of the most high, mighty, invincible, and victorious Prince, Louis the Great, by the grace of God King of France and of Navarre, Fourteenth of that name, I . . . have taken, and do now take . . . possession of this country of Louisiana."

Knowing that rivers are the natural highways of any wilderness, La Salle saw that a French colony at the mouth of the Mississippi would ensure French control of the greater interior of North America. He therefore returned to Canada and sailed for France, where he proposed such a colony to Louis XIV. He stressed that such a colony would prove a counterpoise to Spanish power in the New World, that it might serve as a staging area for the conquest of Mexican silver mines, that missionaries could win a rich harvest of converts in the region—all in addition to ensuring French control of the interior of North America. The king agreed to La Salle's proposal, and on July 24, 1684, the explorer sailed from La Rochelle with four ships and four hundred colonists.

The expedition was ill-fated from the start. Quarrels with the naval commander of the ships, Sieur de Beaujeu; sickness; one ship captured by a Spanish freebooter—all were a mere prelude to the greatest disaster, La Salle's failure to find the mouth of the Mississippi. One ship was wrecked in navigating the entrance to Matagorda Bay on the Texas coast, where La Salle determined to settle, and Beaujeu quickly left with many of the more faint-hearted colonists. A small fort was erected from driftwood and the remains of the wrecked ship, but the site proved unhealthy. Five or six colonists a day were perishing from fever, and the Karankawa Indians were attacking at every opportunity. La Salle moved his encampment a short distance up Garcitas Creek and erected a palisaded encampment which was named Fort Saint Louis. Crops were planted and steps taken to discourage Indian depredations.

Despite such steps, the worst was to come for the little colony. Their crops failed, and the Karankawas increased their ambushes. Then late in the year La Salle attempted to find by land the river he had missed at sea and failed miserably. Another such trip the following spring also resulted in failure. Finally in desperation he decided to try to reach Canada; in January 1687 he set out with twenty men, including his trusted lieutenant Henri Joutel, promising the twenty-five remaining at Fort Saint Louis that he would soon return for them. This promise was not fulfilled, however, for on March 20, not far from the Brazos River, the intrepid explorer was murdered by a group of conspirators within his own party. Seven of the survivors, led by Joutel, later made their way to Canada and France; the murderers chose to cast their lot with the natives of East Texas and remained in that vicinity. Joutel related this tale of ill-fortune and disaster to the king and asked that aid be rushed to those still on the coast of Texas, but Louis had lost interest and nothing was done.

Spanish officials in Madrid and Mexico City, however, were interested in the fate of Fort Saint Louis. In fact, they were in a frenzy of excitement in their desire to find and destroy the French colony, for they were not aware of the sad fate that had befallen La Salle and his dream. The task of conducting the search for the French colony fell to Captain Alonso de León at Cadereyta in the province of Coahuila. On June 27, 1686, he set out with a party of fifty soldiers, twenty-two assistants, and a chaplain. León led these men to the Rio Grande, then turned down the right bank and trekked to the Gulf; although they found no evidence of French intrusion, they did hear rumors from the Indians about a colony of Europeans to the northeast. They then returned to Cadereyta, arriving on July 27, where León made his report.

Near the end of February, 1687, Captain León again was on the march for Texas, this time with an increased number of soldiers. The rumors of Frenchmen in Texas had to be investigated. On this expedition León crossed the Rio Grande and pushed as far north as the Nueces River; there he found his way blocked by floods. Since the natives in that vicinity had no knowledge of a French settlement in the vicinity, he returned to Cadereyta and made a negative report.

Meanwhile, Spanish officials in Mexico City were also dispatching naval expeditions to search for the reported La Salle colony. In January of 1686 Captain Juan Enriquez Barroto sailed from Vera Cruz, proceeding directly to Apalache Bay in Florida, then following the coastline back to his starting point. He reported no success. A year later, however, two new searches were conducted in the Gulf. Two brigantines sailed from Vera Cruz northward along the coast to Matagorda Bay, where they found the remains of the wrecked French ship; deciding that the French had perished in an attempt to land, the Spaniards returned to Mexico. Shortly after their return, the viceroy sent two frigates to conduct another search from Florida back to Vera Cruz; they too saw the wreckage in Matagorda Bay, but did not push inland to find Fort Saint Louis.

Spanish fears of French intrusion were somewhat allayed after this initial flurry of activity. Then on May 18, 1688, an Indian named Augustín de la Cruz, a guide for one of the Spanish units fighting in Coahuila near the Rio Grande, reported to Alonso de León, now the governor of the province, that while lost he had wandered into a village ruled by a European. At first de la Cruz assumed the white man was Spanish, but he learned through an interpreter that the European was French. In great haste Governor León gathered seventeen soldiers and a missionary and, on May 19, guided by de la Cruz, set out from San Francisco de Coahuila for Texas. Crossing the Rio Grande and pushing northeastward, he arrived at the village de la Cruz had found on May 30, and there he confronted the Frenchman. This survivor of the La Salle colony, named Jean Henri, was arrested and sent to Mexico City for interrogation. After questioning the prisoner the viceroy concluded that a new expedition was in order and that Henri should act as its guide.

On March 29, 1689, Governor León set out for Texas with eighty-eight soldiers, twelve armed mule skinners, two priests, and thirteen unarmed attendants. Henri accepted the inevitable and guided the expedition in the right direction, so that on April 22, León finally found Fort Saint Louis. In his report to the viceroy, the governor wrote:

> We . . . found all the houses sacked, all the chests, bottle-cases, and all the rest of the settlers' furniture broken; apparently more than two hundred books, torn apart and with the rotten leaves scattered through the patios—all in French. . . . We found three dead bodies scattered over the plain. One of these, from the dress that still clung to the bones, appeared to be that of a woman. We took the bodies up . . . and buried them. We looked for the other dead bodies but could not find them; whence we supposed that they had been thrown into the creek and had been eaten by alligators, of which there are a great many.

Thus had ended La Salle's little colony, the victim of Indian wrath. León spent a few days exploring in the vicinity. From Indians nearby he heard of a few French survivors living with natives of the region, and he found two of them, Jean L'Archeveque and Santiago Groslet.

Near the spot where he found the two French survivors, the

Spaniards met a large band of Tejas Indians. León took time to exhort the natives to be loyal to Spain, while Father Damián Massanet tried to win their friendship. Already the priest envisioned a mission in the area, and before leaving he promised the Tejas that he would return. Then León led his expedition back to Coahuila. There he made his report, which he sent, along with the two Frenchmen, to the viceroy in Mexico City, the Conde de Galve.

Galve carefully considered León's report, and he interrogated the two Frenchmen personally. His decision was that León should return to Fort Saint Louis and destroy it so completely that the French could never reoccupy it; and Father Massanet was to be allowed to build a mission in the vicinity for the Tejas Indians. For a fourth time Alonso de León prepared to march for Texas; this time he took one hundred and ten soldiers, Father Massanet, and three Franciscan missionaries from the College of the Holy Cross at Querétaro. Setting out on March 27, 1690, they arrived at Fort Saint Louis on April 30 and Father Massanet personally burned the French buildings, and the soldiers thoroughly destroyed all traces of the settlement. Then moving eastward, they met the Tejas Indians on the bank of the Trinity River on May 22. León there divided his soldiers into two parties, one to construct Mission San Francisco de los Tejas, the other to explore in the vicinity for evidences of French penetration. Then leaving the three Franciscan missionaries to their work, León led his men back to Coahuila, ransoming three French boys and a girl from the Indians along the way.

Still Viceroy Galve was not satisfied. He ordered that Texas should be established as a province on a still more formal basis. To command this expedition he chose Captain Domingo Terán de los Rios, who was appointed governor of the province, and with him went Father Massanet as superintendent of the Texas mission field. De los Rios left Monclova on May 16, 1691, with fifty soldiers and nine Franciscan missionaries. On August 4, after stopping at Matagorda Bay where they secured the release of another two French survivors from the Indians, the expedition arrived at San Francisco de los Tejas. De los Rios found that the missions were in a sad condition; the Indians had turned hostile after an epidemic and a drought the previous year. After a thorough search in that vicinity, he departed early in 1692, leaving behind Father Massanet, two other missionaries, and nine soldiers.

This attempt to settle Texas proved abortive. A supply expedition to the missionaries among the Tejas in the spring of 1693 found that the natives were even more hostile. The leader of this relief column, Captain Gregorio de Salinas Varona, reported that he found the situation hopeless; when he returned he brought with him a letter from Father Massanet declaring that the East Texas Indians could be converted only with the assistance of a large number of soldiers who would force the natives to live in closely regulated missions. The viceroy called a council which decided that this mission field be abandoned. Before the order could be transmitted to Texas, however, the abandonment was already a fact. On October 25, 1693, fearing an imminent uprising, the missionaries in Texas buried their church bells and other religious articles and hurriedly fled toward Coahuila under cover of darkness. For the next twenty years Texas was left to the Indians.

During the years between 1693 and 1713, several events occurred which forced a resettlement of the province of Texas. In 1699 the French founded the colony of Biloxi (Mississippi), and in 1702 they established Mobile (Alabama). Gradually the French spread north and west, founding trading posts among the Indians. In 1712 the French king, Louis XIV, granted the colony of Louisiana to Antoine Crozat as a private monopoly. Crozat sent Sieur Antoine de la Mothe Cadillac to govern the area with instructions to increase the trade with the Indians and to establish commercial relations with the Spaniards of Mexico if possible. Cadillac quickly discovered, however, that Spain's mercantile laws forbade any foreign trade with its New World colonies. At this juncture Cadillac received a very welcome letter from Father Francisco Hidalgo, a Franciscan padre at the Spanish outpost of San Juan Bautista, founded in 1699 on the south side of the Rio Grande (opposite present-day Eagle Pass.) Father Hidalgo had been one of the missionaries at San Francisco de los Tejas and hoped to return to labor among these Indians, but for years his requests had been ignored. On January 17, 1711, Father Hidalgo wrote the French governor

of Louisiana requesting co-operation in establishing missions in the
East Texas area. A copy of this letter reached Cadillac early in
1713.

Perhaps Father Hidalgo was sincere in wanting French co-operation; perhaps he thought that if the French expressed interest in
such a project, the Spanish officials would react by recolonizing the
region. At any rate, his letter brought a quick response from Governor Cadillac. The Frenchman decided to use the letter as an excuse to establish relations with the Spanish outpost of San Juan
Bautista, where Father Hidalgo was then residing. For this delicate
mission, Cadillac selected Louis Juchereau de St. Denis, a native of
Canada, who was then commander of Biloxi. St. Denis spoke fluent
Spanish and was conversant in several Indian dialects; in addition,
he was a gentleman of poise, cultivated and diplomatic.

Near the end of September 1713, St. Denis set out from Mobile
with a small party of traders and a large supply of goods. During
the winter of 1713–14 he traded among the natives along the Red
River near the present-day Texas-Louisiana border, naming his
post Natchitoches, after the most numerous tribe in the vicinity.
Then in the spring of 1714, he entered Texas and proceeded to San
Juan Bautista, arriving there in the fall of the year. He presented
his passport and Hidalgo's letter to the presidial commander, Captain Diego Ramón, and inquired about commercial relations. Captain Ramón responded by arresting the Frenchman and his companions, confiscating their goods, and sending their documents and
effects to the viceroy in Mexico City, the Duke de Linares. Six
weeks later Ramón received the viceroy's decision, an order for St.
Denis to be brought from San Juan Bautista to the capital city. The
smooth-tongued Frenchman used this interval to court and win a
promise of marriage from the presidial commander's granddaugh-
ter, the beautiful María Ramón. Then, promising to return, he was
taken southward by a detachment of soldiers.

The viceroy interviewed St. Denis several times. St. Denis declared that the French merely wished to make sure that missions were built among the East Texas Indians, that they had no
intention of settling the area, and that their only interest in the
Spanish outposts in the north was one of trade. The viceroy then
convened a council of war, and decided that four missions should

be built among the Tejas Indians, each to be guarded by two soldiers. On September 30, 1715, the viceroy named as commander of this expedition Captain Domingo Ramón, the uncle of María Ramón, and named St. Denis as guide for the party. The expedition, with a total of sixty-five persons, including St. Denis and his new bride, left Saltillo, Coahuila, on February 17, 1716.

They arrived at the site of San Francisco de los Tejas on June 20, and were greeted warmly by the Indians. Nuestro Padre de San Francisco de los Tejas was built near by, and Father Hidalgo was entrusted with it. Three other missions were built in the area, all of log-cabin construction. Then Ramón and St. Denis visited at Natchitoches and went on to Mobile for talks with the French governor. St. Denis used the trip to procure more goods for trading with the Spaniards in Coahuila. Returning to the East Texas mission field, Ramón learned that two new religious establishments had already been erected, one of them, San Miguel de Linares de los Adaes, only twenty-one miles from Natchitoches. The Spanish captain completed his instructions by building a presidio, Nuestra Señora de los Dolores de los Tejas, at the western end of the line of missions.

Upon returning to San Juan Bautista, St. Denis was immediately arrested by Captains Domingo and Diego Ramón, and his goods were confiscated. He was informed that it was illegal for a Spanish subject to import foreign goods. Again St. Denis was taken to Mexico City for questioning by the viceroy. And once again he managed to talk his way to freedom. His goods had been sold at public auction, and even the money from the sale was given to him. However, he was denied permission to return to Texas. On September 5, 1718, he secretly slipped out of the city and returned to Natchitoches. Later María joined him there. For the next two decades he was a thorn in the Spanish side because of his influence over the local Indians. Not until his death in 1744 were the Spaniards in East Texas able to feel they really controlled the area.

The distance from San Juan Bautista on the Rio Grande to the settlements in East Texas was so great that the Spaniards quickly felt the need of a halfway station. Captain Domingo Ramón recognized the value of such a settlement and of his need for additional soldiers in Texas, and so informed the viceroy in a letter of July 22,

1716. A council of war in Mexico City responded by calling for recommendations from the newly appointed governor of Texas and Coahuila, Martín de Alarcón. While these deliberations were in progress, Father Antonio de San Buenaventura Olivares requested permission to build a mission beside the San Antonio River some one hundred miles above Matagorda Bay. The council of war combined Olivares's mission and the halfway station; they ordered the erection of a presidio and mission on the San Antonio River. Governor Alarcón was entrusted with this task.

On April 9, 1718, Alarcón set out with seventy-two persons, including seven families. This expedition arrived on the San Antonio River on April 25 and soon built a fort named San Antonio de Béxar. Father Olivares established a mission near by named San Antonio de Valero, the chapel of which, the Alamo, later would become famous in Texas history. Crops were planted by the civilians, and Indians soon began gathering at the mission. In fact, by December work had begun on irrigation ditches to ensure good crops each year. Alarcón returned to Coahuila in early 1719, thinking that Texas was a secure province.

A small war in Europe upset Alarcón's expectations. On January 9, 1719, even as the founder of San Antonio was preparing to leave his new settlement, the king of France declared war on Spain because the Spanish had invaded Sardinia and Sicily. The French in Louisiana heard of this war before the Spaniards of Texas did, and in the summer of 1719 St. Denis sent seven soldiers, under the command of Corporal M. Blondel, from Natchitoches to reconnoiter in East Texas. About the middle of June, Blondel and his men approached Mission San Miguel de Linares de los Adaes. There they found one soldier and one lay brother, both of whom surrendered without a struggle. Blondel declared that all the possessions of the mission were the spoils of war, and ordered his men to carry them outside for transportation eastward. In the confusion that resulted, some chickens escaped their pens and ran among the Frenchmen's horses. Blondel's horse reared in fright, and the corporal was thrown. This distraction allowed the lay brother to escape; he fled to a nearby mission where he declared that the French had invaded with a large force.

Captain Domingo Ramón, who commanded the presidio of Dolores, decided to abandon East Texas when he heard of the "invasion." In October 1719 a caravan of refugees from East Texas
arrived at San Antonio in pitiful condition. There they learned that
the war in Europe had already been terminated. Spanish honor had
been offended, however, and the viceroy decided to take vigorous
steps to reoccupy the lost territory. At this juncture a wealthy resident of Coahuila, the Marqués de Aguayo, offered his services and
his money in the reoccupation. The viceroy responded by naming
Aguayo governor of Texas and Coahuila, and instructed him to
recruit sufficient soldiers to re-establish Spanish authority in East
Texas, this time permanently. Aguayo, in a burst of patriotic zeal,
replied that he would do all this entirely out of his own funds.

With a businessman's thoroughness, Aguayo proceeded with his
task, and on March 20, 1721, he was ready. He had gathered five
hundred men and ten times that number of horses. Arriving in San
Antonio, he learned that a new mission had been founded there to
house the refugee neophytes of East Texas; the mission was named
in the new governor's honor: San José y San Miguel de Aguayo.
And he learned there that Captain Domingo Ramón had gone to
La Bahía del Espíritu Santo (as the Spaniards called Matagorda
Bay) and had taken possession of the strategic point where Fort
Saint Louis had once rested. Proceeding into East Texas, Aguayo
re-established all the abandoned missions. Then, only a short distance from Natchitoches, he built a new presidio, Nuestra Señora
del Pílar de los Adaes (near present-day Robeline, Louisiana).
Known as Los Adaes, this fort was the official capital of Texas
until 1773. Next Aguayo held a meeting with St. Denis in which he
protested against the French trading with the natives of Texas. On
his return trip to San Antonio, Aguayo re-established the presidio
of Dolores and left fifty soldiers there. At San Antonio he had the
presidio rebuilt, replacing the wooden palisades with adobes. Then
he toured the La Bahía region, finding that a presidio named Nuestra Señora de Loreto had been constructed by Ramón and that
nearby was Mission Nuestra Señora del Espíritu Santo de Zúñiga.
Satisfied with what had been accomplished, Aguayo returned to
Coahuila. He left behind him two hundred and sixty-eight soldiers,

four presidios, and ten missions, and two of the settlements, San Antonio and Los Adaes, had civilian settlers. Never again would France seriously challenge the Spanish hold on the province.

The one weakness in the Texas colony was that there were few civilians. The Marqués de Aguayo, aware of this, recommended to the king that several hundred families from the Canary Islands be brought to Texas. Not until 1729 did the king act on this recommendation, when he ordered two hundred families to be sent; but the order was cancelled before one-eighth that number had departed. In 1731 fifteen families from the Canary Islands finally arrived at San Antonio. They received small sums of money from the royal treasury to assist them in adjusting to their new home, and they were given seeds, implements, and land grants. In addition, they were conceded the status of *hidalgos,* a minor form of nobility, and San Antonio was designated a *villa,* which carried with it a limited form of local self-government. The arrival of these civilians in 1731 marked the true beginnings of Texas as a permanent colony.

THE SETTLEMENT OF ARIZONA

On May 3, 1700, Father Eusebio Francisco Kino was at San Cayetano de Tumacácori in southern Arizona, saying morning mass, when a messenger arrived with an urgent message. Almost one hundred miles to the south, at San Ignacio, some soldiers had seized an Indian for committing a crime. The soldiers intended to flog the culprit to death on the following morning, as an example. Kino immediately took to the saddle, riding directly south instead of following the trails. After covering almost three-fourths of the distance, he halted at midnight at Imuris to rest a few hours. Before sunrise he mounted again and rode out, reaching San Ignacio in time to say the morning mass and then to save the Indian from a horrible death. This incident occurred when the venerable padre was nearing his fifty-fifth birthday, and it graphically illustrates why the Pima and Papago Indians loved him. Small wonder that Herbert Eugene Bolton entitled a biographical sketch of this heroic Jesuit "The Padre on Horseback." And, considering the area in which

Kino worked, Bolton likewise was correct in entitling Kino's major biography *The Rim of Christendom*. Actually, however, the real monument to Father Eusebio Francisco Kino is the entire area that would come to be known as Arizona, for the story of its settlement is the story of Kino's missionary life.

Born in the Austrian Tyrol of Italian parentage on August 10, 1645, Kino was educated at the universities of Ingolstadt and Freiburg. Quite early in life he distinguished himself in mathematics, and could have had a very comfortable life as a professor. But just as he reached manhood he became seriously ill. He prayed for recovery, promising that he would enter the Society of Jesus and become a missionary. When he was healthy again, he kept his vow and was assigned to New Spain, where he arrived in 1681. Two years later he was sent with the expedition attempting to found a settlement at La Paz, Baja California; he was the superior of the mission, the royal astronomer, the surveyor, and the cartographer. The Indians of the area were hostile and the effort was abandoned, much to the grief of Kino and his fellow Jesuits. Returning to Mexico, he was assigned to Pimería Alta, the upper Pima country, that is, northern Sonora and southern Arizona.

Arriving at the edge of the Spanish settlement in northern Sonora in 1687, Kino began his work by founding the mission of Nuestra Señora de los Dolores, which became the parent mission for all his other religious establishments and *visitas* (regularly visited preaching stations). North and west from Dolores he pushed the work of exploration and conversion, often with no other European companion. By January 1691 he was in Arizona working at the Indian village of San Cayetano del Tumacácori; later he founded a mission there of the same name. In April 1700 he was farther down the Santa Cruz River, establishing the mission of San Xavier del Bac. Within a year he added a third mission in Arizona, known as Guevavi. At each of these points he supplied the Indians with cattle and sheep, and taught them how to look after the animals. He introduced new crops and new farming techniques, and instructed the natives how to store the harvested fruits and grains.

Hand in hand with his work as a missionary went his work of exploration. Of course, Fray Marcos, Coronado, and Melchior Díaz had passed through southern Arizona, but not since Oñate had reached the mouth of the Colorado in 1604–5 had any European seen the Gila River. The reports of at least six expeditions by Kino to that river have been preserved, and twice he penetrated as far west as the Colorado. These westward treks were prompted partly by Kino's desire to reach still more heathens, and partly by his interest in converting the natives of Baja California. He was always interested in finding a way to the region where he had first been assigned. On one of his trips to the Gila River, he found the Indians in possession of "blue shells" such as he had seen in Baja California; these, he reasoned, could have reached Pimería Alta only by a land route. *"California no es ysla!"* he wrote in his report of the trip, and soon thereafter he proved his point by journeying to the mouth of the Colorado, crossing over, and seeing that Baja was a peninsula, not an island as he had been taught in Europe and as was believed in Mexico City and Madrid.

Kino drew maps of Pimería Alta, eighteen of them in all. Many of these, especially his last of 1710, were widely circulated in Europe and had great influence on the cartography of the New World, even a century later when they were copied by Alexander von Humboldt. The Jesuit explorer was rarely given proper credit for his maps, but those plagiarizing his work copied his peculiar place names to such an extent that his touch can easily be detected.

The Pima and the Papago Indians of southern Arizona and northern Sonora recognized Kino's love and concern for them. And they knew they were eating better and more regularly as a result of his efforts. They begged him to visit their villages; they begged him to stay when he arrived; when he departed they begged him to return. Of course, there were times when his life was in danger, but he faced such moments with a calm courage and escaped unharmed. He died at the age of sixty-seven at Magdalena, Sonora. Father Luis Velarde, who knew him well, wrote of his last moments: "His deathbed, as his bed had always been, consisted of two calfskins for a mattress, two blankets such as the Indians used for cover, and a pack-saddle for a pillow." One Spanish historian declared of Kino, "He labored with apostolic zeal." Such would have been a fitting epitaph.

For almost twenty-five years after Kino's death, little was done in Arizona. Periodically the area was visited by Jesuit missionaries who would say mass at the missions or *visitas,* perform marriages, and baptize the children. These were years of consolidation in the Spanish empire, years when the wars of Europe necessitated a certain retrenchment on the further frontiers.

CONSOLIDATION, RETRENCHMENT, AND EXPANSION

Early in 1724 the viceroy of New Spain, the Marqués de Casa-fuerte, received orders to seek ways to reduce expenses on the northern frontiers. Casafuerte appointed Brigadier General Pedro de Rivera to conduct a tour of inspection from the Gulf of California to the Gulf of Mexico for this purpose. Rivera left Mexico City on November 21, 1724, and during the next four years he personally visited each of the twenty presidios that constituted the northern cordon of defense.

Rivera reached New Mexico in the summer of 1726. He noted that Albuquerque had been founded exactly twenty years previously, and had become a thriving city. It was the focal point for expansion in the Rio Abajo area, while Santa Fe was the focal point of the Rio Arriba region. Rivera cut the number of troops in New Mexico to eighty before departing, a move which the citizens protested loudly but with no success. Despite this reduction in military strength, the province prospered and expanded, overflowing the confines of the Rio Grande valley. The Apaches continued to prove invincible to the east, and the New Mexicans were forced north and west. The Navajo, who at first had been extremely hostile, decided in the second quarter of the eighteenth century that peace had many advantages, and New Mexicans began settling around the Cebolleta Mountains. By mid-century settlements were founded at the pueblo of Sandía and in the Sangre de Cristo Mountains, as well as along the Rio Chama.

Rivera reached San Antonio in August of 1728 to inspect the last province on his itinerary. He spent the next several months visiting the three areas of settlement, then made his recommendations. As a result, Dolores presidio was abandoned and more than

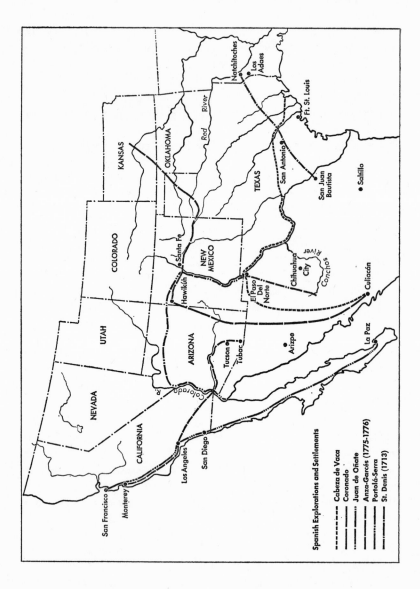

Spanish Explorations and Settlements

- - - - - - Cabeza de Vaca
— · — · — Coronado
· · · · · · · Juan de Oñate
— — — — Anza-Garcés (1775-1776)
· · · · · · · Portolá-Serra
———— St. Denis (1713)

one-half the troops in the province were withdrawn. Because of the reduction in troops in East Texas, three missions there were removed first to the Colorado River of Texas, then to San Antonio, bringing the total number of religious establishments there to five. This reduction in troops emboldened the Apache, and they increased their raids considerably. The arrival of fifteen families from the Canary Islands in 1731 helped lessen this menace, however, for all male civilians automatically were a part of the militia.

The fifteen-year period from 1731 to 1745 was one of consolidation and slow expansion in Texas. During this time the missionaries at San Antonio carried on an ambitious building program that resulted in structures renowned for their grace and beauty. And they constructed irrigation ditches there that made it possible to grow crops even in years of drought. The French threat was more commercial than military during this period, for they continued to dominate the Indian trade and they continued to expand their field of dominance. In fact, as early as 1719, Bernardo de la Harpe worked his way up the Red River and reached Santa Fe. The Spaniards hated these traders because they gave weapons, powder, and shot to the Indians in exchange for horses, cattle, and goods the Indians took in raids in Texas, New Mexico, and in the interior of New Spain.

Because of the English settlement of Georgia in 1733, an area that Spaniards considered a part of Florida, officials in Madrid feared foreign intrusion in the Seno Mexicano, a deserted strip of land stretching from Támpico, Mexico, to Matagorda Bay in Texas. Not until 1746 was a contract let for Spanish settlement, however. José de Escandón was named head of the project, and in December of 1748 he set out. Taking with him 750 soldiers and 2500 civilians, he founded twenty-three towns and fifteen missions in the next several years. Two of these towns were in Texas —Laredo and Dolores—but during the Spanish period these were never governed from Texas. They were attached to the province of Nuevo Santander (Tamaulipas).

As a part of this same colonization project, the presidio and mission of La Bahía were moved in 1749 to the San Antonio River a few miles up from the Gulf (at present-day Goliad, Texas). They retained the old name of La Bahía despite the fact that they no longer were at Matagorda Bay. And in 1754, near the new location, a second mission, Nuestra Señora del Rosario, was established.

Meanwhile there was increasing Indian hostility in the north. The Comanche had originally lived in the mountains of present-day Wyoming alongside their Cheyenne cousins, but they moved out onto the Great Plains when they started to capture wild horses. Soon they were excellent cavalrymen and began pushing southward in search of better land and a warmer climate, a move that brought them into contact and conflict with the Apache. In 1706 they made their first recorded appearance at Santa Fe. A legendary battle was fought between the Comanche and the Apache in 1725, at a river designated the Fierro (probably the Wichita). This battle reportedly lasted nine days and resulted in a decisive Comanche victory. By 1743 the Comanche were at San Antonio. The hard-pressed eastern Apache were forced onto marginal lands lying along the Rio Grande in the Big Bend country and extending across the river into Coahuila and Chihuahua, and thereafter they followed a policy of peace when other tribes were quiet and of war when raids began elsewhere and diverted Spanish attention.

The beleaguered Spanish officials at San Antonio petitioned for help in combating this new menace. Then on June 2, 1745, four Tonkawa Indian chieftains appeared in San Antonio and asked for missions. As these Indians lived north of San Antonio, their request seemed heaven-sent; such a mission might serve as a buffer against the Comanche raiders. Without awaiting official sanction, Father Mariano Francisco de los Dolores y Viana, a Franciscan, hurried north and in April 1746 he unofficially opened San Francisco Xavier de Horcasitas on the San Gabriel River. Two years later, on May 7, 1748, the viceroy gave his approval for the mission. It grew so rapidly that by the following year two additional religious establishments were operating in the area, and in 1750 the jubilant Franciscans reported 502 converts were living in these missions. On March 30, 1750, the viceroy ordered a presidio to be established beside the San Xavier missions. The province of Texas was growing.

There was also growth in the area later to be known as Arizona during this second quarter of the eighteenth century. In 1736 a wandering Yaqui Indian found silver in an arroyo known as Arizona. He revealed his discovery to a Sonoran merchant, who in turn told others, and soon there was a rush to the area (now thought to have been on the Arizona-Sonora border just west of Nogales). Numbering an estimated five to ten thousand, many of these treasure-seekers were *gambucinos,* footloose individuals who rushed to any area showing promise of quick wealth—and who hoped to escape payment of the royal taxes of 20 per cent on minerals.

Many of these *gambucinos* found the wealth they sought. In the arroyo and surrounding hills they found sheets of pure silver, one "nugget" weighing an estimated 425 pounds. Knowledgeable observers estimated that approximately ten thousand pounds of silver were taken from the Real de Arizona, as the area was named. This was accomplished in only a few months and with very little expense. The strangest circumstance of all in this incredible story was the report that some of the pieces of silver when taken from the ground were flexible and resembled a mass of soft wax; but soon it became inflexible as if hardened by exposure to the air.

When word of the strike spread, Captain Juan Bautista de Anza of the Sonoran presidio of Fronteras, which had been founded in 1692, brought a detachment of troops to the area and began confiscating all the silver he could find. He did this pending an official ruling on the "nuggets." A ruling was needed, for under Spanish law the discoverers of ore paid 20 per cent to the royal treasury, but the finders of "treasure" paid a tax of 95 per cent. Anza wanted official clarification as to whether these *planchas de plata* (sheets of silver) constituted ore or treasure. In Mexico City the ruling was that the Real de Arizona was ore; however, Philip V ruled that the find was a "curiosity" and therefore a treasure.

By the time the king's decision could reach the northwest frontier of New Spain, it was meaningless. The Real de Arizona had been abandoned, for the easily discovered silver had been extracted and no one wished to remain in the area to dig for more because of the extreme danger from the Apaches. In addition, the area was far from the interior, and freighting costs were prohibitive for the furnaces, machinery, and supplies needed to maintain a mining settlement. (The story of the Real de Arizona first appeared in the anonymous *Apostolic Labors of the Company of Jesus,* published in Barcelona, Spain, in 1754; in 1850 José Francisco Velasco retold the saga in his *Noticias Estadísticas del Estado de Sonora.* Many of the early American speculators in Arizona mining were inspired by Velasco's tale, and the story was widely circulated, popularizing the name "Arizona" for this region. In 1861 William F. Ney translated several chapters of Velasco's book into English, further emphasizing the name "Arizona," and in 1863, when Congress gave this area separate territorial status, it used this name.)

Following this exciting interlude, Arizona again reverted to its former status as an area with only a few functioning missions and nothing more. Not until mid-century did official attention once again devolve on this "Rim of Christendom." On November 21, 1750, the Pima Indians attempted to imitate the New Mexican Pueblo Revolt of 1680. Led by Luis Oacpicagigua, the Spanish-recognized governor and captain general of the Pima, these Indians rose in a determined effort to kill or drive from their land all missionaries, soldiers, ranchers, and Spanish sympathizers. Within a week they had laid waste the larger settlements of western Pimería Alta, killing more than a hundred persons and burning or carrying away most of the property. The padre at San Xavier del Bac, along with his three soldiers, escaped to Guevavi, where he joined with the padre who served that mission and Tumacácori; together they fled down the ruined chain of missions to safety of the presidio of Terrenate, which had been founded in 1742.

When news of this uprising reached Mexico City, the viceroy immediately ordered measures taken to repair the damage that had been inflicted and to prevent such uprisings in the future. Governor Diego Ortiz de Parrilla of Sonora was ordered to move at once. He quickly gathered an army and marched to San Ignacio, which he made his headquarters. A force under Captain José Díaz del Carpio of the presidio of Terrenate was sent northward to find the Pima. Carpio proceeded down the valley of the Santa Cruz River to an abandoned Pima village named Tubac, approximately three miles north of Tumacácori; there he learned that the Pima had taken refuge in the Santa Catalina Mountains and that they could be reached only through Indian scouts. From Tubac through these

Indian scouts word was sent to Luis Oacpicagigua that all would be forgiven if the Pima would return to their villages and swear allegiance to Spain once again. On March 18 Luís came to Tubac for a conference with Carpio and there announced his readiness to accept the terms offered. His followers returned to their homes, and peace was restored.

The cause of the rebellion was debated in the capital of Sonora and in Mexico City. Governor Parrilla blamed the Jesuits for their cruel treatment of the natives; the Jesuits in turn blamed the governor and the army for military blunders and for naming Luis governor and captain general of the Pima. An investigation followed which resulted in both the Jesuits and the governor being partly blamed and partly absolved. The report of this investigation stated that the Pima were unhappy because some of their best lands had been taken by Spaniards; that they were angry at the punishments meted out by the Spanish missionaries to backsliding converts; and that Luís had been offended by the padres' refusal to recognize his leadership of his nation. The viceroy, the Conde de Revilla Gigedo (the elder), was more concerned with preventing future uprisings than with the causes of the last one. He proposed to the king that a new presidio be established in the northwest, one that would "facilitate Spanish advance to the Gila and Colorado Rivers." The father provincial of the Pimería Alta missions, Juan Antonio Balthasar, declared that a garrison of fifty men would be sufficient, and suggested that Captain Tómas de Beldarráin be placed in command of the new post. On January 31, 1752, the new presidio received official sanction. Beldarráin was to command it, Governor Parrilla was to choose the site, and four cannons were to be sent to it.

On March 26, 1752, Parrilla chose the abandoned Pima village of Tubac, renamed San Ignacio de Tubac. This location was thought ideal: it was situated beside the Santa Cruz River, which had sufficient water even for irrigation; good agricultural land was available in the vicinity; it was in the heart of the Pima country, where any new revolt could be detected immediately; and it was on the edge of the Apache raiding paths and would thus serve as a deterrent to them. Beldarráin proceeded with his task with thoroughness and efficiency, and a civilian population was attracted to the area. By 1757 the settlement had 411 residents, including the troops. Garrison quarters and fortifications were completed by Beldarráin before his death in 1759.

The building of this presidio did not enable the Spaniards to advance northward, however. The Pima uprising of 1751 had reduced the influence of the Jesuit missionaries in the region, and there was no expansion in the years that followed; there was no further talk of new missions, of penetrating as far north as the Hopi country, even of reaching the Gila and Colorado rivers. The natives for the most part lived as they pleased, not molesting the padres, but not living at the religious establishments. They simply considered the missions convenient places for protecting their aged and ill from raiding bands of Apaches. Missionary work was at a standstill.

Following the death of Beldarráin, the presidio of Tubac was commanded by Juan Bautista de Anza, the son of the presidial commander of the same name who had been sent to the Real de Arizona in 1736. Anza thus was the son—and the grandson—of a presidial commander. Born in 1735, he grew to manhood on the frontier and had an intimate knowledge of the Indians. He entered the army at the age of eighteen and served in many campaigns on the northern frontier. On February 19, 1760, he was promoted to captain and sent to Tubac to replace Beldarráin. All records indicate that Anza was a man of great ability and strong character, willing to pursue the Apaches to their strongholds and wage war on them. Father Pedro Font, a Franciscan missionary later to serve in Sonora, Arizona, and California, called Anza "an able and courageous officer." Coming from a padre such words were high praise, for few missionaries found anything worthy of commendation about military figures. Anza proved equal to the task in Arizona, and by vigorous measures held the frontier in check.

The Pima uprising of 1751 in Arizona was nothing compared with the Comanche difficulties in Texas of approximately the same period. The Comanche confrontation with the Spaniards grew out of the founding, in 1746, of the San Xavier missions north of San Antonio, which proved so successful by 1750. On March 30 of that year the viceroy ordered the establishment of a presidio in the vicinity, and placed Captain Felipe de Rábago y Terán in command of it. Rábago y Terán's orders directed him to recruit fifty soldiers and to secure as many civilians as possible, then proceed to the San Xavier area and build the presidio at a site to be selected jointly by himself and the missionaries. He was also instructed to co-operate with the Franciscans in every possible way.

Rábago y Terán arrived at the San Xavier area on December 11, 1751, with his soldiers and a few civilians. But he did not carry out his orders to co-operate with the padres—or even to proceed with the construction of a presidio. Quarrelsome and arrogant, he was bent on making a fortune through graft, and almost immediately he began quarreling with the Franciscans. He wrote the viceroy that the San Xavier site was poorly chosen, that the presidio and missions instead should be situated on the nearby San Marcos River. Meanwhile Father Mariano, the founder of these missions, was also writing to the viceroy, requesting that Rábago y Terán be replaced as presidial commander. While the viceroy was pondering the difficulty, matters came to a head at San Xavier. The missionaries excommunicated the entire garrison of soldiers for their dissolute conduct, and in the ensuing quarrel the Indians at the missions began fleeing into the wilderness. Then two missionaries were murdered, and in the immediate investigation four soldiers declared they had committed the deed at the instigation of Captain Rábago y Terán.

The captain apparently had friends in high places, however, for the man sent to replace him and to hold a formal investigation was his brother, Captain Pedro de Rábago y Terán. He arrived on August 11, 1754, and within a month had his report ready. It completely absolved Felipe of all blame, declared that the missions were in a bad location, and recommended that the establishment be moved to the San Marcos River. In fact, with no official sanction he moved the presidio to the San Marcos River the following year; the missionaries had little choice but to follow. The viceroy finally approved this change on February 6, 1756, but three months later he changed his mind. For some time there had been talk of establishing a mission and presidio in the Apache country, and in May the viceroy ordered the San Xavier complex to be moved to the San Sabá River, to the northwest of San Antonio. Father Mariano disagreed violently with this change, and he, too, made an unofficial move—to the Guadalupe River, thirty-one miles from San Antonio (near present-day New Braunfels). Named Nuestra Señora de Guadalupe, the mission had a tenuous existence until March 1758, when it was finally closed.

Despite these violations of his orders, the viceroy did not lose interest in a mission and presidio for the Apache. To his delight a wealthy Mexican stepped forward with an offer to underwrite the cost of a religious establishment for the Apache for three years, provided that his cousin, Father Alonso Giraldo de Terreros, would be placed in charge of it, and provided that the government would establish and support a presidio in the vicinity. The viceroy accepted this offer and agreed to the conditions set. The troops from the presidio at San Marcos were transferred to San Antonio, where Colonel Diego Ortiz de Parrilla, perhaps as punishment for his mishandling of the Pima Uprising of 1751, was placed in command, Captain Pedro de Rábago y Terán having died in 1756.

Parrilla, Father Terreros, and a large party arrived at the specified site on the San Sabá River (near present-day Menard) on April 18, 1757. Soon they had erected Mission San Sabá de Santa Cruz, and almost two miles upriver on the opposite bank of the stream was built the presidio of San Luis de las Amarillas de San Sabá. But no Apaches came to the mission. Finally in June some three thousand Lipan Apaches arrived, but they informed the missionaries that they were on the annual buffalo hunt. They promised to return in the fall and settle in the vicinity, but they never did. During the winter of 1757–58 the Spaniards heard rumors of Comanche plans to attack the establishment because of its connections with the Apaches, but the Spaniards paid little attention to these rumors. Then, on March 2, 1758, the Comanches drove off the presidial horse herd, and Parrilla took defensive measures, even attempting to persuade the missionaries to move within the walls of the presidio. They refused, preferring, so they said, to stay at their place of duty.

On the morning of March 16 two thousand Comanches appeared at the mission. The priests met them with presents of tobacco and trinkets, but the Comanches were not satisfied. One chief demanded a letter from Father Terreros to the presidial commander stating that the Comanches came in peace and should be admitted inside the fort. Terreros gave the desired letter; but when its bearers returned stating that Parrilla had refused to honor it, the Indians began murdering everyone in sight. One missionary and eight Spaniards barricaded themselves inside one of the rooms and escaped the Indians, but the rest were killed. Parrilla waited until the night of March 17–18 before sending a scouting party to investigate. This party found four of the nine Spaniards inside the room still alive.

When the viceroy received Parrilla's report of the attack, he called a council of war. On June 27, 1758, this council decided that San Sabá should not be abandoned and that a large campaign should be mounted against the Comanche in order to salvage Spanish honor and prestige in the province. By August 1759 more than five hundred Spanish soldiers were at San Antonio and ready for the campaign. But, these were not professional soldiers for the most part; one officer declared that they consisted of "cowboys, tailors, laborers, cigar-dealers, hatters, peons from the mines, and persons of similar occupations." With them when they marched were 134 Apache allies willing to fight their enemy, the Comanche, and they took with them several cannon.

For 350 miles they met no resistance. Then emerging on the banks of the Red River on October 7, they were greeted by a strange sight. The Comanches were gathered in a fortified emplacement surrounded by a palisade and a moat; overhead flew the French flag—no doubt in deference to French advisers. The battle that followed was a disaster for Parrilla and the Spaniards. "After eleven volleys," he wrote later of his cannon, "the Indians still greeted each shot with a shout of laughter." The "Santiago" was given and a charge made, but the Comanches easily repulsed it. When darkness fell, Parrilla found that neither side had won a clear decision, but his own position was very tenuous. The Comanches were maneuvering to encircle him, some of his troops were deserting, and his Apache allies had abandoned him, taking with them a large part of his horse herd. On the morning of October 8 he ordered a withdrawal. But the return to San Antonio proved more a rout than a retreat, for the Comanches followed, killing stragglers and harassing the Spaniards at every turn.

This disgraceful defeat was never avenged. Instead the Spaniards sent emissaries among the Comanche urging a treaty of peace, and in 1760 the captured cannon were returned. Two years later came a formal agreement that the Comanche would not "persecute the Apaches who have been reduced to missions." The presidio at San Sabá was re-garrisoned under Captain Felipe de Rábago y Terán and remained in existence until 1768. The mission was abandoned, but farther south on the banks of the Nueces River two new Apache missions were built, Nuestra Señora de la Candelaria del Cañon and San Lorenzo de la Santa Cruz. The former lasted four years, the latter seven; only a few Apaches ever settled in them, and they were finally abandoned.

The Spaniards had been more successful along the Gulf Coast. Fearing French intrusion near the mouth of the Trinity River, the viceroy issued an order on February 4, 1756, for the founding of a presidio there. In addition, there was to be a mission, and a civil settlement of fifty families was to be established. The presidio, named San Augustín de Ahumada, was constructed in July of that year, and near by rose Mission Nuestra Señora de la Luz. No civilians ever came to the region, however.

The years of consolidation, retrenchment, and expansion came to an end in the northern provinces in the 1760's. In 1763 the Seven Years War was concluded by the Peace of Paris; the Spaniards during this conflict had joined with their French cousins and had lost Florida to England as a result. To compensate for this loss, France gave Spain the Louisiana Territory west of the Mississippi River. This transfer of territory necessitated a new look at policy in Texas. Then, in 1767, the Jesuits were expelled from all Spanish colonies, and Pimería Alta and Baja California became mission fields for the Franciscans. Finally, the Spaniards heard rumors of Russian interest in California, rumors which would make them pursue a policy of "defensive expansion." The last third of the eighteenth century saw drastic changes in the northern provinces of New Spain.

THE SETTLEMENT OF CALIFORNIA

The existence of California had been known since the days of Hernán Cortés, and from time to time it had been visited by naval expeditions. Juan Rodríguez Cabrillo, a Portuguese employed by the Spanish, sailed up the west coast of North America in 1542, reaching San Diego Bay on September 28. Just how far north he proceeded is not known, although it is generally conceded that he was at Monterey harbor. He died on January 3, 1543, and was succeeded by Bartolomé Ferrelo (Ferrer), who again sailed northward to approximately the 41st parallel (about the Eel River or the Mad River) before returning home. The next major visitation was made by Sebastián Vizcaíno, a merchant seeking pearls in Baja California. In 1602 he took three vessels and a large party of soldiers and slowly beat his way northward against unfavorable winds. Late in the year he reached the harbor at Monterey. His report described this as "the best port that could be desired, for besides being sheltered from all the winds, it has many pines for masts and yards, and live oaks and white oaks, and water in great quantity, all near the shore." He declared the land was fertile, the climate hospitable, the Indians friendly, and the harbor ideal for ships coming from the Philippine Islands. Vizcaíno left Monterey in January of 1603 and went up to 42 or 43 degrees north latitude before returning. His report about Monterey harbor, which was a gross exaggeration, was seized upon by the viceroy; for a century and a half thereafter the major Spanish goal in California was to plant a colony in Monterey.

Always, however, there were more pressing commitments elsewhere, and funds were not available from the royal treasury. Settlement proceeded slowly up the west coast of Mexico into Sinaloa and Sonora during the seventeenth century, but there were attempts to jump across the Gulf and found colonies in Baja California. In 1683 Father Eusebio Francisco Kino, the missionary to whose name Arizona is inseparably linked, had accompanied a projected colony to the La Paz region, only to meet with failure. The sterile mountains and deserts of Baja, coupled with the hostility of the natives, made the project a formidable one. Finally the goal was accomplished by Father Juan María de Salvatierra, like Kino, a

Jesuit brother, in 1697. The administration of Baja California was unique in New Spain: as provided by royal concession, the province was controlled exclusively by the Jesuits. All soldiers, all civilians, and all mission activities were under the full control of the order, and the crown subsidized the effort.

In the seventy years that followed, the Jesuits continued to expand northward, finally reaching almost to the present boundary dividing Upper and Lower California. Finally, in 1767, the Jesuits were expelled from all Spanish territory. This momentous undertaking in New Spain was entrusted to José de Gálvez, who had arrived in Mexico City in 1765 with a commission as *visitador-general* and orders to overhaul the administration of the entire viceroyalty. Gálvez, an Andalusian of humble origins, had risen to prominence through his own merits which had been recognized by the capable and energetic Charles III of Spain.

The visitor-general knew that the expulsion of the Jesuits would cause a violent reaction among the natives under their care, but that it might cause an explosion in Baja California particularly, where the order had enjoyed exclusive control. Therefore he chose his men for the task very carefully. Captain Gaspar de Portolá was named governor of the province, and given orders to get the Jesuits out. Portolá proceeded to do this with considerable smoothness; the black-robed friars sailed away on January 3, 1768. To care for the spiritual needs of the converts at the many missions in the province, as well as in Pimería Alta, Franciscans were assigned from the colleges of New Spain. Those bound for Baja California were headed by Father Junípero Serra, one of the great men of Southwestern history.

Born in Mallorca in 1713, Serra entered the Franciscan order at the age of seventeen, where he gained a reputation as a philosopher and orator. He arrived at Vera Cruz in 1749 in good health, but during the walk to Mexico City he was bitten by a scorpion and the sore never healed; for the rest of his life he walked with a limp and with considerable pain. In New Spain he studied the life of Father Kino and concluded that the great Jesuit had the right idea: the Indians could best be converted when they were shown that Christianity brought with it a more abundant material life as well as increased spiritual riches. In the years that followed he gained fame for his work among the Pame tribe in the Sierra Gorda Mountains; within ten years he not only had made this nation one of the most civilized in Mexico but had transformed the region into a productive and cultivated area.

When appointed to the Baja California missions in 1767, Serra organized a band of sixteen priests and walked overland the five hundred miles to San Blas. They arrived at Loreto in Lower California in April 1768 and soon began their spiritual task in the province. Even before Serra could complete a tour of inspection, however, he received a message from José de Gálvez: "The King has need of you. Come at once. We are going to found new missions."

Once again a policy of "defensive expansion" was to push the frontier northward. Russian fur traders had begun working in Alaska and the Aleutians in the 1740's, and were expanding their operations. The Spanish minister at St. Petersburg heard disturbing rumors of a threatened move by these traders southward into California. These rumors he forwarded to the court at Madrid; the king in turn sent an order to the viceroy of New Spain to investigate, who passed it along to Gálvez. The visitor-general interpreted the order to investigate as a mandate for the colonization of Vizcaíno's fine harbor of Monterey. With a vigor not usually found in the Spanish empire, Gálvez set about the task. Portolá would be in command of the military occupation of the province, while Father Serra would serve as *presidente* of the missions there. Two expeditions were to go by land, one led by Captain Fernando de Rivera y Moncada, to consist of twenty-five soldiers, forty mission Indians, and four hundred head of livestock; and the other led by Portolá and Serra, to consist of twelve soldiers, forty-four mission Indians, and all the livestock Serra could requisition from the Baja California missions. Gálvez also commandeered three ships, the *San Carlos,* the *San Antonio,* and the *San José.* He worked with such a fury readying the ships and the land parties that he inspired terror in the hearts of his underlings; in fact, at times his behavior bordered on complete insanity. He claimed revelations from Saint Francis; on one occasion he even claimed to be King of Prussia.

The *San Antonio* was the first to reach the harbor at San Diego; it arrived after a voyage of fifty-four days. Shortly afterward the *San Carlos* arrived in terrible condition; the vessel had required 110 days to reach the port, unfavorable winds having driven it almost to Panama before it could beat its way northward. The *San José* with its crew and passengers, numbering ninety-three in all, simply disappeared with all hands. Scurvy had ravaged the *San Carlos* on its voyage, and soon those aboard the *San Antonio* suffered from it. Before long only twelve men were left alive from the combined crews of the two ships, and thirteen soldiers had died from the disease. The land parties fared better. Rivera y Moncada's division blazed a trail northward, and it was easily followed by Portolá and Serra. On July 1 all four parties were reunited at San Diego, and the following day a formal ceremony was held to mark the founding of a colony there.

Soon after the ceremony, the colony again split. Portolá led most of the soldiers northward toward Monterey, leaving Serra and a few soldiers, along with the five missionaries, to care for the sick. In his diary Portolá declared that he "went on by land to Monterey with that small company of persons, or rather say skeletons, who had been spared by scurvy, hunger, and thirst." Every step of their six-hundred-mile trek was one of discovery, for no European had ever walked the shoreline of California before. Fortunately most of the natives were friendly or were so frightened that they hid. On October 1 they reached the harbor at Monterey, but it proved a severe disappointment. There was no fine harbor. Thinking they had not yet reached the port described by Vizcaíno, Portolá and his men went on up the coast as far as San Francisco Bay. Then they returned to San Diego, living on rotting mule meat most of the way.

He found the situation at San Diego desperate. Serra had founded Mission San Diego de Alcalá on July 16, and the *San Antonio* had been sent for more supplies. The *San Carlos* was left at San Diego for want of a crew. During the six months Portolá was gone, nineteen more persons had died of scurvy, no Indians had been baptized at the mission, and the *San Antonio* had not returned. Captain Rivera y Moncada was sent overland to Baja California for help, and the little colony waited anxiously. Finally Portolá set March 20 as the date for abandoning California, but on March 19 the *San Antonio* hove into sight, bearing provisions. Spirits quickly revived with food, and Portolá ordered the *San An-*

tonio to sail for Monterey. Father Serra went with the ship, while the captain took sixteen soldiers with him overland to the same destination. Portolá arrived first, to be joined a week later by Serra; and on June 3, 1770, a presidio and mission were declared to be in existence. Portolá thereupon invested Lieutenant Pedro Fages with the governorship of the province and sailed aboard the *San Antonio* for Mexico. There he reported the successful colonization of California to the viceroy, the Marqués de Croix. The viceroy, in a special tribute to Gálvez, ordered the church bells of the capital city rung and flags flown to signalize this advance of the frontier. In addition, a special high mass was held and attended by the viceroy and his court.

There was little celebrating in California, however. Life there was very precarious owing to the shortage of supplies and the small number of settlers. Procuring supplies locally was difficult, and the colony was dependent upon Mexico for most of the necessities of life. In addition, soldiers and missionaries soon began to quarrel. Governor Fages insisted that he alone had the right to decide when and where a mission was to be built, while Father Serra insisted that such was his own prerogative. Misconduct in the private lives of the soldiers at the new missions hampered the work of the padres, but Fages turned a deaf ear to all complaints. By the end of 1773 there were two presidios and five missions in existence— seemingly an impressive record. But the forts were wooden stockades surrounding shacks of sticks and mud, and there were only sixty-one soldiers in the province. The missions had converted only five hundred natives, almost all of whom were women, children, and the aged. In addition to the religious establishments at San Diego and Monterey, three others had been built: Mission San Antonio was constructed in 1771, San Gabriel the same year, and San Luis Obispo two years later. But despite the labors of Serra and his fellow Franciscan workers, few men had been converted.

In constructing these seven establishments more than half a million pesos had been expended, and yet the colony was not self-supporting. When the supply ships were late, the settlers went hungry. For example, in 1772 when the ships failed to arrive at the appointed date, Governor Fages sent several soldiers into Cañada de los Osos to hunt bear and send the meat back to the colonists.

For three months this continued, until the arrival of a ship brought more palatable food. By the end of 1773 José de Gálvez had returned to Spain, and officials in Mexico City were not enthusiastic about the continued expenditures needed to keep the colony going. The Dominican order asked to be allowed to work in the Californias, and an agreement that turned over to them all of the lower peninsula was worked out. This freed eight more Franciscans for work in the new colony, but what was desperately needed was a permanent supply route, one not subject to the caprices of wind and waves. From Mexico came disturbing rumors that Viceroy Carlos Francisco de Croix intended the abandonment of the province.

In 1772 Serra journeyed to Mexico City for talks with the new viceroy, Antonio María de Bucareli y Ursúa. As a result Fages was removed from his post as governor of the province, and Rivera y Moncada assumed it with orders to help convert the natives by establishing new missions. Bucareli also sent reinforcements to the colony, consisting of fifty-one persons, most of them married soldiers and their families. Serra returned to California in 1774 secure in the knowledge that the viceroy was sympathetic, but still more was needed. A land route had to be secured to the new province. At this juncture a proposal came to the viceroy's attention from Captain Juan Bautista de Anza at the presidio of Tubac. A Franciscan priest at San Xavier del Bac had penetrated to the Colorado River and beyond, and he thought that California could be reached from Arizona. The viceroy was interested and requested more particulars.

When the Jesuits had been removed from Pimería Alta, their place had been taken by fourteen Franciscans from the college of Querétaro. Among these padres was Father Francisco Garcés, who was assigned to the mission of San Xavier del Bac (near present Tucson). Although he was still under thirty, Garcés became affectionately known as "Old Man" to the Pima and Papago Indians. He was an admirable successor to Kino in the work of conversion and exploration. Twice he visited the Pima on the Gila River. On his third trip he journeyed down the Gila to its junction with the Colorado, crossing near its mouth and proceeding as far west as the termination of the Cocopah range at Signal Mountain. Along this route he met Indians who told him of white men to the west, and they showed a knowledge of the compass and the burning glass. Garcés concluded that there was an easy route overland to California, for looking westward he could see two gaps in the sierra. Returning to San Xavier, he informed Captain Anza of his adventures. Anza wrote the viceroy requesting to be allowed to pursue the project. Bucareli gladly gave the necessary permission, and an expedition was prepared at Tubac.

On January 8, 1774, Captain Anza, Father Garcés, and thirty-four soldiers left the Arizona presidio, journeying to the southwest to Caborca, Sonora. Then going along the route followed by Melchior Díaz in 1540, known as the Devil's Highway (el Camino del Diablo), they trekked west-northwest to the juncture of the Gila and Colorado rivers. There they were met by the Yuma Indians and their Chief Salvador Palma. Palma was invited to the Spanish camp, where he was given a medal and other trinkets by Anza, treated to a demonstration of target practice by the soldiers, and preached a sermon on the greatness of God and the brotherhood of Spaniard and Indian by Garcés. Palma responded by declaring the Yuma were friendly to the Spaniards, and the following day his tribesmen aided the expedition in crossing the Colorado. After great hardship in the desert of the Imperial Valley, the Anza-Garcés expedition reached San Gabriel Mission in the spring of 1774. The return trip proved little different from the outward journey, and was accomplished without incident. Anza thereupon hurried to Mexico City to make his report in person. The viceroy was so pleased that he promoted the presidial commander to lieutenant colonel—and ordered him to take settlers and supplies to California by the new road.

During the spring and summer of 1775 Anza was in Sinaloa and Sonora, gathering colonists, horses, mules, and cattle. At Tubac more settlers joined his caravan, so that when it left that outpost he had 240 people, 695 horses and mules, and 355 cattle. Leaving Tubac on October 23, Anza led his followers northward down the Santa Cruz River. During the first night one of the women gave birth to a son, Anza acting as midwife, but despite his care she died before morning; hers was the only death on the trip, although two more children were born on the trail. Proceeding down the Santa

Cruz, Anza reached the Gila and turned westward. The Yuma were still friendly when he arrived at the Colorado; in fact, Chief Palma said he was disappointed that the expedition was bound for California and was not staying among his tribesmen. However, he was delighted when he was given Viceroy Bucareli's present: shirt and trousers, jacket with yellow front, blue cape with gold braid, and black velvet cap.

Once across the river, Father Garcés and another Franciscan decided to stay among the Yuma. Anza set soldiers to work constructing a rude cabin for them, which was designated Mission Purisimo de la Concepción. Leaving the two men behind, the colonists proceeded across the desert of Southern California. They suffered from snow and intense cold rather than heat. Part of the cattle herd stampeded, and more than fifty mired in a bog and died. Finally, on New Year's Day of 1776, the caravan reached Mission San Gabriel. The remaining five hundred miles of the trip northward to Monterey was over a well-traveled road, and was made without incident. They arrived at the capital of the province in March. These colonists were destined to be the founders of a new settlement at San Francisco Bay, a settlement that itself became known as San Francisco. Having fulfilled his commission, Anza returned to make a report to the viceroy. At the crossing of the Colorado, he heard that Father Garcés had gone on a trip of exploration, but Chief Palma was anxious to go with him to Mexico City to meet Bucareli. Anza agreed to the request, and Palma subsequently was baptized in the cathedral of Mexico. Kneeling there, he said that he loved the Spaniards, that he recognized their great power, and that he wanted missions for himself and his people. Anza was rewarded for his efforts with the governorship of New Mexico, which he assumed in 1778.

Father Garcés, left behind at Mission Purisimo de la Concepción, had conceived the idea of linking Santa Fe and California by an overland route, and had set out to see if it could be done. Leaving the Yuma Indians on February 14, 1776, with only two native interpreters, he journeyed up the Colorado for fifteen days to the vicinity of present-day Needles, California. There he secured guides from the Mojave Indians, and headed west. On March 22 he saw the ocean in the distance, and a short time later he was at Mission

San Gabriel. After resting for two weeks, he returned to the Colorado, making a trip northward to the vicinity of present-day Bakersfield, on the way. Then following much the same route used by Juan de Oñate in 1604–5, he journeyed to the Hopi pueblos of northeastern Arizona. These Indians were unfriendly, and he decided he could go no farther. There at Oraibe on July 3, 1776, he penned a letter to the Franciscan padre at the nearby Zuñi pueblos telling of his journey and recommending that a road be opened from New Mexico to California. He then returned to the Colorado, went down it to Yuma Crossing, and arrived at San Xavier del Bac on September 17. He had been on the trail for eleven months and had traveled more than two thousand miles—without a single European companion.

Father Francisco Silvestre Vélez de Escalante, the Franciscan at the Zuñi pueblos, received the letter from Garcés and thought the suggestion of a road from Santa Fe to California a good one. He wrote the governor of New Mexico and his ecclesiastical superior requesting the necessary permission, which was granted. The expedition consisted of six soldiers under the command of Bernardo Miera y Pacheco, a retired militia captain, Father Francisco Atanasio Domínguez, and Father Escalante. Leaving Santa Fe on July 29, 1776, the party moved up the Chama Valley and crossed present southwestern Colorado, reaching the Wasatch Mountains of Utah and the Great Salt Lake. Winter was approaching, their provisions were low, and no one had heard of other Spaniards among the Indians. Lots were cast, and the decision was to return to New Mexico instead of pushing westward to Monterey. Proceeding by way of the Hopi villages, Zuñi, Ácoma, and Albuquerque, they reached Santa Fe on January 2, 1777.

In the immediate aftermath of the Anza-Garcés expeditions and explorations, nothing was done about Chief Palma's request for missions among the Yuma. Viceroy Bucareli saw the usefulness of the Yuma route and wished to plant settlements along the trail, but there were more pressing problems elsewhere and the necessary pesos could not be spared. Not until 1780 was permission given for this advance of the Pimería Alta and California frontier, and then it was done on an experimental basis. The colony at Yuma Crossing was to be part presidio, part mission, and part civil settlement

—but not really any one or all three. A few soldiers with their families would be sent with four Franciscans, all to live within two establishments. This innovation was justified on the basis of economy; funds were not available for missions and presidios, so they would be combined. Further savings were effected by sending fewer presents for the Indians.

These two "missions" were constructed on the California side of the river. Named La Purísima Concepción and San Pedro y San Pablo de Bicuñer, the missions each had two padres and ten soldiers with their families. Father Garcés was assigned to this effort and labored hard to make them a success. But the experiment was doomed to failure. Almost immediately it was apparent that the Yuma desire for missions had waned, and the miserly allotment of presents caused much resentment. Then the soldiers began appropriating the best lands for their own use, and they disregarded the Indians' rights to firewood and the mesquite beans that all were soon living on. Occasional floggings of the natives for infractions increased the tension.

The Yuma discontent came to a head in early July, 1781, when Captain Fernando de Rivera y Moncada, the lieutenant governor of California, arrived with an immigrant party bound for the West Coast. Camping on the east side of the river, the captain did little to restrain his soldiers from antagonizing the Yumas, and he did not lavish presents on them. Determined on retaliation, the Indians plotted in secret, then struck on the morning of July 17. At San Pedro y San Pablo they clubbed priests, soldiers, and civilians to death. At Concepción Father Garcés was spared temporarily but most of the other Spaniards were killed. On the following morning the Yumas struck the unsuspecting soldiers on the east bank of the river; fortunately the colonists had already left for California, for no one in the camp survived. On the morning of July 19 Father Garcés was killed. Only three soldiers and four settlers escaped the massacre, though the women and children were spared, an act almost unparalleled in Indian uprisings.

Governor Felipe de Neve of Sonora, formerly a governor of California refused to avenge this massacre. He sent Lieutenant Colonel Pedro Fages from Arizpe to recover the bodies for Christian burial and to ransom the captives. In the recriminations that followed, the blame for this disaster was placed on Garcés and Anza; it was said that these two men had misrepresented the Yuma. Thus the Anza-Garcés route to California was broken, leaving the province to develop along far different lines than other Spanish areas on the northern frontier. Linked to New Spain only by a tenuous sea route, the province was left to its own resources and its own devices. The influx of settlers while the land route was open, however, had of course greatly influenced its early development.

During the years after the initial settlement, Father Serra continued his work of building, preaching, and planting. Fages, the first governor, had retarded the mission work, as had his successor, Rivera y Moncada. Then in February 1777, Felipe de Neve had been assigned the governorship, and he pushed ahead with the building. El Pueblo de San José de Guadalupe and El Pueblo de Nuestra Señora la Reina de los Ángeles de Porciúncula (soon shortened to San Jose and Los Angeles) were the result of his energy. Father Serra likewise was busy until his death on August 28, 1784. By that time nine missions had been set up, more than six thousand Indians had been baptized (five thousand of them also confirmed), more than thirty thousand head of livestock roamed on mission property, and more than thirty thousand bushels of grain and vegetables were being harvested annually from mission fields. Father Serra was a meek, humble, unassuming man whose works earned for him the title "The Gentle Conquistador."

THE INTERIOR PROVINCES

Following the close of the Seven Years War and the transfer of Louisiana to Spanish control, drastic changes were needed in the northern provinces of New Spain. The first consideration was economy; the royal treasury was sadly depleted by the wars in Europe, and cuts were necessary on the fringes of the empire. The second was a solution to the impasse with the natives; the missions had not successfully converted them to Christianity and Spanish civilization. Furthermore, the province of Texas was now no longer needed as a buffer against the French—the French were gone; thus Louisiana had become a buffer province against English neighbors.

To search for ways to economize and to seek a solution to the Indian problem, the Marqués de Rubí was sent to inspect the entire area from the Gulf of California to the Gulf of Mexico and to make recommendations concerning the region. Between 1766 and 1768 the indefatigable Rubí trekked from Sonora to Texas, accompanied by a trained military engineer, Nicolás de Lafora. They talked with presidial commanders, merchants, civilians, and Indians, and they estimated the strengths and weaknesses of the missions, presidios, and civil settlements. Then in 1769 they presented their report in Mexico City, with the best map yet made of the northern province.

True enough, the Rubí report asserted, the foreign menace was gone. But the Indian menace was greater than ever before. Thus the frontier provinces should be maintained not as a buffer against French or English or Russian encroachment, but as a buffer against Indian penetrations into the interior of New Spain. Rubí proposed that existing presidios be consolidated into a cordon of defense stretching from gulf to gulf; some forts would have to be moved, some founded, and some eliminated. East Texas could be abandoned entirely, the settlers being moved to San Antonio to strengthen what would become the capital city of the province. As a solution to the Indian problem, Rubí suggested an alliance with the Comanche against the Apache; in fact, he thought the Spaniards should work everywhere on the frontier to foment intertribal warfare, keeping all tribes friendly to Spain. And he suggested that the methods of presidial supply should be changed and that more civilians should be moved to the frontier.

While Rubí was inspecting the northern provinces, Visitor-general José de Gálvez was in New Spain instituting administrative reforms, a commission which he interpreted to include the northern frontier as well as the more settled regions of the viceroyalty. He saw that the area was far from Mexico City, that it was not receiving the close personal attention of the viceroy, and that disaster—if not total depopulation—was imminent. He recommended that the entire chain of provinces be detached from the control of the viceroy and placed under the command of an army brigadier whose headquarters would be in this area under his control; this officer, Gálvez thought, would have the authority to take quick action at critical moments, performing some of the functions of the viceroy, and some of an army field commander, and having judicial and civil powers. The viceroy, Antonio Bucareli, quite naturally opposed changes which would divest him of part of his powers, and worked against the Gálvez recommendations.

The result of the Rubí and Gálvez reports was the issuance in 1772 of the Royal Regulations for presidios. First published in January of that year, this plan created the Interior Provinces, consisting of Texas, New Mexico, California, Sonora, Sinaloa, Nueva Vizcaya, Coahuila, Chihuahua, Nuevo León, and Nuveo Santander. In charge would be a commandant-inspector, not a commandant-general, functioning directly under the supervision of the viceroy. The king had listened to the protests of the viceroy and was willing to try less drastic changes at first. The officer selected for the post of commandant-inspector was Colonel Hugo O'Conor, an Irish mercenary who had been in Spanish service for a long time on the New Spain frontier.

O'Conor worked energetically to effect the changes. East Texas was abandoned in 1773, although some of the civilians were permitted to move back to the Trinity River in 1774. Five years later they returned to their former homes and established the settlement of Nacogdoches without official sanction. The presidio of San Agustín de Ahumada (Orcoquisac) had already been deserted in February 1771, and it remained closed. O'Conor also moved certain presidios in accordance with the Royal Regulations, which specified that the forts be forty leagues apart (approximately one hundred miles); for example, in 1776 the presidio of Tubac was moved down the Santa Cruz Vally to Tucson, which soon had a small civil settlement in the vicinity.

The promulgation of the Royal Regulations of 1772 meant that the mission would no longer be the major arm of the Spanish government in pacifying the Interior Provinces; the army was to do the job. In line with this policy, O'Conor instituted a number of campaigns against the natives committing the raids. In the fall of 1775 he was on the offensive all along the frontier from Sonora to Texas with 1228 soldiers, achieving some positive results. The following year in a similar offensive he had some successes again. Yet despite these victories, the reports show that between 1771 and 1776 the situation continued to deteriorate in the Interior Provinces. The Navajo of New Mexico took to the warpath, the Comanche continued to plunder and kill almost at will, and the Apache followed a policy of raiding whenever Spanish attention was diverted from them.

Because of this continued deterioration, the king in 1776 separated the Interior Provinces from the viceroyalty of New Spain and placed them under the command of a commandant-general. First to occupy this post was Brigadier General Teodoro de Croix, a native of France who had entered the Spanish army at the age of seventeen. Croix had served in many campaigns in Europe; he had arrived in the New World in 1766 with his uncle, the Marqués de Croix, the newly appointed viceroy of New Spain. He returned to Spain four years later, where he remained until his appointment as commandant-general. Croix was an excellent choice for this post: his loyalty had been proven, his ability was a matter of record, and his courage was unquestioned. Yet from the first he was hampered in his new position by the fact that he was given no additional troops for his undertaking, and he was dependent upon the viceroy for all funds—and the viceroy was not generous in dealing with an area not under his own command.

Arriving in Mexico City in December of 1776, Croix spent several months studying reports, then set out to visit the area under his jurisdiction. In his judgment the most pressing problem in the Interior Provinces was that presented by the Apache, and at Monclova, San Antonio, and Chihuahua City he held conferences on how to deal with this tribe. The decision to wage a general campaign against the Lipan and Mescalero Apache, employing Comanche allies, was put into effect early in 1779 and continued until the middle of 1780. The Comanche, with Spanish encouragement, engaged in relentless battles against the Apache, penetrating as far south as Coahuila in their search for their ancient enemies. Finally the Apache came to San Antonio seeking peace. Croix ordered Governor Domingo Cabello y Robles of Texas to give the Apache presents and to settle them along the Rio Grande to serve as a barrier against Comanche raids in Coahuila and Nuevo Santander.

To contain the Navajo and the Comanche in New Mexico, Croix gave as much support as possible to Governor Juan Bautista de

Anza. With his usual energy, Anza applied the divide-and-conquer tactics, which had worked against the Apache, to the western Comanche who were raiding in his province. Allying with the Ute Indians, he campaigned against the plains raiders in August and September of 1779, and defeated them soundly. The following year he was marching west to the Hopi pueblos; there he found these once-numerous Indians had been almost annihilated by the Navajo. Anza kept up the pressure on both Navajo and Comanche during his tenure as governor, but without a drastic increase in the number of troops in his province he could not win a decisive victory.

Commandant-general Croix could obtain few additional men from the viceroy, so he coped with the problem by shifting his available troops to those locations where they were most needed. By various devices he tried to increase the number of regulars at critical points in the cordon of frontier presidios. By 1783 he could report that total strength in the Interior Provinces was 4686 men, including regulars, militia, and Indian allies. Yet this was not enough. Nor was the shifting of presidios into a cordon working as planned; the Indians simply rode around them, or they drove off the presidial horse herds and left the soldiers afoot. What high Spanish officials had overlooked in their strategy of relocating presidios was the fact that the precise placing of forts would prove far less important than the competence of the soldiers garrisoning them. It was the fighting capacity of each private, corporal, sergeant, and officer that would mean the difference between victory and defeat in engagements with hostile Indians. And defeat came more often than victory. This ineffectiveness of the Spanish army in combating the Indians was the result of poor training, inadequate supplies, and official negligence.

Recruits for the frontier army were drawn almost entirely from within the Interior Provinces, the troops enlisting for ten-year terms. These men generally were excellent horsemen and accustomed to the harsh climate and the crude frontier conditions. They had been subjected to close discipline all their lives, for the Spanish system allowed little economic, religious, or social deviation. Most of these troops were mestizos (part Spanish, part Indian), and they came from poor families. They joined the army because it was the best life open to them. A soldier had steady employment, retirement benefits, and access to the only skilled medical attention on the frontier. If he died, his widow received a pension. There was also the chance of promotion, for most junior officers in the Interior Provinces had risen through the ranks. In addition, a trooper could easily obtain land near the presidio where he was stationed. In fact, the Spanish system encouraged such practice, for officials at Mexico City and Madrid hoped the soldiers would remain near the presidios after their discharge and thus contribute to the colonization of the region.

For his service the newly enlisted soldier received 290 pesos annually. From this he received one-fourth peso daily for his and his family's subsistence. The remainder was kept by the paymaster to be used to purchase the horses, articles of uniform, armament, and equipment he needed. Unlike the regular Spanish army, the troops of the Interior Provinces were enlisted into presidial garrisons and had no regimental or larger unit designations. At each presidio the Royal Regulations prescribed four officers, including a chaplain, forty-three enlisted men, and ten Indian scouts. By royal decree these men were to be accorded the ranks and privileges of the regular Spanish army. This practice, as well as the many benefits, should have contributed to a high *esprit de corps*. Yet such was not the case.

The training of new soldiers was rigidly prescribed by the Royal Regulations of 1772, but in reality it varied from presidio to presidio, depending on the zeal and diligence of each captain. These commanders were expected to drill their men in the handling of firearms, in target practice, in mounted tactics, and in military discipline and procedures. Weekly reviews were to be held to inspect equipment and to see that unserviceable items were replaced. But in many cases these regulations were disregarded, and the new soldier learned his profession from his fellow enlisted men in barracks discussions. Training in warfare came most often on the field of combat against an actual enemy. Nor was his equipment maintained, even on that bloody frontier. The practice of paying soldiers partly in cash and partly in goods worked to the benefit of paymasters, presidial officers, and local merchants, many of whom connived together to set exorbitantly high prices for goods of inferior quality. The temptation for officers to engage in this practice was strong since inspections were rare, punishment for those caught was light, and examples of others getting rich were ever at hand. Paymasters frequently spent the money entrusted to them for pay purposes so that deficits were common and salaries often fell in arrears. Because of these abuses, the soldier received so little money that they and their families lived on the edge of starvation, their equipment deteriorated, and they came to despise their service.

Corporal punishment was still practiced on the troops, inflicted by the officers against whom an abuse was committed. The sentencing of criminals to terms in the presidial armies was a common practice; even the presidial troopers themselves when convicted of crimes were given additional terms in the army. Those officers who came from Spain were often arrogant and regarded the common soldiers as contemptible colonials. Such officers frequently made derogatory judgments of the provincials under their command, attributing failures to racial factors.

The soldier's armament consisted of a short-barreled, smooth-bore, *escopeta,* or carbine, and two heavy, large-caliber pistols; in addition, he carried a short, wide-bladed, heavy sword—the *espada ancha*—and a lance. Spanish regulations provided that each soldier be issued three pounds of gunpowder annually; any he expended in excess of this amount he paid for from his own pocket. Therefore he had little interest in firing at targets and perfecting his aim, and in combat he tended to rely on his sword and his lance. Both of these weapons were efficient only in close, hand-to-hand combat—tactics which were common in European battles of the day. In the Interior Provinces, however, the two weapons were almost useless, for the nomadic Indians rarely fought in the open or made a stand unless trapped. They preferred hit-and-run tactics and the ambush; rarely would they attack unless the odds were heavily in their favor. Thus the Spaniards were generally at a disadvantage, equipped and encumbered by two weapons of little practical value.

The defensive equipment supplied to the presidial soldiers was also traditional in design. The *adarga,* or leather shield, was meant to deflect arrows and lance thrusts, and was made of four to six thicknesses of bull hide. In preparing for battle the presidial soldier also donned a *cuera,* a three-quarter-length sleeveless coat also made of four to six thicknesses of leather. Commandant-general Croix criticized both these items of equipment, saying they were outmoded and a hindrance. He urged the use of lightly equipped, mounted troops employing the latest firearms and the best horses in order to pursue and defeat the Indians—mobility was the key to victory with the Comanche and the Apache. Some units were organized on this plan; called *compañías volantes,* they were, in effect, light cavalry units, and they performed excellently. Yet most officers on the frontier were bound by tradition and never adopted the new tactics suggested by Croix. Under such conditions it is little wonder that the military pacification of the Indians failed, just as had the mission system.

Croix was rewarded for his small success by promotion in 1783 to the post of viceroy of Peru. Following his departure, the Interior Provinces were divided, later reunited, and then divided again. When the viceroy had the king's confidence, he was given control of the region; when he did not, the region was separate. Finally in 1785 a viceroy was appointed who had both the king's confidence and a new plan for controlling the Interior Provinces.

Bernardo de Gálvez, a cousin of the visitor-general responsible for the colonization of California, assumed the office of viceroy in 1785. He had seen service on the northern frontier and had gained a reputation as a capable Indian fighter; then he had served as governor of Louisiana. Gálvez issued his plan as a decree entitled *Instructions for Governing the Interior Provinces.* He ordered a vigorous war on those Indians not at peace with Spain. Once these Indians asked for peace, he decreed, they would be settled in villages in the shadow of the presidio. There they would be given presents regularly, along with inferior firearms and alcoholic beverages. Gálvez reasoned that if the presents were of sufficient value the Indians would prize peace more than war. The arms supplied them would quickly become inoperative, and only the Spaniards could repair them; in addition, when the Indians went on the warpath, they could not obtain gunpowder and shot.

For those natives too numerous or too powerful to be reduced to such villages, Gálvez decreed the establishment of trading posts near their villages. From such posts the Indians would receive their annual distribution of presents; but the traders were in reality to be spies for the army. From such vantage points the traders could keep a watchful eye on the activities of the Indians, get news of impending raids, and work to civilize the natives. Another part of the Gálvez plan was to keep all tribes friendly to Spain but unfriendly toward each other. As General Pedro de Nava, commandant-general of the Eastern Interior Provinces, ordered in 1796: "One of the maxims that should always be observed on our part, with respect to the nations of Indians, is to allow them to make reciprocal war on each other in order in this way to bring about a diminution of their forces, to energize their mutual hatreds, and to avoid their union and alliance; we should, however, take the lead in keeping them constantly in our friendship and in our debt."

The Gálvez plan was put into effect on the northern frontier, and it accomplished what neither cross nor sword had been able to do. Although the soldiers could not permanently defeat the Indians in the campaigns that followed, they could keep up sufficient pressure to compel the warring tribes to ask for peace. Then began the annual distribution of presents, gifts of firearms, and supplying of firewater. The Indians, as Gálvez had reasoned, did indeed realize that peace had more attractions than war. Thus the Southwest knew a period of relative calm between 1787 and 1810. Peace was achieved by the Spaniards for more than two decades, but it was by purchase, not force of arms. It was during this period that many of the beautiful missions of Arizona and New Mexico were constructed, missions such as San Xavier del Bac. This was the time that ranching expanded with relative security, and when prospectors ventured into the mineral-rich hills to make a few minor discoveries. Yet when the Mexican War for Independence began in 1810, and the Spaniards stopped distributing presents, the Indians again took to the warpath, thundering past the useless cordon of presidios into the Interior Provinces.

The necessary ingredients for a successful army were available to Spain in the Interior Provinces, but those officials at the policy level did not make proper use of them. Through a reliance on traditional weapons and equipment, and an improper and inadequate training of the common soldiers—who did have high potential— peace had to be purchased ingloriously. In 1777–78, on his first tour of inspection, Commandant-general Croix noted that the soldiers of the Interior Provinces were without training in handling firearms and were ignorant of military tactics. Thirty years later, in 1807, Lieutenant Zebulon Montgomery Pike, during his momentous trek through the Southwest, commented that the soldiers he saw in the province of New Mexico would have been outstanding if they had been trained properly. In 1817, just four years before the Spanish empire crumbled away, Governor Antonio María Martínez of Texas wrote to his superiors:

> . . . The troops which make up the garrison of this province are in the most deplorable condition. They are absolutely unclothed except the veteran company of [San Antonio de] Béxar, the 1st militia company, and the pickets from Aguaverde and Rio Grande. The cloth coats and breeches worn by the men in these companies are full of holes, and the material is practically rotten. The other troops in the companies of La Bahía, Monclova, and Colonia have absolutely nothing, and neither the former nor the latter has hats or shoes, or even a single shirt. . . . The terrible condition of these troops has created a state of general dissatisfaction in the province and is the cause of the many desertions which occur daily and retard the efficiency of the service. Sometimes I cannot get together a party of twenty-five men to send to Rio Grande to escort convoys or execute any other mission because I cannot trust that many individuals to return. Invariably, there are some men in every party who do not wish to come back.

Clearly the military problems on the frontier had not been solved by the end of the colonial era.

LIFE IN THE SPANISH PROVINCES

The original reasons for settling most of the Interior Provinces were either missionary or military. The pioneers—missionaries, neophytes, and soldiers—were faced with the necessity of earning their daily bread, just as were the Americans who came to the region later. In theory the missions were to be self-supporting, and soon they developed a healthy pastoral economy; the soldiers received parcels of land on which they farmed or ranched, attempting to supplement their meager income by growing their own food. Settlements sprang up near the presidios and missions, producing a merchant class and an artisan class. Yet the Interior Provinces were different in climate and geography from the regions from which these Spaniards came, and the civilian colonists found it necessary to adapt themselves to the new environment. In this process of adaptation they borrowed heavily from the native population to produce pioneering techniques which later would be adopted and adapted by the Americans who inherited the region.

Without question the largest single industry in the Southwest during the Spanish period was ranching. The animals were brought to the region by the early Spanish expeditions. Beginning with Coronado, almost every Spanish *entrada* during the age of conquest and exploration was accompanied by horses and cows, many of which escaped to find themselves in a pastoral paradise. Southwestern conditions were ideal for their increase, and by the end of the eighteenth century they roamed the thousand hills of the region in enormous numbers. Among these animals were longhorn cows and Spanish mustangs. The longhorns, made famous in the post-Civil War period of American history, had been brought to Mexico from Spain. The breed that survived the rigors of the Southwest were descended from the Spanish cattle that had the longest horns, and their bodies were larger, rangier, leaner than those of the cattle originally imported. Except for a few choice cuts, their meat was tough almost to the point of inedibility. The horses were Arabian-Spanish in origin, of clean, sharp lines, fleet, and by English standards somewhat small. The sheep were of Peninsular extraction; however, sheep required close tending for they were not capable of self-defense and fell prey to predators very easily. Only in New Mexico did sheep-raising become widespread.

The Southwest, covered as it then was with so much grass, should have been a rancher's paradise. Shortage of water was no great deterrent, for the settled areas tended to be near lakes or streams. Furthermore, the longhorn was capable of walking up to sixty miles between drinks. However, the ranching industry prospered—or declined—not because of geographic conditions, but according to the whims of the nomadic Indians. The Apache and Comanche quickly learned to appreciate a good steak, and they always needed horses to ride—and they preferred stealing from the Spaniards to catching the fleet-footed, untamed animals on the prairies. In California, despite some thievery by the Indians, the ranching industry prospered beyond all Serra's dreams. By his death in 1784 his mission herds already numbered more than thirty thousand animals.

In perfecting the methods of ranching in the Interior Provinces, Spanish and Indian *vaqueros* drew heavily on Spanish techniques brought to Mexico and then adapted them as they made their way northward. This process evolved almost all of the techniques and paraphernalia associated with the cowboy complex of the American post-Civil War period: a broad-brimmed sombrero to shade the eyes from the blazing sun, a bandana to protect the nose and mouth from dust, *chaparajos* (chaps) to ward off thorns, pointed boots suited to the stirrup, and spurs with big two-inch rowels; a lariat (*la riata*) for roping, a saddle with a horn for dallying a rope (very different from the type used by Englishmen), a hackamore (*jáquima*) of rope without a metal bit. The branding of livestock dated from the Roman era and had come to the New World by way of Spain; it was not in common use in England or in English colonies. The rounding up of livestock from an unfenced range became a standard procedure in the Southwest, quite distinct from the fenced-pasture methods employed on the East Coast by English colonists. In short, the American cowboy of a later period rode a Spanish mount, and the longhorn he tended and the tools of his trade had come from Spain by way of Mexico to the Interior Provinces.

Even the long trail drive of cattle to market began during this period. In June 1779, Bernardo de Gálvez, then governor of Louisiana, sent messengers to Texas to purchase 1500 to 2000 head of Texas cattle. Commandant-general Croix approved the project, and that fall the animals were driven eastward over the *camino real* from the San Antonio–La Bahía region by Francisco García. Following this successful effort, Texas cattle were driven to Louisiana at the rate of fifteen to twenty thousand head annually. California unfortunately had no such market for its livestock since it was connected with the outside world only by sea. The Arizona area developed a ranching industry for a short time, but Apache hostility caused most of the outlying *haciendas* to be abandoned; the Marqués de Rubí on his tour of inspection in 1767 noted that the area around the presidio of Tubac contained many ranches deserted because of Indian raids, and that the cattle had become wild.

The raising of horses never became widespread in the Interior Provinces because a large herd of these animals was certain to attract Apache or Comanche raiders. Therefore, despite the fact that large numbers of these animals ran wild on the plains and in the mountains, Spanish military commanders were forced to import their horses from the interior of Mexico. Presidial horse herds were generally pastured away from the forts for grazing and were favorite targets for Indian raids; as a result, the soldiers frequently were unable to pursue the Indians because they had no mounts.

Commandant-general Croix on his first tour of inspection of the provinces under his command noted the large herds of unbranded livestock roaming the area. They included both wild animals and those that the ranchers had been unable to brand because of Indian raids. Croix decided that he had found a new source of revenue for the hard-pressed royal treasury, and on January 12, 1778, issued a decree declaring all unbranded stock the property of the king. For the privilege of capturing such animals, individuals had to pay a fee of four silver *reales* (one-half peso) per head for cattle, and six *reales* for horses. (Later he lowered the fee for horses to two *reales* to encourage the capturing of mustangs worthy of use by the army, and because he felt that wild horses were twice as difficult to corral as wild cattle.)

The howl of protests from ranchers and missionaries that greeted Croix's decree resulted in its revocation in 1786. The joy occasioned by the rescinding of this law was short-lived, however. Shortly afterward, the viceroy convened a council in Mexico City to settle the question of ownership of unbranded animals in the Interior Provinces. The decision of this council was that unbranded stock was the property of whoever could capture it; however, anyone who wanted to do so had to have a separate license for each animal—a license that cost four *reales* for each cow and two *reales* for each horse. And the viceroy so decreed in 1795.

New Mexico alone developed an extensive sheep industry. There, in the semi-arid country, sheep were able to find sufficient pasture, and mutton became a basic food and woolen garments the most common apparel. The Indians were taught to be herders and learned to weave fine blankets. Large *haciendas* devoted to the raising of sheep became common, some of them having as many as a million head. One Spanish governor reportedly had flocks numbering more than two million. Normally about two thousand sheep would be sent out under the care of two men to graze in dry areas; the sheep could go long distances without water, and the men carried their own supply. The Navajos acquired a taste for mutton and stole hundreds of thousands of the animals, but the annual increase was sufficient to take care of the wants of both Indian and New Mexican.

Although not as widespread as ranching, farming was practiced in the Interior Provinces on a wide scale. Spaniards had learned the techniques of irrigation from the Moorish invaders of their country in centuries past, and introduced the *acequia* to the Southwest. Centuries before, in central Arizona, the Hohokam—"those who have gone"—had built extensive canals, as sophisticated as any dug by Spaniards, but the Hohokam culture had vanished by the time Father Kino came to plant his missions, and the ruins of these canals had filled with dust. Those Indians in the Southwest who practiced irrigated farming relied on the annual spring flooding of the river bottoms, or a more esoteric form of securing water—the rain dance.

Another major Spanish contribution to Southwestern agriculture was the introduction of new crops—wheat, barley, and other grains, and fruit trees of many varieties. Perhaps even more revolutionary in the long run was the animal power that the Spaniards supplied; the plow was not used by the American Indians before the Spaniards came. New crops, new planting and harvesting techniques, and a knowledge of irrigation revolutionized Southwestern agriculture. Nevertheless, the staple crop of the entire region remained the same: corn. This native American grain was the major item in the diet of both Spaniard and Indian, and whether the provinces feasted or starved depended upon how much of this crop was harvested each year.

Despite the fertility of Southwestern soil and the ease with which bounteous harvests could be obtained once irrigation was arranged, the Interior Provinces never became entirely self-supporting in their agriculture. This was due primarily to the laziness of the citizens in New Mexico and Texas; in these two colonies the governors and inspectors reported that in years of good crops the farmers did not bother to harvest the entire crop, and in bad years they merely petitioned the government for aid. The Arizona missions and presidios never became self-supporting because the Apache raids would not permit extended agricultural activity. Only the Californians managed to feed themselves adequately, but this was due to a generous natural environment and to isolation; the only supply route was by sea, a hazardous and tenuous connection at best, and thus they had to feed themselves or go hungry. Fortunately the Indians were no major threat there.

Every Spaniard who came north to the Interior Provinces, no matter whether he was a soldier, a missionary, or a civilian, had some hopes of discovering mineral deposits. The dream of quick wealth had brought Cabeza de Vaca, Coronado, Oñate, and other *conquistadores* into the region initially, and it permeated every facet of Spanish endeavor in the provinces after they were permanently settled. These Spaniards had a long history of mining activity, both in the Old World and the New. The mines of Galicia and Asturia in the Mother Country had been worked for centuries before the discovery of America, and following the conquest of Mexico and Peru the Spaniards had prospected over most of Central and South America. These centuries had yielded a considerable body of knowledge about mining and mining techniques which were brought into the Interior Provinces, and wherever they went these pioneers looked for mineral wealth. Every friendly Indian was trained to recognize ore, and was rewarded for bringing in likely specimens.

Once gold was found in placer deposits (i.e. in stream beds), it was extracted by means of a *batea,* a shallow, conical bowl which dated from the Roman era. Extensive placer deposits were worked by means of the sluice, or rifflebox. This consisted of a trough whose bottom was crossed with wooden bars at the top end and with a coarse woolen blanket at the bottom end; the water flow was carefully gauged, for if it flowed too fast it would wash away the smaller particles and if it flowed too slowly it would allow other matter to be retained. Then paydirt and water were run through the box by the miner, who periodically halted the process to collect his gold dust. The tailings (the material, mostly dirt, that ran on through the sluicebox) were worked again and again until not a grain of gold escaped.

Hard-rock ore (that deposited in quartz) was first crushed in an *arrastra,* then run through a sluicebox. An *arrastra* was a crude ore-crushing device that cost little to construct and operate. It consisted of a circular pit with a center stone pivot with drag-stones to crush the ore. Horses or mules were attached to one end of the horizontal pole and furnished the power to turn it around and around. The *arrastra* was not very efficient, but it was inexpensive.

One other process was in widespread use to extract mineral wealth. If silver was found in the form of lead-silver sulphides, it was difficult to refine. For example, silver found at San Luis Potosí in Mexico was locked in ores which refused to be worked by any of the usual procedures; the problem was solved by means of the "patio process," first perfected by Bartolomé Medina of Pachuca in 1557. The first step in this process was grinding the ore; then it was spread on a stone platform, or patio, and mixed with large quantities of salt, copper sulphate (bluestone), and mercury. After these ingredients were carefully worked into the mixture, it was then exposed to heat and sunlight for fifteen to forty-five days. During this period a chemical reaction separated the silver from the quartz, changing the mixture to a grey color. Then it was washed and the silver extracted. Most of the mercury was recovered, although a set percentage was lost in each use during the process. Because mercury was a necessary part of extracting silver through this method, and because the loss of a part of it occurred when it was used, the Spanish monarch declared a royal monopoly on mercury; purchasers were required to pay a 20 per cent tax on all bullion they extracted, and a check on the amount of mercury used would show how much silver they had mined.

It is ironic that, although the American miners of the post-Mexican War era employed Spanish mining techniques almost exclusively, the Spaniards made very few mineral discoveries in the Southwest. Had such discoveries been made, the history of the region would have been far different, for Spaniards in great numbers would have rushed to the area, settlements would have grown up, and the area would not have been so sparsely populated when the Americans came. In California the first colonists had occupied only the coastal strip; later, when the ranchers extended settlement farther inland, even they entered the Mother Lode country only rarely. Texas, as subsequent development would show, had no substantial deposits of gold or silver. There is little documentary evidence of mining activity in New Mexico, except at Santa Rita del Cobre, in the southwestern corner of the province, where there was a copper deposit. Work began in earnest there in 1804. And Arizona was never sufficiently populated to allow extensive mining activity, although the *Real de Arizona,* the one major Spanish strike in the Southwest, did occur there.

Soldiers, ranchers, farmers, miners, missionaries—all were present in the Interior Provinces in large numbers. Census returns show merchants, tailors, shoemakers, teamsters, fishermen, carpenters, blacksmiths, and barbers—and a horde of government officials selling tobacco and paper (both royal monopolies), collecting taxes and the tithe (church and state were one, so the tithe was a regular part of the taxes), and overseeing almost every facet of the social, economic, religious, and cultural life of the provinces. And there were a few Negro slaves working along with those Indians sentenced to "personal service." In 1783 the king decreed that, because of his concern for the prosperity of his vassals in the Americas, he would encourage the importation of Negro slaves for agricultural labor and to work in the mines, even allowing them to be transported in foreign ships.

Manufacturing was almost nonexistent in the Interior Provinces except for metalworking, the weaving of blankets, and some leatherworking. The Spanish mercantile system militated against the growth of an independent economy in any part of the colonies, and the tax structure practically killed incentive. Goods could be imported into New Spain only at Vera Cruz, and on these goods, which were often manufactured in France or England, one had to pay an import tax into Spain, an export tax leaving that country, an import tax on arrival in Mexico, and a tax at every crossing of a provincial boundary (the *alcabala*) between Vera Cruz and the Interior Provinces. Such a system resulted in overpriced goods of inferior quality, but royal law forbade direct trade with any foreign

power. As a result the economy stagnated, and smuggling became a
way of life. In Texas the colonists procured their goods in nearby
Louisiana, while in California the officials frequently ignored the
foreign vessels unloading cargoes in that province.

The heavy hand of bureaucracy, the unrealistic tax structure,
and the rigid supervision of every phase of life, coupled with the
ever-present Indian menace, allowed the typical pioneer of the Interior Provinces little reason for joy or laughter. Nor could he even
consider his home safe. Except for the very few wealthy dwellers of
the cities, these squalid homes more often than not had dirt floors,
mud and brush ceilings, and unplastered adobe walls. Census reports accurately reflected this fact by classifying most homes as
jacales—huts. Married soldiers living outside the presidios endured
the same hardships, their homes no better than those of their civilian neighbors. Soldiers and civilians slept on the floor, rolled in
blankets. A small fireplace built in one corner served as cookstove
and source of heat. Chairs and tables, except those that were
homemade, were in short supply; therefore most sat on the floor or
on the ground outside the hut to eat their meals. Perhaps a trunk or
chest served to hold the family's few possessions, which seldom
included more than a few pieces of clothing, cooking utensils, and
religious objects. Candles, when they could be had, provided a
source of light during the evening hours.

When supplies could be obtained from the south—and when the
soldier or civilian was not too deeply in debt to pay for them—
some luxuries could be secured. Hot chocolate, served in the morning and evening, supplemented a diet largely made up of frijoles,
ground corn, beef or mutton, and sometimes fruit from mission
orchards. Grain for tortillas was ground in stone metates in the
house, or in nearby mule-powered stone mills. Small plots of land
could be had almost for the asking, and on these the pioneer tried
to raise beans, corn, chiles, and local crops. When the Indian raids
became too intense, he had to rely on stored foods or what could be
secured from the nearby desert—generally mesquite beans and
what wild vegetables grew in the region. In such circumstances the
Spanish colonist eked out an existence—with little hope of improv-
ing his living conditions. And only in California, where peace with
the Indians made life more settled and where the missions could

supply certain luxuries, for a price, were conditions much better.

Except that the soldier was paid for his service, there was very little difference between the army troops and the civilians on the frontier. According to royal law, all settlers in the Interior Provinces were considered to be a part of the militia. The ownership of land carried with it an obligation to keep arms and horses ready to assist the military when expeditions were necessary. But the civilians tended to be timorous, impoverished peasants, more a source of weakness than of strength; most of them would not join in forays against the enemy except under coercion, and yet they had to be protected. In point of truth, the civilian, like the soldier, stayed fairly close to the presidio, rushing behind its walls when the Indians attacked. Both were trying to stay alive. These people found little relief from the hard monotony of their lives even in their leisure moments.

Yet despite the hardships these pioneers found reason for hope, for laughter, and for enjoyment. Very slowly the population grew in the provinces. Almost every week a *fandango,* an informal dance, was held, but women were always in short supply on the frontier except in the few towns of considerable size, such as Santa Fe, San Antonio, and San Diego. In searching for a bride, the colonist, part Indian, frequently married a mission native and raised children who were even more Indian than he. Mescal, either brewed locally or brought up from the south, drowned many sorrows and insults. Gambling was so widespread that officials quit trying to stop it, although the laws strictly forbade games of chance. Other forms of amusement included cock fights, horse races, and the observance of the local patron saint's day or the various religious holidays.

With the Gálvez policy of buying peace, the pioneers gained some respite from Indian attack and life became better. But across the Atlantic a storm of revolutionary ideas and lengthy wars was brewing which was to disturb even this remote corner of the world —some of the European-born officers referred to it as *"el fin del mundo"* (the end of the world).

THE LAST YEARS OF THE SPANISH SOUTHWEST

On the morning of March 21, 1801, Lieutenant Manuel de Múzquiz and 150 Spanish soldiers surrounded an American party near present-day Waco, Texas. Múzquiz called on the Americans to surrender, and some of them did so. But their leader, Philip Nolan, and nineteen of his men firmly refused. In the ensuing struggle Nolan was killed and the remainder of his party captured. These prisoners subsequently were taken to San Antonio, then to Chihuahua City, where some died and others spent years in captivity. In 1807 one of the nine survivors, Ephraim Blackburn, was executed to satisfy a royal order that one of every five members of the party be hanged. Philip Nolan, a name later given to the fictional "Man Without a Country," had been entering Texas since 1785 to capture wild horses on the prairies; he had been trusted by governors and commandants-general and had moved about freely. His death at the hands of Spanish muskets was a minor by-product of the French Revolution, which instilled a fear—almost a hysteria—in Spanish officials in the Interior Provinces that the doctrines of liberty, equality, and fraternity might corrupt the minds of loyal subjects in the New World. The death of Nolan, however, did not prevent the entrance of such ideas—or of other Americans.

The outbreak of the French Revolution in Europe brought Spain into the wars that followed, first on the side of England, then as allies of the French. Both viceroys and commandants-general sent orders to the governors to arrest all foreigners and to halt the spread of seditious books and writings. Then, in 1798, when the United States almost went to war with France, these same Spanish officials naturally feared that the Americans might invade the Interior Provinces, for Spain and France were allies. Philip Nolan was the first to suffer from this Spanish distrust of the United States, a distrust which intensified immediately after the Louisiana Purchase of 1803.

By 1800 Napoleon was so powerful that he was able to force Spain to cede Louisiana back to France, but because of his numerous European commitments he could not take advantage of the new acquisition. Not until November 30, 1803, did the French take control of the Territory, and then only for the purpose of transferring it to the United States, to whom Napoleon on April 30 of that year had sold it for fifteen million dollars. On December 15, 1803, American commissioners took formal control of Louisiana, thereby inheriting a boundary dispute with Spain. No definite boundary existed between Louisiana and Texas. Spain claimed all territory east to the Arroyo Hondo; while some Americans argued that the true boundary of Louisiana was the Rio Grande, the government was willing to settle for the Sabine River as the dividing line. For almost three years this dispute raged. Gradually the number of Spanish troops in Texas was increased until it numbered 1368. In Louisiana the American military commander was the enigmatic General James Wilkinson of Aaron Burr Conspiracy fame. On October 29, 1806, General Wilkinson proposed a compromise; he would withdraw American troops east of the Arroyo Hondo if Spain would move its troops west of the Sabine. On November 4 Lieutenant Colonel Simón Herrera, commander of the Spanish force in Texas, agreed to the compromise, thus creating the Neutral Ground between the two countries.

Hardly had Spain settled this difficulty in the New World when an even more serious threat to its dominion arose—not from without but from within. On September 16, 1810, Father Miguel Hidalgo y Costillo called upon the masses of Mexico to revolt and throw off the yoke of Spanish tyranny. Soon he found himself commanding a rabble army of some one hundred thousand men, mainly composed of Indians happy to have the chance to strike back after centuries of subjugation. These insurgents captured Guanajuato and Guadalajara, and the provinces of Nuevo Santander (Tamaulipas) and Coahuila fell into their hands.

In far-off California, separated from the mainstream of life in New Spain, the events of the Mexican War for Independence caused little stir. By and large the Californians' sentiment was loyalist, for they had benefited from Spanish paternalism; furthermore, the missionaries, soldiers, and officials were all appointed by the king. To the Californians the war meant only that the supply ships from Mexico stopped coming annually, but this caused little hardship; by now the province was easily self-supporting, the missions possessing large herds and extensive fields. Only the soldiers suffered, for their pay fell in arrears and they were forced to live off the charity of the missions—which made them hate missions and eventually get rid of them. To make up for the outside supplies that no longer were reaching the province, the officials there merely winked at royal regulations prohibiting trade with foreign countries; ships from the United States, England, and Russia were permitted to land their cargoes and exchange them for hides and tallow.

It was during this eleven-year interval of the Mexican Revolution that the Russian settlement, so feared in the 1760's and 1770's, finally became a reality. By 1803 agents of the Russian American Fur Company were pushing southward to California in search of furs. Two years later Nikolai Rezánof, an inspector for the czar, visited San Francisco to arrange an extension of the Russian fur trade to California and to trade for foodstuff in the province. And in 1808 Ivan Kuskoff came to Bodega Bay, in northern California, where he stayed for eight months, trading and trapping. In 1811 he journeyed to San Francisco, where he purchased land from the Indians for a permanent post; the price was three blankets, two axes, three hoes, and some beads. The land was located about nineteen miles north of San Francisco. The following year Kuskoff brought one hundred Russians and eighty Aleutian Indians south and established Fort Ross on this land. Primarily this was an agricultural colony, the purpose being to grow sufficient grain and raise enough stock to feed the company's outpost in Alaska, but there was also considerable trade both with the Spaniards and the California natives. The Spanish officials in California were not particularly cordial to the Russians, nor were their Mexican replacements, but the fort remained a Russian outpost until 1841.

Very early in the year 1822 the California officials were notified that Mexican independence had been won. Governor Pablo Vicente de Solá convened a council to discuss the matter; it recommended that the province recognize the change, declare itself a part of the Mexican empire, and take the oath of independence. Solá and the members of this council took the prescribed oath at Monterey on April 11, 1822, and shortly thereafter everyone in the province likewise swore loyalty to Mexico. There was no difficulty and little hesitation about taking this oath, even among the missionaries.

In New Mexico the revolution likewise passed with no real disturbances. By January 6, 1822, when a formal celebration of independence was held in Santa Fe, the population of New Mexico numbered almost 30,000 *gente de razón* (i.e. Spaniards, mestizos, and Christian Indians), making it the most populous of the provinces in the Southwest. The period of peace that had begun about 1790 was broken by troubles with the Navajo from 1800 to 1805, but there was a certain amount of prosperity which was reflected in a growing affluence among the upper class. Yet, because of the closed economic system in the Spanish colonies, these wealthy New Mexicans could not spend their coins on anything but inferior goods which cost far more than they were worth. Therefore they showed an inclination to welcome overland traders from the United States, although some of those who came during this period were arrested by zealous officers of the army. Also, it was during this period of the revolution that the first American mountain men began making their way into the province in search of beaver pelts. Spanish regulations likewise forbade their entry and some were arrested, but several officials in the province saw another path to wealth being opened.

In all the northern tier of New Spain's provinces, the revolution caused the greatest disturbance in Texas. On January 22, 1811, a group of men who sympathized with the Hidalgo revolt staged a successful coup. Led by Juan Bautista de Las Casas, a retired army captain, the conspirators arrested Governor Manuel María de Salcedo, military commander Simón de Herrera, six captains, five lieutenants, and all loyalists in the capital city of San Antonio. Similar arrests were made at the other two areas of settlement, La Bahía and Nacogdoches, and Las Casas assumed the title of governor. His glory was short-lived, however, for on March 2 a counterrevolution took place under the direction of Juan Manuel Zambrano, and the province once again came under the loyalist banner. Las Casas, like Father Hidalgo, was executed for his part in the rebellion—but the battle for independence did not die in New Spain or in Texas.

At the start of his uprising, Father Hidalgo had sent Bernardo Gutiérrez de Lara to the United States to seek aid. After a warm but unofficial welcome in Washington, Gutiérrez returned to Louisiana and made his headquarters at the old French outpost of Natchitoches. The death of Hidalgo did not put a halt to his activities, for he still plotted a coup in Texas, either to make it a separate republic or a state in the republic of Mexico. Aiding him in this enterprise was Augustus William Magee, a graduate of the United States Military Academy who, in 1812, at the age of twenty-three, was bitter because he had not been promoted. Magee became the colonel and military commander of the projected invasion force; Gutiérrez was named general and given the task of winning over the Spanish residents of Texas to the cause. With a rabble army of Americans, Frenchmen, Mexican revolutionists, Indians, and disreputable characters from the Neutral Ground, the two men crossed the Sabine River on August 12, 1812, and marched to Nacogdoches. This town was taken with no resistance.

A beachhead established, the insurgents rested and recruited more men, then marched on La Bahía in September. It too fell without a fight. Three days later, however, a royalist force led by Lieutenant Colonel Herrera arrived, and the Gutiérrez-Magee forces were besieged for four months. Then, in early February, Magee died under mysterious circumstances. He was succeeded by Samuel Kemper. Soon afterward the royalists raised the siege, and the rebels, eight hundred strong, marched for San Antonio on February 21, 1813. Herrera came out from the city with an army to meet them, and on March 2 a battle was fought with disastrous results for the royalists. Governor Salcedo agreed to terms of surrender, and on March 6 Gutiérrez assumed political control of the province. Soon afterward he declared the Republic of Texas with himself as president, and he had an underling murder Herrera, Governor Salcedo, and ten other high officials. These acts disgusted the better element in the rebel army, and they left the province for Louisiana. Those who remained behind joined in a successful conspiracy to overthrow the president, and José Álvarez de Toledo was installed as president on August 4. The army of insurgents, numbering more than 1700 by this time, was actually little more than a mob, having little discipline or organization; on August 18, it fell easy prey to a royalist army brought to the province by Brigadier Joaquín de Arredondo, commandant-general of the Eastern Interior Provinces. A battle was fought on the banks of the Medina

River near San Antonio, total victory going to the Spanish army.

Following the Gutiérrez-Magee filibuster, the province of Texas was swept clean of rebel sympathizers by Commandant-general Arredondo. Many citizens were arrested; some were shot, and others sent to prison. The result of this vengeance was an exodus of Texans to Louisiana. This brought a measure of peace—but not prosperity—to the province for the next six years. Only Galveston Island remained a stronghold of resistance to the Spanish regime. Luis Aury secured a commission in the "Mexican Navy" from Hidalgo's successor as leader of the revolution, Father José María Morelos, and set up his headquarters at Galveston. From this port he carried on piratical raids on Spanish shipping, disguised under the cloak of patriotism. The cargoes were smuggled to New Orleans and sold at a handsome profit.

Still other revolutionaries under Francisco Xavier Mina decided that Galveston would be a good staging area for an invasion of Mexico. They arrived at the island on November 22, 1816, and soon afterward joined forces with another adventurer, Henry Perry, a native of Connecticut who had participated in the Gutiérrez-Magee expedition. Perry reached Galveston probably in September of 1816, bringing with him about 150 men. Perry joined Mina in a plan to invade Mexico, the two groups leaving Galveston on April 7, 1817, in Aury's ships. Galveston was left in the hands of still another adventurer, Jean Lafitte. Perry became convinced that Mina's invasion was doomed to failure, and when the insurgents landed at the mouth of the Santander River of Mexico he and forty-three of his men set out for Texas. Mina was quickly defeated, captured, tried, and executed. Perry's force reached La Bahía on June 18, 1817, and demanded that the presidial garrison surrender. However, Governor Antonio Martínez and a force of Spanish soldiers arrived, and the Americans fled toward Louisiana. Before they could escape they were surrounded and all but four were killed or wounded. To avoid capture Perry committed suicide on June 19.

Aury, upon his return to Galveston Island, found Lafitte securely in control of the port, and thus had to sail away. The new master of Galveston continued the profitable business of seizing ships in the Gulf and selling the booty in New Orleans, all under the pretext of Mexican patriotism. The government of the United

States became convinced that Lafitte was not always careful about the nationality of the ships he attacked, and they planned to evict him; in May of 1820 the pirate abandoned the island, sailing to Yucatán.

The year previous to Lafitte's withdrawal from the Texas scene, the Spaniards achieved two triumphs: they settled the long-standing boundary controversy with the United States, and they defeated yet another filibuster. Officials of the two nations had been meeting since shortly after the conclusion of the Wilkinson-Herrera agreement of 1806, though they were interrupted, of course, by the Napoleonic wars of Europe. The talks finally achieved a positive result on February 22, 1819, with the signing of the Adams-Onís Treaty (also called the Florida Treaty, or the Treaty of 1819). Besides settling the Florida question and other points of dispute between the two nations, this treaty delineated a boundary between the Louisiana Territory and the Interior Provinces of Spain. This boundary began in the Gulf of Mexico, proceeded up the west bank of the Sabine River to the 32nd parallel, then went due north to the Red River, turned west up the south bank of that river to 100° west longitude, proceeded due north up the south or west bank of the Arkansas River to its source, then went due north to 42nd parallel, and followed that line to the Pacific ocean.

The Spaniards' triumph over a filibustering expedition grew out of this agreement. Many Americans, especially Southerners, were angry at what they considered to be the surrender by the United States of a just claim to Texas; they believed that the La Salle colony of 1685–87 entitled the United States to claim as part of the Louisiana Territory all land westward to the Rio Grande. A group of citizens in Natchez, Mississippi, organized an expedition of approximately seventy-five men who, under the command of Dr. James Long, set out for Nacogdoches to free the province from Spanish control. The United States government made only half-hearted efforts to halt this expedition, and it moved across Louisiana with little difficulty, entered Texas, and captured Nacogdoches in June 1819. Long immediately proclaimed the Republic of Texas, promulgated a declaration of independence, established a civil government, and invited settlers to come to the area with assurances of generous land grants. Then the president of this republic went to Galveston to invite Lafitte to join the movement. Lafitte politely declined, whereupon Long returned to Nacogdoches. There he discovered that his army had been scattered by a Spanish force commanded by Colonel Ygnacio Pérez. Long fled to Louisiana, but he planned a return.

Late in 1820 Long raised another army and marched them to Point Bolivar, on the Texas coast. In the summer of 1821 he attacked and captured the presidio of La Bahía, only to learn shortly thereafter that Mexico had achieved its independence. He was persuaded to journey to Mexico City; there in 1822 he was shot in the streets by a soldier who went berserk. But the news he had heard— that Mexico was free—was correct. Through the efforts of Colonel Agustín de Iturbide, the revolutionary forces in Mexico had united under the Plan de Iguala, and a new nation was born. On July 17, 1821, the governor and other officials of Texas took the oath of independence, just as would the officials of New Mexico, California, and Sonora (Arizona) shortly afterward.

THE SPANISH HERITAGE

From 1519, when Piñeda landed on the coast of Texas, to 1821, when Mexico won its independence, the Southwest was part of the Spanish empire. Spanish settlers actually occupied parts of the area as early as 1598. Yet they did not find the area uninhabited; tens of thousands of Indians of various tribes lived in the region. Spaniards attempted to Christianize, civilize, and Hispanicize these natives, but in the attempt both European and Indian were changed; there was a blending of Spanish and Indian blood and cultures, the Spanish predominating. During these three centuries, the Southwest was traversed time and again until the geography was well known. Spanish names still predominate on the maps of the region—mountains, rivers, cities, and streets have titles that bear witness to the Spanish heritage. The surprising percentage of the population that still speaks the language of Castile, either as a native tongue or as a second language, shows that descendants of the *conquistadores* still live in the region.

Other evidences of the long Spanish ownership may be seen in the unique methods of handling cattle, of mining, and of irrigated farming which the Spanish settlers either brought with them or evolved in the area. The architecture of the region known as "hacienda" or "rancho" in California, "territorial" in Arizona, and "territorial" and "pueblo" in New Mexico, is basically Spanish-Indian in origin. The music of the Southwest, filled with the strains of the guitar, is far more Spanish than English in origin. The American pioneers of the Southwest also adopted the foods of their Indian and Spanish predecessors, and the "Mexican food" of today is another part of the Spanish heritage, as is so-called Western clothing, which evolved from the apparel of the *vaqueros*. Everywhere in the Southwest are echoes of those three centuries of Spanish rule.

3

THE MEXICAN ERA
1821–1848

THE ARRIVAL OF THE ANGLO-AMERICANS

In the late fall of 1821, William Becknell, a trader with several pack-loads of merchandise who was intent upon bartering with the Indians, happened to meet a party of scouts from the New Mexican presidio of Santa Fe. There in the mountains of Colorado these soldiers informed Becknell that the old Spanish restrictions on trading with foreigners had fallen along with the Spanish flag. Assured of a welcome, Becknell accompanied the scouts to the ancient pueblo-capital of New Mexico, where he sold his cotton goods and trinkets for a handsome profit. Returning to Franklin, Missouri, with specie, mules, blankets, and other items, Becknell found a willing audience for the news that Santa Fe would welcome American traders. Such a reception was not what the first Americans had received there; some of them had arrived in the capital of New

Mexico as early as 1804, but had been jailed and had had their merchandise confiscated.

In the spring of 1822 Becknell secured credit to the amount of five thousand dollars, money he used to buy more trade merchandise, three wagons, and stock, and to hire twenty-one men to accompany him. Late in May of 1822 he started from Missouri, proceeded to the Big Bend of the Arkansas River, and crossed at a point known as the "caches." Here he diverged from his route of the former year, venturing across the Cimarron Desert straight toward Santa Fe, instead of going up the Arkansas to the point where Bent's Fort later would be located and then turning south through Raton Pass to Las Vegas and Santa Fe. He and his men suffered greatly that year, but they succeeded in opening a wagon road along what would be the major route of the Santa Fe Trail. Becknell reached his destination on November 16, with his three wagons still in good condition, and he sold his merchandise quickly and at very favorable prices.

Four other trading parties reached Santa Fe in 1822, the major one led by Stephen Cooper. The thirty traders in this party exchanged their goods for four hundred jacks, jennies, and mules, a quantity of beaver pelts, and a large sum of specie. Such success encouraged still more traders to go down what has been called the "Turquois Trail" in 1823, and they too met with success. In 1824 the trade organized still more formally, and thereby set the pattern for the next two decades. Early in April the traders began assembling their wagons in Franklin, Missouri, departing on May 16 with eighty-three men and twenty-four wagons. To protect themselves from the Indians, they organized in semi-military style, adopting a constitution and electing officers. No difficulties were encountered, and on July 28 they reached Santa Fe, where they disposed of their goods, valued at $30,000 in Missouri, for $180,000 in specie and furs worth another $10,000.

Such profits encouraged still more traders to wish to venture down the Trail, but the danger of hostile plains Indians caused the Missourians to demand protection from the United States government. Senator Thomas Hart Benton of Missouri responded by introducing legislation to mark the Trail and to secure peace treaties with the plains tribes guaranteeing the traders' right of transit without molestation. Congress passed this act on March 3, 1825, along with an appropriation of $30,000. Three commissioners subsequently were appointed, and they left Franklin on July 4, 1825. Following the Trail already laid out, they heaped up mounds of rocks or dirt along the way (permission was secured from Mexico to continue the survey to Santa Fe in 1826), and they met with the Osage and the Kansas tribes to make treaties. The result of this federal interest was a doubling of the traffic in 1825, followed by still greater increases in 1826 and 1827. However, the Comanche and the Kiowa had not been parties to the treaties granting unmolested passage to the traders, and each year they increased their depredations. In 1828 they attacked several parties of returning traders, driving off horses and mules and killing several men. These attacks raised a storm of protests to Washington, accompanied by demands for military protection, but it was not until 1829, with the inauguration of Andrew Jackson, that troops were provided. That year Major Bennett Riley and four companies of infantry accompanied the caravan to the international boundary (the 100th meridian) where they stopped; however, when the traders were attacked six hours later on the Mexican side of the boundary, Riley led his troops across and saved the caravan. Then he returned to the American side and waited until the traders returned in October, escorting them back to Franklin without incident. Despite this success, no further military protection was afforded the traders, who thereafter relied upon their own strength of arms and semi-military organization to ward off Indian attacks.

One of those traders in the caravan of 1829 was William Bent, a former mountain man who realized that greater profits lay in trading than in trapping beaver. He and his brother Charles, in partnership with Ceran St. Vrain, decided to locate a permanent trading post on the upper Arkansas River (at the site of present-day La Junta, Colorado); their fort was completed by the spring of 1834, although they had been doing business at the site for more than a year by that time. The post was almost an exact duplicate of a Spanish presidio, showing not only that Bent was familiar with such architecture but also that the Spanish design was eminently practical for Southwestern conditions. After the completion of this post, many of the Santa Fe traders each year chose not to cross the

Arkansas River at the "caches," but instead to continue up the river along its north bank to Bent's Fort, then turn southward to Las Vegas and Santa Fe. The fort protected both traders and friendly Indians from attacks by the several warlike nations in that vicinity.

While the many traders who came down the trail from Missouri found the province of New Mexico open to them, they had to pay a price. Government officials there wanted a share of the profits—a share which they exacted in the form of taxes and fees. New Mexico remained a province until 1824, when it became a territory of the Republic of Mexico, a designation it held until 1836 when it was declared a department. During the years it was a territory its chief official was a *jefe político,* while in the latter period he was given the title of governor; in reality, there was little difference which title the official bore, for his powers were approximately the same. First to occupy the post after independence was José Antonio Vizcarra (1822–25), who campaigned successfully against the Navajo and Hopi in 1823. After Vizcarra came a long list of men, none of them very distinguished; most were interested only in increasing their private fortunes through levies on the Santa Fe traders. The officials who imposed the custom laws were arbitrary and capricious, the amount to be paid depending primarily upon the balance in the provincial treasury or upon the governor's personal needs. Those Americans who protested too violently found themselves in prison with their goods confiscated.

In 1837 the Pueblo Indians and settlers north of Santa Fe revolted, and the government reacted strongly. Albino Pérez, an outsider sent to the province as governor, had the unhappy task of imposing the direct taxes decreed in Mexico City. The Indians of the northern pueblos, possibly inspired by Father Antonio Martínez, the padre of that vicinity, marched on Santa Fe in July 1837, demanding an end to the burdensome taxes. Governor Pérez gathered a force of approximately 150 men, mostly soldiers, but was defeated in the ensuing battle. Pérez was captured and killed. Manuel Armijo, also rumored to have been a part of the conspiracy with Father Martínez, suddenly appeared as the champion of the New Mexican forces; in January 1838 he led soldiers and volunteers to victory in a battle with the Indians, and shortly thereafter he was made governor. He maintained his rule until 1846 and the coming of the Mexican War.

Governor Armijo was a man who understood the Santa Fe trade. Not only had he been a customs official, but he was involved in the Mexican mule trade—and the Americans wanted mules almost as much as they wanted gold and silver. Because of their qualities of endurance and surefootedness, these hardy animals had quickly become very popular with the traders, as well as with mountain men and other frontiersmen, who rode them and used them for carrying loads. Missourians found the animal useful for the same reasons, as well as for plowing on the plains; therefore the jacks and jennies coming up the Trail were bought by Missourians, who also began raising mules in such numbers that the animals became a virtual trademark of the state. The Santa Fe traders found no difficulty in disposing of all the mules they brought back up the Trail and every year the number of these animals coming from Santa Fe increased.

At first the supply of mules in New Mexico seemed inexhaustible. Every *hacienda* raised the animals in large numbers. But within a decade of the start of the trade the New Mexicans found the demand much greater than the supply, and they began buying them from ranchers in Chihuahua and Sonora. Even this failed to supply all the mules that were needed, however. In 1829, in an attempt to secure still more mules, Antonio Armijo organized a party of sixty men and a large pack train of New Mexican goods, mostly blankets and *serapes,* which he took overland to California, in the process opening a new route that, surprisingly, bore the name "The Old Spanish Trail." Setting out from Abiquiú early in November, Armijo went northwestward to what is now the Four-Corners Country (where present-day Colorado, New Mexico, Arizona, and Utah come together), turned west along the present-day Arizona-Utah border to the Virgin River, which he followed along its northern bank to the Grand Canyon, pushed across with Indian guides to the vicinity of what is now Las Vegas, then crossed the torturously dry Mohave Desert, arriving at Mission San Gabriel near Los Angeles in February 1830. This crossing led to regular overland commerce between New Mexico and California, for Armijo had significantly improved the route pioneered by Garcés, Escalante, and other explorers of the eighteenth century, and by some of the mountain men of the early nineteenth century.

The Old Spanish Trail was passable with little danger from the Indians because it went north of the Apache and Navajo country in New Mexico and eastern Arizona, and north of the Quechan tribes of the Colorado River. The Yuma, the principal nation of the Quechan groups, had prevented the use of the Anza-Garcés route that crossed the Colorado at that river with the Gila; rising in rebellion against Spanish domination in 1781, they had remained enemies of the Spaniards and of their heirs, the Mexicans. They were still hostile in 1823–26, when Captain José Romero, commander of the presidio of Tucson, and Father Felix Caballero, a Dominican serving at Mission Santa Catalina in northern Baja California, had attempted to reopen this route. Romero and Caballero had crossed the Colorado near its mouth to avoid the Yuma, but they had found the natives at that point were also hostile. They had reached California safely, however, only to be prevented from making their return for three years by Indian uprisings in inland California and by tribal warfare among the Indian nations along the Colorado. Although Captain Romero was promoted to lieutenant colonel for this feat and was hailed as a "Mexican Anza," the trail he used remained closed except for brief intervals. So Armijo's crossing in 1829–30 was very important.

The ranchers of Mexican California were delighted when they learned that Armijo would trade fine woolen blankets for their mules and horses. By 1830 these animals were so numerous in California that they were considered a nuisance; in fact, in years of drought the *hacendados* there had to slaughter great numbers of wild horses and mules in order to keep all available grass for their cattle. Armijo made his return in March and April of 1830 "with no more mishap than the loss of tired animals." Other New Mexicans, along with a number of American frontiersmen, were soon plying the "Old Spanish Trail" regularly, exchanging trade goods for mules and horses for the Santa Fe trade; a mule worth only ten dollars in Los Angeles sold readily in Santa Fe for five times that amount. Even this fantastic profit was not enough for some of those engaged in the California trade; during the 1830's the California authorities frequently complained that the theft of mules and horses for the Santa Fe trade was more widespread than the purchase of animals.

Traders in mules and horses were not the only ones to penetrate California during the Mexican period. Fur trappers came in large numbers to the coastal province. These mountain men, like the Santa Fe traders, had reached the capital of New Mexico even before the end of the Spanish years, then had spread across the Southwest in search of their quarry, the beaver. Zebulon Montgomery Pike, while in Santa Fe in 1806, reported the presence of two mountain men, Jean Baptiste Lelande and James Purcell. In the next fifteen years other trappers reached New Mexico in search of fur or of trade with Indians for fur, but like the first traders to the province they did not find a warm welcome. Some were imprisoned and their pelts confiscated.

When Mexico gained independence, restrictions on foreign interlopers, like the restrictions on trade, were relaxed. Soon mountain men in ever-increasing numbers were pushing southward from Colorado into New Mexico. These men came farther into the Southwest because of the competitive pressures of the British companies working in the Pacific Northwest and in the northern Rocky Mountains, and because the upper reaches of the Missouri River had been thoroughly trapped out. In the Southwest they hoped to find large numbers of beaver to supply the hat industry of the East and of Europe.

Taos and Sante Fe soon became headquarters for these Americans, as well as for New Mexican and Indian trappers. Supplies and trade goods were purchased in the two towns, parties were organized there, and the pelts were brought there for marketing to Santa Fe traders returning to Missouri. Several of the American fur traders who moved to Taos or Santa Fe became Mexican citizens in order to secure more favorable treatment from government officials or simply because they liked the area. Most notable among these was Kit Carson, destined for fame as a trapper, Indian fighter, guide, and soldier. Settling in Taos, he married a local girl and became a nominal Catholic. James Baird of Missouri also became a Mexican citizen, and in 1826 he protested to the New Mexican officials that Americans were trapping beaver; he asked that these "foreigners" be excluded so that "we Mexicans may peacefully profit by the goods with which the merciful God has been pleased to enrich our soil."

Few of the mountain men cared a great deal about what laws the Mexican government might pass, however. With or without permission, they spread across the Southwest in search of beaver; by 1824 they had trapped out the headwaters of the Rio Grande until few of the animals were left there. Next they transferred their activities to the Gila Valley of Arizona, reaching as far south as Sonora and as far west as California. In the forefront of this vanguard of American expansion was Jedediah Strong Smith, a native of New Hampshire. Born in 1798, Smith had received a fair education, including some Latin. At the age of thirteen he had become a clerk on a Lake Erie freighter. Later he moved to St. Louis, which, during the first two decades of the nineteenth century, was the capital of the Western fur trade. There, in 1822, he became an employee of William H. Ashley's Rocky Mountain Company. In the following year they trapped along the upper Missouri River and into present-day Wyoming. Crossing the Continental Divide at South Pass, the party also worked the upper Green River country, which was rich in beaver. The next three years found Smith in other parts of the West in search of pelts for Ashley's company. Then in 1826 in partnership with David E. Jackson and William L. Sublette, Smith bought the business from Ashley. These three men carried on the trapping and trading until 1830, when they sold the firm to another group of mountain men.

It was while he was a partner in the Rocky Mountain company that Smith began a series of explorations that earned him enduring fame. In August of 1826, accompanied by seventeen men, Smith left the Salt Lake basin and crossed into California by way of the Mohave Desert. Reaching Mission San Gabriel on November 27, he was imprisoned by a suspicious governor. After his release he made his way back to Salt Lake in the spring of 1827, and in the year that followed he retraced the same route, though in that expedition he lost men during an attack by the Mohave Indians. In April of 1828, instead of returning to Salt Lake as he left California, he turned north and reached the Klamath River. In Oregon all but two of his men were massacred by the Umpqua Indians. Perhaps it was because of these setbacks that Smith retired from the fur trade in 1830; the following year he became a Santa Fe trader, but in May 1831, near the Cimarron River, he was surrounded by Comanche Indians and killed. His explorations materially advanced American knowledge of the Southwest, however, and his routes were well traveled by those who followed.

Another fur trapper who reached California in search of beaver was James Ohio Pattie. He came down the Santa Fe Trail with his father, and in New Mexico they worked the Santa Rita del Cobre mines for a time. Then in 1825 young Pattie joined a party bound for the Gila Valley in search of beaver. They found many, but lost most of their pelts in an Indian attack; and they returned to New Mexico with little to show for their efforts. The next year, 1826, Pattie again joined the trappers bound for the Gila Valley. This time they followed the river all the way to its junction with the Colorado, turned north along the river into the Mohave Indian Country (where they were attacked), then skirted the Grand Canyon and made their way back to New Mexico—only to have their furs confiscated because they had no license to trap in Mexican territory.

In September 1827 Pattie again joined a party bound for the Gila. Passing down the river, the party had no trouble with Indians and secured a large number of pelts. Then at the junction of the Gila and Colorado rivers, the Yuma Indians stampeded their horses and left them afoot with more pelts than they could carry. Caching their furs, they went overland to California. In his recollection of this trek (in his *Personal Narrative*), Pattie describes the terrible hardships the party endured and overcame before reaching San Diego—where they were imprisoned by Governor José María Echeandía. In that prison his father, Sylvester Pattie, died. Governor Echeandía sent part of the group to the Colorado to recover the furs that had been cached, but they discovered that flood waters had ruined the pelts. According to his *Narrative,* Pattie secured his release when a smallpox epidemic struck California and he let it be known that he had a supply of vaccine; the governor contracted with Pattie to vaccinate the Californians, which he did. He states that he administered the vaccine to 22,000 persons, most of them Indians. Among the others were the Russians at Fort Ross. When

the governor refused to pay Pattie's fee for this service, he journeyed to Mexico City to plead his case—but to no avail. He returned to his native Tennessee by way of steamer to New Orleans,
discouraged and impoverished.

The Pattie route to California was improved in 1829 by Ewing
Young, who led a group westward that year. Young and his men
trapped the Salt River first, then cut across the mountains to the
Mohave villages on the Colorado and proceeded across the desert
to Mission San Gabriel. Turning north, he and his men worked the
San Joaquin Valley early in 1830 before returning to Los Angeles.
There local authorities threatened to arrest them for trapping without the proper papers, but with the aid of young Kit Carson, a
member of the party, Young managed to get his men safely out of
town. They returned to Taos without further incident arriving in
April 1831. Young made two other visits to Los Angeles, once in
1832 trapping, again in 1834 to purchase horses and mules for the
Santa Fe trade. Then in 1837 he passed through California buying
stock for a ranch he was building in Oregon.

Other mountain men were crossing the Southwest to California
in the 1830's. In 1833 Joseph Reddeford Walker reached San
Francisco and Monterey and wintered in the province before returning to Salt Lake. Paulino Weaver carved his name on the Casa
Grande ruins in central Arizona in 1832. William Sherley ("Old
Bill") Williams, a lone wolf, trapped the mountains of northern
Arizona without any partners, returning to Taos to drink and gam-
ble until his funds ran out; then he would set out on another soli-
tary trapping venture. Men such as these performed a vital service
for the United States government, for when the Americans began
coming into the region as part of the army or on scientific expeditions they found a number of experienced guides familiar with the
geography and the Indians. Still later they would serve immigrant
wagon trains in the same capacity.

Other Americans venturing across the Rockies to California
came not for furs but in search of land. Many of these men were
immigrants along the Oregon Trail who never got to the Columbia
River; instead they turned off the trail to Oregon, crossed the Sier-
ras into California, and liked what they found so well that they
stayed. They found several of their countrymen already there, men

who had come originally for the hide and tallow trade but had stayed to become Mexican citizens and large land owners. William E. P. Hartnell and William A. Gale arrived in California in 1822 as resident agents for the hide and tallow trade; American ships from New England found Californians of the Mexican period very anxious to trade their only marketable commodity, the hides and tallow from their large cattle herds, for merchandise of any type. These hides were taken back to Boston, which became a shoe manufacturing center as a result; the tallow was used to make candles. Hartnell became a Mexican citizen in 1830, eight years after he moved to California. He married a local girl and received a large land grant, Rancho Patrocinio del Alisal, near Monterey.

William Goodwin Dana, uncle of the author of *Two Years Before the Mast* (a classic story of the hide and tallow trade), came to California in 1826, was naturalized and baptized, married into the prominent Estudillo family in San Diego, and received Rancho Nipomo as a land grant. Abel Stearns of Massachusetts arrived in Monterey in 1829; instead of staying there to become a rancher, he chose to live at Los Angeles where he became a wealthy merchant, trader, and smuggler. He acquired so much land that he was the wealthiest man in southern California. John Marsh, a Harvard graduate, came to Los Angeles in 1836 to practice medicine, then moved to northern California where he practiced ranching and irrigated farming on a large scale along the slopes of the western Sierra. John A. Sutter, a Swiss by birth, arrived in California in 1840 and settled in the Sacramento Valley; purchasing Fort Ross from the Russians, he founded a ranching and farming complex that was virtually an empire, including trapping, distilling, a tannery, a mill, and a blanket factory. By 1840 there were approximately 380 foreign-born residents of California, some of them extremely wealthy and influential.

Beginning in 1841 these early arrivals were joined by a large number of Americans coming overland. Propelled by the hard times following the Panic of 1837, these pioneers found California a paradise of free—or virtually free—land and of opportunity. Those first arrivals became advertisers of the province, and the number of immigrants a year increased to a total of at least 250 persons by 1845. Many of these new arrivals refused to become

Catholics or to embrace Mexican citizenship, which worked against them in obtaining land; many of them drifted on to Oregon or returned to the East. Nevertheless, by 1846 there were approximately 680 foreigners in Mexican California, many of them ready to join in a revolution to annex the province to the United States.

California during the Mexican period continued to be isolated from the mainstream of national events. There was no dependable land route linking the province with the Mexican interior, only the tenuous connection by sea. In addition, the steaming cauldron of Mexico City politics between 1821 and 1846 left national politicians little time to worry about the needs of outlying areas such as California; as a result the province was left to work out its own destiny. Upon receipt of the news of Mexican independence early in 1822, Governor Pablo Vicente de Solá and his advisers accepted the accomplished fact and took the oath of independence on April 11. An agent of the new government, Agustín Fernández de San Vicente, visited the province soon afterward, but after his departure the Californians were by and large left to their own devices. During the twenty-five years of Mexican rule, the province had a number of revolutions, most of them small ones, as governor succeeded governor by force of arms.

The first such scramble for the chief executive's office came in 1831. While he was governor, José María Echeandía had moved the capital from Monterey to San Diego on the pretext that his health would be better away from the fogs of the north. His successor, Manuel Victoria, returned the capital to Monterey, whereupon Echeandía headed a southern revolt; at the ensuing Battle of Cahuenga the rebels won and Echeandía again became governor. Then Agustín Zamorano, a native of Florida who came to California in 1825, led a northern uprising that resulted in a temporary division of California, Echeandía controlling the area from San Diego to San Gabriel, and Zamorano from Santa Barbara to the north. From this period dates the historic division of northern and southern California; unlike in geography and economy, the two regions of the province had dissimilar attitudes and needs. The southern part of the province became conservative and insular, while the northern part looked outward on the world from its seaports. The gold rush, with its influx of foreigners and foreign ideas, would give the north a permanently liberal attitude.

Under Governor José Figueroa (1833–35) the two halves of the province were reunited in fact, but never in spirit. It was during Figueroa's administration that the greatest change in California's history formally began—the secularization of the missions. Church and state were unified under the Spaniards, and the missions had been established as an integral part of the government's efforts to civilize, Christianize, and Hispanicize the Indians on the frontier. No changes in this relationship came with Mexican independence. There was, however, a growing demand among the liberals of Mexico that church and state be separated. The demand was unsatisfied for more than a century. A Mexican decree of 1828 called for the expulsion of all Spaniards, which included many of the Franciscans working in Pimería Alta (Sonora and Arizona) and California. This decree had an effect only in Arizona, for in the Pacific Coast province Governor Echeandía made no attempt to enforce it. Yet there was a growing demand for secularization of the missions in California among the *hacendados* (the landed class) and among those who aspired to be *hacendados*. These people coveted the thousands of fertile acres owned by the missions, and believed that with an end to the mission system the land would easily fall into their hands. In large measure it was this local pressure which resulted in the secularization of the missions in 1834, but the action was also caused by the political situation in Mexico.

Shortly after Mexico won its independence, Agustín de Iturbide rose to power as Emperor Agustín I, but he was forced into exile in 1823. A constituent congress convened that year hammered out the first great Mexican constitution, that of 1824, which provided for a federal republic. Only the first president under this document managed to serve out his four-year term of office. After 1828 revolutions and counterrevolutions came with increasing frequency. The major cause of these upheavals was a struggle between centralists and federalists: the conservative element wanted a strong central government, a continuation of the union of church and state, and little power in the provinces; while the liberals wanted a federal republic, separation of church and state, land reform, and a host of other changes. A revolution in 1832 swept Antonio López de Santa Anna into the presidency at the head of the liberal faction, but the wily politician decided to allow his vice-president, Gómez Farías, to institute the liberal reforms. While Santa Anna waited at his plantation of Mango de Clavo, Gómez and the Congress enacted a secularization law, another law providing for secular education, and several other changes that would lead to a conservative uprising in 1835 (under the leadership of none other than President Santa Anna).

Governor José Figueroa had advised against secularization, but upon receiving the congressional decree he had no choice but to proceed. On August 9, 1834, he issued a proclamation ordering ten missions to be secularized, half the property to go to the Indians and the other half to be administered by secular officials. In 1835 and 1836 all but one of the remaining missions were secularized. Figueroa tried to avoid Indian excesses and the swindling of these new citizens by decreeing that the natives could not dispose of their property nor could cattle be killed unless it was necessary. However, Figueroa died before the task of secularization was completed, and his successors in the task, working during a period of political instability in Mexico, were not sympathetic to the Indians. The former mission property rapidly found its way into the hands of the Californians, most of the cattle were butchered in an orgy of Indian feasting, and the natives suffered terribly. They had not yet learned the ways of civilization well enough to compete with Californians. A few of the Indians found employment as ranch hands; the rest, including a majority of the former mission neophytes, either joined tribes in the interior or lived on the fringes of civilization in a state of degradation. In 1844 came the final disposition of all remaining mission property; Governor Manuel Micheltorena used the threatening war with the United States as a pretext for an order to dispose of it. The Franciscans managed to retain only Santa Barbara.

During the Mexican era, there were no innovations in dealing with the Indians of the Southwest. The political situation in Mexico City prevented any new concepts from being put into effect—or even an effective use of the older Spanish triad of mission, presidio, and civil settlement. The missions were secularized, and the presidios and pueblos allowed to work out their own destinies as best they could. The Royal Regulations of 1772, a military guide and handbook for the frontier, were continued in force just as if there had been no change of governments; in fact, these Regulations were reprinted in Mexico City in 1834 with no changes whatsoever, even to the signature of *Yo, El Rey* (I, the King) at the end. The presidios were left with insufficient garrisons which were inadequately supplied, infrequently paid, and ill-trained. With the exception of California, where the natives near the settlements had taken to the mission system, the provinces of the Southwest were as much, if not more, the property of the nomadic Apache and Comanche as they were of Mexico. Raiding, pillaging, and looting led to a reduction in the number of *gente de razon* (reasonable people —i.e. Mexicans and friendly Indians) in Arizona-Sonora, and very little expansion in New Mexico. Only in Texas did the raiding Indians meet resistance, and that came not from the Mexicans but from the encroaching Anglo-American frontiersmen.

THE COLONIZATION OF TEXAS, THE REVOLUTION, AND THE REPUBLIC

On December 23, 1820, while the flag of Spain still flew above the governor's mansion in San Antonio, Moses Austin appeared in the dusty streets of the capital city of Texas. Making his way to Governor Antonio María Martínez's office, he made a bold proposal: he wished to bring three hundred American families to the province and establish a colony. Such settlers would, of course, become Spanish citizens and members of the Catholic church. Austin justified his request by stating that he was a former Spanish citizen himself; although born in Connecticut and later engaged in business in Virginia, in 1798 he had moved to Missouri to mine lead, and at that time the area still belonged to Spain. Governor Martínez at first refused to consider the request, but Austin persevered with the aid of an old friend, the Baron de Bastrop, whom he happened to meet in San Antonio. Finally the governor gave his endorsement to the project and forwarded it to his superiors. On January 17, 1821, Austin's request received final approval from officials at Monterey.

Moses Austin did not live to see his colonization scheme carried into effect. On his return trip to Missouri he died of pneumonia, leaving his son, Stephen Fuller Austin, the task of colonizing Texas with Anglo-Americans. Stephen Austin in 1821 was only twenty-seven years of age, but already he had served five years in the Missouri Territorial Legislature and had been a district judge in Arkansas Territory. In 1821 he was engaged in business in New Orleans. That summer he journeyed to San Antonio where he had a cordial meeting with Governor Martínez; he was recognized as the heir to his father's commission, and was authorized to explore in Texas for a location. Upon his return to Natchitoches, Louisiana, he found more than a hundred letters from Americans interested in settling in Texas. The hard times engendered by the Panic of 1819 had not abated, and in 1820 the United States government had passed a new land law stating that the smallest tract that could be purchased was eighty acres at $1.25 an acre; this meant that a frontiersman needed one hundred dollars in cash to purchase a farm, a sum of money very difficult to acquire during the depression then prevailing.

Austin was back in Texas in the fall of 1821 at the site he had chosen for his colony, the land lying between the Brazos and Colorado rivers near the Gulf Coast. This area was well watered and heavily timbered, thus very similar to that part of the United States already settled by frontiersmen; in Texas he could build a log cabin, erect split-rail fences, and raise cotton just as he had in Arkansas, Tennessee, or Georgia. In Missouri and Iowa he was at the edge of the Great Plains where timber became scarce and the rainfall dropped to twenty inches a year, an area where his pioneering techniques could not be applied so readily. The Austin colony attracted many settlers during that first winter, and by the spring he felt able to journey to San Antonio for another conference with the governor.

At the capital the young colonizer learned of Mexican independence and the resulting political instability at Mexico City. Martínez advised him to journey to the national capital where he could look after his interests. Because of the Iturbide interlude, Austin made little headway in his quest to have the Spanish colonization grant recognized and himself authorized as his father's heir. Austin did use his time to good advantage, however. He learned the Spanish language thoroughly, and he made friends with many influential men. Finally, on January 4, 1823, the Austin grant was approved by Iturbide's forty-five-member *junta* (council), which had replaced the imperial Congress; because this was the only colonization permit approved while Iturbide was emperor, it was referred to as the Imperial Colonization Law. Austin was aware, however, that a reaction was developing against Iturbide, and he stayed in Mexico City to await developments. In March of 1823 the emperor was forced to abdicate, but the Congress, which reconvened, recognized Austin's grant as valid on April 14, and two weeks later Austin left for Texas.

Arriving at his infant colony in August, accompanied by the Baron de Bastrop, who had been named commissioner to issue land titles, Austin found conditions critical. Many of the first colonists to journey to Texas in 1821, as well as those who came the following year, had become discouraged at the delay in receiving titles to their land and had returned to the United States. However, the colonizer's appearance with a commissioner ended the uncertainty, and soon many new pioneers were arriving. A town was established as a seat of government for the colony, christened San Felipe de Austin, and by the end of the summer of 1824 Bastrop had issued 272 land titles. Eventually all three hundred families were settled in the confines of the grant.

To provide for further colonization of the relatively empty province of Texas, the Mexican Congress, on August 18, 1824, passed a new law which provided for further empresarial contracts (an *empresario* was a colonization agent holding such a contract with the state). The law established general guidelines, leaving specific details to be settled by the various states. This general colonization law did provide that no foreigners could settle within ten leagues (twenty-six miles) of the coast or twenty leagues of the international boundary. The old Spanish provinces of Texas and Coahuila were joined as one state in the Mexican Republic created by the constitution of 1824, and on March 24, 1825, the state of

Coahuila y Texas passed a state law for colonization. This provided for immigration either individually or through an *empresario*. Under it a rancher was to receive a square league of land (4428 acres) and a farmer a *labor* of land (177 acres). An *empresario* was to receive five square leagues and five *labors* of land for each one hundred families he brought. Such contracts were to run for six years and to be voided if less than one hundred families had been brought in that period of time. No person, however, could receive more than eleven square leagues of land.

Stephen F. Austin became the most active *empresario*. In addition to his original Imperial Colonization grant, he received several contracts from the state of Coahuila y Texas. By December of 1833 he was responsible for the issuance of 1055 land titles. Another colonizer of importance was Green DeWitt, a Missourian, who settled American immigrants along the Lavaca and Guadalupe rivers. Martin de León and Lorenzo de Zavala, both Mexicans, likewise received grants and brought new settlers to Texas, mainly from the interior of Mexico. The most troublesome *empresario* was Hayden Edwards, who, on April 15, 1825, secured a grant to bring eight hundred families to the unoccupied lands in the vicinity of Nacogdoches in East Texas. Already in that area there were settlers, some of whom had been there for half a century or more. Edwards began charging a higher fee for the land than allowed in his contract, and he threatened to expel those already there who did not pay him, even if they held a valid title to their lands. He also found evidences of fraud in the titles of many persons in the area and began questioning the validity of some. All this became an issue in the election of an *alcalde* (an officer who combined the functions of mayor, sheriff, and justice of the peace) for Nacogdoches in 1826. When the anti-Edwards candidate was declared elected and began validating all contested land titles, Edwards's brother complained to the governor, but the governor took offense at the tone of the letter and, on October 2, 1826, cancelled Edwards's contract. The standard of revolt was raised, Edwards declaring a Republic of Fredonia and calling for all "Americans" to join his cause. Edwards negotiated a treaty with the nearby Cherokee Indians, who were resentful that a land title had never been given them. However, most Americans had nothing to do with Edwards; in fact, Austin sent his militia to help put down this rebellion, and in January 1827 the insurgents fled across the border to the United States.

The Fredonian Rebellion created alarm in the minds of many Mexicans concerning the loyalties of the new arrivals in Texas. To inspect the colony the government in Mexico City sent General Manuel Mier y Terán, a soldier and scholar, who visited the settlements in 1828 and 1829. His report stated that he found Anglo-Americans predominating in most parts of the province, that the Americans had schools, were building homes and acquiring property, and that the local government was weak and its officials venal. He recommended drastic reforms: "either the government occupies Texas *now,* or it is lost forever." On April 6, 1830, the Mexican Congress, in secret session, passed a law which followed Terán's suggestions closely: more troops were to be sent to Texas, among them convict soldiers who would be encouraged to settle there when their terms were completed; the coastal trade between Mexico and Texas was to be encouraged by allowing such goods to enter free of duty, while those from elsewhere had to pay duties; and Article 11 stated: "it is prohibited that emigrants from nations bordering on this Republic shall settle in the states or territory adjacent to their own nations." The Anglo-Americans in Texas particularly resented Article 11, for it clearly was aimed at preventing more of their countrymen—friends and relatives—from joining them in Texas. Only Guatemala and the United States bordered Mexico, and few Guatemalans were immigrating. And the Anglo-Americans were going to have to pay more import duties on goods coming from the United States, duties which they had often been able to avoid.

Customs collectors arrived in Texas by May of that year, followed closely by more troops. Both actions were bad enough in the eyes of the new Texans, but were made even worse by the caliber of both sets of officials. A high percentage of the troops were convict soldiers, which the Anglo-Americans bitterly resented. And the customs collectors were high-handed martinets: George Fisher, a Serbian adventurer sent to Anahuac, decided that all ships clearing Texas ports had to see him at that one port, while Colonel John Davis Bradburn, a Kentuckian in the Mexican army, refused to allow any land titles to be issued in his district and suppressed the *ayuntamiento* (city council) at Liberty, Texas. When some of the Texans protested, Bradburn arrested two of them and refused to allow them a civil trial. The Texans gathered and surrounded Anahuac where Bradburn was holding the two prisoners. A clash of arms was narrowly averted by the arrival of Colonel José de las Piedras, commander of the Mexican troops at Nacogdoches, who countermanded Bradburn's acts and so humiliated him that he resigned soon afterward. But the Texans insisted that all troops leave Texas, and by the summer of 1832 there were no Mexicans left in the American part of the province.

Colonel José Antonio Mexia, commander of the forces at Matamoros in Mexico, became alarmed at this activity and gathered an army of four hundred troops to put down what he feared was an insurrection. Stephen F. Austin, who happened to be returning from a meeting of the legislative session of the state of Coahuila y Texas at Saltillo, joined Mexia on the march northward. Austin used the time to convince Mexia that the Texans were loyal, that they merely had been fighting a local tyrant who was taking orders from President Anastacio Bustamante, recently deposed in the coup of 1832 that installed Antonio López de Santa Anna in power. The rebellious force at Anahuac in fact adopted the "Turtle Bayou Resolutions," a declaration that the Texans were fighting as loyal Mexicans in the cause of General Santa Anna, liberty, and freedom. When Mexia arrived at the scene of disorder, he received a very cordial welcome spiced at every hand with declarations of loyalty and displays of enthusiasm for Mexico. Mexia's report was very favorable.

Despite the fact that they had cleared the province of all troops and had ended the collection of customs duties, the colonists were still not satisfied. They wanted an end to the provisions of Article 11 of the Law of April 6, 1830. Therefore on August 22, 1832, just a month after Mexia's departure, the city council of San Felipe de Austin issued a call for election of delegates to a convention, which was to meet at San Felipe on October 1 that year. In traditional American frontiersman fashion, they planned a convention to draft a petition to the central government stating their wishes. The fifty-five delegates gathered on the appointed day, and Stephen

F. Austin was elected president. The convention proceeded to enact several resolutions, principal among which were a call for repeal of Article 11 and a request for separate statehood for Texas. In the joint state of Coahuila y Texas, the Texans had little voice since Coahuila had the greater population and since the capital (Saltillo) was so far away. At the end of the convention, three men were elected to take the resolutions to Mexico City, chief among whom was Stephen F. Austin. They did not leave Texas immediately, however, for it was thought unwise to forward a petition on which there were no Spanish names. Another convention was called to meet on April 1, 1833, at San Felipe, this one with representatives from San Antonio.

The Convention of 1833 was even more militant than the first. Although the resolutions adopted at this body were similar to those accepted at the meeting the year before, they were couched in stronger language. And the second convention proceeded to write a constitution for the proposed separate state of Texas; on the committee that prepared this document was a newcomer to Texas, former governor of Tennessee Sam Houston. Again the burden of taking the request to Mexico City fell on Austin, and on April 22 he set out, arriving at the capital on July 18. General Santa Anna was not in the capital, so Austin dealt with Vice-President Gómez Farías. The proposal for separate statehood was introduced in the House of the Mexican Congress, but a cholera epidemic brought its progress to a halt. Austin, impatient at the delay, wrote the city council at San Antonio urging that body to begin organizing a state government. On November 5 the Texas colonizer had a conference with Santa Anna in which the Mexican president agreed to the repeal of the ban on further immigration, but refused separate statehood for Texas.

Austin left Mexico City on December 10, happy with what had been accomplished. On the return trip he stopped at Saltillo to see the commandant, who promptly arrested the Texan and sent him back down the road to Mexico City under guard. Austin's letter urging the city council at San Antonio to organize a state government for Texas had been sent to officials in Mexico City, who regarded it as a gesture of treason. In fact, Santa Anna and Gómez were unsympathetic to the methods of the Texans in calling con-

ventions and sending petitions to Mexico City. While such practices were a common part of the American frontier heritage, they
were unknown in the Spanish-Mexican tradition—and therefore
suspect. For his rashness in writing the letter, Austin was kept in-
communicado in prison until Christmas Day, 1834. In July of
1835 he was allowed to return to Texas—but he never received a
trial, for no Mexican court would accept jurisdiction in the case.

While Austin was in prison, Santa Anna was forwarding his plan
of dictatorship. In April of 1834 he ousted Gómez and assumed the
presidency to which he had been elected in 1832 as a liberal feder-
alist; however, when he assumed the office, it was as a conservative
centralist. He exiled Gómez, dissolved Congress, disbanded the
state legislatures, and usurped the powers of the government. A
hand-picked Congress finally legalized these actions in October of
1835 by declaring federalism at an end; Santa Anna was recognized as leader of a centralist government, and the militia was reduced to one soldier for every five hundred inhabitants. This action
precipitated armed uprisings in no less than seven different Mexican states, of which Texas was one.

The Texas Revolution—for such it would come to be—was the
outgrowth of a long series of real and imagined grievances against
the government of Mexico. In part it came from a different cultural
heritage: the Texas colonists were angry in their new home because
they had no trial by jury, no public education system, no freedom
of religion; they resented the instability of the national government,
the jailing of citizens for exercising the right of assembly and
petition, and their own inability to get separate statehood for
Texas. But most of all, they revolted because of Santa Anna's ab-
rogation of the republican Constitution of 1824 and his subsequent
attempt to suppress the militia—which, in effect, meant an attempt
to disarm the civil populace.

Many historians have attempted to show that the Texas Revolution was actually an attempt to win more slave territory for the
United States, that it was a conspiracy to wrest land from Mexico,
annex it to the United States, and thereby expand the institution of
slavery to include still another state. This "slaveocracy conspiracy"
theory as an explanation of the Texas Revolution has no basis in
fact. The Texas colonists, most of them from Southern states, had

brought their slaves across the international boundary along with the rest of their property. Then in 1829, in the face of a threatened Spanish invasion, President Vicente Guerrero of Mexico on September 15 had issued a decree abolishing slavery everywhere in the Republic except one state in the far south; however, even before this decree was promulgated, Texas was also exempted. And one part of the Law of April 6, 1830, had forbade the further importation of slaves into Mexico; but this, like other parts of the law, was soon lifted. No further action had been taken against the slaveholding rights of Texas colonists, and when the Revolution started in 1835 it was because of an attempt to take away weapons, not slaves. There was no planned immigration to Texas by Southerners who plotted to start a revolution, then annex the area to the United States in order to expand the number of slave states in the Union. The Texas Revolution began as part of a bigger war against the usurpation by a dictator of those freedoms which Anglo-Americans, as well as many Mexicans, felt to be the fundamental birthright of men everywhere. Just as residents of the thirteen colonies rebelled against the tyranny of George III sixty years earlier, so the Texans (many of whom were of Spanish descent) fought against the tyranny of Antonio López de Santa Anna.

The fighting actually began on October 2, 1835, when a Mexican force of one hundred dragoons came to impound a cannon at Gonzales, Texas. Led by Colonel John H. Moore, a group of Texan volunteers routed the Mexican force. The Texans struck their first offensive blow on October 9, when a force of fifty men under George Collinsworth captured a fort at Goliad which contained valuable military supplies. The snowballing Texan force, now commanded by Stephen F. Austin, who reluctantly had come over to the warhawks' side, approached and surrounded San Antonio late in October. When Austin was deputized to go to the United States in search of aid by a provisional government, Edward Burleson and Ben Milam took command of the volunteers of San Antonio. After five days of hard fighting, beginning on December 5, the troops at San Antonio under General Martín Pérfecto de Cós surrendered and marched out of the province under parole, leaving the province completely free of Mexican soldiers.

The Texans were not as successful politically as they were militarily. On October 11 a so-called permanent council was organized with no real legal justification. For three weeks it exercised sovereignty over the province, then passed out of existence upon the convocation of an elected body of delegates at San Felipe on November 3. Branch T. Archer was elected president of the "Consultation," which declared by a vote of thirty-three to fifteen that the Texans were fighting for the Mexican Constitution of 1824 and not independence; it also selected Sam Houston to serve as commander in chief of the army and created a provisional government to serve either until the differences with Mexico were resolved or until March 1, 1836, when a new convention would meet. To head this provisional government, the Consultation chose the quarrelsome Henry Smith as governor, along with a council to assist him. However, the powers of each were not clearly defined, and difficulties soon arose. The governor denounced the council, and the council retaliated by declaring the governor impeached. The result was political indecision and inactivity during that critical winter. Additional problems were created by the volunteer companies of soldiers who rushed to Texas from the United States; they refused to accept the orders of General Sam Houston, and they proposed an invasion of Mexico to capture Matamoros, south of the Rio Grande. The result was that there was no military activity during the months from November to March.

On March 1, 1836, fifty-nine delegates with plenary powers met at Washington-on-the-Brazos, Texas, and solved the governmental deadlock. A declaration of independence, written mainly by George C. Childress, was passed on March 2 without a dissenting vote; the change in attitude regarding independence came about because the emissaries to the United States reported that such a declaration was necessary if the Texans were to secure aid in their struggle. The American colonists had found such a step necessary to secure French support in 1776, and the Texans found the same half a century later. Then in quick order the convention reappointed General Houston commander in chief of all Texan forces in the field, wrote a constitution, and, shortly before adjourning on March 17, created an *ad interim* government with David G. Burnet as president and Lorenzo de Zavala as vice-president.

While these delegates were meeting, military reverses were

suffered in the field. General Santa Anna appeared outside San Antonio on February 23, 1836, months before anyone thought he possibly could reach that far north. Immediately he laid siege to the Alamo where the Texan defenders, led by William Barrett Travis, James Bowie, and Davy Crockett, had taken refuge. On the morning of March 6 to the nerve-tingling strains of the *"Deguello,"* a song signifying that no quarter would be given, the final assault on the chapel of Mission San Antonio de Valero came, and the 187 Texans inside were killed. Santa Anna's victory was costly, however; estimates of his casualties run as high as sixteen hundred. More important than the Mexican losses, however, was the time which these lives bought—time for the convention at Washington-on-the-Brazos to complete its affairs and time for General Sam Houston to begin preparations for a decisive battle.

While Santa Anna was occupied at San Antonio, along the Texas coast to the south a separate Mexican force under General José Urrea was winning an easy victory over Francis W. Johnson and fifty men of the proposed Matamoros expedition at San Patricio and another victory at Agua Dulce over Dr. James Grant and one hundred men. Urrea continued eastward and on March 20 captured Colonel James W. Fannin and approximately 450 volunteers after a sharp fight at Coleto Creek. On March 27 at Goliad, under explicit orders from Santa Anna, Urrea executed almost all the prisoners he had taken. The "Goliad Massacre," as it was called, and the bloody assault of the Alamo proved to be Santa Anna's great blunders. Had he taken prisoners at the Alamo, put them with those taken along the coast, and shipped them to New Orleans, he would have made them a laughing stock; instead he made them martyrs, stiffened the back of the Texans to resist, and saw a flood of aid and supplies pour into Texas from the United States.

Sam Houston was appointed commander in chief of the Texan army on March 6, 1836, and he immediately left for Gonzales where the troops were encamped. There he found 374 ill-clad men, most of whom were raw recruits with no military experience, many without guns, others without ammunition, and only two days' rations on hand. Within moments after his arrival he heard rumors that the Alamo had fallen. Publicly the commander pretended not to believe such rumors; privately he dispatched three scouts to ascertain the truth. On March 13 the scouts returned with confirmation of the bloody Mexican victory at San Antonio, and with news that Santa Anna was moving eastward to pacify the rebellious province. Houston thereupon began a series of retreats which carried his small army eastward to the Brazos River; there he encamped for two weeks to drill his army and to discipline it for battle.

After the fall of the Alamo, Santa Anna thought the backbone of resistance had been broken in Texas. Rashly he split his army into small detachments, personally leading one part in a futile attempt to capture the *ad interim* government at Harrisburg. On April 18 the Texan army arrived at Harrisburg, and the two forces converged near San Jacinto Bayou. Early on the morning of April 21, Santa Anna's forces happily cheered the arrival of General Martín Pérfecto de Cós and four hundred troops, bringing the Mexican force to a total of approximately fifteen hundred men. That afternoon at about three-thirty, to the tune of "Will You Come to the Bower I Have Shaded for You" and shouts of "Remember the Alamo; Remember Goliad," the seven hundred eighty-three Texans led by Houston swept across the two hundred yards separating the two forces and with blazing guns and flashing knives began to slay the enemy. The Mexicans, taken by surprise during their afternoon *siesta,* broke in panic and ran. Eighteen minutes later the battle was over, but the pursuit and slaughter of retreating Mexicans continued until nightfall. Of the Mexican army, six hundred thirty died, two hundred eight were wounded, and seven hundred thirty were taken prisoner; in Houston's army two were killed and twenty-three wounded, six of them mortally.

The following day, April 22, independence was assured when the jubilant Texans captured President Santa Anna. The proud general, taken in the uniform of a private soldier, found himself a prisoner of the compatriots of the men he so recently had ordered to be executed at Goliad and the Alamo, and he rightly feared for his life. General Houston, however, ordered the tyrant to be turned over to the provisional government, and subsequently two treaties, one public and one secret, were signed by Santa Anna at Velasco whereby all Mexican troops were ordered to leave Texas and prisoners were to be exchanged. In return for his release, Santa Anna, by the terms of the secret treaty, agreed to work in Mexico for a recognition of the independence of Texas. The Battle of San Jacinto was the only decisive battle ever fought on American soil west of the Mississippi River; as a result of it a territory larger than most European nations was taken from Mexican control and established, *de facto,* as an independent nation.

Texas was free—but independence brought many problems. To the west were hostile Indians ready to plunder and kill; to the south were Mexicans determined to regain their lost province—for the Treaties of Velasco were never ratified by the Mexican Congress; and at home there was an empty treasury and an unruly army. In the decade that followed two men emerged as leaders of the Republic of Texas: Sam Houston and Mirabeau Bonaparte Lamar. Bitter enemies both personally and politically, the two represented aspects of the American frontier which had given them their background and training. Houston was born in Virginia on March 2, 1793; he was a veteran of the War of 1812 and of numerous Indian campaigns with Andrew Jackson, and a former governor of Tennessee; he had lived with the Indians on several occasions and had arrived in Texas in 1833 to become the major hero of the Revolution. Lamar was a Georgian, born there on August 16, 1798, had tried his hand at mercantile activity, had been a private secretary to Governor George M. Troup of Georgia, and had actively participated in the expulsion of the Creek and Cherokee from Georgia. After his wife died in 1833, he ran unsuccessfully for Congress, then migrated to Texas, arriving in March of 1836 in time to participate in the Battle of San Jacinto as commander of the cavalry unit. Houston favored peace with the Indians; Lamar hated them bitterly. Houston favored releasing Santa Anna; Lamar wanted the Mexican president executed. Houston wanted peace with Mexico; Lamar favored an invasion. Houston favored economy in government; Lamar believed in deficit spending to finance an expansion of Texas.

In winning the presidency in 1836, San Houston had defeated candidate Stephen F. Austin; but Houston made Austin Secretary of State for the Republic. However, Austin died late in December of that same year. In that same election of 1836 Lamar was made vice-president of the Republic, the constitution which had been written during the Revolution was approved by the voters, and a referendum on annexation to the United States was overwhelmingly passed.

In the first year of the Republic, the immediate danger was a military rebellion against the civil authorities. Volunteer soldiers, disappointed at arriving from the United States too late to participate in the Revolution, proposed an invasion of Mexico. When their proposal was rejected, they talked of replacing President Houston with a fighting general. Houston finally resolved this crisis by furloughing all except six hundred soldiers and appointing a loyal commander in chief. He tried to solve the Indian, Mexican, and currency problems by annexation to the United States, but this move was blocked by New Englanders who said that the Texas Revolution was a "slaveocracy conspiracy." Disappointed at this rejection in the United States Congress, Houston turned to a policy of conciliating the Indians and Mexicans. These expedients freed him to contend with the growing public debt and the empty treasury. Paper money was issued based on expected tariff revenues and on the public domain, and loans were sought unsuccessfully from England and France. By the end of his two years in office (the constitution provided that the first president of the Republic would serve two years; thereafter the term would be three years), the public debt stood at two million dollars, and the value of paper currency had depreciated to sixty-five cents on the dollar. However, Houston did manage to secure recognition of Texas' independence from the United States just before Andrew Jackson went out of office.

Because the constitution of Texas forbade a president from succeeding himself, Houston was not a candidate for re-election. Lamar won the contest without opposition, for death and suicide removed his opponents. But Houston used the inaugural ball on December 1, 1838 to rob Lamar of his moment of glory and to perpetrate one of the greatest practical jokes in Texas history. Houston knew that Lamar took considerable pride in his ability as a writer, and that he had worked hard to make his inaugural address a literary masterpiece. At the inaugural party Houston arrived dressed in a wig and knee-length breeches, the only person in costume. As George Washington, he interrupted the proceedings to make a "farewell address." He spoke for three hours, recounted tall stories, told jokes, and defended his administration. By the time he had finished speaking, Lamar was too nervous with frustration to read his speech. A friend did the job for him—in such a dead monotone that most of the audience left before it was completed.

Once in office, however, Lamar had things his own way. Despite Houston's opposition in the Congress (he was elected to the House in 1838), the new president pursued a vigorous war against the Cherokee in East Texas, forcing them to move to Oklahoma. In March of 1840 the Comanche met with Lamar's representatives at the Council House in San Antonio, but a fight broke out in which a chief and several warriors were slain; the Comanche believed a massacre had been planned and took to the warpath in great numbers seeking revenge. Lamar's Indian wars alone cost the Republic $2,500,000, and countless lives were lost on either side. To finance these campaigns, as well as his foreign adventures, he issued still more paper money, and the dollar dropped to a value of twelve to fifteen cents.

In foreign affairs Lamar enjoyed both successes and failures. His diplomatic agents in Europe managed to secure recognition of the Republic by France, England, the Netherlands, and Belgium, and arranged favorable commercial treaties with France, England, and the Netherlands. These were only minor considerations in Lamar's mind, however, for his major drive was southward and westward. He dreamed of a Texas that extended westward to the Pacific. To carry out this policy—and to snub his opponent Houston—he moved the capital of the Republic from the city of Houston to the far western edge of the frontier at a village named Austin. To secure recognition from Mexico of Texas' independence, he sent diplomatic agents southward early in his administration. When such attempts failed, he sought to force the issue by arms. On June 21, 1841, he dispatched an army of 270 men under the command of Colonel Hugh McLeod to the capital of New Mexico; McLeod had orders to use force only if necessary *and* to occupy Santa Fe only if he thought a majority of the New Mexicans favored joining with Texas. Journeying northward, then westward, these troops arrived in New Mexico completely exhausted from their ordeal (New

Mexican spies posing as scouts led them over a tortuous route) and surrendered to Governor Armijo's forces without firing a shot. They were marched to Mexico City and imprisoned in Perote Castle. This disastrous expedition so stirred up Mexico that retaliation was planned, but Lamar went out of office before overt hostilities occurred.

In the election of 1841, Sam Houston was again returned to the chief executive's office. Immediately he took steps to retrench, to economize, and to repair the harm to Texas-Mexican relations. The Texas navy, which Lamar had rented to a rebellious faction in the Mexican state of Yucután, was sold at public auction. Meetings were arranged with various Indian tribes, and peace treaties were signed with most of them. But the Mexicans refused to be placated. Early in 1842 President Santa Anna, back in power once more, sent an army northward which captured Goliad, Refugio, and San Antonio, held them a few days, then retreated south of the border. Houston managed to prevent Texans from marching against Mexico, hoping that the Mexican incursion would satisfy Mexican honor and peace would return. Then in September of 1842 another force, commanded by General Adrian Woll, crossed the Rio Grande from Mexico and captured San Antonio. After nine days Woll also retreated across the Rio Grande, taking with him a number of prisoners who were sent to Perote Castle. Houston could not prevent a Texas army from retaliating. In mid-November that year a force of 750 men under General Alexander Somervell marched to Laredo, which they captured on December 8. Somervell, probably on orders from Houston, at that point announced that he was going home, and approximately half the army went with him. The remainder elected W. S. Fisher their colonel and marched to Mier, Mexico, which they surrounded on December 25. A fierce battle against the forces of General Ampudia followed, and on the morning of December 26 the Texans surrendered—to join their fellow Texans in Perote Prison.

In the election of 1844 a Houston man, Dr. Anson Jones, was elected president of the Republic. During his term the major events centered on the annexation of Texas to the United States. Perhaps it was the ill-fated Texian-Santa Fe expedition which revived interest in annexation, for certainly the people of the United States became more aware of Texas and its fate following this disaster; also, a growing British involvement in the affairs of the Lone Star Republic caused concern in Washington. On October 16, 1843, President John Tyler had opened negotiations with the Houston administration for annexation by treaty. This treaty was signed on April 12 of the following year; it provided for Texas to enter the Union as a territory, for the United States to pay the Texas public debt, and for the public domain of Texas to become a part of the national public domain. However, this treaty failed to win the necessary two-thirds majority vote in the United States Senate. Because of the strong feelings which the annexation of Texas raised in the United States, both pro and con, the question became a strong issue in the election of 1844. James K. Polk, nominee of the Democratic party, warmly endorsed annexation, while Henry Clay, the Whig standard bearer, opposed immediate annexation. Polk's victory at the polls was interpreted as a mandate for annexation, and Tyler began the necessary steps before going out of office. In his last annual message to Congress, delivered in December 1844, he recommended the passage of a joint resolution (which required only a simple majority in both houses, and thus had more chance of passage than a treaty did) embodying the major features of the rejected treaty. The measure passed on February 28, 1845, and Tyler signed it the following day, March 1. It provided that Texas would enter the Union as a state, but would retain both its public land and its public debt, and that the United States would adjust all questions concerning its international boundary.

England and France joined Mexico in urging the Texans to reject the offer, though for different reasons. The European powers opposed the move because it would strengthen the United States, and because they would lose a profitable "most favored nation" trade status in Texas; Mexico, of course, still hoped somehow to reestablish control over its lost province. At the urging of British and French agents, the Mexican government became resigned to the permanent loss of Texas and offered the Lone Star Republic a treaty recognizing its independence provided that it never joined the United States. President Anson Jones convened the Congress of the Republic on June 16 and submitted both proposals to it. The delegates overwhelmingly accepted the offer of the United States. A

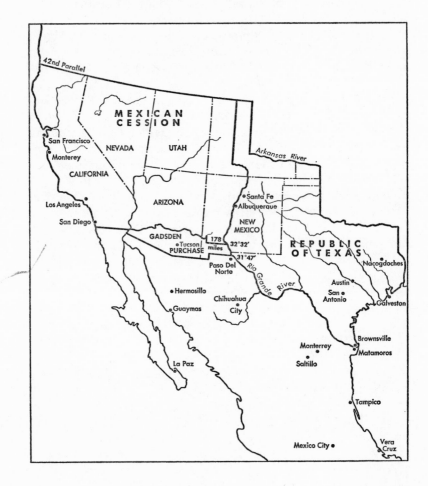

constitutional convention, which met on July 4, likewise accepted the American offer, and proceeded to write a state constitution. Then on October 13 the voters of the Republic went to the polls and ratified the annexation agreement as well as the proposed constitution. On December 29, following congressional acceptance of the Texas constitution, President Polk formally signed the act making Texas the twenty-eighth state. Almost two months later, on February 19, 1846, President Jones participated in a ceremony in Austin in which he formally turned the affairs of Texas over to Governor J. Pinckney Henderson. Concluding his address, Jones declared, "The final act in this great drama is now performed; the Republic of Texas is no more."

But the final act was not over in the drama of annexation. Just five days after Congress passed the joint resolution, on March 6, 1845, the Mexican minister in Washington demanded his passport and left for home, thus severing relations between the two republics. The American Congress could vote on the measure, the President could sign it, and the Texans could agree to it, but a war had to be fought to ratify the annexation of Texas, as well as settle a number of other differences between the United States and Mexico.

THE MEXICAN WAR

On April 24, 1846, a detachment of Mexican cavalry, acting under official orders from President Mariano Paredes and General Mariano Arista, crossed the Rio Grande into Texas, where they ambushed an American patrol led by Captain S. B. Thornton, and killed or wounded sixteen men. Then the Mexicans withdrew south of the river. This act of war signaled the beginning of a conflict that would last almost two years, would cost thousands of lives and millions of dollars, and would redraw the maps of the Southwest. Yet that action of April 24 was but the start of the last act—not the first—of a drama that had begun more than three centuries earlier. The discovery of America had started a contest for the continent between France, Spain, and England. The French were eliminated in 1763, and two decades later the United States inherited a large part of the British claim. A cultural conflict had smoldered for generations, engendering hatred and distrust and causing numerous personal battles between "gringo" and "greaser." The settlement of Texas and the subsequent revolution added to the inherent cultural conflict between Mexicans and Americans. But the war between Mexico and the United States cannot be explained by this one factor alone, nor can it be explained as "nature abhoring a vacuum"—that is, Mexico failing to fill the region with people and develop its resources.

Relations between the United States and Mexico had begun warmly when the United States promptly recognized its southern neighbor's declaration of independence. The first note of discord was sounded in 1829 when the American minister opened discussion of the claims question—i.e. the payment of debts owed to United States citizens by the Mexican government. Nothing came of the effort. Then, in 1837, just before going out of office, President Andrew Jackson again made an attempt to collect these debts, and he too was unsuccessful. That the claims question alone justified war according to international usages of the day is shown by the fact that France invaded Mexico in 1838 to collect the debts owed to its citizens, and England by show of force convinced Mexico to pay the debts owed to Englishmen. In 1839 the Mexican government agreed to an arbitration of the American claims by the King of Prussia; Mexico delayed eighteen months before coming to the conference table, argued four months over procedure, and settled less than one-third of the cases before the arbitration process broke down. President Santa Anna, back in power in the early 1840's, refused to pay even the $2,000,000 agreed upon. Finally, in June 1843, Mexico made the first payment on this settlement, but refused the following April to make the second payment. There the matter rested when Texas entered the Union and diplomatic relations were severed.

Another factor causing the war, at least according to some apologists for American actions, was the California question. This school of historians states that the United States wanted California, which is true enough. On October 19, 1842, Commodore Thomas A. C. Jones, commanding the American naval forces in the Pacific, sailed into Monterey and seized the town, believing that the United States and Mexico had gone to war and anxious to prevent England

from getting the Pacific Coast province first—and England defi-
nitely had designs on California. On discovering his mistake, Jones
had apologized and paid for what damage he had done. James K.
Polk, when he took office, had his eye on California, and is often
charged with being a member of the "Manifest Destiny" school of
politics; some Americans did believe that the United States had a
"Manifest Destiny" to acquire all of the North American continent
and extend to it the enlightened Anglo-Saxon, Protestant system of
free enterprise and good government. But Polk would not have
waged a war for California. He wanted California, but he hoped to
acquire it either through diplomacy or by promoting a revolution
and annexation as had happened in Texas without American help.

Polk's hope of a revolution in California was not far-fetched. In
1835 when Santa Anna had abolished the Constitution of 1824,
young Juan Bautista Alvarado, a native of the province, led a revolution which declared California a "free and sovereign" state until
Mexico should return to the Constitution of 1824. Later he modi-
fied this stand to mean merely the right of local self-government.
Mexico's hold was so weak that no attempt was made to suppress
the Alvarado revolt; instead the central government recognized his
regime and made him governor of California. After he retired from
office in 1842, local uprisings continued to plague Mexican appointees to the extent that the province was ripe for such a revolution as Polk hoped to see. Perhaps it was the hope of such an event
that led the American President to send Captain John Charles
Frémont westward in 1845, ostensibly on a journey of exploration.

Polk's choice of Frémont for this task was both fortunate and
unfortunate. Frémont, born in Virginia in 1813, had a gift for
mathematics and managed to secure an appointment as second
lieutenant in the United States Topographical Corps in 1838. In
1841, through the influence of Senator Thomas Hart Benton of
Missouri, whose daughter Frémont would marry later that same
year, he received his first appointment of exploration, a commission to explore the Des Moines River. The following year he was
sent to explore the Wind River chain of the Rocky Mountains, a
task widely publicized through his report, largely written by his
talented wife Jessie and published at government expense in an edi-
tion of ten thousand copies thanks to his father-in-law. Now hailed

by some as "The Great Pathfinder"—but in reality much closer to what his detractors have called him: "The Great Pathfollower"—Frémont was fortunate enough in his explorations to have secured the services of mountain men as guides; his maps were valuable and his wife's prose was brilliant, but he opened no new routes in the West nor were his adventures as thrilling as his reports pictured them. Nevertheless, in 1843 he was sent on still another expedition, this time to Colorado, the Great Salt Lake, and Oregon, returning by way of Nevada and California. A third western expedition was ordered in 1845; with Kit Carson as guide and an escort of sixty men, the young army officer proceeded to Salt Lake, then went up the Humboldt, and crossed the Sierra, reaching Sutter's Fort in California on December 9, 1845. At Monterey he was ordered out of the province by Mexican authorities, whereupon he went north to Klamath Lake in Oregon (just north of the forty-second parallel) and encamped. Obviously he was poised for action in California whenever Polk should order it.

The American desire for California caused concern and hostility in Mexico, but it does not account for the virulent hatred of Americans that was so prevalent in Mexico City. Polk sought to combine the claims question with his desire for California in 1845 by offering a trade. President José Herrera, who succeeded the ousted Santa Anna in 1844, was a moderate and seemed inclined to settle differences with the United States by diplomacy. Polk therefore sent John Slidell to Mexico with instructions to trade the claims for California if possible. Yet when Slidell arrived in Mexico—after private assurances that he would be received—Herrera refused to see him; so strong was the anti-American feeling that any government which would treat with agents of the United States would have been toppled immediately. In fact, late in 1845 the Herrera regime was turned out of office by a popular uprising in favor of the more militant General Mariano Paredes, who declared that he would see the Eagle and Serpent of Mexico flying over the American White House before he would give up the claim to Texas. Because of the kaleidoscope of revolutions, counter-revolutions, *juntas,* constitutions, and dictators which had troubled Mexico in the two-and-a-half decades of its independence, there could be no diplomatic settlement of differences with the United States. The demagoguery of Mexican politicians had so inflamed the populace that no peaceful settlement could be reached.

But it was the Texas question that started the fighting. More specifically, it was the question of the Texas boundary. Texas claimed that its southern and western boundary was the Rio Grande to its source, then north to the 42nd parallel. By the end of the Texas Revolution this river had become the accepted dividing line. General Cós, when he retreated from San Antonio in December of 1835, had moved south of the Rio Grande. Santa Anna after the disaster at San Jacinto had issued an order to his army to retreat across this river, and the order was obeyed. The Treaties of Velasco likewise recognized the Rio Grande as the border between Texas and Mexico, and in December of 1836 the first Texan Congress had asserted that the Rio Grande was the international boundary. True enough, Texas had never really asserted jurisdiction over the area between the Nueces River and the Rio Grande (or in the far west in New Mexico), but neither had Mexico exercised authority in the lower Rio Grande Valley. Finally, when Mexico offered recognition to Texas in return for not joining the Union, the proffered treaty specified the Rio Grande as the boundary.

While the annexation proceedings between Texas and the United States were concluded, President Polk instructed General Zachary Taylor to move his troops, numbering approximately 1500, to the mouth of the Nueces River. When the Slidell mission failed, Polk ordered Taylor to move to the Rio Grande to protect the boundary of Texas. Paredes thereupon countered, on April 4, 1846, with an order to General Arista to attack the Americans; the result was the first skirmish of the war on April 24 in which Captain Thornton's dragoons were attacked. Informed of this attack, Polk went before Congress on May 11 and asked for a declaration of war, stating that American blood had been shed on American soil. That same day the House passed the bill by a vote of 174 to 14, and the next day the Senate concurred by a vote of 40 to 2. Angry abolitionists in the Senate did manage to delay temporarily an appropriations bill of ten million dollars for the war, charging that the conflict had been promoted by Southern slaveowners to acquire more slave territory.

General Taylor did not wait for a declaration of war. He knew hostilities had commenced and acted accordingly. On May 8 and 9 he fought battles north of the Rio Grande at Palo Alto and Resaca de la Palma, and won both. Crossing the river, he captured Matamoros, then marched on Monterrey. Texans by the thousands flocked to the American standard, wanting to even old scores with Mexico, and many of them fought with Taylor as Texas Rangers in the campaigns at Monterrey and at Buena Vista. Even Governor J. Pinckney Henderson took a leave of absence from his duties to fight in the war. When Taylor began gaining too much popular acclaim for his victories, the Democrat Polk halted the Whig general in northern Mexico and sent another Whig general, Winfield Scott, to invade Mexico at Vera Cruz. This second major offensive was equally successful, for Scott's expeditionary force met little resistance in its march from Vera Cruz to the Mexican capital.

The third major offensive of the war was aimed at winning the Southwest, and it succeeded. It was led by Colonel, later General, Stephen Watts Kearny. At Fort Leavenworth, Kansas, he assembled a rag-tag army, designated the "Army of the West," of some 2700 men, most of whom were mounted. Also included in this number was a battalion of five hundred Mormons, enlisted at the request of Brigham Young, whose salaries were paid to the Mormon church to help finance the move westward from Illinois to the Great Salt Lake area. When the major portion of this army marched toward Santa Fe on June 26, it was accompanied by a large wagon train of traders anxious to transact business in New Mexico. After a hot, thirsty march of 565 miles, the Army of the West reached Bent's Fort on the upper Arkansas. There they rested while Kearny and his staff pondered reports that three thousand men had marched north from Chihuahua to defend New Mexico.

At the same time in Santa Fe, Governor Manuel Armijo was aware of the march of the Americans—and no doubt wished that his forces had been augmented by troops from Chihuahua. He had at his command only two to three hundred regulars, mostly ill-equipped and poorly trained, and approximately two thousand militia, most of whom had no firearms. Still he might have won a contest of arms with the Americans had he utilized his geographical advantages. A short distance east of Santa Fe was Apache Canyon, a narrow pass in the mountains through which the American army had to pass. A handful of loyal Mexicans could have held off Kearny's army until heat, hunger, and thirst forced their retreat or surrender. But Armijo made no stand, thanks to the persuasions of James W. Magoffin, a Santa Fe trader accompanying Kearny by virtue of an order from President Polk. Magoffin left the army at Bent's Fort with a twenty-man escort under Captain Philip St. George Cooke. Under a flag of truce he and the escort made their way to Armijo's headquarters, where Magoffin, an old friend of the New Mexican governor, and Captain Cooke were hospitably received. That evening the trader persuaded Armijo that resistance was useless (according to legend the persuasion was a satchel of gold). One Mexican officer, Colonel Diego Archuleta, wanted to fight anyway; to him Magoffin held out the promise of governing an area west of the Rio Grande, either deliberately misleading Archuleta or not knowing that Kearny had orders to continue to California. As a result of Magoffin's persuasion, the American army encountered no resistance when it passed through Apache Canyon on August 17; Governor Armijo had fled southward to Chihuahua. Santa Fe fell into American hands on the afternoon of August 18 without a shot having been fired.

At ceremonies in the capital of the province on August 19, General Kearny tried to settle all doubts in the minds of the New Mexicans regarding the government of the territory. He guaranteed them freedom of religion, recognition of their land titles, and full rights of American citizenship. Most local officials were left in office once they took the oath of allegiance. Kearny also organized a civil government, appointing Charles Bent governor and Preston Blair, Jr., attorney general. Blair was ordered to compile a code of laws for the territory recognizing the Spanish heritage, but reconciling it with English common law. Once the chiefs of the leading pueblos came to Santa Fe and took the oath of allegiance to the United States there was no reason for Kearny to remain in New Mexico, especially since he had orders to march to California. According to his orders from Washington, he divided his army into four parts: three hundred dragoons under his personal command would march to California; one portion under Colonel Alexander W. Doniphan would move southward into Chihuahua in December; the Mormon Battalion under Cooke, now a lieutenant colonel, was to follow

Kearny to California, opening a usable wagon road in the process; the remainder of the troops, all too few in number, were to remain on garrison duty in New Mexico under Colonel Sterling Price.

On September 25, after checking on a rumored uprising of New Mexicans in the southern part of the territory, Kearny departed for California with three hundred dragoons. Down the Rio Grande they marched to Socorro, then turned westward toward the Gila River Valley. A short distance out of Socorro this column was met by Kit Carson, who was returning from California with dispatches from Frémont concerning the war on the Pacific Coast. Frémont and his party of "explorers" had been ordered out of California in the spring of 1846 by the governor and had moved across the boundary into Oregon at Klamath Lake. There on May 8 he was reached by Lieutenant A. H. Gillespie, sent west by President Polk with secret instructions for Commodore J. D. Sloat, commander of the American Pacific squadron, Thomas O. Larkin, American consul at Monterey, and Frémont. According to Gillespie, the instructions he brought Frémont from the President and secretary of state were "to watch over the interest of the United States, and counteract the influence of any foreign agents who might be in the country with objects prejudicial to the United States."

Frémont immediately marched southward to the American settlements on the Sacramento River, while Lieutenant Gillespie went aboard an American warship at San Francisco where he was furnished arms, ammunition, and money which he then took to Frémont on the Sacramento. On June 11 the Americans began an uprising against the Mexican forces of Governor José de Castro. On July 4 Frémont addressed the revolutionists at Sonoma, advising them to declare their independence from Mexico and to drive out Governor Castro and his adherents. This the group attempted, proclaiming the existence of the "Bear Flag Republic" and raising one hundred and fifty men, among them Captain Frémont's sixty followers. Two days previously, Commodore Sloat had received definite information that the United States was at war with Mexico, and on July 7 he took Monterey and ran up the American flag. Two days afterward there was a ceremony at San Francisco and Sonoma, and on July 11 the Stars and Stripes were raised at Sutter's Fort. Sloat's proclamation to the people declared that he came as a "friend," that Californians would have full citizenship and the right of free worship, and that their property would be respected.

This action presaged a change in the Bear Flag Revolt. On July 15 Sloat was replaced by Commodore Robert F. Stockton. A few days later the volunteers in the Bear Flag Revolt were enlisted as volunteers in the American army with Frémont as their major and Gillespie their captain. On July 25 Stockton sent a warship, the *Cayane,* sailing south to San Diego with Frémont and the volunteers, hoping to cut off the retreating Castro. The Mexicans halted and encamped near Los Angeles, whereupon Stockton sailed the *Congress* to San Pedro and disembarked his sailors and marines to do battle. Castro preferred to retreat southward, however, and on August 13, accompanied now by Frémont, Stockton entered Los Angeles, where he declared martial law and forbade the carrying of weapons. Thus the war was over, they thought, and Carson was sent east with dispatches to that effect.

Upon receipt of this news, Kearny sent two hundred of his dragoons back to Santa Fe and proceeded west with the remaining one hundred. His orders specified that he was to continue from New Mexico to California, where he was to act as military governor. He persuaded Kit Carson to forgo seeing his wife in Taos; the famous scout reluctantly agreed to guide Kearny across the desert to his destination. Along the Gila they met roving bands of Apaches who were peaceful but not friendly. In central Arizona they entered the land of the Pima who were more than friendly; when Carson tried to bargain for provisions for the soldiers, the Pimas replied, "Bread is to eat, not to sell. Take what you want." Near the Colorado River four prisoners were taken. These Mexican herders, under questioning, told of a native Californian uprising at Los Angeles against American authority. Kearny crossed the Colorado in a hurry and pushed into the burning hell of the real desert. After a week of hardship almost beyond description, his column entered the last range of mountains—to be met by fog, cold, and heavy rains. One officer commented about the men after an inspection: "Poor fellows. They are well-nigh naked—some of them barefooted—a sorry looking set."

On December 6 and 7 at San Pascual, Kearny's "sorry looking

set" encountered the insurgent Mexicans, led by Andrés Pico. Unaccountably the American dragoons had allowed their powder to get wet, and the Mexican lancers charged with devastating results. Sixteen Americans were killed in the first onslaught, and as many more were wounded. The little force was surrounded and besieged atop a hill. Only with difficulty were Kit Carson and Lieutenant Edward Fitzgerald Beale able to slip through the lines and reach San Diego, where they called on Commodore Stockton for aid. In the early morning hours of December 10 help arrived and the Mexicans were routed. Other skirmishes followed in which Kearny acquitted himself more admirably, and on January 10 Los Angeles surrendered to him. The northern part of the province was also pacified, and the American conquest of California was complete.

Almost immediately a quarrel began among the victors to determine who was to govern California. Stockton claimed his orders entitled him to name the military governor of the area, and he chose Frémont. The thirty-three-year-old army captain—and major of volunteers—chose to side with Stockton against army Brigadier General Kearny, and accepted the appointment. Kearny fumed and ranted, demanding the surrender of all documents and authority to himself, but Frémont stood adamant. The dispute was settled in February of 1847 by orders from Washington confirming Kearny as governor, whereupon the general humiliated Frémont, detained him in defiance of the President's order, and took him to Fort Leavenworth, where he arrested him on charges of mutiny and insubordination. From November 1847 to January 1848 Frémont's case was tried by court martial in Washington before a board of regular army officers; he was found guilty and given a stiff sentence. Although President Polk remitted the penalty (for bravery during the war), Frémont was so enraged that he resigned from the service.

Shortly after Kearny had left New Mexico for California, Lieutenant Colonel Philip St. George Cooke had set out with the Mormon Battalion in accordance with his orders to open a wagon road to California. Cooke was a strong-willed commander, and only the fact that Brigham Young had enjoined the members of the battalion to remain obedient prevented a mutiny, for the Mormons were equally strong-willed and were distrustful of their gentile commander. Setting out on October 21, 1846, they followed the Rio

Grande southward below Socorro, then turned southwest to Playas Lake in present Hidalgo County. There they found the old Spanish-Mexican road that ran to Janos in Chihuahua, where they turned westward and pushed across to San Bernardino, an abandoned ranch (near where Arizona and New Mexico now join on the Mexican border). They found many wild cattle and deserted ranch buildings at that point, showing that there had been ranching activity at that point sometime previously, no doubt abandoned because of Apache hostility. In the San Pedro Valley to the west, the battalion was attacked by wild bulls, one of which almost gored Cooke; he referred to the incident in his journal as the "battle of bull run." Casualties in the encounter included a private who was wounded in the leg, a sergeant who received broken ribs, and Lieutenant George Stoneman (later a governor of California) who nearly shot off his thumb with his own rifle.

On December 12 the guide, Antoine Leroux, returned from a scout with information that he had discovered some Mexicans making mescal. They had informed him that a force of two hundred Mexican soldiers had been gathered at the presidio of Tucson to oppose the march of the Americans. Two days later Mexican officers from the presidio arrived at Cooke's camp with word from their commander at Tucson, Captain José Antonio Comaduran, that he had orders to prevent the Americans from marching through Tucson; however, if they would pass quietly by the town, Comaduran said he would not oppose them. Cooke's reply was a demand that the presidio surrender and the town be thrown open for trade and refreshment. This the Mexican emissaries refused. On the morning of December 16, Cooke came within sight of the town and prepared for battle, only to be greeted with the news that Captain Comaduran and the garrison had fled southward, leaving the five hundred townspeople at the mercy of the Americans. Cooke informed them that he had not come to make war on Sonorans, much less to destroy an outpost of defense against raiding Indians; but he did open the public stores of food to his battalion, and many of the Mormons gorged themselves sick. On December 18 the soldiers left, moving north up the Santa Cruz River to the Gila, then going down it to Yuma crossing. They proceeded on across the Imperial Valley of southern California, arriving at San Diego on

January 29, 1847. At the end of his report, Cooke commented: ". . . Marching half naked and half fed, and living upon wild animals, we have discovered and made a road of great value to our country. . . ." Indeed they had, for Cooke's Wagon Road, "The Gila Trail," became a principal route to California soon afterward.

Meanwhile, blood was being shed in New Mexico. Colonel Diego Archuleta was the principal instigator; his anger stemmed from his failure to gain political control of New Mexico west of the Rio Grande as had been hinted to him by James Magoffin. He found supporters among those New Mexicans who felt that Governor Armijo's refusal to fight and subsequent flight southward had impugned Mexican honor. In secret the conspirators gathered an army and weapons and drilled their troops. At a secret meeting in Santa Fe, held early in December 1846, plans for the uprising were formulated: Governor Charles Bent and Colonel Sterling Price were to be killed immediately; then all American soldiers would be exterminated or driven out of the province in the ensuing confusion. The date for the uprising was set first for December 19, then for Christmas Eve. The American authorities learned of the plot, however, and some of the conspirators were arrested, ending the planned rebellion—or so Governor Bent thought. On January 5, 1847, he issued a proclamation describing what had happened and asking the people to remain loyal to the new regime.

Thinking all danger past, Bent decided to visit his family and friends in Taos early in January. There on January 19 the uprising occurred. Led by Pablo Montaya, self-styled "Santa Anna of the North," the Indians at Taos Pueblo marched into town where they killed and scalped Governor Bent. Five others in the town, including the sheriff, the circuit attorney, and an army captain, were murdered. Seven other Americans were killed at Turley's Mill in the Arroyo Hondo, and about the same number died at the town of Mora. Colonel Price at Santa Fe heard of the outbreak the following day, and he quickly gathered an army to crush the rebels. Marching nearly five hundred men northward through bitter winter cold, he met fifteen hundred rebels at La Cañada on January 24, and won a decisive victory over them. Five days later another battle was fought with the same result. The rebels thereupon entrenched themselves in the Taos Pueblo. Price brought up his artillery to batter down the walls, but the thick adobe refused to give way before the shells. Ladders were employed, and the fortress was stormed. Seven Americans were killed and forty-five were wounded in the battle, but approximately one hundred fifty rebels died before the fighting ceased. Fifteen of the ringleaders of the revolt, including Montaya, were sentenced by a makeshift court and hanged. Archuleta, who was waiting in the south, heard of the defeat at Taos and fled the province, leaving it securely within American hands. A few other skirmishes were fought by the Americans, including a battle that saw the destruction of Mora, but the victory at Taos really marked the close of the Mexican War in the Southwest.

Meanwhile, Scott had fought his way to Mexico City, and on February 2, 1848, the Treaty of Guadalupe Hidalgo was concluded between the warring republics. This treaty of "peace and friendship" provided for an end to the conflict and, in theory, settled all matters of dispute between Mexico and the United States. By the terms of this agreement, Mexico gave up all claims to Texas; the new boundary would begin three marine leagues from shore in the Gulf of Mexico, proceed up the deepest channel of the Rio Grande to the southern boundary of New Mexico, turn west at that point for three degrees of longitude, then run due north to the nearest branch of the Gila River, proceed down the Gila to its junction with the Colorado, and divide Upper and Lower California by a line running straight from the Gila-Colorado junction to a point one marine league south of the southernmost point of the port of San Diego. For this cession of territory the United States agreed to pay fifteen million dollars and to assume payment of all claims owed to American citizens (these totaled $3,208,315). The United States Senate approved the treaty on March 10, 1848 by a vote of thirty-eight to fourteen, and on May 26 ratifications were exchanged at Querétaro, the temporary seat of Mexican government. President Polk officially proclaimed the treaty to be in existence on July 4, 1848, the seventy-third anniversary of the independence of the United States. Except for a small slice of territory in southern New Mexico and Arizona, the Southwest had become American.

4

THE CONSOLIDATION OF
AMERICAN CONTROL

1848–1863

THE COMPROMISE OF 1850

The legislature of the state of Texas met in special session on August 13, 1850, to hear a report from the governor, Peter H. Bell,
regarding the attempts to organize Santa Fe County. Governor Bell
summarized the efforts that had been made and the resistance
offered, mainly by officials of the United States, to the organization
of this county, and stated:

> Difficult and embarrassing then, as the question undoubtedly is,
> and however fraught its contemplation with painful solicitude, we
> have left us no choice, but to meet it. It must be met boldly, and
> fearlessly and determined. Not by further supplications or discus-
> sion with Federal authorities; not by renewed appeals to their gen-
> erosity and sympathy; not by a longer reliance on the delusive

hope, that justice will yet be extended to us; but by action—manly
and determined action on our part, by a prompt assertion of our
rights and a practical maintenance of them with all the means we
can command, *"at all hazards and to the last extremity."*

What Governor Bell was proposing was armed insurrection against
the government of the United States because of what he and other
Texans felt to be a grave injustice: the taking from Texas of that
portion of New Mexico east of the Rio Grande, an area claimed by
the Lone Star State at the time of its annexation to the United
States. And the legislature overwhelmingly responded by endorsing
this policy. Very shortly the assembly was debating measures to
organize a militia and send it into New Mexico, a course of action
that certainly would have led to Civil War, for other Southern
states were supporting the Texas claim to eastern New Mexico.

This near insurrection was caused by the successful termination
of the Mexican War and by the slavery controversy. Texas entered
the Union with the understanding that its southern and western
boundary was the Rio Grande from its mouth to its source, thence
north to the 42nd parallel; from there eastward it followed the
Adams-Onís boundary line of the Treaty of 1819. Indeed, the
United States had gone to war with Mexico on the premise that
American blood had been shed on American soil, a premise that
could have been true only if the southern boundary of Texas in fact
was the Rio Grande. But the end of the war, terminating the fighting with a foreign enemy, allowed the Americans to begin quarreling among themselves. Northern abolitionists were determined that
New Mexico would not become a part of Texas—and thus a part
of the country open to slavery. Southerners were equally determined
that Texas should get what rightly belonged to it. But this would
have meant extending slave territory north to the 42nd parallel,
and the Missouri Compromise of 1820 had stipulated that 36° 30'
north latitude should be the line dividing slave and free territory.

Without waiting for the United States Senate to ratify the Treaty
of Guadalupe Hidalgo, the Texas legislature on March 15, 1848,
created Santa Fe County, which included almost all of New Mexico
east of the Rio Grande. Judge Spruce M. Baird was sent to organize this county as a representative of the state of Texas. But upon

his arrival at Santa Fe, Baird found his efforts blocked by high
military and civil officials of New Mexico. In fact, so anxious were
these army officers and civilians to prevent Texas from acquiring
jurisdiction over the area that in November of 1848 they had arranged a convention in Santa Fe which adopted petitions to Congress asking that New Mexico be created a separate territory. The
military commander in New Mexico, Colonel John M. Washington,
informed Baird that he would support the government established
in New Mexico by General Kearny until ordered to desist by the
federal government—an order that he had already received from
President Polk, but which he chose to disregard. Baird finally grew
discouraged and left New Mexico without accomplishing his goal.

The inauguration of the Taylor administration in Washington
marked a change in the federal attitude toward the Texas claims to
New Mexico. Polk had instructed military authorities in Santa Fe
not to contest the Texas claims, although his instructions were not
heeded; Taylor wished to get New Mexico into the Union as a separate state as quickly as possible, just as he similarly favored statehood for California. The Texas legislature responded to this threat
by designating new boundaries for Santa Fe County and by creating three new counties to the south of it between the Pecos River
and the Rio Grande. Robert S. Neighbors was appointed the new
commissioner of Texas to effect the organization of these four
counties. Neighbors was a happy choice, for he had both courage
and a knowledge of the area, having just completed laying out a
trail from San Antonio to El Paso. He quickly organized El Paso
County, meeting no resistance either from the local citizens or from
the army; the county seat was the town of San Elizario, downriver from the little village of Franklin established by James Magoffin just across from the Mexican village of El Paso del Norte.

In New Mexico, however, Neighbors met hostility at every turn.
Colonel Washington, in fact, had issued orders that no army officer
or post was to aid the Texan in any way. At Santa Fe Neighbors
discovered that Colonel John Monroe, Washington's successor,
had issued a call for a constitutional convention in New Mexico,
and likewise would give him no assistance. He thereupon withdrew
from Santa Fe, returning to Austin to make his report. It was this

report which inflamed Governor Bell and which led to his speech before a special session of the legislature. The Texas delegation in Washington was appraised of the situation and made formal protests to President Taylor, but they were ignored. At this critical juncture came word of Taylor's death and the inauguration of Millard Fillmore as chief executive of the nation. Fillmore proved even more adamant on the question of jurisdiction in New Mexico; he declared that Texas had no claim whatsoever to New Mexico, and he sent 750 additional troops to the area with orders to "use force" to expel any Texas intruders. Other Southerners joined the Texans in pressing the claim to eastern New Mexico, and civil conflict became a distinct possibility. Alexander H. Stevens of Georgia (later to be a vice-president of the Confederacy) declared in the House, "The first federal gun that shall be fired against the people of Texas without the authority of law will be a signal for the free man from the Delaware to the Rio Grande to rally to the rescue."

In the meantime, New Mexicans were proceeding with plans for statehood. They were very anxious for some form of stable civilian rule, for by 1850 they had been under military rule more than two years. The death of Governor Charles Bent at the hands of the Taos insurgents in January of 1847 had left the Territory without a governor. Secretary Juan Bautista Vigil assumed the office as acting governor, without any real authority, recommending to Washington the appointment of Céran St. Vrain. Nothing was done at that level, however, and in December 1847 Vigil was appointed governor by the military commander, General Sterling Price. He could accomplish very little, and finally resigned in October 1848. The only important feature of his administration was a convention which met on October 10, 1848, and petitioned Congress for the "speedy organization by law of a territorial civil government" and asked for protection from Texas and a prevention of the introduction of slavery. After Vigil stepped aside, the area came under the military governorship first of Colonel Washington and then of Colonel Monroe.

In September 1849 another convention met at Santa Fe at the call of the military governor. It elected Hugh N. Smith the delegate to Congress and instructed him to seek the formal creation of the

Territory of New Mexico. In July 1850 the House refused, by a vote of 92 to 86, to seat Smith. The next step in this drama occurred in April 1850, when Colonel Monroe issued a call for a constitutional convention. An election followed, and the convention gathered in Santa Fe on May 15. It took this group of delegates only ten days to frame a constitution for the "state" of New Mexico. They generously set their boundary on the east at the 100th meridian and on the west at the 111th meridian; their constitution also prohibited slavery. This document was submitted to the people for ratification on June 20, elections to be held on the same day for a full slate of state officials. The people responded by ratifying the constitution by a vote of 8371 to 39, and by electing Henry Connelly governor and Manuel Álvarez lieutenant governor. The newly elected "state" legislature convened in Santa Fe on July 1, and immediately began issuing orders and directives through the chief executive. This action, of course, brought them into conflict with Colonel Monroe, who asserted that his administration would continue until Congress should admit New Mexico as a state. Thus matters stood in August 1850 when Governor Peter H. Bell of Texas declared before the legislature of that state his willingness to use military force to assert jurisdiction over New Mexico east of the Rio Grande. Fortunately for all, a compromise was reached in Washington, not only with respect to the Texas-New Mexico boundary and the political status of New Mexico, but with respect to California and a number of other problems as well.

Like the New Mexicans, the Californians had undergone a military governorship and an uncertain status between 1846 and 1850. The court martial of John Charles Frémont had left General Stephen Watts Kearny in complete control, but this did not please the Californians, who demanded civil government at once. Commodore Sloat had promised this when he landed at Monterey, and Commodore Stockton had reiterated the promise. *Alcaldes* and other local officials were encouraged to stay at their posts and continue their functions, but even this was protested by the American element in the territory. On August 7, 1848, Colonel R. B. Mason formally announced the Treaty of Guadalupe Hidalgo, and the cession of California to the United States thereby, and he promised that Congress would provide a civil government within a few months. In addition he issued a code entitled *Laws for the Better Government of California*. But even the promise and the code of laws failed to satisfy the demands for civilian rule in California. At this juncture came the discovery of gold, however, and the cry against the military was generally forgotten in the mad rush to the diggings.

Then with the arrival of winter and the resulting inactivity in the gold fields, agitation began again for civilian rule. On February 12, 1849, a self-authorized convention met in San Francisco and organized a town government on the American order. General Persifer F. Smith, Mason's successor as governor and military commander, refused to endorse this action. Mass meetings of protest resulted—at San Jose, Monterey, Sacramento, and elsewhere—and a convention was called to meet on the first Monday in August. When General Bennett Riley assumed the governorship in April, he decided that the best way to control this situation was to go along with it, especially after he learned that Congress had adjourned in the summer of 1849 without acting on the California question. He therefore issued a call for a convention to meet on September 1 at Monterey.

Forty-eight delegates arrived on the appointed day, not more than a dozen of them forty-niners of the gold rush. Three-fourths of the delegates had long been residents of the area, and among them were a few native Californians. The main argument of the convention came from the debate over an eastern boundary for the proposed state. Some of the delegates favored the crest of the Rocky Mountains as the eastern edge of the state, while others favored the crest of the coastal range (the Sierra). The latter group, the small-state faction, argued that their proposed line would throw the burden of protecting immigrants on the federal government, and that any line that included the Mormon settlements in the Great Salt Lake area would be rejected by Congress. A compromise was finally effected that set the boundaries of the state as they yet remain: beginning on the Pacific Coast in the north, the boundary followed the 42nd parallel eastward to the 120th meridian, went south along that line to its intersection with the 39th parallel, proceeded in a direct southeasterly line to the intersection of the 35th parallel with the Colorado River, then followed the middle of the Colorado southward to the boundary between the United States and Mexico, and went westward to the Pacific Ocean along the international boundary.

The convention also drafted a constitution for the proposed state of California. This document drew heavily from the recently approved constitution of the state of Iowa and on that of New York. It was a concise document, unencumbered by technical details, and provided that California would be a free state. Submitted to a popular vote, the constitution met with overwhelming acceptance, then was forwarded to Congress in the hope that federal authorities would overlook the fact that no enabling act had ever been passed authorizing the framing of the document. Thus California's bid for statehood came at approximately the same time that New Mexico was clamoring for equality with the other members of the Union. But there was still another area within the Mexican Cession seeking statehood—Utah.

The vanguard of the Mormon outcasts from Nauvoo, Illinois, arrived at the Great Salt Lake area in 1846 under the leadership of Brigham Young. Soon they had a thriving town established, the government of which was a virtual theocracy, and from this base they began extending their settlements in all directions. The gold rush to California aided the Mormons greatly, for a majority of those forty-niners pursuing an overland route chose the Humboldt Trail. The Mormons sold provisions to these "pilgrims" at handsome prices, the profits used to found more settlements and to extend the work of conversion to their church, thus providing still more settlers for Utah. Although their area was Mexican territory when they settled, they found themselves once more a part of the United States by virtue of the Treaty of Guadalupe Hidalgo. Not wanting Congress to provide for them, the Mormon leaders, headed by Brigham Young, moved to establish their own framework of government. A constitutional convention was called to meet at Salt Lake City on March 4, 1849, and consisted entirely of faithful members of their church.

This convention drafted a constitution for the "Proposed State of Deseret." This document varied but little from other state constitutions then in force, providing for a two-house legislature, a governor and lieutenant-governor chosen for four years, and a standard court system. There was to be, however, a state militia in which all adult males between the ages of eighteen and forty-five had to participate. And in the boundaries these delegates drew for the proposed state of Deseret, they proved very generous. This boundary, too complicated to reduce to words easily, included all of the present states of Utah and Nevada, as well as parts of Oregon, Idaho, Wyoming, Colorado, New Mexico, Arizona, and a strip of California that extended to the port of San Diego. This document was sent to Congress with the request that it be approved.

The Texas boundary dispute and the proposed states of New Mexico, California, and Deseret were not the only problems facing Congress in the late summer of 1850. There was also the Texas debt question. During its years as a republic, Texas had issued millions of dollars of paper money backed by expected revenue from import duties and the sale of public lands. Texans argued that as the federal government was collecting their import duties and New Mexico east of the Rio Grande had been taken from them, their ability to repay the public debt was reduced. They reminded the federal government that at the time of their annexation they had retained their public lands on the ground that this was necessary to repay the debts, which they agreed would remain a Texas debt. This argument found favor in the North, especially since many Northern speculators bought up these Texas indebtedness certificates with the hope of being repaid at face value. They added their support to the Texans on the question of the New Mexican boundary.

The slavery issue was also before Congress in the summer of 1850, in two forms: Southerners wanted the federal government to be responsible for returning to their masters the runaway slaves who escaped to the North, and Northerners wanted to end the slave trade in the District of Columbia, which was then legal. These six problems before Congress were inflaming passions both Northern and Southern, and talk of civil war was current. Henry Clay, three times a presidential candidate and in 1850 a Senator from his adopted state of Kentucky, paired off the problems of the Southwest and introduced them in the form of an "Omnibus Bill." The South got its Fugitive Slave Law, while the North was satisfied with the abolition of the slave trade in the District of Columbia. The Texas boundary in the northwest was redrawn; starting at the 100th meridian, it proceeded west along 36° 30′ north latitude (the Missouri Compromise line) to the 103rd meridian, went south along this meridian to the 32nd parallel, then proceeded directly west to the Rio Grande. New Mexico received the land west of the 103rd meridian and north of the 32nd parallel, for which Texas was paid ten million dollars, enough to satisfy the indebtedness inherited from its days as a republic. The Mormon desire for statehood was thwarted, Congress choosing instead to establish it as a territory and naming it Utah, for the Ute Indians; and its boundaries were much reduced, to include only the present Utah, most of present Nevada, about a third of Colorado, and a corner of Wyoming. New Mexico likewise did not achieve statehood, receiving territorial status with borders that included all of present-day New Mexico and Arizona and a portion of Nevada and Colorado. California entered the Union as a free state, but Southerners were pacified because the question of slavery in New Mexico and Utah territories was left unsettled; the act creating these two territories stipulated that when they were admitted as states they "should be received into the Union, with or without slavery, as their constitution may prescribe at the time of their admission." This meant that slaves could be taken into these territories, implying the doctrine that later came to be known as "popular sovereignty."

The Compromise of 1850, as the Omnibus Bill came to be known, was signed by President Fillmore on September 9, 1850, and temporarily settled all disputes in the Southwest. Civil war was thereby averted for another decade, California and Texas received their permanent boundaries, and two new territories filled that part of the Mexican Cession lying between the two states. Yet there was another boundary problem in the Southwest, one that Congress alone could not settle—the boundary between the United States and Mexico. Seemingly this line had been drawn by the Treaty of

Guadalupe Hidalgo, but surveying the boundary set at the end of the Mexican War proved more difficult than anticipated and almost led to a second clash of arms between the two republics.

THE CONTROVERSIAL BOUNDARY SURVEY AND THE GADSDEN PURCHASE

Article V of the Treaty of Guadalupe Hidalgo delineated a new boundary between the United States and Mexico, a line that was to commence three marine leagues from land in the Gulf of Mexico, proceed up the deepest channel of the Rio Grande "to the point where it strikes the southern boundary of New Mexico; thence westwardly along the whole southern boundary of New Mexico (which runs north of the town called *Paso*) to its western termination; thence northward along the western line of New Mexico until it intersects the first branch of the River Gila," then down the deepest channel of the Gila to its junction with the Colorado River. On the California coast the boundary was to begin one marine league south of the bay of San Diego and run in a straight line to the junction of the Gila and the Colorado. The Treaty further provided that each nation was to appoint a Boundary Commissioner and a Surveyor to run and mark the international line; the record of their acts then would become a part of the treaty, having "the same force as if it were inserted therein."

Before leaving office in the spring of 1849, President James K. Polk offered the post of Commissioner to Major William H. Emory, on condition that he resign his commission. But Emory was a native of Maryland, a graduate of West Point, class of 1831, a respected member of the Army Corps of Topographical Engineers, and a seasoned veteran of the Mexican War. In that conflict he had served in Kearny's Army of the West, out of which experience had come Emory's *Notes of a Military Reconnaissance from Fort Leavenworth, in Missouri, to San Diego, in California,* a work that popularized the Southwest and established Emory's reputation. Emory had chosen the life of a soldier, and he politely declined Polk's offer that would have meant his resignation. Thereupon Polk appointed John B. Weller, a Democrat from Ohio, the Boundary Commissioner. Weller was a political choice, although he had served with some distinction in the war with Mexico; following that conflict, he had made an unsuccessful bid for the governorship of Ohio, a state he had served as congressman before the war. The post of Surveyor went to Andrew B. Gray, a much happier choice; Gray, a Virginian by birth, had been the Surveyor for the Republic of Texas in running and marking the boundary between that nation and the United States and had worked in the exploration and survey of the Keweenaw Peninsula of Michigan. He had also served in the Texas Rangers during Indian campaigns, so he was both qualified as a surveyor and familiar with frontier conditions.

The American Boundary Commission set out for California by way of Panama, which they found crowded with gold seekers bound for the newly discovered riches of California. After troublesome delays the Commission reached San Diego where, following Article V of the Treaty of Guadalupe Hidalgo, they met their Mexican counterparts, General Pedro García Conde and José Salazar Larregui, on July 6, 1849. Conde, the Mexican Commissioner, was a native of Sonora, an army brigadier general with much frontier service, had been both Secretary of War and Marine and a national senator, and was a qualified topographical engineer. Salazar, the Surveyor, was also an extremely competent engineer and a native of Sonora. Both men were ardent Mexican patriots, and General Conde even paid the costs of the survey out of his own pocket when funds failed to arrive from the politically divided capital of his nation.

The Joint Boundary Commission quickly agreed on the initial point of the line dividing Upper and Lower California, one marine league south of San Diego Bay. At the same time a party under the command of Lieutenant Amiel Weeks Whipple, another graduate of West Point, veteran of the Mexican War, and member of the Corps of Topographical Engineers, was establishing the exact latitude and longitude of the junction of the Gila and Colorado rivers. Still a third party was busy at the same time; this group, under the command of Captain Edmund La Fayette Hardcastle, whose background was similar to that of Whipple, was sent to reconnoiter the

145 miles of country between the two extremities and to select elevated points from which both ends of the line could be sighted directly. Though Emory did decline the Commissionership, he was attached to the Commission as the chief astronomer and commander of the military detachment. He had chosen a unique method for drawing the correct boundary. Gunpowder was ignited at set intervals at the two extremities, and from these points of elevation sightings were taken that enabled Emory to draw an accurate map of the boundary. When he had completed this survey, his work was accepted by the Mexican Commission without correction; and when it was put to the test of actual surveying and marking by two parties, one pushing east from San Diego and the other west from the Colorado, they met within inches of one another—an error that Emory attributed to the natural inaccuracy of prolonging a straight line over a long distance.

This work of the Joint Boundary Commission had begun in July of 1849, four months after the change of administrations in Washington, D. C. The Whigs had assumed control in March of that year, and they began harassing the Democrat Weller by withholding funds for the survey. Unpaid personnel of the American Commission began deserting for the gold fields, and the activities of hostile Indians in the area further hampered the work. In September word arrived that Weller had been removed and the position of Commissioner had been offered to John Charles Frémont, who had settled in California after his resignation from the army. The Great Pathfinder at first accepted the post, feeling that the appointment was a vindication of his conduct during the Mexican War; however, he resigned before actually assuming the office because he was elected to the United States Senate from California. Then in February 1850 word came that Weller had been removed as Commissioner by the Whigs without a successor being named. Emory was to act as temporary Commissioner to supervise the completion of the work on the Pacific Coast. Thereupon the Joint Boundary Commission adjourned in mid-February 1850 after agreeing to meet again in El Paso on the first Monday in November of that same year.

Emory and Surveyor Gray completed the running and marking

of the line dividing Upper and Lower California despite severe handicaps and hindrances, then made their way at their own expense to Washington, arriving at the capital on November 4, 1850. Their instruments they sent to El Paso under the supervision of Lieutenant Whipple. In Washington, Emory requested to be relieved of further connection with the Boundary Commission; he was disgusted by what he thought to be the outrageous treatment he had received at the hands of the government, especially from political appointees who had no knowledge of surveying. Gray was ordered to resume his office with the Commission, then in the field at El Paso under the supervision of Commissioner John Russell Bartlett.

After Frémont had resigned the post of Boundary Commissioner, the Whigs arranged the appointment of Bartlett, a member of their party and a New Englander of scholarly inclinations. A native of Providence, Rhode Island, Bartlett had received a good education, then had become a clerk in a bank. In Providence he had become an active member of the Rhode Island Historical Society, and after moving to New York City where he was a bookseller, he affiliated with other historical societies. With Albert Gallatin, the Secretary of the Treasury under Presidents Jefferson and Madison, Bartlett founded the American Ethnological Society in 1842. In the 1840's Bartlett gained some literary fame for his *Progress of Ethnology, Dictionary of Americanisms,* and *Reminiscences of Albert Gallatin.* In 1849, owing to financial difficulties, he journeyed to Washington seeking the post of minister to Denmark. He failed in this, but was offered the position of Boundary Commissioner as consolation. He accepted the offer because, according to his own statements, he had led a sedentary life and wanted to travel for a change, and the post offered him a chance to see for himself the object of his long interest and admiration, the American Indian.

Appointed on June 15, 1850, Bartlett was directed to proceed to El Paso by the nearest route in order to reach that place by November 1, if possible. Unaccustomed to government service, ignorant of conditions in the Southwest, and incapable of doing the task to which he had been appointed, Bartlett proceeded to make blunder after blunder. Political pressures led him to employ many workmen unsuited to the work their contracts obligated them to perform, workmen who signed up only for the adventure they thought they would find, workmen who had powerful Whig relatives and patrons. Once in the field near El Paso, the Commissioner discovered his mistake and had to fire several of these workers, some of whom turned "Robin Hood" bandits. The son of Senator John H. Clarke of Rhode Island was one such young man—and he paid for his ignorance with his life; in a fight with a group of frontiersmen over dancehall girls, the lad was stabbed nine times in the breast and abdomen.

Bartlett and General Conde held their first meeting on December 3, 1850. Shortly afterward they discovered two errors in Disturnell's map of 1847, the one used by the treaty-makers at Guadalupe Hidalgo, which made it very difficult to determine the line dividing New Mexico from Chihuahua. As drawn on the treaty map this line began eight miles north of El Paso (present-day Juarez), at a point on the Rio Grande 32° 15′ north latitude. But actual surveying showed the town to be at 31° 45′. Moreover the map showed the Rio Grande at the initial point to be located at 104° 39′ west longitude, while its true location was 106° 29′. This error of half a degree of latitude placed El Paso on the map thirty-four miles too far north, and the error of almost two degrees in longitude put the initial point on the Rio Grande well over a hundred miles too far east.

To General Conde the solution was simple: the lines of longitude and latitude in the treaty map should be used as drawn regardless of errors. Start the boundary at 32° 22′ north of El Paso on the Rio Grande and run it west three degrees of longitude from 104° 39′, then proceed north to intersect the Gila. Bartlett at first argued that the line should begin eight miles north of El Paso and run west for three entire degrees of longitude, that the obvious intent of the Mexican negotiators of the Treaty of Guadalupe Hidalgo was to get for their nation the town of El Paso, and that the lines of longitude and latitude in Disturnell's map should be ignored. Finally the inexperienced American Commissioner was persuaded to "compromise" by Conde: the United States would accept a boundary beginning forty-two miles north of El Paso, and Mexico would agree to running the line westward from that point for the full three degrees of longitude. Not only did Bartlett agree to this boundary, he actually began surveying it.

When Surveyor Gray arrived on the scene, he protested this agreement—generally called the Bartlett-Conde Compromise line. Gray stated that by the terms of this agreement the United States would lose land actually belonging to it, land needed for the building of a transcontinental railroad. He also stated that the Bartlett-Conde line was not valid, for the Treaty of Guadalupe Hidalgo stated that the acts of the Joint Boundary Commission had to be signed by the Commissioners *and* Surveyors of both nations to be valid. Both men appealed to Washington for support, each confident that his opponent would be reprimanded. Whig administrators, anxious to protect one of their own appointees, first ordered Gray to sign the agreement, then fired him from the Commission. In replacing Gray, Secretary of the Interior H. H. Stuart selected Major William H. Emory, naming him not only Surveyor but also chief astronomer. Emory was given a copy of the order which Stuart had sent Gray regarding the signing of the Bartlett-Conde Compromise Line, and was told that if Gray had persisted in his refusal to ratify the agreement, then he, Emory, was to "sign the official documents . . . which require the signature of the surveyor to settle this important point."

Emory arrived at El Paso on November 25, 1851, to take up his new duties with the Boundary Commission. Having studied the relevant documents concerning the Bartlett-Conde agreement, he concluded that Gray's stand was the correct one, that Bartlett was trying to sign away six thousand square miles of territory rightfully belonging to the United States. To comply with his orders, however, he did sign the document, but he appended thereto a proviso stating that the initial point of the boundary as agreed upon was not the decision of the Joint Commission, only that of the commissioners. To prevent any possible misunderstanding of his signature on the document, Emory obtained a statement from Mexican Surveyor Salazar confirming that the compromise line was that "agreed upon by the two commissioners, and nothing else." This proviso, Emory wrote, allowed him to comply with his orders from Secretary Stuart, but left the United States free to repudiate the Bartlett-Conde agreement.

The surveying party at El Paso, which fell immediately under the command of Emory, was very disorganized and demoralized. Approximately one hundred employees of the Boundary Commission were idle there for lack of direction; they had no knowledge of the whereabouts of Commissioner Bartlett. After his argument with Gray the Commissioner had left them in El Paso and had moved westward. He had sent Gray and Whipple to survey the Gila, while he proceeded into the interior of Sonora in search of supplies—of which there was more than a sufficiency at El Paso, but which had been left behind by the Commissioner's oversight. While Gray and Whipple contended with nature and Indians on the Gila, Bartlett went to Hermosillo, Guaymas, Mazatlan, and Acapulco; from Acapulco he sailed for San Diego, arriving in the California port in February 1852 to find Gray and Whipple had run out of supplies and had journeyed to San Diego in search of the Commissioner. Bartlett found it necessary to go to San Francisco in search of more supplies before rejoining his group at San Diego and proceeding eastward late in May 1852. After several adventures and one Indian attack, he arrived at Ringgold Barracks, only 241 miles from the mouth of the Rio Grande, just before Christmas of 1852; there he met Surveyor Emory, who had organized the workers at El Paso and had proceeded downriver with the work of running and marking the boundary.

At this juncture important dispatches arrived from Washington notifying Bartlett that additional funds for the Boundary Commission were being withheld by Congress. Since 1849 Congress from time to time had taken notice of the survey because of the many complaints that had been lodged against Bartlett by ex-members of the Commission. John B. Weller, the first head of the survey, had been elected to the United States Senate from California after his appointment had been revoked by the Whigs, and from that vantage point he had been a severe critic of subsequent work. Others had also advanced charges against Bartlett, who, by the summer of 1852, stood accused of making private use of government transportation, of unpardonable mismanagement of the public funds entrusted to him, of disregard for the health, comfort, and safety of those under him, and of general negligence. Such charges led to a senatorial investigation in 1852, and on July 26 of that year the

Secretary of the Interior had to deliver a full report with supporting documents on the activities of the Commission to the Senate.

As a result of this investigation, the Bartlett critics were able to attach a restraining clause in the deficiency appropriation bill for the fiscal year 1851–52, which allocated $80,000 for the Boundary Commission, to the effect that "nothing herein contained shall be so construed as to sanction a departure from the point on the Rio Grande north of the town called [El] Paso, designated in the said treaty." Then when the regular appropriation bill for the fiscal year 1852–53 was voted, these critics were able to insert a clause in that section of the act giving $125,000 to the Boundary Commission making it impossible to spend any of the money "until it shall be made to appear to the President of the United States that the southern boundary is not established . . . further north of the town called Paso than the [boundary] is laid down" in the map accompanying the Treaty of Guadalupe Hidalgo.

Secretary Stuart had no recourse, after reading this proviso, but to inform Bartlett that President Fillmore was forced to conclude that the money could not legally be spent. Therefore the survey came to a halt. Bartlett sold the field equipment and the Commission's animals at San Antonio, disbanded the crews in his employ, and retired from the field to his home in Rhode Island where he wrote an account of the boundary survey under his directorship. Entitled *Personal Narrative of Exploration and Incidents in Texas, New Mexico, California, Sonora, and Chihuahua* . . . , the two-volume work was an explanation and, hopefully, a vindication of his work as Boundary Commissioner.

While Bartlett was traveling in Mexico and California and Emory was surveying the Rio Grande, a quarrel had developed between the governors of New Mexico and Chihuahua over the Mesilla Strip, as the area under dispute came to be known. William Carr Lane, governor of New Mexico, believed the area to be under his jurisdiction and insisted that the people in the valley wished to be American citizens. Governor Angél Trias of Chihuahua believed the opposite; in fact, he had moved troops to the area shortly after the Bartlett-Conde agreement had been reached, and was exercising authority over the people there. However, the five hundred men he had sent could not be supplied and had to be withdrawn to

El Paso. Then when Lane heard that Congress seemingly had repudiated the Bartlett-Conde agreement by withholding funds from the Boundary Commission, he called on Colonel Edwin V. Sumner, commandant of the military district of New Mexico, for aid in asserting American jurisdiction over the Mesilla Valley. Sumner refused, having no instructions from his superiors to give such aid. Lane therefore organized a group of New Mexican and Texan volunteers and marched to the village of Doña Ana where he issued a proclamation claiming the Mesilla Valley for the United States.

When a copy of Lane's proclamation reached Governor Trias, the Mexican reacted sharply with a declaration of his own. He asserted that Mexico had always owned the territory in dispute, that the boundary had legally been set at 32° 22', that Chihuahua had occupied the area without opposition in 1851, and that the people in the area desired to be Mexican citizens. He also strengthened his garrison at El Paso and called on his national government for support. At this point a second war between the United States and Mexico seemed imminent. So certain were Mexican officials of this impending conflict that instructions were sent to the Mexican diplomatic agents abroad instructing them to seek aid from European nations in case of war with the United States.

At this critical juncture, both the United States and Mexico took a second look at the situation. Newly inaugurated President Franklin Pierce saw that another war with Mexico would wreck the Democratic party—the New England branch of the party had given only lukewarm support to the first one—and it might possibly split the nation in two because of the slavery controversy. President Antonio López de Santa Anna likewise did not want war; he knew that Mexico could not win such a conflict, and, besides, he desperately needed money to continue his recently installed dictatorship in office. A diplomatic settlement seemed the best solution to both sides, and in March 1853 the United States sent James Gadsden of South Carolina to Mexico with instructions to negotiate a settlement of all differences outstanding. Gadsden negotiated the treaty that bears his name. It provided that the United States would pay Mexico fifteen million dollars for land south of the Gila River; the new boundary would begin at 31° 47' 30" north latitude, proceed in a direct line to the intersection of the 31st parallel with the

111th meridian, then go in a straight line to the middle of the Colorado River at a point six miles above its mouth, and proceed up the middle of the river until it reached the junction of the Gila and Colorado (which was the start of the line dividing Upper and Lower California). This treaty also provided that the United States was not liable for the damages inflicted in Mexico by Indians raiding from the United States; Mexico had tried to file claims for these, but the United States took the position that it could not compensate Mexico for such raids since it did not pay its own citizens for such damages.

The Gadsden Treaty, signed on December 30, 1853, went to the United States Senate in the spring of 1854, where the senators redrew the boundary line and cut the amount to be paid to ten million dollars. The Mexican ambassador to the United States, Juan N. Almonte, lobbied very effectively to get a different boundary drawn between the United States and Mexico; he believed, and probably correctly, that unless Mexico had a land link with Baja California (and no bridge could be built across the Colorado within six miles of its mouth because of the huge tides), the territory eventually would fall to the United States. The boundary drawn by the United States Senate started in the middle of the Rio Grande at $31° 47'$ north latitude, proceeded due west for one hundred miles, turned due south to $31° 20'$ north latitude, went west from there until it intersected the 111th meridian, then went in a straight line to a point in the middle of the Colorado River twenty English miles below its junction with the Gila; it then went up the middle of the Colorado until it intersected the surveyed line between Upper and Lower California. The reason this particular line was drawn was because certain Senators thought this boundary would include all of Cooke's Wagon Road, which then was in use by forty-niners bound for the gold fields of California.

Even before Gadsden went to Mexico, Congress had voted funds for completing the survey of the Rio Grande. General Robert B. Campbell, a man of considerable experience, was appointed the new Commissioner and Major Emory the Surveyor. They organized a new party, much smaller than the one led by Bartlett, and completed all field work by the middle of December 1853. After the ratification of the Gadsden Treaty in June 1854, an entirely new Boundary Commission was appointed. President Pierce on August 15 appointed Emory to head this new effort to complete the work begun six years earlier, and to avoid quarrels he also named Emory Surveyor and chief astronomer. His Mexican counterpart was José Salazar—Conde had died in December of 1851. They met in El Paso on December 2, and without argument they proceeded with the work. On August 16, 1855, the Joint Commission met for the last time for the signing of the documents certifying that the entire boundary between the United States and Mexico had been surveyed and marked with appropriate monuments. Emory then returned to Washington where he busied himself for two years in preparing a report of the survey, a three-volume work printed in 1857 and 1859 which is far superior to Bartlett's *Personal Narrative*. It contains both a report of the work of the Boundary Commission and a long description of the geology, birds, mammals, and geography of the boundary area.

Although the Gadsden Treaty was ratified and exchanged in the summer of 1854, the Mexican garrison did not leave Tucson, the only military post in the area, until March 1856. And the residents of the pueblo protested this withdrawal loudly, for American troops had not yet arrived to protect them from Apache hostility. Finally on November 14, 1856, Major Enoch Steen and three companies of the First Dragoons reached the village from New Mexico, and the American flag was unfurled there for the first time. The American boundaries of the Southwest had been completed.

THE GOLD RUSH

"Gold! Gold! Gold on the American River!" shouted Sam Brannan as he strode down a San Francisco street in the spring of 1848, holding aloft a bottle containing a sample of the precious metal by way of proof. Quickly a crowd gathered around him demanding more information. Brannan told them that gold had been discovered on land belonging to John A. Sutter, the Swiss immigrant who was farming and ranching along the American River. Brannan's announcement started a stampede that almost depopulated San

Francisco, a stampede of individuals who within months had un-
earthed enough gold to more than repay the fifteen million dollars
the United States had given Mexico for almost the entire American
Southwest.

The gold fever that started in San Francisco quickly spread, the
germ seemingly borne on the wind in every direction. From Mexico, British Columbia, Australia, China, South America, and every
country in Europe they swarmed to the new Eldorado, but
especially from the eastern part of the United States. In December
1848 President James K. Polk confirmed the discovery in his last
annual message to Congress—thus ending all lingering doubts in
the East as to the authenticity of the strike. By the hundreds, thousands, and tens of thousands, both in the North and in the South,
merchants boarded their windows, farmers dropped their plows,
doctors and lawyers quit their practices, teamsters left their
wagons, and mechanics abandoned their tools. As one newspaper
editor commented, "Everything [is] neglected but the manufacture
of shovels and pick-axes."

Three routes westward "to see the elephant" emerged as the
most popular: by sea to Panama, overland to the Pacific, and
thence by boat to California; overland via the Humboldt Trail, an
offshoot of the Oregon Trail so popular in the 1840's, which passed
through Salt Lake City and followed the Humboldt River across
Nevada to the Sierra; and the Gila Trail, which in effect was
Cooke's Wagon Road across the Southwest. This latter trail was
used by an estimated sixty thousand "pilgrims" during the period
1849–51. It was a popular route because there were fewer mountains to cross, the weather was more tolerable than the weather to
the north where the intense cold of winter killed so many, and there
were towns along the way where food and other supplies could be
purchased. Following the custom of the Santa Fe traders, these
"argonauts" traveled by groups in semi-military style. They bought
what they could along the way—corn, barley, eggs, dried beef, and,
as one man said, "miserable coffee." The price of such commodi-
ties doubled and doubled again, as did the price of mules and
horses. There were obviously some women in these parties, for in
1849 as one group drifted down the Gila River from the Pima vil-

lages of central Arizona the first American child was born in Arizona; he was named "Gila Howard."

The Comanche roaming West Texas and northward to Kansas were not friendly to these passing waves of humanity, but the Apache of New Mexico and Arizona apparently looked upon the Americans as allies in their long fight against the Mexicans. So long as the forty-niners traveled in large parties, they suffered few indignities. The story was different with stragglers, however. In March of 1851 the Oatman family started down the Gila River with no other companions. Mohave Apaches attacked the family, killing the father, mother, and three youngest children; an older boy was clubbed and left for dead, while Olive Oatman, aged twelve, and Mary, aged eight, were carried away into captivity. Subsequently the two girls were sold to the Mohave Indians, where Mary died under the harsh treatment they received. After five years of slavery Olive Oatman was rescued.

Lieutenant Cave J. Couts, who in the fall of 1849 commanded the military detachment guarding Lieutenant Amiel Weeks Whipple during the survey of the confluence of the Gila and Colorado rivers, commented in his diary that the Yuma tribe admitted ambushing Americans caught alone. He added, however, that the Americans had recently killed five of the same tribe of Indians, had stolen their horses, and robbed the natives of food. Despite the Indian menace, it was Couts's opinion that the greatest menace to the gold-seekers was the gold-seekers themselves; they came without knowledge of the route ("they . . . are willing to keep me talking and making way-bills for them from sun-up until sun-down."), without enough provisions ("The emigrants! Ah! Still they come! . . . begging for sugar, flour, molasses, pork, a little fresh beef, rice, coffee, etc. and God only knows how they have the face to push such entreaties as they do."), and without an appreciation of the dangers of Southwestern geography (many were drowned crossing the Colorado; others died of thirst).

One bizarre aspect of this overland traffic was the scalp bounty system, which induced many forty-niners to work their way westward as employees of the state governments of Chihuahua and Sonora. Because of the Indian raids, both these states were offering

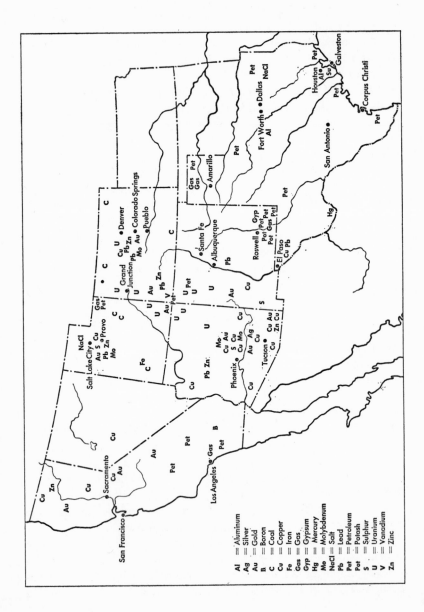

bounties for Indian scalps by 1850. Not a few of the gold-seekers paused to collect this reward, which was exceedingly high: two hundred and fifty dollars for a live warrior, two hundred dollars for the scalp of a warrior, one hundred and fifty dollars for a live squaw or child, and one hundred dollars for the scalp of a woman or child. Not only were there scores of Americans in this "profession," but also many Mexicans, who had never seen so much money, turned to "backyard barbering" as an occupation. There even were runaway slaves, and even other tribes of Indians, among them the Delaware, who entered the chase. James Johnson had first shown the huge profits to be reaped when in 1837 he gathered a group of Apaches near the Santa Rita Copper Mines for a "picnic." When the Indians crowded around the packmules to receive presents, Johnson touched off a blunderbuss loaded with shot, slugs, and bits of chain, and killed almost the entire band; one of the few Indians to escape was Mangas Colorado, who never forgot this act of treachery by an American.

Perhaps the most famous of the scalp hunters was James Kirker, a former mountain man, who gathered a company numbering almost two hundred and brought in thousands of dollars worth of hair. He, along with other American scalp hunters, soon discovered that the Mexican examining committees could not distinguish between the scalp of an unfriendly Indian and that of a friendly one; soon almost every tribe in the American Southwest and in the northern states of Mexico was on the warpath because of the slaughter. Then the scalp hunters found that these same examining committees could not distinguish between Apache hair and Mexican hair. The greedy hunters were surrounding outlying villages to prevent anyone escaping, killing the entire population, and collecting their grisly reward. Some of the hunters had to flee Mexico with a price on their own heads.

One such scalp hunter, John Joel Glanton, who fled Chihuahua with a price of $8,000 on his own hair, transferred his activities to Sonora. There after a trip through the countryside he turned in enough scalps to collect $6,550 from the government. Moving on, he arrived at Yuma crossing on the Colorado where he found two ferries in operation, one by the Yuma Indians and another in the hands of an American. Glanton took over the ferry being operated by the American and made huge profits by taxing Mexicans returning from the California mines and by robbing and even killing immigrants bound for the gold fields, blaming the Yuma for such depredations. Then Glanton killed the manager of the Yuma ferry, bringing the Indians' fury down on himself and his gang of cutthroats. On April 23, 1850, the Yuma killed fifteen members of the Glanton gang, and, according to one survivor, Glanton in the attack lost his scalp "at the adam's apple level."

Armed men came from California to punish the Yuma for this "massacre," but soon left. Then late in the fall Major Samuel P. Heintzelman brought soldiers from San Diego and established Camp Independence on December 1, 1850, at the site occupied by Couts a year earlier, known as Camp Calhoun. In March of 1851 the temporary post was renamed Camp Yuma, then was abandoned late that year. It was re-established on a permanent basis as Fort Yuma on February 28, 1852, with the stated purpose of providing protection for the gold-seekers bound for California.

Once in California most of the immigrants pushed immediately north to the gold fields. Among the first to arrive there were Mexicans from Sonora, who established the town of that name and introduced Spanish techniques of mining in the diggings. But they suffered greatly owing to the Americans' hostility against "foreigners," and the Spanish influence in northern California was practically obliterated. Only in southern California did this influence linger. Although California became a state in 1850 because of the tremendous influx of population, it was a state divided into two distinct parts. Northern California was almost totally American in its society and its institutions; southern California, not endowed by nature with rich mineral deposits, retained its Spanish heritage, its leisurely way of life, its insularity, and its agricultural and pastoral economy. The large land holdings dating from the Spanish and Mexican period were not overrun by squatters and claim-jumpers as were those in the north, and thus survived intact, although many of them fell into the hands of enterprising Anglo-Americans. Farming was extended to large areas near Los Angeles and San Diego because high prices were paid for anything edible in the gold fields, and there was a resulting boom in the south—but of a very different nature, one contributing to and increasing the old divergence between north and south in the new state. Ranching likewise received a strong impetus, but this also increased the split in California: sheep ranching predominated in the northern part of the state, cattle raising in the south.

There were more than just agricultural benefits for the Southwest in the California gold rush, however. Mining methods and techniques learned from the Mexicans would serve prospectors in Nevada, Colorado, and Arizona, while the legal code pertaining to mining, evolved in California, would spread all across the West and beyond, even to Alaska and Australia. Under Spanish law all subsurface deposits belonged to the crown, and a 20 per cent tax had to be paid on all wealth extracted. However, the federal government of the United States never attempted to collect anything for the gold and silver taken from the public domain in the American Southwest. Nor were federal and state officials quick to follow the miners into the mountains other than to impose the foreign miners' tax, which meant that officers of the law were almost unknown at the diggings. To curtail lawlessness the miners evolved their own legal code; each mining "district" had its registrar of claims, regulated the size of a "claim," and enforced rough justice through the "miners' court" (and through vigilante action). Because of the rapid shifting of argonauts from one strike to another and the very real and very strong desire to see law and order prevail, the "miner's code," as these rules of procedure came to be called, were roughly standardized. Not until 1866 did the United States government attempt to impose laws on mining in the public domain, and then it was to enact into federal statute the miners' code almost verbatim.

As the boom in California reached a peak and then began to decline, many of the disappointed argonauts pushed east across the Sierra to prospect in other areas. First to benefit from the California experience was Arizona, and from a non-miner. Working as chief clerk in the surveyor's office of the custom's house in San Francisco late in 1853 was twenty-eight-year-old Charles Debrille Poston, a native of Kentucky who had been infected with gold fever in 1851 and had gone west. When news of the Gadsden Purchase reached that port city, Poston became very excited and was easily persuaded by a French syndicate to lead an expedition to the area to search for mineral wealth. Recruiting some twenty-five adventuresome young men, he sailed for Guaymas, Sonora, in February of 1854. They survived successively shipwreck, the attitude of Mexican officials suspicious of an armed party of Americans, and the long journey northward through Sinaloa and Sonora, eventually reaching the Santa Cruz Valley of southern Arizona. There they found exciting indications of silver deposits. At the junction of the Gila and Colorado rivers, Poston mapped a town known first as Colorado City, then as Arizona City, finally as Yuma, Arizona, and he met and talked with Major Samuel P. Heintzelman, the commanding officer at Fort Yuma.

At San Francisco Poston made his report to the syndicate that had hired him, then hurried to Cincinnati, Ohio, where he was instrumental in organizing the Sonora Exploring and Mining Company, capitalized at one million dollars, one hundred thousand dollars paid in. Heintzelman was president of the company; Poston as general manager had orders to return to Arizona and open mines. By May 1, 1856, he was in San Antonio where he recruited a group of Texas frontiersmen, "armed," as he later wrote, "with Sharp's rifles, Colt's revolvers, and the recklessness of youth." Proceeding to Tucson without incident, he turned south in search of a suitable location. At Tubac he found what he wanted. The abandoned presidio's buildings became headquarters for the company: the guardhouse became a storeroom for company property, the main building became a large dining room and lounge for officials, and the enlisted men's rooms became quarters for the workers. Atop the presidial tower a sentinel could keep watch for Apache raiders. Food could be had cheaply from nearby Sonora, a two-acre garden was cleared, and fruit was secured from the orchard left by the mission fathers at nearby Tumácacori.

Mines were quickly staked out, the richest located to the west and named the Heintzelman. It produced about seven thousand dollars to the ton of ore. In 1859 the company bought a European barrel amalgamating works in San Francisco for $39,000, shipped to Fort Yuma by boat, then freighted overland to a site eight miles from the Heintzelman Mine where it was placed in operation; it yielded about three thousand dollars a day in silver from the various mines worked by the company. Of these pre-Civil War years at

Tubac, Poston later declared wistfully: "We had no law but love, and no occupation but labor. No government, no taxes, no public debt, no politics. It was a community in a perfect state of nature."

Another mining entrepreneur of southern Arizona was Sylvester Mowry. A Rhode Islander and a graduate of West Point, Mowry was sent to Fort Yuma in 1855 for romantic indiscretions at Salt Lake City, and like most army officers in the Southwest he had dreams of gaining wealth from mining ventures. Learning that a public meeting in Tucson was petitioning for separate territorial status, Mowry secured a sick leave from the army, managed an appointment as "Territorial Delegate from Arizona," and left for the nation's capital. He was also empowered to sell the Sopori Grant, a Spanish land grant in southern Arizona containing approximately 220 square miles and reported to be rich in silver. At his home town of Providence, Mowry sold the grant—to the Arizona Land and Mining Company, of which he emerged as half owner. One of the investors in this venture was John Russell Bartlett, former United States Boundary Commissioner. By July of 1858 Lieutenant Mowry was so involved in this affair that he resigned his commission, and by the following year he had opened the Mowry Mine and had it producing handsomely.

Ironically the first gold strike in Arizona came within twenty-five miles of the post where Mowry had served, Fort Yuma. In 1858 a Texan, Jacob Snively, struck paydirt on the river about twenty miles upstream from the junction of the Gila with the Colorado, and near by was born Gila City to accommodate those who rushed to the spot. The strike was so rich that even inexperienced miners could work twenty dollars of gold from a few shovelsful of dirt; in 1861 there were some 1200 miners in the area making from $30 to $125 a day. Gila City was typical of the boom towns of the mining frontier; one traveler described it in this fashion: "There was everything in Gila City within a few months but a church and a jail, which were accounted barbarisms by the mass of the population." Soon the rich placers were exhausted, however, and when in 1864 J. Ross Browne visited the spot he wrote: "The promising Metropolis of Arizona consisted of three chimneys and a coyote."

The silver deposits of southern Arizona did not play out before the coming of the Civil War, and were worked quite profitably until the summer of 1861. At that time the removal of the army troops from the area and the commencement of Indian hostilities forced Poston's Sonora Exploring and Mining Company to shut down its operations. Mowry barricaded himself at his mine, along with a few faithful employees, and continued his work on a much-reduced scale.

By the 1850's some New Mexicans had pushed northward to settle in the southern part of what eventually would become the Territory of Colorado. In fact, New Mexico Territory as created in 1850 contained a considerable portion of land above the thirty-seventh parallel. The place names still in use reflect the Spanish influences that these pioneers introduced. However, they were farmers, not miners. The discovery of paydirt in Colorado, just as in Arizona, was made by disappointed argonauts from California. In 1850 a group of Cherokee Indians bound for the "Golden West" paused in the vicinity of what would become the site of Denver and panned in the streams. They found a little "color," but not enough to keep them from pushing on. Eight years later, however, one of these Cherokees, Captain John Beck, disappointed in California and now living in the Indian Territory (Oklahoma), remembered the promise of Colorado and proposed to return. Joined by W. Green Russell and a group from Georgia, the party numbered more than one hundred when it reached the headwaters of the South Platte and its tributaries.

Disappointment seemed to be their only reward by July of that year, and all but thirteen, under the leadership of Russell, left for home. A few days later Russell made a strike on Dry Creek (now inside the city limits of Denver), triggering the usual stampede to the area. Soon the towns of Denver, Pueblo, and Boulder had been established, and enough gold returned eastward to prompt the "Pike's Peak or Bust" rush of the spring of 1859. One authority declares that one hundred thousand started from the Missouri River in this rush, that fifty thousand actually reached their goal, but the disappointment was so great that about half immediately left for home. With so many prospecting the hills, however, a strike was inevitable if there actually was any gold to be had—and it was. On May 6, 1859, John H. Gregory discovered the Central City lode, and the rush at last had an actual reason for existence. Other towns developed—Cañon City, Golden, Central City. The farmers of southern Colorado prospered from the boom prices of the gold fields, causing some of the later arrivals to decide that agriculture was more lucrative than mining. The spring of 1860 saw an even larger immigration to Colorado, and demands for self-government soon were heard.

The first non-Indian settlers of Nevada were Mormons from the Salt Lake City area. Arriving in 1851, their endeavors were more agricultural and missionary than mineral, and they were ordered to return to Utah in 1857 during the so-called Mormon War episode. The first prospecting in Nevada came early in the 1850's when small amounts of placer gold were found on the eastern side of the Sierra in Gold Canyon and Six Mile Canyon. A few hopeful argonauts continued to work their way up these canyons. Among them was Henry T. P. Comstock, who with several others built a small village named Gold Hill near the head of Gold Canyon. In the spring of 1859, while digging a reservoir to hold water for their placer operations, they found a rich vein of what they thought was gold ore, but which was lodged in heavy bluish-black rock. In June a shipment of the ore was sent to California for assay; the report showed $876 per ton in gold—and $3,000 per ton in silver. The Comstock Lode, as it came to be known, was located in Washoe Indian territory, and thus the district came to be known as the Washoe Mines.

During the rest of 1859 and early in 1860 the rush was on. The town that sprang into existence was called Virginia City, and the population in the vicinity soon numbered an estimated ten thousand. The Esmeralda mines were opened near Walker Lake, while discoveries also were made in the Humboldt Mountains—but the Comstock Lode and the Washoe Mines proved the most productive, created many millionaires, and financed the buildings on Nob Hill in San Francisco.

New Mexico alone failed to benefit greatly from the gold rush of the pre-Civil War period. Actually the oldest gold-mining district in the United States lay in that territory, the yellow metal having been discovered there in 1828 in the Ortiz Mountains (between Albuquerque and Santa Fe). Gold valued at sixty to eighty thousand dollars was taken annually from these mountains between 1832 and 1835, and by 1846 the total output was estimated at three million dollars. Energetic Americans took over the operation after the Mexican War, but the shortage of water in the vicinity greatly curtailed the placer mining. Adding to the hazards of wresting mineral wealth from New Mexico's mountains was the continual threat of Indian raids. Thus the territory saw no booms, no rushes, and no great mining prosperity prior to the end of civil conflict in 1865.

EXPLORERS, SURVEYORS, AND FILIBUSTERS

Shortly after the war with Mexico ended, it became obvious both at the state and national levels that little was known about the newly acquired Southwest. The region needed to be explored and mapped, and roads to be laid out. First to be traversed was West Texas, a deed accomplished within a remarkably short time. On February 12, 1849, a military expedition set out from San Antonio, its object to open a wagon road to Franklin, Texas (later to become El Paso, Texas). Led by Lieutenants William F. Smith and William H. C. Whiting, both of the United States Army Corps of Topographical Engineers, the military expedition reached its goal on April 12, then returned to San Antonio late in May. The trip was made without incident, at approximately the same time as another expedition, jointly sponsored by the federal government and the citizens of Austin, Texas, was performing the same task. Commanded by Major Robert S. Neighbors and Ranger Captain John S. (Rip) Ford, the second expedition left San Antonio on March 23, 1849, reached Franklin on May 2, and returned to Austin on June 2. The Neighbors-Ford route, north of that traveled by Smith and Whiting, became known as the Upper Road, while the army's route was labeled the Lower Road. Thus by the summer of 1849 two practical wagon roads had been opened from the settlements of Texas to the eastern end of Cooke's Wagon Road to California.

To test the practicability of the new military road, Brevet Major Jefferson Van Horn left San Antonio late in May 1849 with six companies of infantry, two hundred and seventy-five wagons, and two thousand five hundred animals. In September, after a march of one hundred days, he reached the area of Franklin, and established the Post of El Paso, later to be known as Fort Bliss. Van Horn's task was to halt Indian raids into Mexico, to protect travelers, and to assert American authority in the region. In addition, he proved the success of the Smith-Whiting route westward across Texas. Besides this lonely outpost, other forts were established in West Texas very soon after the Treaty of Guadalupe Hidalgo was signed: Davis, Duncan, Inge, Lincoln, Martin Scott, Croghan, Gates, Graham, and Worth. These posts, each strategically located either to protect the settlements or to command various Indian trails, were poorly manned and ill-equipped to perform their task. Policymakers in Washington, for reasons known only to themselves, decided that foot soldiers could best cope with the mounted and mobile natives of the Southwest. The mistakes were many and costly, and the list of casualties in this decade was long. The first settlers to push past the timber and out onto the plains complained repeatedly of Indian attacks. State officials in Austin finally ordered the Texas Rangers to take the field. On horseback and armed with the latest weapons, including Colt's revolvers, the Rangers pursued the Indians to their home territory and attacked them in their own villages. The state billed the federal government for this service, but it was not until 1906 that the $375,000 was paid.

On February 6, 1854, the state legislature of Texas established two Indian reservations. The first, known as the Brazos Indian Agency, was located twelve miles south of Fort Belknap on the Brazos River (near present-day Graham), and two thousand members of the Caddo, Waco, Tonkawa, and Anadarko tribes gladly went there, hoping for protection from the Comanche. Forty-five miles to the west on the Clear Fork of the Brazos was the second preserve; it was intended for the fierce Comanche nation, but only about four hundred and fifty of their number settled there. Raids by the Kickapoo and the northern Comanche on the settlements, with the blame being placed on reservation Indians, division among the tribes on the preserves, and the tendency of young warriors to join parties raiding the settlements, all contributed to the abandonment of this system, as did the white hunger for the land given the Indians, the selling of liquor to reservation Indians by unprincipled white traders, and attacks on the reservation Indians by nearby white settlers. In 1858 Governor Hardin Runnels and Senator Sam Houston appealed to the federal government to move all Indians out of Texas. But before the Indian Bureau officials could find a suitable location in the Indian Territory (Oklahoma) for them, angry Texans took matters into their own hands. Led by a former agent on the reservation, now turned rancher, John Robert Baylor, the settlers on May 23, 1859, attacked the Brazos Agency. Major Neighbors, who was acting as chief Indian agent in Texas, immediately ordered the reservations to be closed. This order was effected on July 31, 1859, and control over these tribes was formally given to officials of the Indian Territory on September 1, 1859. In theory all Indians except the Alabama-Coushatta were thereby removed from the state of Texas.

Military exploration was also taking place to the north of this activity in central West Texas. In 1849 Captain Randolph B. Marcy led a small command of soldiers from Fort Smith, Arkansas, to Santa Fe, New Mexico, by way of the Canadian River. On his return, Marcy followed a different route: he marched downriver to Doña Ana, marched to the Pecos River at its junction with the 32nd parallel, turned to the northeast to the headwaters of the Colorado and Brazos rivers, crossed the Red River at Preston, and returned to Fort Smith. Known as Marcy's Trail, this southern route soon had a line of forts along it to protect immigrants and traders: Belknap, Cooper, Phantom Hill, and Chadbourne.

The need for good wagon roads west was so pressing—Cooke's Wagon Road ran mostly through Mexico until after the Gadsden Purchase was ratified in June of 1854—that new ones were constantly being sought. In this search the Corps of Topographical Engineers of the United States Army was in the forefront. Captain Lorenzo Sitgreaves set out from the Zuñi villages of New Mexico along the 35th parallel in September of 1851 with a party of twenty men. Proceeding westward, he passed through Arizona where later would be located the towns of Flagstaff, Williams, and Kingman, arriving at the Mohave Indian villages on the Colorado River, then turning south to Fort Yuma, which he reached in December. This trek proved that wagons could travel west from Santa Fe to Albuquerque and directly across to California; getting across the Mohave Desert of California was the big problem.

Another 35th parallel survey came two years later because of the national desire for a transcontinental railroad. Beginning in the early 1850's, the clamor grew louder and louder for "linking the nation together with rails of steel," as political orators put it. This task also fell to the Corps of Topographical Engineers, and two routes across the Southwest were surveyed, one along the 35th parallel and one across the 32nd parallel. In 1853 Lieutenant Amiel Weeks Whipple, assisted by Lieutenant Joseph Christmas Ives, surveyed a route from Fort Smith, Arkansas, to California. They crossed the Colorado River near present-day Needles and braved the Mohave Desert to reach their destination. The following year, with the permission of the Mexican government (for the official transfer of the Gadsden Purchase had not yet been made), Lieutenants John G. Parke and George Stoneman came across the 32nd parallel from west to east—much of their trip along Cooke's Wagon Road—to the Rio Grande.

And there was one private railroad survey in the 1850's. Because the state containing the eastern terminus of a transcontinental railroad would profit so greatly, Texas, which owned all its public land, offered sixteen sections of land to the Texas Western Railroad Company for each mile of track it would lay. Chartered in New York in February of 1852, this company hired Andrew B. Gray, the former United States Boundary Surveyor, to survey a route from Indianola, Texas, to San Diego, California, mainly along the 32nd parallel. During 1853–54 Gray organized a party and completed the trek from the Gulf of Mexico to the Pacific Ocean. The reports of the surveys of both civilian and army officers were published either as government documents or as company promotional pieces, and they contributed substantially to the growing knowledge of the geography, native tribes, and conditions in the Southwest.

To protect the emerging routes of travel and commerce in New Mexico and Arizona—the 35th parallel, the 32nd parallel, and the Rio Grande—several army posts were established following the close of the Mexican War. Along the Rio Grande were Fort Craig, Fort Fillmore, and Fort Marcy (at Santa Fe). In northeastern New Mexico was the principal supply depot for that territory, Fort Union, while east of the Rio Grande in the White Mountains was placed Fort Stanton, to keep watch over the Apaches in that vicinity. The first post in what would become Arizona was Fort Defiance, located in northeastern Arizona in 1852 in the Navajo country. After the Gadsden Purchase, the first troops to arrive in southern Arizona, in May 1857, located permanently at Fort Buchanan (southeast of Tucson). Fort Mohave was established in April of 1859 on the east bank of the Colorado River near its junction with the 35th parallel. Finally, there was Camp Tucson, established in 1860.

While army officers and civilians, including the members of the various boundary commissions between 1848 and 1855, were surveying, exploring, and mapping the Southwest, and while the army was establishing posts to contain its Indians and provide a measure of stability, still other newcomers to the region were trying to extend the limits of the United States through extra-legal measures. Some of these filibusters may have been motivated by the doctrine of Manifest Destiny, which stated that Americans had almost a divine mandate to acquire and govern the whole of North America, extending to the entire continent the enlightened institutions of liberty, equality, the pursuit of happiness, and free enterprise. In examining the lives and statements of these filibusters, however, it is difficult—if not impossible—to find a single one who in any way paid even lip service to this concept. Most, if not all, of them were involved for the adventure, still wishing "to see the elephant," and for whatever personal gain might be involved. The doctrine of Manifest Destiny as an explanation for such activities has generally been hypothesized by historians unaware of the *ex post facto* nature of their attempt. After the first flurry of mining had died in California, the state was filled with restless, adventurous young men ready for any endeavor promising or even hinting at booty to be divided.

First to be involved in such activity was Joseph C. Morehead, whose eyes were turned toward Baja California. As quartermaster-general of California, Morehead early in 1851 had at his disposal weapons, equipment, and funds left over from the expedition of the year before which went to punish the Yuma Indians following the "massacre" of the Glanton gang. He went south at the head of an army at the invitation of malcontents in Baja and Sonora who wanted either an independent republic—"as Texas had been," declared one Sonoran official—or annexation to the United States, as another report had it. During March and April of 1851 several parties ranging in size from twenty-five to one hundred men—there was no shortage of volunteers—left for Sonora or Baja. The *Josephine*, a bark purchased by Morehead with the funds at his disposal, landed two hundred troops at La Paz who, when questioned by the authorities, declared themselves to be traders and dispersed. A second force at Los Angeles began marching for Yuma, intending to go into Sonora, while Morehead gathered a third army at San Diego. Most of his men deserted at that port. American customs officials came aboard the *Josephine* at San Diego and searched it thoroughly for the munitions and weapons it reportedly was carrying, but could find none. Morehead sailed on May 11, bound for Mazatlán. Mexican officials at that port were sufficiently alarmed to place the city in a state of defense, and when Morehead arrived they too searched in vain for weapons. At this point the filibuster collapsed, and Morehead was heard of no more.

Mexican officials decided that the best defense against future "invasions" was a strengthening of defenses in their northwest. In Baja California geography would serve their purpose; Sonora they decided to populate with colonists recruited from among the French immigrants to California. Numerous in the gold fields, but suffering from the foreign miners' tax and other forms of discrimination, the French were susceptible to Mexican offers of land and financial aid. In November 1851 eighty-five of them sailed for Guaymas under the command of Charles Pindray. They were settled near Cocóspera, Sonora, where their number grew to more than one hundred and fifty. But the Apache attacked and the promised Mexican aid never materialized. Pindray was shot under suspicious circumstances, and the colony dissolved.

Many Frenchmen in California were still willing to emigrate to Mexico, however. Under a new leader, Count Gaston de Raousset-Boulbon, an impoverished, reckless French nobleman, expeditions left San Francisco in 1852 and 1854 to Guaymas and thence inland, ostensibly to mine. Friction soon developed between the volatile Frenchmen and the equally volatile Mexicans, leading to the capture of Hermosillo by Raousset-Boulbon. Then began a retreat to Guaymas by the French, many of whom surrendered in discouragement along the way. The Count made his way to San Francisco where he began recruiting an army of one thousand men, some said for the purpose of making himself "Sultan of Sonora." In the midst of these preparations he was invited to Mexico City to confer with President Santa Anna about bringing five hundred Frenchmen south to protect Sonora. The two men failed to agree, and the count returned to San Francisco to continue his recruiting.

Simultaneously, another filibuster was recruiting, William Walker, later called the "grey-eyed man of destiny." Most of the biographical encyclopedias list his occupation as "adventurer," and so indeed he was. Born in Tennessee in 1824, Walker earned a doctorate of medicine from the University of Pennsylvania by the age of nineteen, and later was admitted to the bar in New Orleans. Next he turned to journalism, becoming one of the editors and owners of the New Orleans *Daily Crescent.* Then in 1850 he joined the gold rush, and at Marysville, California, he engaged in law and politics—which involved him in several duels. Becoming interested in "colonizing" in northern Mexico, he gathered forty-five men and sailed from San Francisco in October 1853, aboard the brig *Caroline,* claiming that Mexicans had invited him down to protect them from the Apache. Landing at La Paz on November 3, he captured the local governor and began issuing proclamations as "President of the Republic of Baja California." Threatened by hostile Mexican forces and prevented from receiving needed supplies and reinforcements by customs officials in San Francisco, he retreated northward to Ensenada, just south of San Diego, where on January 18, 1854, he annexed Sonora to his republic by proclamation. In May he ingloriously fled across the border—into the waiting arms of the United States army. He was brought to trial in San Francisco for violating the neutrality laws, but was acquitted by a sympathetic jury. The following year he left and had incredible adventures in Central America that eventually brought him the actual presidency of Nicaragua—and death by firing squad in Honduras on September 12, 1860.

Walker's filibuster in Baja California caused the Mexicans to make another attempt to get Raousset-Boulbon and the French to settle in Sonora. In the spring of 1854 the count set out from San Francisco with four hundred men, but at Guaymas the reception was not friendly, and on July 13 the Battle of Guaymas was fought.

The French were decisively defeated, and thirty days later the count was executed. Raousset-Boulbon's death marked an end to French filibustering from California, but not to the filibustering itself. One more tragic *entrada* was to be made.

Henry Alexander Crabb, a Tennessean trained in law, came to San Francisco in 1849. He became successful in California politics and married a daughter of the Aiensa family, which was prominent in commerce both in that state and in Sonora. Crabb became interested in Sonora because of his wife's property holdings there, especially after he was defeated for a seat in the United States Senate, and in 1856 he led a party of fifty colonists into the northwestern Mexican state. While he was there he met General Ygnacio Pesqueira, one of the revolutionaries contending for the governorship in the unstable political situation there. Pesqueira persuaded Crabb to return to California for the purpose of raising an army to help drive the rival contender, Manuel María Gandara, out of Sonora; in return for this help, Crabb and his men were to be given mining concessions and extensive grants of land along the northern border, where they would protect Sonorans from Apache raiders.

In California Crabb raised an army of approximately one hundred disappointed gold-seekers and marched them to Sonora by the Los Angeles-Yuma route. Arriving at the border, he found unexpected opposition. Pesqueira had defeated Gandara without outside help, and once in power had turned violently anti-American, probably for political reasons. Crabb nevertheless led his army, somewhat reduced by desertion, southward. At Caborca, on April 6, 1857, partly by force and partly by treachery, the Americans were induced to surrender. The next morning the fifty-nine prisoners were taken out in small groups and shot in the back. Crabb was reserved for last; his head was preserved in vinegar for a time and exhibited to an exulting populace. Some thirty Tucsonans, hearing of Crabb's initial difficulties, decided to come to his rescue. They barely escaped a similar fate and returned empty-handed. The United States government made only a weak protest about this incident, lending strength to the feeling that Crabb's fate was deserved; actually he and his followers for the most part were men of high reputation, who had gone to Sonora by semi-official invitation; they died because Pesqueira wished to cover his invitation to

Americans to help him achieve the governorship. If this fact had become widely known, Pesqueira would probably have lost his office and his reputation.

The Crabb expedition brought to a close almost a decade of expansionist activities in the Southwest, but parts of Mexico were still coveted. When the second legislature of the Territory of Arizona convened in Prescott on December 6, 1865, the members heard Acting Governor Richard C. McCormick declare:

> For the accommodation of the southern part of the territory, the acquisition of the port of Libertad, upon the Gulf of California, is a matter of the first importance, and, whatever the controlling power in Mexico, it should be negotiated for at the earliest practicable moment. Its acquisition, with that part of the State of Sonora which lies between it and our present line, would give new life and importance to the region below the Gila River, and be largely beneficial to the whole territory.

McCormick was right in saying that such an acquisition would have proven beneficial, but the time for moving the American boundary southward, either by force or by negotiation, had passed forever.

TRANSPORTATION

Upon reaching California with the Duval Party of 1849, young Benjamin Butler Harris spent a considerable time traveling in the gold fields. He noted that the heavy rains of the winter of 1849–50 had rendered almost every thoroughfare there impassable. One pilgrim, traveling by horse and buggy, whose horse almost drowned at a swampy stretch of road, according to Harris paused to post a notice: "This place is not crossible, not even horsible." Not far behind him came another argonaut, this one astride a burro; struggling out of the same boggy stretch, the second traveler appended a postscript to the sign: "This place is not passable, Not even Jackassable."

Under such conditions, it is not surprising that almost all freight bound for California came by sea. The rest of the Southwest was supplied either through Texas Gulf ports or by way of the Santa Fe Trail. But commercial transportation did develop, first in California, then throughout the Southwest. Within a remarkably short time steamboats were running on the streams leading to the gold fields, and Abbott and Downing's famous stage, the Concord, was struggling to keep posted schedules between the cities and the mining camps. The impetus was gold—fortunes could be made by anyone who could move humans and mail from one place to another. Alexander Todd, for example, decided to leave the diggings for San Francisco; he announced that he would carry letters out for an ounce of dust per letter—and had more than one hundred customers. Next he purchased a skiff for three hundred dollars in which to make the trip to Sacramento; his charge to passengers, who also had to man the oars, was sixteen dollars a head—and he collected more than twice the sum he had paid for the craft.

While the profit motive stimulated the development of several commercial carriers within California, no such motive existed for transcontinental ambitions. The distance was so great and the passengers and freight so negligible that either a stage line or a railroad required huge federal subsidies, but the growing disagreement between North and South prevented agreement on the route to be followed; the profits to be made by having the eastern terminus of such a carrier in the area caused Southerners to want a southern route, while Northerners wanted the line to begin either in Missouri (St. Louis) or Illinois (Chicago). Yet the clamor for some form of communication and transportation with the East steadily grew louder in California. The government responded by ordering the Army to make the necessary surveys, and in 1853 $150,000 was appropriated for this purpose. The Corps of Topographical Engineers performed the task in their usual competent fashion, then made reports. These bulged with facts about the geography, geology, botany, zoology, and climate of the West, but merely gathered dust in the files while the sectional controversy raged.

The pressure for some form of transcontinental link with California led Congress on March 3, 1857, to pass an act subsidizing a mail route to the Pacific Coast. The Postmaster-General was authorized by the terms of this act to make a six-year contract for his service—with a subsidy of $600,000 per year—on a twice-weekly basis, the run to be made in twenty-five days or less. Aaron Brown of Tennessee was Postmaster-General at this time, and it was widely predicted that he would dictate a Southern route. Furthermore, it was believed that the contract would go to James Birch, a Californian. The route chosen was indeed a southern one, but the contract went to John Butterfield. The agreement was signed on September 16, 1857, and called for service to begin within one year.

Though Birch did not get this transcontinental contract, he did not come away empty-handed. Just before the big contract was granted to Butterfield, Birch and Brown made an agreement whereby the Californian was to receive a $150,000 subsidy to run a monthly mail stage from San Antonio to San Diego. The first coaches of the San Antonio and San Diego Mail Line—"from nowhere to nowhere," some Californians said—began operating late in 1857, and soon was dubbed the "Jackass Mail" because certain sections of the route were unfit for wheeled vehicles, and there the passengers were supplied with mules for transportation. Birch thus had the honor of operating the first transcontinental, but he did not live to enjoy it; in the fall of 1857 he died at sea in the wreck of the *Central America*. The Jackass Mail did not long survive him, dying quietly when the Butterfield began operating the following year.

Even Butterfield's friends told him that he could never build a line of way-stations, acquire the necessary stock and coaches, and hire competent men to operate a stage line some 2800 miles in length within one year's time. Even if he did, they added, the line would be too long, too unwieldy, and thus doomed to failure. But John Butterfield had great determination, years of experience, and organizing ability. Born in New York in 1801, he had received little formal education, becoming a stage driver at an early age. He rose rapidly to own several New York lines, and in 1850 he was one of the founders of the American Express Company. In the year that followed the signing of the contract, Butterfield did all that his friends claimed he could not. On September 16, 1858, the first westbound coach was ready to roll from Tipton, Missouri, the railhead west of St. Louis, and the first eastbound from San Francisco. The route west ran from Tipton to Fort Smith, Arkansas, crossed the Red River to follow the line of army posts across Texas to El

Paso, turned north to Mesilla, proceeded west to Tucson, thence to San Diego by Cooke's Wagon Road, and reached San Francisco along the mission route laid out almost a century before by Father Serra.

For this ride across the Southwest, the passenger paid two hundred dollars; in addition, he was expected to help fight any troublesome Indians encountered, to push when the stage became stuck, and to give aid in any emergency. The stages ran day and night, and the passenger who gave up his seat to rest a few days at a way-station might have to wait for a month or more before another stage passed with an empty seat. Waterman L. Ormsby, a reporter for the New York *Herald,* rode that first stage coach all the way from Tipton to San Francisco, a run that was made in twenty-four days. Ormsby's exciting trip was described in dispatches he sent back to his paper; later these were put together in book form under the title *The Butterfield Overland Mail.* His description of the trip, along with that of subsequent passengers, tells of the hardships encountered: no facilities for sleeping, food that consisted primarily of beans and salt pork, breathing dust day after day, the threat—on occasion, the reality—of Indian attack. Occasionally a traveler with a weak constitution simply went insane, jumped out of the stage, and disappeared into the desert never to be seen again. Others said the trip was an exciting adventure.

Whether adventure or hardship, the Butterfield route did not please northern Californians. They said that a line running directly west from St. Louis to Salt Lake City and Sacramento could make the run in several days less time and could be kept open the year around. Southern Californians were jubilant, however, and the Southern-oriented administration of President James Buchanan echoed their sentiment; the Butterfield continued to be the only line drawing a regular subsidy until the coming of the Civil War. Just before that conflict started, northern California did get the Pony Express along the route it wished. This dramatic transcontinental mail service began on April 3, 1860, and ended a year and a half later—October 26, 1861—upon the completion of the overland telegraph, the lines of which also followed a northern route.

Another type of transportation in the Southwest before the Civil War was the steamboat—on the Colorado River. This came out of the need for an inexpensive means of transporting supplies to Fort Yuma. In the fall of 1850 it was costing the army seventy-five dollars per ton to freight goods from the mouth of the Colorado, whence they had been brought by sea-going vessels, to the outpost. Brevet Major General P. F. Smith, commander of the Department of the Pacific, ordered Lieutenant George H. Derby (who had already gained some fame for his humorous writings about the army in the West under the pen-name of John Phoenix) to explore the Colorado for a water route to Yuma and beyond. Derby left San Francisco aboard the schooner *Invincible* early in 1851 and came upriver to a point about eighty miles below Yuma. There he boarded a small boat and proceeded another sixty miles upriver. He reported that boats of a shallow draft could reach the fort easily.

Derby's report caused the army to award a contract to Captain George Alonso Johnson to supply Fort Yuma by water. Johnson brought freight to the mouth of the Colorado in ocean-going vessels, then transferred it to a fifty-foot barge which was poled upriver. Indian attacks and the difficulties of using manpower against the swift current of the Colorado made the journeys unsatisfactory, however, and Johnson terminated his contract with the army. Early in 1852, after the re-establishment of Fort Yuma, Captain James Turnbull took up the challenge. He brought the *Uncle Sam,* a twenty-horsepower stern-wheeler, sixty-five feet long, with a draft of only twenty-two inches, to the mouth of the Colorado and easily made the run to Yuma. Turnbull had no difficulty with the Indians; he noted that at sight of the craft the natives ran, yelling "The devil is coming, blowing fire and smoke out of his nose and kicking the water back with his feet." Later, when their fear had been overcome by familiarity, the Indians cut and sold wood to the captain at designated points along the Colorado's banks.

In 1853 George A. Johnson once again received the contract to supply the army post at Yuma. He attracted outside capital to his venture, and the firm was named George A. Johnson and Company. It purchased the *General Jessup,* a seventy-five-horsepower craft, measuring one hundred and eight feet, drawing only thirty inches of water, and capable of carrying tons of cargo and pulling two barges. For more than a year this one boat handled all freighting chores on the river; then the firm acquired the *Colorado,* a one-hundred-and-twenty-foot stern-wheeler sporting two steam engines.

The federal government wanted to open the Colorado River above Fort Yuma to navigation, so in 1857 Congress appropriated funds for exploration. Lieutenant Joseph Christmas Ives was assigned the task. His vessel, the *Explorer,* was specially built at Philadelphia, then disassembled and transported to the mouth of the Colorado by way of Panama; at Port Isabel it was reassembled, and on December 21, 1857, Ives set out upriver. It took the *Explorer* nineteen days to reach Fort Yuma, from which point the trip northward began early in 1858. Reaching Black Canyon, the *Explorer* on March 12 struck a submerged reef—the place came to be known as Explorer's Rock—and Ives concluded that he had reached the head of navigable water. Finally freeing the *Explorer* and making the necessary repairs, Ives returned to Yuma. His report had a lasting influence; for several years thereafter Black Canyon was accepted as the head of navigation on the Colorado. Fifty-two miles downriver, outside the Canyon, William H. Hardy laid out Hardyville (or Hardy's Landing) and grew rich from the passage of goods to the interior through his landing.

One other mode of transportation was tried in the Southwest prior to the Civil War—one of a more experimental nature. During the years immediately following the Treaty of Guadalupe Hidalgo, the years of military and civilian parties of exploration and the westward movement of California-bound gold-seekers, the Americans discovered what the Indians had known for centuries: water was the key to survival in the West. It is not surprising that an experiment was conducted to determine the usefulness of camels as beasts of burden in an area labeled in textbooks, "The Great American Desert." As early as 1836 Major George H. Crossman had proposed their use to his Washington superiors; twelve years later Major Henry C. Wayne made the same suggestion—but no one listened to either man. Then in 1854 Lieutenant Edward Fitzgerald Beale, a veteran of the Mexican War who thought camels might prove useful in the Southwest, found a ready supporter in Jefferson Davis, Secretary of War in the Franklin Pierce administration, who recommended to Congress the appropriation of funds for this purpose. Thirty thousand dollars were made available for an experiment, and on May 14, 1856, thirty-three camels were led ashore at Indianola, Texas. On February 17 of the following year, forty-four more of the beasts arrived, and Beale had seventy-seven animals with which to found the "Camel Military Corps."

The animals were stabled at Camp Verde, Texas (about sixty miles northwest of San Antonio), where for several months Beale and his men conducted experiments and trained themselves in the ways of the dromedary. Two drovers imported from Egypt, nicknamed Greek George and Hi-Jolly, taught the troopers the proper placement of packs on the beasts, and they stayed to accompany Beale on the first test of the fitness of the camels in the Southwest. In the spring of 1857 Beale was given orders to survey a wagon route from Camp Verde along the 35th parallel to the Colorado River. They left on June 25, 1857, and reached the Colorado in January of 1858, then returned to Texas by the same route. Beale's report was enthusiastic:

> My admiration for the camels increases daily with my experience with them. The harder the test they are put to, the more fully they seem to justify all that can be said of them. They pack water for others four days under a hot sun and never get a drop; they pack heavy burdens of corn and oats for months and never get a grain; and on the bitter greasewood and other worthless shrubs not only subsist but keep fat; with all, they are so perfectly docile and so admirably contented with whatever fate befalls them. No one could do justice to their merits or value in expeditions of this kind, and I look forward to the day when every mail route across the continent will be conducted and worked altogether with this economical and noble brute.

The Secretary of War at that time, John B. Floyd, in 1858 recommended to Congress the immediate purchase of one thousand camels, but his plea went unheeded owing to the sectional controversy. Those animals already in the United States continued to be tested. Beale was stationed at Fort Tejon, California, with twenty camels, and he used them for surveying expeditions and wagon road construction. In the summer of 1859 Lieutenant William H. Echols of the Topographical Engineers made a patrol from the Pecos River to the Rio Grande and back, using twenty-four camels to carry loads of four to six hundred pounds. The quartermaster of this expedition made a glowing report, just as had Beale; he stated that the animals often went without water from two to five days without impaired efficiency, that they traveled across rough country easily, and that they thrived on food unfit for horses or mules.

Not everyone in the Southwest thought so highly of the camels, however. The packers detested them because of the difficulties of loading them correctly. Many a soldier developed a hatred of them because of their sharp teeth, which they were inclined to use without provocation. Teamsters wanted to shoot the camels on sight because their appearance often caused placid horses and mules to rear and bolt. The Civil War intervened before the experiment could convince the army or civilians of the value of the beasts, and they were turned over to the Quartermaster Corps for sale at public auction. Some were purchased by a company in Nevada, which used them to carry salt from a marsh in Esmeralda County to the Washoe silver mill, a distance of two hundred miles. They did their work satisfactorily, but the packers hated and mistreated them. Still other camels were used to pack ore in Arizona. Some escaped to run wild in the desert, to be shot on sight by prospectors and hunters who regarded them as pests. Not a few were purchased individually by saloon-keepers who stabled them as a kind of sideshow attraction for patrons.

By one form of transportation or another—mostly by horseback and by wagon—the Americans made their way into the Southwest during the decade preceding the Civil War, and the population increased tremendously. The Republic of Texas boasted 135,000 residents when it ceased to exist; the census of 1860 showed a total of 602,000 within the state. New Mexico also showed a gain, but not as spectacular; in 1850 it had a population of 61,547, while by 1860 the number was 80,567. The figures for New Mexico included the population of Arizona, which was negligible owing to the harshness of the land and the hostility of the Apache. The number of Californians, estimated at slightly more than 100,000 in 1849, had risen to 380,015 by the census of 1860. Of course, these totals do not include the Indians. Nor are they indicative of the true population of the Southwest; a majority of those people in Texas lived in the eastern part of the state, just as a majority of those in California lived north of the area with a strong Spanish influence.

Most of those persons moving into West Texas, southern New Mexico, Arizona, and southern California came from the southern part of the United States, bringing with them their proslavery and pro-Southern sympathies. In the northern parts of New Mexico and California, however, most of the settlers were from the Midwest or the North, and they were abolitionist and Unionist in sentiment.

CIVIL WAR IN THE SOUTHWEST

In 1882—seventeen years after the last gun had been fired in the Civil War—General William T. Sherman visited Tucson. When the train stopped, a delegation of local dignitaries, chief among them Granville H. Oury, moved forward to welcome the Union hero to Arizona Territory. When Oury was introduced to Sherman, the general asked if he was "one of my boys in the late unpleasantness." Oury replied, "No, General, I was on the opposite side of the conflict in that sad affair, but I am here to extend you greetings and the hospitality of the Old Pueblo of Tucson." As they moved toward the waiting carriage, the band struck up "Marching Through Georgia." Oury remarked, "General Sherman, many a time I marched to that tune," to which Sherman replied, "Beg pardon, Sir, didn't I understand you to say that you were on the opposite side in the War?" "I was, General," Oury said. "I was just ahead of you in Georgia, and marching like Hell." Oury's statement was true not only of those who went East to fight in the Civil War, but also of those who stayed behind. Despite their distance from the well-known battlefields and the centers of government, despite their relative isolation and their lack of affiliation with the conflicting philosophies of the war, Southwesterners nonetheless were also "marching like Hell."

A growing dissatisfaction in the South over the issue of states' rights was brought to a climax in 1860 by the election of Abraham Lincoln. Southern leaders, who till then had contented themselves with theoretical statements about the right of a state to secede, transformed words into action after the results of the election were announced, and for the first and only time in its history the democratic process broke down in the United States. South Carolina led the way, and one by one other Southern states followed. In Austin, Texas, on January 26, a secession convention met with the reluctant approval of Governor Sam Houston, the aging hero of San Jacinto. Four days later, with only eight negative votes, this convention voted a resolution of secession. In the subsequent popular vote on the issue, the people favored it by a margin of three to one. Texas became the seventh Southern state to secede.

Many Southerners, especially Texans, believed that the Territory of New Mexico (which also included all of Arizona) would side with the Confederacy, and the Texas Secession Convention appointed two commissioners to journey to New Mexico for the purpose of inviting it to do so. One of these men, Philemon T. Herbert, an El Paso attorney, wrote an inflamatory letter to the *Mesilla Times* on February 1, 1861, calling for a secession convention to be held in Mesilla on March 16; he urged the people of the Gadsden Purchase area, which was being called Arizona, to join with "those who have ever sympathized with you" against the "fanaticism of the North." Local citizens from the area also promoted a secession convention, chief among whom was Dr. Lewis S. Owings, provisional governor of the "Territory of Arizona" locally organized in 1860 but never approved. The convention was held on schedule with James A. Lucas, a prominent Arizonan, presiding. The principal address was delivered by W. Claude Jones, law partner of Philemon T. Herbert, who declared: "Has not [the North] treated us with cold and criminal neglect, and has this corrupt sectional [Republican] party taken any steps toward our organization? . . . For six years we have petitioned, pleaded, prayed for protection and some kind of organization. . . . The hell of abolitionism glooms to the north—the Eden of liberty, equality, and right smiles upon you from the south! Choose ye between them." By unanimous resolution the convention voted to repudiate the Republican party, to sever ties with the Union, and to unite with the Confederacy. This resolution was sent to Montgomery, Alabama, where the Provisional Congress of the Confederate States was then in session.

A similar meeting was held in Tucson on March 23. Presiding was Mark Aldrich, the first American merchant in the Old Pueblo. It enthusiastically joined with the citizens of Mesilla in denouncing the North: "[We have] nothing to hope for from Northern legislation," it said, asking that the Confederacy extend to the area "the protection necessary to the proper development and advancement of the Territory."

The Texas secession convention had done more than vote a resolution to withdraw from the Union and elect commissioners to Arizona. It had voted into existence two regiments of Texas Mounted Rifles. The First Regiment was placed under the command of Colonel Ben McCulloch, a veteran of the Mexican War and frontier duty with the Texas Rangers; he moved quickly to secure the surrender of all Federal posts in Texas. There were approximately 2700 Federal troops in the state, but their commander was Major General D. E. Twiggs, a Georgian whose sympathies lay with the South. On February 18 Twiggs agreed to the evacuation of all Federal posts in Texas and the surrender of military supplies and property valued at three million dollars. The Second Regiment was divided into two parts, the first under the command of Colonel John S. "Rip" Ford and the other half under Lieutenant Colonel John R. Baylor. Ford was sent to the lower Rio Grande Valley, while Baylor was ordered to the far western part of the state. Thus McCulloch received the surrender of Federal troops in North Texas, Ford the surrender of the posts in the southern part of the state, and Baylor the surrender of Fort Bliss, near El Paso.

While there was no question about which side of the Civil War the Texans would join, the outcome was doubtful for a time in New Mexico, Colorado, and California. In New Mexico the public attitude had been decidedly pro-Northern in 1850, but the passage of a decade had brought a change. In 1856 New Mexico had enacted legislation restricting the rights of free Negroes; three years later came a slave code spelling out the treatment and punishment of African property. Thus by 1861 most knowledgeable observers believed New Mexico would side with the South. But when the time came for a decision, the most noticeable attitude was apathy—the Indians and the Mexican-born population did not care where the Territory's loyalties lay; they were more interested in their own day-to-day lot. The biggest surprise in the struggle for New Mexico's allegiance came from Miguel A. Otero, the Territory's delegate to

Congress. Otero proposed to ignore both North and South, forming instead a confederacy of the Pacific States.

After the resignations of several high-ranking officers from the Federal force in New Mexico, Colonel E. R. S. Canby was left in command. His situation was anything but favorable. In the face of almost certain Confederate invasion, he had less than three thousand men, the militia was unreliable, he was short of funds, provisions, and supplies, and there was little prospect of help from the East. Canby consolidated his troops, pulling them back to the central portion of the Territory with headquarters at Fort Craig; thereby he abandoned all of Arizona to the mercy of the Apache, who had recently gone on the warpath because of what became known as the Bascom Affair. Started by a drunken rancher, John Ward, who falsely accused Cochise and the Chiricahua Apache of kidnapping his stepson, and culminating in bloody tragedy in Apache Pass, this incident in southern Arizona in February of 1861 brought a period of terror to the area. Then in June the Federal troops were recalled to New Mexico, and Arizonans were left without protection. Canby also issued a call for New Mexican volunteers, and, without authority, asked the assistance of the governor of Colorado, William Gilpin, in repelling any Confederate invaders.

The census of 1860 had shown that there were 34,277 persons in Colorado, most of whom were clamoring for self-government. The withdrawal of Southern delegates from Congress allowed the passage of a territorial act, which the President signed on February 28, 1861. Gilpin, the first governor, was given virtual dictatorial powers by Lincoln, who wanted Colorado kept loyal to the Union whatever the means employed. Gilpin arrived in Denver on May 29 to learn that on April 24 a Confederate flag had been run up over a building in the city; however, it had been pulled down by an angry crowd of Union sympathizers. The pro-Southern element soon found itself in the minority, and many of them left the Territory to fight for the Confederate cause. Gilpin secured credit and began collecting arms and ammunition for a volunteer force which he was raising. By the fall of 1861 he was ready to assist Canby.

Otero's call for a Pacific Republic had far more supporters in

California than in New Mexico. Dreams of independence there dated from the Revolution of 1836, and had risen again during the period of military government (1846–50) and during the days of the Second Vigilance Committee (1855). Even Governor John B. Weller declared in 1861 that California should not choose between North and South, but establish on the Pacific shore "a mighty republic, which may in the end prove the greatest of all." However, the greatest threat in California was not separatism. Of more concern to Federal officials than a Pacific Republic was the strong and very real pro-Southern sentiment in the lower half of the state. During the decade and a half preceding the Civil War, southern Californians had harbored a hatred of the northern half of the state, a desire for the division of California into two separate political entities, and a proslavery attitude that fitted their agrarian economy. At the constitutional convention of 1849 the southern delegates raised the question of a division of the area, feeling that a territorial government would be more suited to their needs than statehood. They felt that they would be dominated by the northern half of California; in this they were right, for when the state government was organized they were given less than their due share of representation in the legislature. In addition, the tax structure of the state was based primarily on land; in 1852 the six thousand residents of southern California paid $42,000 in property taxes and $4,000 in poll taxes, while the people of northern California, who numbered one hundred and twenty thousand, paid only $21,000 in property taxes and $3,500 in poll taxes. These southern Californians were bitter because of the treatment they had received, and were vocal in their support of the South.

Another factor that made California anything but certain to remain in the Union was the rule by Democrats during the 1850's. The Democratic party had been dominated by the pro-Southern faction. Under their leadership the legislature in 1852 had passed an effective fugitive slave law, and in 1858 had instructed its Washington delegation to vote for the admission of Kansas under the Lecompton (proslavery) constitution. Abraham Lincoln and the Republican party did carry California in the election of 1860, but only because the Democrats were badly split.

Secession editorials, speeches, and pronouncements continued to be heard in California after the Southern states seceded. General George Wright, commanding the Department of the Pacific, excluded half a dozen papers from the mails for their vicious attacks on the Union, but the tirade continued. For this reason few of the sixteen thousand volunteers for the Union Army saw service in the East. The national draft law was never applied in California. The most famous unit from the state to see service in the war was the "California Column" commanded by Colonel James H. Carleton, a regular Army major and a Down-East Yankee with political and financial ambitions. When the Confederates invaded New Mexico and Arizona, Carleton was ready to make an eastward thrust to repel them.

By the first week in July 1861, Lieutenant Colonel John R. Baylor and his four companies—two hundred and fifty-eight men— were securely in command at Fort Bliss at El Paso. Baylor was ambitious, however, and soon he was collecting information about conditions in southern New Mexico—the area coming to be known as Arizona. The nearest Union troops were at Fort Fillmore, some forty miles up the Rio Grande. In command of a force of more than five hundred and fifty troops at Fort Fillmore was Major Isaac Lynde, who had orders from Canby to defend the region. Baylor decided to take the post, hopefully by surprise. He failed, and so he occupied the nearby town of Mesilla instead. Marching into the village on the morning of July 25, he and his men were greeted with "vivas and hurrahs," according to the *Mesilla Times*. That afternoon Major Lynde moved up to do battle, sending emissaries forward under a flag of truce to ask an unconditional surrender of the Confederates. Baylor reportedly replied, "We will fight first and surrender afterwards." After a short skirmish, Lynde retreated ingloriously.

The following evening, July 26, the timorous Lynde set fire to the military stores at Fort Fillmore, and during the early morning hours of July 27 began marching his men eastward toward Fort Stanton, the nearest Union outpost. When Baylor heard this, he gathered one hundred and sixty-two of his men and gave chase. Lynde's trail was easy to follow, for it was lined with straggling Yanks who had fallen out due to heat and exhaustion. When Baylor reached the head of the column, Lynde decided resistance was hopeless and surrendered unconditionally without firing a shot. "Honor did not demand the sacrifice of blood after the terrible suffering," Lynde later wrote. In addition to the captives, Baylor acquired all the Federal's transportation equipment, arms, ammunition, commissary and quartermaster stores, along with $9,500 in United States drafts. The *Mesilla Times* headlined Baylor's victory: "ARIZONA IS FREE AT LAST."

As a result of Lynde's blundering, Union government and control collapsed in southern New Mexico, leaving Baylor in complete command of the area. The Texan proceeded to establish a semi-military government. On August 1 he issued a proclamation stating that he had taken possession of the "Territory of Arizona" for the Confederacy. The boundary for the Territory was set at the 34th parallel on the north, stretching from the Panhandle of Texas to the Colorado River in the west. The proclamation declared that Baylor was governor, the capital of Arizona would be Mesilla, and that all United States civil and military offices were vacated. On August 14 Baylor wrote Brigadier General Earl Van Dorn, Confederate commander of the Department of Texas, that he had a functioning provisional government.

Within a week of the establishment of the Confederate Territory of Arizona, a mass meeting was held at Tucson at which Granville H. Oury was elected delegate to the Confederate Congress. Oury, who was a former Texan, proceeded to Richmond, where on November 22, 1861, John H. Reagan, another Texan, introduced a bill in the Confederate Congress providing for the organization of the Territory of Arizona. This bill subsequently passed both houses and was signed by President Jefferson Davis on January 18, 1862, to take effect on February 14. The act declared the northern boundary of the Territory to be 34° north latitude, but stipulated that the Confederacy reserved the right to occupy all or any part of the former Territory of New Mexico north of that line; and the act stipulated that slavery was to be protected in the Territory. Oury then took his seat in the Confederate Congress as the official delegate of the Territory. Soon after the passage of this act, President Davis named Baylor the governor of Arizona with an annual salary of $1,500, plus an additional $500 as Commissioner of Indian Affairs for the Territory.

Baylor faced two major problems as governor of Confederate Arizona. The first was a threat from the north. Canby had gathered approximately two thousand five hundred men at Fort Craig, only one hundred and seventeen miles upriver, and rumor had it that he planned to drive the Texans out. During the fall of 1861 Baylor commenced preparations to abandon Mesilla and fall back to West Texas should Canby begin marching downstream. Robert P. Kelley, the editor of the *Mesilla Times* and a rabid Southern patriot, published a strong criticism of these preparations in his issue of December 12, intimating that Baylor was motivated more by fear than military necessity. Kelley refused to retract his statement, and the two men fought a duel. Kelley died on January 1, 1862, from the wound he received.

Even more urgent than the threat from Canby were the roving bands of Apaches who made life and property unsafe anywhere in the Confederate Territory of Arizona. Baylor's answer was to raise a group of volunteers from within Arizona, whom he designated the "Arizona Guards" and the "Arizona Rangers," consisting of thirty-five and thirty men, respectively. These units Baylor ordered to reopen the road between Mesilla and Tucson, and especially to rout the Indians from Apache Pass. However, the situation continued to deteriorate. By the spring of 1862 the Indians controlled almost every acre of land in Confederate Arizona; only in Tucson and Mesilla, where there was safety in numbers, could non-Indians feel safe. On March 20, 1862, from his home in Mesilla, Baylor wrote Captain Thomas Helm of the Arizona Guards at Tucson his proposed solution:

> You will . . . use all means to persuade the Apaches or any tribe to come in for the purpose of making peace, and when you get them together kill all the grown Indians and take the children prisoners and sell them to defray the expense of killing the Indians. Buy whiskey and such other goods as may be necessary for the Indians and I will order vouchers given to cover the amount expended. Leave nothing undone to insure success, and have a sufficient number of men around to allow no Indian to escape.

Baylor was a whole-hearted subscriber to the frontier philosophy that "The only good Indian is a dead Indian." Despite such efforts, however, the Confederates did not stop the Apache.

President Jefferson Davis decided to follow up Baylor's success in Arizona with another force which would strike northward and capture the rest of New Mexico Territory. To head this venture he chose Henry Hopkins Sibley. A West Point graduate in the class of 1838 and a regular army officer for many years, Sibley had seen service in the Mexican War and in various Indian campaigns. At the outbreak of the Civil War he was serving in New Mexico, bitter at his failure to be promoted beyond the rank of major. He resigned his commission on May 13, 1861, and hurried to Richmond, where he convinced President Davis of the ease with which all of New Mexico would fall into Confederate hands. He was commissioned a brigadier general and authorized to raise three regiments of cavalry in Texas for the purpose of conquering New Mexico, which he was then to govern. During the summer and early autumn of 1861 Sibley organized his "Army of New Mexico" at San Antonio, then marched it north and west, arriving at Fort Bliss on December 14. There he assumed command of all Confederate forces in West Texas, Arizona, and New Mexico. On December 20 he issued a proclamation to the people of New Mexico which listed the many "benefits" of Confederate rule and protection and invited one and all—Union soldiers as well as civilians—to join with him. On the same day he promulgated General Order No. 12, which stated that his proclamation was "not . . . intended to abrogate or supersede the powers of Col. John R. Baylor, as civil and military governor of Arizona." However, all of Baylor's men were mustered into the Army of New Mexico.

Pausing at Mesilla only long enough to dispatch a company of "Arizona Volunteers" westward to Tucson under the command of Captain Sherrod Hunter, Sibley moved his army northward toward Fort Craig. There Canby—who was Sibley's brother-in-law—waited, and on February 21 they fought the Battle of Val Verde. During the morning and early afternoon it appeared that Canby and the Federals would win. Sensing defeat, the Confederate general declared that he was "completely exhausted and . . . no longer able to keep the saddle." His men called him "The Walking Whiskey Keg," and there is reason to believe that he was almost an alcoholic by this time; anyway he turned the command over to Colonel Tom Green and retired to his tent. Green was a veteran of

San Jacinto and the Mexican War, and knew only one battle tactic: "Charge." This was enough, for it turned the tide of battle. New Mexican volunteers under Canby's command failed to hold their position, and the Union troops broke and ran for the protection of the walls of the fort. About seven o'clock that evening Sibley felt well enough to resume command, and his first order was to break off the engagement. Then leaving Canby and the Federals inside the fort—and astride his line of supply and communication—Sibley headed north. Albuquerque and Santa Fe fell into his possession without bloodshed, leaving only Fort Union still in Union hands. At this post, some ninety miles east of Santa Fe, were concentrated the supplies and stores for the Department, a tempting prize which Sibley determined to have. Seemingly there was no force in New Mexico capable of stopping him, and Union officers at the post made plans to destroy it and the supplies.

Meanwhile Captain Sherrod Hunter and his two hundred "Arizona Volunteers" were carrying out their orders. They arrived in Tucson on February 28 to be greeted enthusiastically by a majority of the population. Union sympathizers either remained silent, or else they slipped away to Sonora or California to await better days. Colonel James Reily, who at Sibley's orders had accompanied Hunter to Tucson, proceeded south to Sonora where he met with Governor Ignacio Pesqueira of Sonora. The Confederate officer persuaded Pesqueira to sell supplies to the Southerners, but the treaty to this effect was rendered almost meaningless by a clause which called for all payments for goods to be in gold; Pesqueira would not accept Confederate currency or bonds. News of this bit of diplomacy reached General George Wright at San Francisco, who immediately addressed a strong letter to Pesqueira warning the Sonoran to allow no rebels to cross the border. And from Fort Yuma Colonel Carleton wrote the Sonoran governor that the seven thousand Federal troops at Yuma (a gross exaggeration) were ready to aid him in expelling unwanted Confederate emissaries. Pesqueira apparently got the message, for her had no further dealings with the Southerners.

In Tucson Captain Hunter busied himself seizing the property of Union sympathizers, confiscating their mines, animals, and supplies. And he made a token show of fighting the Apache. But he kept hearing of a large Union contingent on the march from California. He detached a detail to the Pima villages on the Gila River to capture a supply of flour being collected there to feed Carleton's army when it arrived at that point. A scouting party of Federals under the command of Captain William McCleave also arrived at the Pima villages, and was captured by the Confederates. Thereby Hunter learned of the danger from the west. Carleton in the meantime had sent Lieutenant Colonel Joseph R. West with an advance party to open the road to Tucson. Hearing of Confederates in the area, West sent a detachment under Lieutenant James Barrett to investigate. Barrett and twelve men encountered a Confederate detail of some fifteen troopers at Picacho Peak, and there on April 15th was fought "the westernmost battle of the Civil War." Barrett and two of his men were killed, while two Confederates were killed and three captured. It was the Union force which broke off the engagement and fled, but despite their victory the Confederates knew their days were numbered. On May 4 Hunter ordered the retreat. On their way out of Arizona the force was attacked by Chiricahua Apaches in the southeastern part of the Territory and suffered heavy losses.

Carleton started the main body of his troops up the Gila from Fort Yuma in the middle of May. Despite dust and heat, they followed the Butterfield route to Tucson, where on June 8 Carleton issued a proclamation declaring a Federal "Territory of Arizona" and himself the governor. The boundaries of this "Territory" were the same as those set by Baylor: all of New Mexico Territory south of the 34th parallel. In Tucson Colonel Carleton asked all citizens to take the oath of allegiance to the United States, he collected a tax from the merchants of the town for war expenses (with an especially heavy levy on gamblers and saloon-keepers, to be used to care for sick and wounded Union soldiers), and he took some political prisoners. Chief among the latter was Sylvester Mowry, who had barricaded himself at his mine along with some of his employees and had fought the Apaches. Mowry had written first to the United States government asking protection, then had appealed to Confederate authorities, including Baylor, Sibley, and Hunter. Carleton arrested the former army officer and charged him with treasonable complicity with the rebels. Mowry was confined at the post he had once commanded, Fort Yuma. Then in November 1862 he was unconditionally released, but he found that his mine had been seized and stripped of its most valuable ore. Carleton then prepared to march east and link up with Canby to drive Sibley's force out of New Mexico. The job had already been done, however.

In mid March Sibley had sent a large portion of his army from Santa Fe to take Fort Union. Twenty-three miles east of Santa Fe at Glorieta Pass, this force unexpectedly met the enemy—the First Regiment of Colorado Mounted Volunteers. Governor Gilpin of Colorado had responded to Canby's call for help by sending his volunteers south under the command of Colonel J. P. Slough and the militant Methodist minister, Major John M. Chivington, later to lead the whites at the Sand Creek Massacre of Cheyenne men, women, and children. On March 26, while a preliminary skirmish was taking place, the Texans' wagon train was captured, leaving them without even their blankets. Two days later, when the major battle was fought, the Federals were driven from the field in defeat, but the Confederates had to withdraw to Santa Fe because of the loss of their supplies.

Before another attempt could be made at capturing Fort Union, Sibley learned that a Union force was marching toward New Mexico from Missouri—Secretary of War Edwin Stanton had finally heeded Canby's requests for reinforcements. From the west Carleton was marching. And from the south Canby, aware that fresh troops were coming, was moving toward Albuquerque. At a council of war the Confederates decided to abandon New Mexico. Their retreat was a series of horrors: no food, little water, disease, and harassment by the Indians. Sibley decided to hurry ahead and make his report, leaving Colonel Green to command the retreat. In June and July of 1862 the "Army of New Mexico" returned to San Antonio. They had been victorious in every engagement with the enemy, but had been defeated—primarily by poor leadership and overwhelming odds. One-third to one-half the original force remained in New Mexico, either dead or in Union prisons.

Baylor likewise was forced to withdraw, and in May 1862 he journeyed to Richmond, Virginia, where he promoted a plan to recapture the Southwest for the Confederacy. On May 29 he was authorized to raise five battalions of rangers for the purpose, Baylor to be their colonel as well as governor of Arizona. His plans were hampered first by a shortage of fighting men to volunteer for such an adventure. Few were left in Texas. Then came severe criticism from Richmond because of his Indian policy. In fact, President Davis finally removed him from office because of his "kill the Indian" policy. Baylor thereupon enlisted as a private, and as such he fought in the Battle of Galveston on January 1, 1863. Shortly before this contest, he answered his critics in a letter to General John B. Magruder, commander of the Department of Texas. He declared: "If the [Confederate] Government had the combined wealth of the world it could not purchase peace with the Indians, and in my humble opinion it would be far cheaper to board the savages (were that possible) at first-class hotels than to continue the reservation, feeding, paint, and blanket system longer. . . ." With this letter he enclosed the scalp of a white woman which he personally had taken from an Indian chief; he asked that the grisly bit of evidence be forwarded to President Davis. Later Baylor was elected to the Confederate Congress, and on March 25, 1865, just fifteen days before Appomattox, he received an appointment as colonel with authority to raise a regiment for recapturing the Territory of Arizona. By then, of course, it was much too late.

By the time Carleton was proclaiming his Territory of Arizona, on June 8, 1862, Confederate control of the area had evaporated. The Californian immediately began making plans to link up with Canby in New Mexico, and on June 21 he ordered Colonel Edward E. Eyre to march one hundred and forty-three men from Tucson to the Rio Grande. Eight days later Eyre met a party of scouts from Major Chivington's Colorado Volunteers at Cow Springs, New Mexico. Together they returned to Fort Thorn. The only casualties on the march were three men lost to raiding Apaches and one coyote shot by a nervous recruit. In July Carleton began marching other detachments toward New Mexico. At Apache Pass on July 15 one group of one hundred and twenty-six men was attacked by Apaches under the leadership of Mangas Coloradas and Cochise, but they drove off the Indians with cannon fire. Carleton himself paused in Apache Pass to order the erection of Fort Bowie in the vain hope that such a post would control the Apaches. Once at Fort Thorn, where he arrived on February 9, he began probing southward to El Paso for rebels, and even penetrated West Texas and took Fort Davis. His hastily organized military government of the "Territory of Arizona" confiscated the property of all known Southern sympathizers, then turned its attention to the Indian problem.

Like Baylor, Brevet Brigadier General Carleton—he had been promoted—instituted a ruthless extermination policy against Indians. Unlike Baylor, however, his campaign was relentless, for he had more troops. Early in 1863 one of his subordinates led soldiers to the Santa Rita Copper Mine area, and there in a battle managed to capture the seventy-year-old Mangas Coloradas. According to official army reports, Mangas was killed when he tried to rush a guard. One soldier who was present stated that Mangas was lured into camp on the pretext of making peace, that he was seized, and that General T. R. West, who commanded the troops, told the guards: "Men, that old murderer has got away from every soldier command and has left a trail of blood for five hundred miles on the old stage line. I want him dead or alive tomorrow morning, do you understand. *I want him dead.*" The next morning the Apache chief was found shot.

By mid March 1863 Carleton had four hundred Mescalero Apaches at Bosque Redondo, a reservation he had established on the Pecos River far from any settlements. Fort Sumner was erected nearby to watch over the Indians. Also at the same reservation were the Navajos rounded up by Kit Carson. While Carleton was dealing with the Apache, the Navajos had continued their centuries-old habit of pillaging and stealing along the upper Rio Grande. Carleton sent an order to the Navajo to report for transfer to Bosque Redondo or they would be treated as hostiles after July 20, 1863. A few responded, but most of them sought refuge in their usual hideouts. Carleton thereupon commissioned Colonel Kit Carson to raise volunteers and seek out the Indians. During the fall and winter of 1863 Carson tracked the Navajos to their winter homes, particularly the Canyon de Chelly of northeastern Arizona, and waged relentless war on them. Eventually more than eight thousand Navajos had surrendered—to be ordered to walk four hundred miles to Bosque Redondo where they were enclosed on a small reservation with their traditional enemies, the Apache.

While the Navajo campaign was under way, Comanche raiders took advantage of the distraction to attack supply wagons on the Santa Fe Trail. Carleton again turned to Kit Carson, who in the summer of 1864 marched eastward with three hundred and thirty-five soldiers and seventy-five Ute and Jicarilla Apache volunteers. Near Adobe Walls, an abandoned fort on the Canadian River in the Panhandle of Texas, Carson's force was attacked by an estimated one thousand Comanche warriors. Carson later declared that his men would have been massacred had it not been for the two howitzers he had brought; the firing of these cannon frightened the Indians, who broke off the engagement and fled. Perhaps the penetration of the Comanche country by a large army did some good, however, for in January 1865 Comanche chieftains came to Fort Bascom and asked for a peace treaty. Thus through the efforts of Canby and Carleton, much of the Southwest was retained by the Union, and a measure of relative peace settled over New Mexico and Arizona. But Carleton's "Territory of Arizona" was never sanctioned officially. As usual, politicians in Washington would have the last word.

Even before Carleton began his march toward Tucson—and while the Confederate flag was still flying over the Old Pueblo—a bill to create a Federal Territory of Arizona was introduced in the House of Representatives in Washington: H.R. 357, dated March 12, 1862. Charles D. Poston, after being driven from his mine in southern Arizona in the summer of 1861, made his way to the national capital where, with Samuel P. Heintzelman, he began lobbying for separate territorial status for Arizona. The reason for this move was simple: if Arizona was made a territory, then sufficient troops would be sent to the area to give the miners protection from the Indians. And as the Sonora Exploring and Mining Company was headquartered in Cincinnati, it is not surprising to find that the bill to create the Territory of Arizona was pushed through by Ohioans. H.R. 357 was introduced by James M. Ashley of Ohio, and he steered it toward a final vote in the spring of 1862.

The principal argument against the bill was that there were not sufficient people there to warrant separate organization. But with the support of John Addison Gurley, another representative from Ohio, and John S. Watts, territorial delegate from New Mexico, H.R. 357 passed by a vote of seventy-two to fifty-two on May 8. The passage of the bill in the Senate was another matter. Despite the fact that the principal backer of the bill was the powerful Benjamin Franklin Wade, Senator from Ohio, it was tabled and did not come up again for consideration until February 19, 1863. The following day the measure carried by a vote of twenty-five to twelve, and on February 24 President Lincoln signed it. The act provided that New Mexico Territory would be divided by a north-south line (approximately 109° west longitude) instead of an east-west line as Baylor and Carleton had chosen; the northern boundary was the 37th parallel, the western boundary was the California state line (thus what would become the southern tip of Nevada originally belonged to Arizona), and in the south the United States-Mexican boundary marked the limits of the Territory.

Arizona was not alone in benefiting politically from the Civil War. Nevada did even better, achieving both separate territorial status and statehood. Just as Colorado was created a territory at the outbreak of the Civil War, after opposition had disappeared with the resignation of Southern Congressmen, so likewise was Nevada. The discovery of silver in the western part of Utah Territory in 1859 and the rush that followed brought thousands of non-Mormons to the area. These newcomers did not want to be a part of Brigham Young's empire, and delegations were sent to Washington demanding territorial status to ensure law and order, which Mormons could not enforce. Then with the start of the Civil War, a few people in the Washoe District expressed Confederate sympathies. Washington officials were horrified to think that the output of the Nevada mines might fall into Southern hands, and although the "rebels" were badly outnumbered in Nevada and no real threat of a Confederate coup existed, a bill passed Congress and was signed by the President on March 2, 1861, creating the Territory of Nevada. The original boundaries were the 42nd parallel on the north, the 37th parallel on the south, California to the west, and the 39th meridian west from Washington to the east (the eastern boundary twice was moved, both times at the expense of Utah, to the 38th and 37th meridians west from Washington, respectively).

On March 3, 1863, came the first enabling act for "the State of Nevada," passed because the Republican party already had an eye on the national election of the following year. However, after the constitutional convention had completed its work, toward the end of 1863, the voters rejected the document; it called for the voters to elect state officials at the same time they adopted or rejected the constitution, and certain politicians so opposed this plan that they managed to get the constitution defeated. As the year 1864 began, President Lincoln was very much in doubt about his own re-election; also, he needed votes to pass the Thirteenth Amendment (abolishing slavery). Therefore he pushed Congress to pass another enabling act. There was strong opposition to the plan, however, for Nevada had less than twenty thousand people, while the current quota for one representative in the House was 127,381. Lincoln used the patronage power to secure the necessary votes, and another enabling act for Nevada passed in March. The next constitutional convention met in July and completed its work in a record twenty-three days. Then in order that Nevada might vote in the national election of 1864, the entire constitution was telegraphed to Washington—at a cost of $3,416.77—passed Congress, and was signed by Lincoln on October 31. On November 8 Nevada repaid the president by voting a straight Republican ticket, and subsequently ratified the Thirteenth Amendment. When opponents charged that Nevada did not deserve statehood, Lincoln usually replied that thereby he had assured the passage of the Thirteenth Amendment, and that the constitutional abolition of slavery was the moral equivalent of raising another one million men for the Union army. Critics, with reference to the election of 1864, promptly labeled Nevada "Lincoln's Rotten Borough."

While the political aspects of the Civil War lasted until 1864 in the Southwest, actual fighting had come to an end by the winter of 1862–63 everywhere but along the Gulf Coast of Texas. Part of Lincoln's strategy for ending the conflict was a naval blockade of the entire South along with the occupation of the principal port cities. In line with this policy the city of Galveston was taken by a

Union force late in 1862. General John B. Magruder, Confederate commander of the Department of Texas, immediately took steps to expel the invaders. On January 1, 1863, he attacked the island city, using a collection of river steamers and three hundred veterans of the Sibley Brigade as marines. When the fighting ended, the Texans had reoccupied the town, captured four vessels, and taken three hundred Federal prisoners. Nearby Sabine Pass (at the outlet of the Sabine and Neches rivers) did not have to be retaken; there Lieutenant Dick Dowling and forty-seven men stood off a Federal force of four gunboats and transports carrying five thousand troops, in the process capturing two enemy craft and taking three hundred and fifty prisoners.

Victory went to the invaders at only one point on the Texas coast, Brownsville, at the mouth of the Rio Grande. Six thousand men landed at that point on November 1, 1863, and Colonel Rip Ford was forced to retreat. From Brownsville the United States troops moved up the coast to occupy Corpus Christi and Indianola. Ford and the Texans took the offensive in June 1864, and by the spring of 1865 they had regained some of the lost territory. The last battle of the Civil War was fought by Ford's troops on May 13, 1865—almost two months after Appomattox—at Palmito Ranch near Brownsville. The Texans won the engagement, but from their prisoners they learned that the war was over.

Much bloodier than the battles between Yanks and Rebels in Texas during the Civil War were the encounters with Indians. The war caused many of the frontier posts which had offered protection to the settlers moving westward to be abandoned. In fact, shortly after the outbreak of the war, the western line of settlement had regressed more than one hundred miles. A Confederate conscription law, along with the fighting spirit that caused many to volunteer, had virtually depopulated Texas of men capable of halting the Indian terror. Of the approximately ninety thousand men between the ages of eighteen and forty-five in the state in 1861, more than sixty thousand saw military service, most of them outside Texas. Rip Ford's regiment had orders to protect the Rio Grande Valley from Brownsville to El Paso, while a Frontier Regiment served along the former line of Army posts that stretched across central Texas from the Rio Grande to the Red River. But by the end of the conflict no real solution had been found, and Comanches and Apaches raided almost at will in most of West Texas.

The Civil War years had a strong effect on the Greater Southwest. California profited from the high prices prevailing for agricultural and mineral products, while its industries grew tremendously. Utah, which contributed few men to the conflict, saw boom years and high profits. Nevada, Colorado, and Arizona reaped political benefit from the conflict, while New Mexico and Texas harvested bloodshed and havoc. Within the Southwest proper, only southern California saw monetary gain. Arizona paid for its separate territorial status with the lives of many citizens, victims of Indian wrath. The Civil War also marked an end and a beginning for the Southwest—the end of the period of Anglo-American occupation, and the beginning of a period of internal growth and development.

5

INTERNAL DEVELOPMENT

1863–1912

THE INDIAN WARS

As the Civil War drew to a close, the Southwest began focusing its attention inward toward developing its resources, building on a permanent basis, much as did the eastern portion of the United States in the decades following the War of 1812. Before the Civil War immigrants to the Southwest came primarily to get quick wealth—in the form of furs or precious metals—and then go elsewhere to enjoy the good life; it was regarded as a colonial area to be exploited, almost entirely dependent upon the "States" to supply the necessities of life. After the war the people came to settle, to build. But, as the frontiersmen in the East had discovered half a century earlier, they found that the native inhabitants had to be dealt with before the mines, farms, and ranches could be worked in safety. Something had to be done with the original owners of the land—on this point all were agreed; but there was no unanimity on the proper solution to the problem.

In 1849, just after most of the Southwest had come under American jurisdiction, Congress had transferred control of the Indians from the War Department to the Department of the Interior on the assumption that civilians could better understand the Indian problem than could military officers. Yet the Indian Office had made no real effort to develop a long-range philosophy for coping with the Southwestern tribes by the outbreak of the Civil War. During that conflict the Indians had taken advantage of the absence of troops to return to their old ways of looting and killing. Immediately after the war came a wave of revulsion in the East against the military coercion of the Indians, a feeling that the natives were Rousseau's "Noble Savages" who would best respond to kindness, religious instruction, and training in agrarian methods. These idealists demanded a "peace policy" toward the natives. Moreover, they wanted army officers to be deprived of the right to act as Indian agents, and these jobs to be taken over by members of the various religious denominations. When Ulysses S. Grant became President in 1869, they got their wish.

Also in transition as the Civil War came to a close was the federal policy of reservations for the Indians. In 1825 Secretary of War John C. Calhoun had conceived the idea of moving all eastern tribes west of the 95th meridian, thus creating one big reservation in the area then labeled "The Great American Desert" in geography books. When white settlers pushed across this meridian in the 1840's and found the land fit for farming, the government turned to a system of two large reservations: one in what is now Oklahoma and part of Kansas, called the Indian Territory, for the southern tribes, the Kiowa, Comanche, and eastern Apache; the other in the Dakotas, Montana, and eastern Colorado for the Sioux, Cheyenne, Arapaho, and Crow Indians. This, of course, was before the acquisition of the Southwest, and thus there were no permanent reservations for Southwestern tribes until 1859, when the Pima and Papago of Arizona were allowed to keep their traditional homelands along the Gila River, and in southwestern Arizona. After the Civil War the federal government continued the policy in the Southwest, as well as elsewhere, of creating small reservations as needed for particular tribes, restricting the Indians to as little land as they would settle for peacefully.

The government's promise of an annual distribution of presents and a regular ration of food was instrumental in persuading the Indians to sign treaties accepting reservations. To oversee the distribution of such rations and presents, as well as to represent the government, the Indian Office placed agents at each reservation. These agents by and large created more problems than they solved. Opportunities for graft were always at hand—at the expense of the Indians, of course—and corruption was rife. Perhaps even harder for the Indians to take was the ignorance and indifference of most of the agents. Appointments were all too frequently made from among easterners who had political pull; such men neither knew nor cared about the Indians' customs, and disregarded them at every turn. Then after Grant instituted the peace policy, the agents provided by the religious denominations frequently were so idealistic that they took no heed of the fact that some of the Indians were using the reservations as convenient and safe resting places between raids; when white settlers complained about raids, as was the case in North Texas with regard to the Comanche, the agents swore that none of their Indians were involved.

Also complicating the situation in the Southwest were the Indian traders. These individuals were frequently shiftless characters who disregarded the government's injunction against the sale of liquor to the Indians. Even worse, they often supplied the natives with arms and ammunition. The Indians found that they did not even mind exchanging these forbidden items for plunder taken from the settlers in raids. So the traders were supplying the Indians with both the means and the motives to loot and kill.

Another cause of the Indian wars in the West following the Civil War was the wanton slaughter of the buffalo in the decade and a half after 1865. The number of these shaggy beasts on the southern plains in 1865 was estimated at seven million, and they constituted an indispensable part of the Indians' way of life. Thousands of the buffalo were killed to feed the workers on the transcontinental railroads, but the mass destruction began when eastern tanners discovered that buffalo hides could be turned into excellent leather. Between 1872 and 1878 the southern herd was virtually

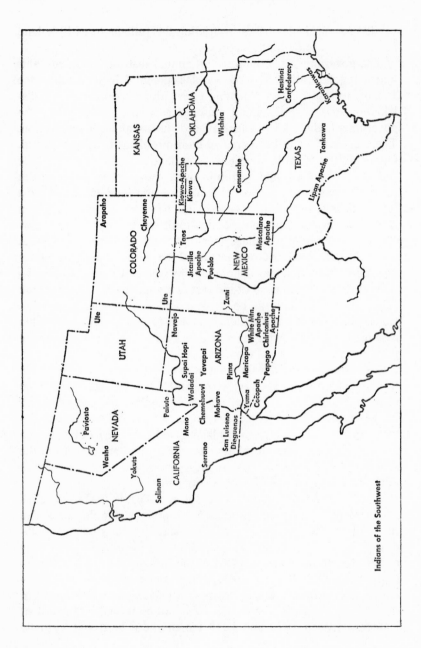

Indians of the Southwest

exterminated by parties of hunters who took only the hides and the choicest cuts of meat, leaving the rest of the animals to rot. Later the bones were collected to be ground up and used as fertilizer. In 1873 alone the Atchison, Topeka and Santa Fe Railroad shipped 754,529 hides to market. The most reliable estimates place the number at well above 7,500,000 buffalo killed. Such slaughter and waste quite naturally angered the plains tribes and sent them thundering along the warpath.

Apologists for the Indians have cited most often as the reason for their raids the relentless push of westward migration, the white settlers encroaching on lands guaranteed to the natives by treaties. This argument has validity when applied in Oklahoma and the Dakotas; the Homestead Act of 1862 guaranteed 160 acres to any adult male American, and often the whites coveted the fertile farmlands and pastures they saw inside the reservations. But in the Southwest proper, the argument does not hold. The population density of the Indians was so small, and the whites who came so few in number, that only rarely did a settler covet reservation lands or attempt to move on to acres guaranteed to the Indians. The truth is that most Southwestern tribes needed no excuse for making war on the whites. The Comanche, Kiowa, and Apache had lived for centuries by murder and theft; in the east they rode down the Comanche War Trail, which led from the Great Plains as far south as Durango, Mexico, and in the west the war trails led from New Mexico and Arizona mountain hideouts into Chihuahua and Sonora. In addition, the Comanche held a grudge against Texans dating from the Council House Fight of 1840, and considered the settlers of the Lone Star State their special enemies. The Navajo had established and enlarged their sheep herds at the expense of New Mexicans shortly after the first Spanish settlement, while the Chiricahua Apache, after the Bascom Affair, took more delight in killing Arizonans than in stealing from them.

In most of the Southwestern tribes, the livestock a brave owned was the index for measuring his wealth—and invariably his horses, mules, and sheep were obtained in raids. A warrior gained not only wealth but also social standing by his success as a thief. In addition, these tribes had accepted the Spanish-Mexican custom of scalping, making it an important part of their warfare and their method of judging a warrior's courage. A brave became a war chief of stature only by gaining a reputation as a thief and a killer. The Indians, of course, not only fought American and Mexicans but also stole from and warred with other tribes. The whites who came to the Southwest found such a way of life barbaric, and concluded that the "only good Indian was a dead one." It was a tragic "clash of civilizations." The Indians were living as they had always lived and on their own land; the whites posed for them a real physical and psychological threat. The whites, on the other hand, believed they owned the land by right of conquest and that the Indians were not making a productive use of it. Might made right in that era, and the two races appealed to the final arbiter of their age: force.

The Indian-fighting army of the post-Civil War period was trying to establish and maintain a lasting—if not completely honorable—peace in this incendiary situation. No longer were these troops a part of the Grand Army of the Republic, patriotically preserving the Union, but a peacetime force with little public appreciation or understanding. Their task was complicated by an economy-minded Congress, which, in 1866, reduced the size of the army to 54,641 men, consisting of ten regiments of cavalry, forty-five of infantry, and five of artillery; the majority of these men were stationed in the conquered South to enforce reconstruction, leaving only a small number available for fighting the Indians. The same Congress added to the problem of fighting the Indians by deciding that the army had to exhaust Civil War surpluses before ordering new materials; thus the soldiers were sent out to do battle with obsolete weapons and equipment, as well as in under-strength numbers. Their pay was small (a private received thirteen dollars a month), corporal punishment was inflicted on them (the branding of deserters and thieves was commonplace), and life was Spartan at frontier posts.

In command of this army during much of the period when the Indians were being pacified was General William T. Sherman, veteran of the scorched-earth policy in Georgia. Regarding the Lone Star State, he commented that if he owned Texas and Hell, he would rent out Texas and live in Hell. He termed New Mexico a "damned ugly elephant," and said that the price of fighting the Indians there was costing annually "more than all the country with its houses, land, cattle, sheep and people would sell for." And of Arizona he said, "We fought one war with Mexico to acquire it, and we ought to fight another war to make them take it back." Clearly he was not in sympathy with the Southwestern point of view.

In California, virtually all Indians had been eliminated or confined by the end of the Civil War. Only in the far northern part of the state would there be hostilities, Indian "massacres," and white "victories." In southern California the continuing fear was caused by depredations by tribes from the desert interior—i.e. the Colorado River tribes. Part of the chore of pacifying the Yuma, Walapai, Mohave, and Yavapai was allotted to troops in California and part accomplished by soldiers in Arizona. The Yuma, who by 1865 had been much reduced by their contacts with "civilization," were given a reservation on the California side of the Colorado River near Fort Yuma shortly after the Civil War, and there they have remained in relative peace. The Walapai and Yavapai revolted in 1871; after being "subdued," the Yavapai were sent to the Apache reservation of San Carlos, and the Walapai were removed to Colorado preserves. Finally the government set aside a tract of two thousand square miles along the bend of the Colorado River (near Grand Canyon) for them. The Mohave were given land at Half Way Bend on the Colorado, while other smaller tribes were situated near Fort Defiance. Southern California was thus early, and almost painlessly, rid of an Indian menace.

A solution in Texas was not so easy. Between the collapse of the Confederacy and the arrival of Union Troops, the frontier of West Texas was ablaze with Comanche and Kiowa raids. The state legislature voted to raise a thousand Rangers, but General Philip H. Sheridan, commanding the Division of the Missouri (which included Texas), vetoed the measure, probably fearing so large a body of recent rebels. Gradually Sheridan had the old cordon of posts across West Texas reoccupied—Forts Richardson, Griffin, Concho, McKavett, Clark, and Duncan, thus stretching from the Red River near Jacksboro to the Rio Grande near Eagle Pass. And in far West Texas, Forts Stockton, Davis, and Bliss were garrisoned once again. These moves were accomplished in 1868. In addition, the government tried to contain the southern plains tribes by the terms of treaties concluded at Medicine Lodge Creek. In

October of 1867 a presidential peace commission met with the Arapaho, Cheyenne, Comanche, and Kiowa and concluded treaties with each, guaranteeing the Comanche and Kiowa some 4,300,000 acres in the western portion of the Indian Territory. These treaties called for the plains nomads to become farmers; they would be provided with farm implements, and would receive an annual distribution of food and clothing until they learned agricultural pursuits. In return the Indians guaranteed they would cease their nomadic ways and their raiding. But while these treaties were signed by the chiefs and adhered to by the old men, the young braves did not recognize the agreements as binding and continued the old ways. The raiders did find one part of the new arrangement helpful, however. Taking charge of the Fort Sill headquarters of the Comanche and Kiowa preserve on July 1, 1869, was Quaker agent Lawrie Tatum, who did not believe in the use of force against the Indians and forbade the troops to attack them on the reservation (in which he was upheld by Washington officials). Because of Tatum and other agents like him, the reservations became sanctuaries for the braves who raided south of the Red River.

By 1871 the Comanche and Kiowa raiders were emboldened by constant success. In May of that year came the Salt Creek Massacre, in which a band of Kiowas, led by the notorious Satanta, Big Tree, and Satank, wiped out a wagon train near Jacksboro. Just a few hours beforehand, General of the Army Sherman had traveled over the road and was resting at Jacksboro; he was on a tour of inspection to see personally if the situation was as bad in Texas as the citizens had reported. Proceeding to the Fort Sill agency, Sherman had the leaders of this raid arrested and sent to Texas for an unprecedented civil trial. Satank was shot and killed while trying to escape en route to the trial; Satanta and Big Tree were tried, convicted, and sentenced to death. However, federal officials brought pressure on Governor E. J. Davis, and he commuted their sentences to life imprisonment. This incident temporarily slowed Kiowa raiding into Texas, but not Comanche raiding. Finally Agent Tatum was forced to acknowledge the guilt of his wards and called in the troops; this act brought the displeasure of his idealistic superiors, and Tatum resigned in disgust.

One reason for the increasing Comanche raids into Texas was

their need for goods to trade with their suppliers from New Mexico, usually called the Comancheros. Shortly after the treaty between New Mexican Governor Juan Bautista de Anza and the Comanche in 1786, a small trade had sprung up between the two groups. At first the New Mexicans had taken buffalo hides from the Comanche in exchange for trade goods and weapons. By the 1820's some cattle were being driven westward by the Comanche and were being accepted by the traders for sale to New Mexican ranchers. Until the post-Civil War period, however, this trade in cattle was so small as to go almost unnoticed, the bulk of the Comanche trade being in buffalo hides. But when the hunters began killing the buffalo, the Comanche turned more and more to stealing Texas cattle. As the trade increased, Texas ranchers grew increasingly bitter. When their appeals to the army proved futile, they took matters into their own hands. One cattle baron, John Hittson, secured powers of attorney from nearly two hundred fellow ranchers, gathered approximately ninety well-armed cattlemen and cowboys, and in the fall of 1872 rode into eastern New Mexico. For six weeks the party rode from one ranch to another, taking cattle with Texas brands, shooting those ranchers who resisted, and drove between five and six thousand cattle home to their owners. While the raid did not end the Comanchero trade, it certainly achieved part of the desired result; the Comanche found the New Mexicans less willing to exchange goods for Texas cattle thereafter.

In the summer of 1874 Kiowa and Comanche warriors decided to rid the Texas Panhandle of the buffalo hunters. Some seven hundred braves came upon a party of twenty-eight hunters encamped at Adobe Walls, about one mile from the point where Kit Carson had fought ten years earlier. The hunters forted up in two stores and a saloon, and with their "big fifty" buffalo guns and their superb marksmanship held off the Indians until help arrived. A month after this incident the Department of the Interior approved an army plan to punish those Comanches and Kiowas not on their reservations. The renegades had taken refuge in Palo Duro Canyon (near present-day Amarillo, Texas). There on September 27 Colonel Ranald S. Mackenzie struck with about four hundred troops; although the Comanche rallied and forced Mackenzie to withdraw, the troops did burn the village and its provisions and captured more than fourteen hundred Comanche horses. These Mackenzie ordered to be slaughtered to prevent the Comanches from stamped-ing and recovering them. While not decisive, this action did lower Comanche morale for they had thought such retreats safe.

During the winter of 1874–75 the army kept up the pressure on the renegades, following them from winter encampment to en-campment, giving them no rest. Relentless campaigning in the spring of 1875 finally brought the last of the troublemakers to the agencies asking peace. Satanta, who, through misguided philan-thropy, had been paroled from the Texas state penitentiary, was found guilty of leading some of the raids and was returned to his prison cell; there he committed suicide. Seventy-four Comanches, Kiowas, and Southern Cheyennes, the worst offenders of the three tribes, were shipped to St. Augustine, Florida, where they were im-prisoned. This Red River Campaign, as it came to be known, effec-tively ended Comanche and Kiowa raiding in Texas. Thereafter the Lone Star State suffered only from Apache raiders who were using the Fort Stanton reservation as a base for their depredations in the trans-Pecos country of West Texas and eastern New Mexico.

At the Bosque Redondo reservation, established by Carleton for the Navajo and Mescalero Apache, quarrels between the two tribes were an almost daily occurrence. So bitter was the feuding that in 1865 the Mescalero fled to the frontier, where they began raiding. They were returned by force. By 1868 the Bosque Redondo was an admitted failure, and General Sherman came to New Mexico to ne-gotiate a new treaty with the Navajo. According to this new agreement, the Navajo were permitted to return to their traditional homelands, receiving a reservation of some five thousand square miles in northwestern New Mexico and northeastern Arizona, plus a generous annual allotment from the government, aid in establish-ing farms and ranches, and funds to facilitate their transfer from the old reservation to the new one. The Navajo, 7304 in number, arrived at Fort Wingate, headquarters of the new agency, on July 23 that same year, and have remained peaceful since.

At the Cimarron agency in New Mexico were the Jicarilla Apache and approximately fifteen hundred Utes. Like the Mesca-lero, these Indians were using their reservation as a base for minor depredations both in New Mexico and Texas. In 1878 the Utes were removed to a reservation in southern Colorado, and two years later the Jicarilla were located at Fort Stanton with the Mescalero. Still another group of Apaches, known collectively as the Gileño, were given a reservation as Tularosa in 1870 at the insistence of Vincent Colyer, a Quaker member of the President's peace commission; but only about five hundred of the fifteen to eighteen hundred of these Indians came to the Tularosa agency, the others breaking into open revolt. The government attempted to placate them by locating them at Ojo Caliente. This move brought a measure of peace until 1877 when the government attempted to move them to San Carlos, Arizona; many of the Gileños went on the warpath in protest.

Victorio, the leader of the Warm Springs Apache, proved the most troublesome Indian leader in New Mexico, terrorizing New Mexico, West Texas and Chihuahua for almost a decade in the post-Civil War period. Joined by renegade Mescaleros, he and the Warm Springs Apache eluded large columns of troops for years. It has been estimated that the soldiers from Fort Davis and other Texas posts marched some ninety thousand miles in pursuit of this one leader. Finally Victorio and his followers were driven into Mexico where in October of 1880 he was trapped in Chihuahua by Mexican troops and killed. Some of his followers under Nana escaped to join Geronimo in Arizona.

Because of the scale of Indian depredations in the territory, in 1865 the district of Arizona, a part of the Department of California, was placed under the command of General John S. Mason, who came east with 2800 men. Then on April 15, 1870, the district was separated from California and made a department by itself. General George Stoneman was sent to take command. Following orders from Washington, Stoneman implemented the peace policy by establishing reservations for such Indians as would accept them and by feeding them when they did. Arizonans were enraged at this practice, believing such reservations to be nothing more than feeding stations for Apaches who were raiding and killing. On April 30, 1871, a citizen's army from Tucson, composed of approximately fifty Americans and almost one hundred Papago Indians, attacked a reservation for the Arivaipa Apache near Camp Grant, Arizona, killing one hundred and eight of the Indians—only eight of them men—and carrying off twenty-nine children into captivity. The perpetrators of this "Camp Grant Massacre," as eastern newspapers headlined it, were arrested and brought to trial in Tucson, but a local jury exonerated them at once. Westerners simply would not convict a man for killing an Indian, even though the Indian was a woman or child.

As a result of the national attention focused on the Apache problem of Arizona by the Camp Grant Massacre, President Grant sent a peace commission to Arizona. Headed by the mild-mannered Quaker, Vincent Colyer, this commission was charged with arranging treaties with the various Apache bands and getting them on reservations. Governor A. P. K. Safford reflected public sentiment in the Territory when he issued a proclamation asking the people to co-operate with the commission despite its members "erroneous opinions upon the Indian question and the condition of affairs in the Territory." One local newspaper editorialized that Arizonans "ought, in justice to our murdered dead, to dump the old devil [Colyer] into the shaft of some mine, and pile rocks upon him until he is dead. A rascal who comes here to thwart the efforts of military and citizens to conquer a peace from our savage foe, deserves to be stoned to death, like the treacherous, black-hearted dog that he is." Despite such opposition, Colyer proceeded to get some four thousand Indians onto reservations, establishing the San Carlos agency as the principal preserve for the Apaches of Arizona. When he departed, the only major tribe of Apache not on reservations was the Chiricahua tribe, still being led by Cochise.

While Colyer was at work, Lieutenant Colonel George Crook had arrived in the Territory, and on June 4, 1871, he took command of the department. A study of the situation convinced Crook that only an army capable of rapid pursuit could cope with the Indians, and he began training his men in suitable tactics, employing mules to carry provisions for extremely mobile units. Crook also concluded that the best trackers of Apaches were other Apaches, and from the White Mountain band and other relatively friendly groups he recruited Apache scouts to work for the army. But before Crook could test his theories in a campaign, still another peace commission arrived, this one headed by General Oliver Otis Howard. He likewise met local resistance, but like Colyer proceeded with his work. He inspected the military posts of the department, then arranged conferences with the Pima, Papago, and Apache. Then with the assistance of Thomas J. Jeffords, a white man who had won the friendship of Cochise, Howard met the aging Chiricahua chieftain and arranged a treaty. The Chiricahuas were given a reservation at Sulphur Springs in the Dragoon and Chiricahua mountain area, their traditional homeland. And until the death of Cochise in 1874 the Chiricahuas honored the agreement.

After Howard had made peace with Cochise, Crook was turned loose to campaign against all renegade Indians in the Territory. Crook pressed the renegades hard during the winter of 1872–73, including a striking victory on December 28 at Skull Cave, where some seventy-five Yavapais were killed. On April 6, 1873, the Yavapai surrendered at Camp Verde, by which time the remaining Apache had quit fighting—bringing a period of relative peace to Arizona. Crook was rewarded with a startling promotion from lieutenant colonel to brigadier general, and in 1875 was sent north to deal with the Sioux.

Just as Crook was leaving Arizona, and contrary to his advice, almost all the Apaches were herded together at the San Carlos agency—four thousand of them grouped where originally only eight hundred had lived. On August 8, 1874, Agent John P. Clum, a twenty-three-year-old representative of the Dutch Reformed Church, assumed charge of the agency. Using twenty-five Apaches as police and allowing the Indians to be their own judges and juries, he managed to keep an uneasy peace for three years. However, there were some renegades who refused to live at the reservation. Clum made a national reputation in April of 1877 when with his Indian policemen he arrested Geronimo and more than 450 renegades. But on August 15, 1877, Clum resigned because of disputes with army officers and Indian Office functionaries.

The next serious incident came in June of 1881, when Nakaidoklini, a medicine man, stirred the White Mountain Apache with a new religion similar to the ghost dance craze that later was introduced to the Sioux and other tribes. Colonel Eugene A. Carr led eighty-five cavalrymen and twenty-three Apache scouts to the Indian camp, arrested Nakaidoklini, and began a return march. At their encampment that night they were attacked by some one hundred followers of the new religion; in the fighting the medicine man was killed by his guard. As a result of this, Nantiatish led fifty-four followers on the warpath in July 1882. At the battle of Big Dry Wash, on July 17, twenty-two Apaches died, but only one trooper was killed. It was the last real battle between Indian and soldier on Arizona soil.

At about the same time Geronimo and seventy-five followers fled from San Carlos to Mexico to begin almost four years of raiding and pursuit. Then on July 29, 1882, a treaty between the United States and Mexico was concluded allowing soldiers of either nation to cross the international boundary when in pursuit of marauding Indians. And on September 4 of that same year General Crook returned to command the Department of Arizona. He took advantage of the new treaty to keep pressure on the renegade Chiricahua, even when they were south of the border, and by the spring of 1884 most of them had surrendered. An uneasy year of peace followed, broken in May of 1885 when some 190 Chiricahuas, drunk on *tiswin,* a native liquor, fled to Mexico under Geronimo's leadership. Again Crook sent units into Mexico in pursuit, and on March 25, 1886, Geronimo and his followers met Crook at Canyon de los Embudos in Mexico to surrender. En route to Fort Bowie, however, a wandering whiskey peddler sold liquor to the Indians, they became drunk, and Geronimo and thirty-five followers fled into the mountains. In the storm of public criticism that followed, Crook resigned his command.

On April 12, 1886, General Nelson A. Miles, a former crockery clerk from Boston who had made a reputation in the Civil War— and who had married into a family with political and military influence—took command in Arizona. Miles spent thousands of dollars on a heliograph system (which never led to a battle or any prisoners), and he organized pursuing columns. Then in the late summer of 1886, largely through the efforts of Lieutenant Charles B. Gatewood, Geronimo was induced to surrender. Miles met Geronimo at Skeleton Canyon on September 4, and the Apache wars were over. Geronimo was sent to Fort Marion, Florida, for imprisonment, along with nearly five hundred Chiricahuas. Later they were moved to the Indian Territory, and there in 1909 Geronimo died.

The end of fighting and the creation of reservations did not settle the basic Indian problem in the Southwest, however. Although the whites had won, the Indians did not simply disappear. They were wards of the federal government, and something had to be done for them. Reformers proposed that they should be made as rapidly as possible, and if necessary by force, to "take the white man's road." They were to become farmers, each family settled on 160 acres owned separately. All traces of the former civilization were to be wiped out; the Indians were to ignore their former leaders ("Every man a chief" was the government's slogan), forget their social and religious customs, and forswear the medicine man. Joining with the reformers in this movement to abolish the communal system of landholding were some western land boomers, who wanted the reservations to be broken into 160-acre parcels and what remained to be thrown open to white settlement.

The proposals of the reformers became law by means of the Dawes Act of 1887. This federal statute provided that land, generally in 160-acre lots, would be granted to individual Indians designated by the President, to be held in trust for a period of twenty-five years; such Indians immediately received citizenship, but they did not get title to their land until the passage of the twenty-five years. Such allotments soon proved too small, and eventually were subdivided into tiny plots through inheritance. Also, the Indians generally were unhappy with the length of the trial period. Therefore in 1906 came the Burke Act which stipulated: (1) no citizenship for the Indians until they got title to their land, (2) ownership of land, and thus citizenship, to come when the president thought them qualified, and (3) no intoxicating liquor to be given or sold to Indians who were not citizens. In 1924, when about half of all the Indians had bowed to the inevitable and accepted citizenship, Congress extended to all of them the title of American citizens.

Despite the idealism that motivated these acts of Congress, few people during the nineteenth century or first three decades of the twentieth had considered the Indian problem from the point of view of the Indian. Always his culture had been in conflict with that of the white invader: the Spaniard had tried to convert him, the Mexican had placed a bounty on his scalp, and the American had thought of him as something more than an animal but less than human, an impediment to civilization, a stumbling block to be removed—even eradicated—as quickly as possible. None of these representatives of white civilization had wished to allow the Indian to be himself—and by the standards of their day they were in the right because they represented "civilization." Even those late-nineteenth-century romanticists in the East who were concerned about the plight of the native believed that the way to help him was to convert him to the "white man's road." Not until the New Deal of Franklin D. Roosevelt, when the Indian Office was placed under the administration of John Collier, did official policy change. Not until this point did anyone seriously consider the damage done to the Indian's pride in the white man's attempt to eradicate his racial heritage. In 1934 the Indian Office began encouraging native crafts and customs, communal land holding, tribal government in the old way—in short, they finally allowed the Indian to be Indian; he could be a part of America, yet separate. And the American public at last came to realize the proud spirit of independence which had motivated the Indian to fight a noble but losing battle against the whites, and to recognize his many contributions to our culture. Today the tourist agencies compete with each other to show the public that the Indian culture is a unique aspect of the Southwest, a part of history to be appreciated.

THE COMING OF THE RAILROADS

The start of the Civil War had seen the Butterfield Overland Mail transferred north, and the Southwest left without commercial transportation. Running from St. Joseph, Missouri, due west to San Francisco, the new route proved satisfactory until the coming of winter, when it broke down. In 1862 the route was acquired by Ben Holladay, called the "Napoleon of the Plains" because he controlled almost five thousand miles of stage lines. He operated until late in 1866, when he sold out to Wells, Fargo and Company, which continued to buy up small lines and to maintain an efficient operation. But when the Civil War ended, stages did not immediately begin running across the Southwest again. Santa Fe was connected with Missouri by a line, and travel in California was never interrupted, but there was no service elsewhere. Finally in 1869 the

Southern Overland U. S. Mail and Express began service between Mesilla, New Mexico, and Tucson, Arizona. The following year the Tucson, Arizona City, and San Diego Stage Company completed the re-establishment of service to the Pacific Coast.

Since most people in the Southwest were accustomed to traveling by horseback, the shortage of scheduled stages was not as severe a handicap as the need for cheap transportation of freight. At the end of the Civil War, Southwesterners were importing almost everything they ate and wore and all their tools and equipment. Isolated army posts depended on contract freighters to bring in their supplies and their ammunition. Prior to the Civil War the firm of Russell, Majors and Waddell had dominated Western freighting, but it had collapsed because of over-investment in the Pony Express, a venture ruined by the opening of the overland telegraph. After the war, posts in New Mexico were supplied out of Missouri, the hauling done by contract with the government. Arizona posts were supplied by way of the Colorado River steamboats; the service on this river had been pushed as far north as Callville (now buried beneath the waters behind Hoover Dam), and freight wagons hauled the merchandise into the interior. The firm of Tully and Ochoa, working out of Tucson, at one time had wagons and teams valued at one hundred thousand dollars, and operated from Kansas City to the Colorado. But both stage lines and freighting firms were doomed when the railroad arrived.

The desire for a transcontinental railroad dated from 1845, when the scheme was first proposed, and it was greatly strengthened by the gold rush. The federal government had underwritten the cost of several surveys in the early 1850's, but no action could be taken at the time because of the sectional controversy. Then in 1862, after the Southern congressional delegation had withdrawn, the first federal charters were voted for a line to run from the Missouri River to Sacramento, California. Building from California eastward was the Central Pacific, while work from the east proceeded westward under the auspicies of the Union Pacific. The federal subsidies were generous: a four-hundred-foot right-of-way free, ten alternate sections of land for each mile of track (later doubled), and a loan of sixteen thousand dollars for each mile of track laid in level country, thirty-two thousand dollars for each mile of track in the foothills, and forty-eight thousand dollars for each mile of track in the mountains (at first this loan was considered a first mortgage, but later it was changed to a second mortgage). Construction moved slowly during the Civil War, but at the end of the conflict track-laying began in earnest. Both the Central Pacific and Union Pacific raced to lay the most track, because huge profits were being made from the construction. Millions of dollars were swindled in the process, but a transcontinental railroad became a reality; the two met at Promontory Point, Utah, on May 10, 1869, with appropriate ceremonies. While this link did not serve the Southwest, it did teach promoters how to build a railroad for a profit.

The first charter to build across the Southwest went to the Atlantic and Pacific on July 27, 1866. This line was authorized to build from Springfield, Missouri, to the Colorado River and thence to San Diego, crossing New Mexico and Arizona along the 35th parallel, and was to receive the usual federal subsidies. However, the company collapsed in the Panic of 1873, before it could really begin work. A 32nd-parallel contract went to the Texas and Pacific in 1871, to run from Marshall, Texas, to San Diego, California, and it too received federal subsidies of land and loans. In March 1872 the Texas and Pacific reorganized and three existing short lines were incorporated into it; but by 1873, when the Panic came and work was halted, track had only reached as far west as Dallas. The Atlantic and Pacific and the Texas and Pacific held federal charters, but neither seemed capable of building transcontinentals across the Southwest. But others could.

The four men who emerged as owners of the Central Pacific had originally intended only to construct that line at a profit; and, since they were merchants, they hoped thereby to dominate the trade with Nevada. The "Big Four," as they came to be known, were veterans of the gold rush who had become businessmen at Sacramento: Mark Hopkins and Collis P. Huntington, owners of a hardware store; Leland Stanford, a wholesale grocer; and Charles Crocker, a dry-goods merchant. Finding no buyer for their Central Pacific, the four decided not only to continue but also to secure a monopoly on railroading in California. They incorporated several short lines and they laid new track to accomplish their purpose.

One of the companies they chartered was the Southern Pacific, which was to build down the coast from San Francisco to San Diego; the state legislature, which the Big Four were beginning to dominate, granted them right-of-way and allowed them to collect bounties from the counties and cities.

The work of laying track was pushed rapidly, for the owners wished to reach Yuma and Needles, California, before any competitors could secure these two sites, the natural routes of entry for 35th- and 32nd-parallel railroads. Town fathers were reminded of the fact that a city not on the railroad was doomed to a slow death, and huge subsidies from counties and cities were collected by the Southern Pacific for building through them. Los Angeles, the largest city in southern California, was threatened with a "run around," and had to pay a bonus of $600,000, give the railroad a sixty-acre depot site, and deed to it the Los Angeles and San Pedro Railroad in order to get the owners of the Southern Pacific to build through it. Reaching San Diego, the line turned eastward, built through San Gorgonio Pass, and approached the Fort Yuma military reservation. There it came to a halt, blocked both by the need for a permit to build across the army post and by the fact that the Texas and Pacific had the charter providing subsidies to build across Arizona and New Mexico.

Aided by money from Fort Worth residents, the Texas and Pacific had reached that city by 1876, but again it was delayed. Huntington, as president of the Southern Pacific, was not content to wait for the Texas line to build west; without a connection eastward from Yuma, the Southern Pacific stood to make no profits from its expensive tracks to the Colorado. Therefore Huntington persuaded the legislatures of New Mexico and Arizona to grant his company a charter to build across those territories, and shortly afterward received permission to build across the military reservation at Yuma; Huntington hoped that thereby he would force the Texas and Pacific to turn over its land grants to him. On March 20, 1880, the first train reached Tucson, and track was pushed eastward by way of Lordsburg and Deming. In the meantime the Texas and Pacific had fallen into the hands of Jay Gould, well known for his railroad promotion schemes in the East. Gould had hired General Grenville M. Dodge to superintend the construction of that line westward, and

Dodge, who had built the Union Pacific, pushed at a very rapid pace. Huntington and his associates in the Southern Pacific came to an agreement with Gould whereby the two lines would meet at El Paso; the western part of the Texas and Pacific land grants were transferred to the Southern Pacific, and a traffic arrangement was made between the two companies. Congress, however, refused to endorse the transfer of the land grant, and the Southern Pacific officials thereupon decided to make their own link with both the Mississippi River and the Gulf Coast. Despite the fact that the Southern Pacific and the Texas and Pacific joined at Sierra Blanca (about ninety miles east of El Paso) on January 1, 1882, the Southern Pacific proceeded to acquire the Galveston, Harrisburg, and San Antonio Railroad, a line built from Galveston to El Paso by 1883. The Texas and Pacific acquired a line running from Shreveport to New Orleans, providing Gould with control of tracks from the Crescent City to El Paso; Huntington and associates controlled track from San Francisco to Galveston—and thus the agreement between these two companies, which included the distribution of traffic and the pooling of receipts, gave them virtual control over much of Southwestern transportation. Their only real rival was the Santa Fe, and even there Huntington and his associates had a stranglehold for a while.

In 1859 Cyrus K. Holliday obtained a charter from the Kansas legislature to construct a railroad between Atchison, on the Missouri River, and Topeka, the state capital. That completed, Holliday dreamed of extending his line to Santa Fe, New Mexico, and thus providing railroad transportation over the old Santa Fe Trail. By 1872, with state aid, he had built across all of Kansas. Easily surviving the Panic of 1873, by 1876 the company built to Pueblo, Colorado, with the aid of bonds voted by two Colorado counties. There it came into conflict with the Denver and Rio Grande, a narrow-gauge line started at Denver in 1870 by William J. Palmer, who hoped to build southward to Mexico City. Both companies needed to build through Raton Pass, and thus had to deal with Richard "Uncle Dick" Wootton.

Raton Pass was the one major obstacle on that branch of the Santa Fe Trail which ran from Bent's Fort in Colorado to Las Vegas, New Mexico. Often it took teamsters a week to make the fifteen miles through it. Seeing a potential profit, Wootton in 1865 had persuaded the legislatures of Colorado and New Mexico to authorize his building a toll road through the Pass. The following year he had completed twenty-seven miles of graded road, and from stage and freighting companies and the army he had collected fees which made him rich.

Not only did both railroads need to buy Wootton's franchise to Raton Pass, both also were anxious to extend their rails to the rich mining district around Leadville in western Colorado. To reach that area a railroad would have to build through the Royal Gorge of the Arkansas River, a narrow defile that would allow only one set of tracks. Each company won and each company lost in the fight. The Santa Fe came to terms with Wootton, tunneled two hundred feet through Raton Pass, and reached Las Vegas in June of 1879; bypassing the city of Santa Fe, the line completed track to Albuquerque in April of the following year. Meanwhile, the Denver and Rio Grande won the right to build through the Royal Gorge and reached Leadville in 1880, continuing on to Salt Lake City in 1883. An agreement between the two companies stated that the Denver and Rio Grande would not attempt to build south to El Paso, while the Santa Fe promised not to build into the Colorado mountains. The Santa Fe did build to Denver in 1887, but in the meantime it had proceeded with its ambitions to be transcontinental in size.

At first the Santa Fe had planned a 32nd-parallel route to California, but the hasty construction of the Southern Pacific across this route forestalled the Sante Fe's ambitions. Continuing south from Albuquerque, Sante Fe track was laid to Deming, New Mexico, where, by an agreement reached with the Southern Pacific in 1882, the company's rolling stock was forwarded westward to San Diego. Blocked in this direction, Santa Fe officials found another way to achieve their goal. The Atlantic and Pacific charter, providing for federal subsidies for a road from St. Louis to the Colorado River along the 35th parallel, was still good. The company was in trouble, however; it had failed in the Panic of 1873, and an attempt to reorganize in 1876 had achieved no success. Affiliating with the Atlantic and Pacific, which it would take over completely in 1897, the Santa Fe began building westward from Albuquerque

in May 1880, thereby gaining control of the ten-million-acre subsidy of the Atlantic and Pacific. Northern Arizona proved a diffi-
cult area to cross, but by August 1883 track was at the Colorado
River. Across the river at Needles, California, was the Southern
Pacific, so once again a compromise had to be reached. On August
20, 1884, the Santa Fe agreed to purchase the Southern Pacific's
Mojave-Needles line; then connections were made at Barstow
with a line running from San Diego by way of San Bernardino. On
November 14, 1885, the Santa Fe had been extended from St.
Louis to the Pacific Coast.

As each of these lines crept across the desert, mountains, and
rivers, railhead towns sprang into existence, housing the families of
the Irish, Chinese, and other immigrant workers, merchants who
sold them goods, gamblers to give them a (theoretical) chance to
be lucky, saloon-keepers to provide them with a solace from their
labors, and ladies of easy virtue. These railhead towns varied little
from the shanty towns around mining strikes or at the end of the
cattle trails; they existed primarily to separate the workers from
their pay, enjoyed a brief boom, then declined almost to nothing as
the end-of-track moved farther away. They were not as dreary and
deadly as they are generally pictured, however. As they reached
maturity each generally had fine restaurants, an opera house where
touring theater troupes or local amateurs performed, churches, and
schools within a remarkably short time. And when the track-laying
crews left, the farmers and ranchers attracted by the railroad stayed
to form a stable community.

The rest of the story of Southwestern railroading is one of building connecting lines between the transcontinentals, of constructing
short lines to outlying mining communities, and of consolidating
these conecting links and small companies into bigger systems.
The Santa Fe eventually reached the Gulf Coast, the Denver and
Rio Grande built into Santa Fe, and the Southern Pacific constructed a link northward from El Paso to Santa Rosa, New Mexico. A subsidiary of the Santa Fe built southward from Ash Fork in
northern Arizona to Phoenix to connect with the Southern Pacific
at Maricopa (near Phoenix). Eventually almost every city of any
size had rail connections with the outside world.

The cost of building these lines was tremendous—most of it

coming out of the public pocket. The railroads received very large subsidies not only from the federal government but also from states, territories, counties, and cities. For example, Texas, which owned all its public domain, gave approximately 32,250,000 acres of land, an area as large as the state of Alabama, to the various railroads, the Texas and Pacific alone receiving 5,167,360 acres. Because of the availability of such subsidies, the building of a railroad, as opposed to its operation, was a profitable venture, and an excess of track was laid. After the construction was completed, many of the lines went into bankruptcy, while those that survived did so because they had a natural monopoly and could charge excessive fees. This stranglehold which the railroads had on transportation in the last quarter of the nineteenth century and first quarter of the twentieth century lent impetus to the progressive movement and to the regulation of big business in general. However, the coming of the railroads marked the end of Southwestern isolation; they meant that the minerals, livestock, and agricultural produce could be shipped to outside markets, while manufactured goods could be brought to the Southwest within a reasonable time. William S. Oury summed up what the arrival of the railroads meant when he declared at Tucson on March 20, 1880, at the celebration of the arrival of the Southern Pacific: "The enterprise of such men as now surround me has penetrated every corner of our broad land, and we now have no frontier to which the pioneer may flee to avoid the tramp of civilized progress."

THE BONANZA YEARS OF MINING

Neither the Civil War nor the Indian campaigns appreciably slowed the quest for precious metals in the Southwest. Prospectors continued to comb the hills and search the arroyos for yellow and silver dust and nuggets while Billy Yank and Johnny Reb settled their quarrel and while Comanche and Apache raiders endangered life and property everywhere. Many of the members of Carleton's California Column and Chivington's Colorado Volunteers were experienced miners, and they brought with them their dreams of striking it rich. One of Carleton's first acts at Tucson was to dispatch a force to establish a protective garrison at Tubac so that the Sonora Exploring and Mining Company, now under the presidency of Samuel Colt, the gun-maker, could resume operations. And across Arizona Territory to the west, a gold strike was made in 1862 at La Paz on the Colorado River, creating the boom towns of Olive City and Mineral City. Once in New Mexico General Carleton gave a safe conduct pass to Joseph Reddeford Walker, a former trapper, who left New Mexico to prospect for—and discover—a bonanza of silver on Lynx Creek, the Big Bug, Agua Fria, and Turkey Creek in northern Arizona. The Walker Mining District sprang up as a result, and General Carleton ordered Fort Whipple to be established nearby to protect the miners.

Another veteran of the mountain-man era, Paulino Weaver, along with A. H. Peeples and Jack Swilling, pushed almost directly east from La Paz, Arizona, to make a fabulous discovery of gold at Antelope Hill in the Weaver Mountains early in 1863. Their strike was said to be the richest placer ever found in Arizona, and was called, appropriately, Rich Hill. Within the space of three months some $100,000 worth of gold nuggets, varying in size from a speck to a hickory nut, were picked up or pried out with hunting knives. Still another member of the California Column, Henry Wickenburg, upon receiving his discharge, went to La Paz hoping to join the Weaver, Peeples, and Swilling party, but arrived too late to get in on the Rich Hill strike. Setting out on his own, he prospected west of the Hassayampa River; there, according to one version of the story, he threw a rock at his mule one day and the rock split open to show gold. He staked out the Vulture claim. However, the mine was too far from water to allow placering, and he sold it for $80,000—and lost a fortune, for the Vulture yielded more than $3,000,000 in the next ten years.

The next real discovery in Arizona to create widespread excitement was the Silver King. Found in 1873, east of Picket Post Mountain, by four farmers from the town of Florence, the ore was almost virgin silver and could easily be pounded flat like lead. James Barney, a Yuma merchant, eventually acquired control of the mine, incorporated it under the laws of California in 1877, and by 1886 had extracted more than $6,000,000 in silver from it. The company paid over $1,500,000 in dividends, and its stock was one of the few Arizona mines regularly quoted on the San Francisco Exchange.

It was during this period that one of the most famous mining districts in Western history, certainly the most famous in Arizona, was discovered. In 1877 Ed Schieffelin, the son of a forty-niner who had prospected in Oregon, Nevada, Utah, Idaho, and California, came to southeastern Arizona to do some assessment work on the Brunckow Mine, filed in 1857 by Fred Brunckow who had died before he could develop it. Schieffelin found some promising ore samples in the vicinity and staked out a few claims. Then he went north to Mohave County to see his brother Al, hoping to interest him in the venture. Al was very reluctant, and joined his brother only after Richard Gird, an assayer and scientist of note, had checked Ed's samples, found them rich, and was eager himself to go south with them. The three agreed to split whatever they found equally. On their way to the San Pedro Valley they stopped in Tucson to see John S. Vosburg, a gun dealer in the Old Pueblo who was always ready to grubstake a good prospect. Vosburg was also a fast friend of former governor A. P. K. Safford, who had financial connections in the East. Vosburg furnished them supplies worth three hundred dollars.

Slipping out of town after dark to avoid being followed, the three made their way to the site where Ed had found the rich samples, but discovered nothing. However, after weeks of searching, they found what they were looking for, and staked out ten claims. They obtained the necessary financing through Vosburg and Safford, erected a stamp mill, and began operations. When the first bar of bullion was poured from the mill, the company they had formed immediately declared a dividend of fifty thousand dollars a month, a dividend that was paid continuously for the next twenty-seven months. Eventually the Schieffelins and Gird sold their interest to the Corbin Brothers of Connecticut.

The news of this strike at Tombstone caused the traditional rush, and within three years the town population was estimated to be ten to fifteen thousand people. Since the area was one of hard-rock mining, the majority of these men were laborers for the big companies that owned the mines; a ten-hour shift underground left little time or energy for gunfighting, gambling, and excessive drinking, although the town had its share of all three. Racketeers, gunmen, rustlers, and petty thieves from all over the West hurried to Tombstone. But their influence has been magnified out of true perspective—these were the parasites, not the heroes of Tombstone. They attracted no capital to the area; they did not cause the railroad to build through southern Arizona; nor did they contribute to a stable economy. They were thugs who did nothing for Tombstone or Arizona; the Earps, the Clantons, Johnny Ringo, and Curly Bill contributed far less than the miners who worked in the tunnels below ground, for the discovery of the Tombstone mines and the bullion that came from them helped pull Arizona out of an economic slump, attracted farmers and ranchers to the area, and contributed to the stable growth of the region.

But the bonanza did not last. In 1882 the output of the mines was five and a quarter million dollars, the zenith of production. The following year the mines began to flood as they approached the five-hundred-foot depth. Expensive pumping systems did not do the job. This, coupled with fires and labor difficulties, almost brought a halt to mining. Then came the disastrous fall in the price of silver after 1893. In 1901 new pumps were installed and for several years did their job. After 1909, however, production was at an end. Tombstone, a "town too tough to die," was left as a tourist center, but from the ground in the vicinity had come precious metal estimated at more than eighty million dollars. In the 1880's silver was discovered in other parts of Arizona—the Bradshaw Mountains, the Patagonias—but there would never be another Tombstone.

New Mexico also shared in the post-Civil War mining boom. Gold was discovered at the Pinos Altos mines in the Black Range (in the southwestern part of the Territory). The Pacific Queen, which had thirty-one stamps in operation, grossed $250,000 during the winter of 1867–68, and an estimated three million dollars would come from it in the next thirty years. Nearby in 1869 came a silver strike, giving rise to Silver City, Georgetown, and Shakespeare (Ralston). In 1881 in the Black Range the Percha District was opened, as was Lake Valley nearby. Some of these mines produced ore so rich that it was sent directly to the mint; one chunk of silver valued at seven thousand dollars was placed on exhibit at the

Denver Exposition of 1882. The American claim was located by Billy Gill, who, with the aid of a mule and an *arrastra*, ground out a fortune for himself. In northern New Mexico there also was activity. On the west side of Mount Baldy in 1866 a prospector found placer gold, and soon Elizabethtown boomed. A ditch was constructed to bring water from the Red River, forty-one miles away, and expensive machinery was installed. When the placers were exhausted, all was abandoned, and today Elizabethtown belongs only to ghosts and its machinery quietly rusts away. At the nearby town of Golden a half million dollars was spent to bring water from the Sandia Mountains; it too had its moment of glory, but is survived only by a quiet, sleepy village of farmers.

From the end of the Civil War to 1893 silver was the glamour metal, although gold held its own. From 1867 to 1873 the price of silver was $1.29 an ounce, at a ratio of sixteen to one with gold, which was priced at $20.64 an ounce. Then in 1873 the government stopped minting silver dollars, and the price dropped. Five years later, in 1878, came the Bland-Allison Act which provided for a government purchasing program of silver, a program that was doubled in 1890 by the Sherman Silver Purchase Act. When the Sherman Act was repealed in 1893, however, the price of silver dropped to sixty-four cents an ounce, and marginal mines were closed all over the West. These same three decades after 1865 saw United States currency actually appreciating in value, causing the birth of the Greenback party and aiding in the growth of the Populist party. The Panic of 1893, coupled with the repeal of the Sherman Silver Purchase Act, brought the hard times that spawned the political career of William Jennings Bryan. The end of this depression and period of monetary appreciation came with the discovery of huge deposits of gold in Colorado and Nevada.

During the quarter of a century following the end of the Civil War, Colorado had enjoyed several mining booms that made towns flourish—and sometimes die—almost overnight. The resulting population and wealth, coupled with the political necessities of the Republican party, saw Colorado enter the Union as a state in 1876, the Centennial State. And still the silver strikes were made, as at Gunnison and Leadville, both in 1878. The first gold strike at Cripple Creek was made in 1878, but nothing of consequence was found until 1890. At first there was no rush; only a handful of prospectors wandered into the area to file claims. Then in 1892 the rush started in earnest, and by the following year the town had a population of five thousand. Finally, in 1893, just as the Sherman Act was being repealed and the national depression setting in, the Portland and Independence mines proved their wealth. By 1910 the Independence alone had a gross output of thirty million dollars and made several millionaires. Despite extreme labor difficulties and lengthy strikes the Cripple Creek district prospered. The Florence and Cripple Creek Railroad, a narrow-gauge, was opened, and the population of the town reached fifty thousand. Between 1890 and 1953 the Cripple Creek district officially produced $412,974,848 in precious metals, 99.5 per cent of it in gold.

To the west, James Butler, a rancher in southern Nevada, tried his hand at prospecting in the spring of 1900. On May 19, while searching for his runaway burros, he found ore that looked promising. At that site the town of Tonopah sprang into existence within a year; the ore was hauled by wagon for sixty miles to the Carson and Colorado Railroad. Butler sold his interests to Eastern investors, who in turn formed the Tonopah Mining Company and extracted millions of dollars in gold. In 1902 William Marsh and Harry Stimler, grubstaked by Butler, found gold ore twenty-five miles to the south of Tonopah; the rush to this area in 1903 brought the town of Goldfield into existence. This area was developed by George Wingfield and George S. Nixon, two financiers who survived labor difficulties and the Panic of 1907 to extract millions from their Goldfield Consolidated Mining Company. Other strikes were made in southern Nevada in the first decade of the twentieth century, and the towns of Rhyolite and Rawhide had their moments of glory, along with some one hundred other towns, but the production did not last and the towns faded away.

Yet of all the metals in the Southwest, it was the ugly duckling that eventually would prove to be the beautiful swan. A table showing the value of mineral production will reveal that copper has produced more wealth than all gold and silver production combined, and stocks that once went begging at fifty cents a share later rose to fifty dollars and more each. The telephone, the telegraph, and electricity were the movers in this copper revolution; wire made of copper was used to transmit speech in 1876, and in 1882 the nation's first electric-light generating plant was opened. The total world consumption of copper in that latter year was approximately the same as was used in two weeks by the late 1950's—and the Southwest, especially Arizona—was rich in this metal.

Copper had been mined in the Southwest even before the Civil War. In fact, the Santa Rita del Cobre mine in New Mexico was the site of perhaps the earliest copper production in the United States; it was worked in the eighteenth century. That one site has remained the chief copper mining area of New Mexico, for 90 per cent of New Mexico's production is still within Grant County. As early as 1905 the value of the copper that had been extracted in the Territory was more than double the value of all the gold and silver that had been mined. By 1936 there were thirty mines in operation in ten counties in New Mexico.

The first copper mining company in Arizona was formed by Charles D. Poston in San Francisco in 1854. The Ajo Copper Company, as it was named, was organized to work the deposits at Ajo, in the southwestern part of Arizona. The ore was transported to Yuma, then shipped round the Horn to Swansea, Wales, for smelting—and still paid a profit to the owners. Eventually, however, the scarcity of water on this desert route forced the owners to suspend work, and even to allow their title to the property to lapse. Others, such as Emerson Oliver Stratton, found ore there, but, as he said, "there was no profit in copper at the time and we did not hold it [the mine]." The Ajo mine had passed through many hands by 1912 when it was acquired by John Campbell Greenway and operated as the New Cornelia Copper Company. Under his management and direction it yielded a fortune.

Copper mining on a large scale began in Arizona in about the mid-1870's. The Arizona Copper Company was organized in 1875 by the brothers Jim and Bob Metcalf, who had discovered copper croppings five years earlier in southeastern Arizona while scouting against the Apaches. When developed, their mines yielded ore so rich that it was "quarried rather than mined." By 1882, the Metcalf-Clifton-Morenci area mines had produced some twenty million pounds of copper, and a railroad was constructed from there to Lordsburg, New Mexico, to transport the output.

Hugh Jones, a prospector looking for silver near the headwaters of the San Pedro River in southern Arizona, discovered copper deposits in 1875, but was so disgusted that he allowed his title to the property to lapse. George Warren, who relocated the claim, thought so little of the future of copper that he lost it by betting on a foot race (it is estimated that he thereby lost thirteen million dollars). James Reilly later bought the claim, and in turn sold it for $1,250,000 to the Copper Queen Mining Company, which was financed by New York interests. This group hired Dr. James Douglas, a physician turned geologist, and by his genius he solved the problem of extracting paying quantities of metal from low-grade ore, which previously had prevented widespread mining; to him Phelps Dodge Corporation owed much for providing the basis of its early success. In the vicinity of that first mining area grew the towns of Bisbee and Douglas.

The first mine in the Globe-Miami-Superior area was located in 1873, but no mining began there until 1878. Within six years this mine was turning out three thousand tons of ore, and the smelter producing 7,400,000 pounds of copper. In 1904 this property was reorganized as the Old Dominion Company. At nearby Superior the Magna Copper Company's mine was first located as a silver mine, but despite the name of the location, the Silver Queen, it was never worked for precious metal. Its progress as a copper producer has been slow but sure. To the north, at Jerome, Arizona, a mine was located about 1880 and worked for precious metals, but it was not profitable, and by 1885 it had been abandoned. Others relocated the claim, but in 1888 William Andrews Clark, the copper baron of Butte, Montana, bought the property for almost nothing after a personal tour of inspection had convinced him of its potential. Clark formed the United Verde Company to develop this holding, operating it for twelve years before paying a dividend; since 1900 it has paid more than $72,000,000 in dividends. The United Verde, a subsidary of Clark's Anaconda Copper Company, has played Santa Claus to many Arizonans who bought the stock prior to 1900.

Utah had not shared in the bonanza of wealth during the first years of the mining of precious metals. During the Civil War gold and silver had been found in Bingham Canyon (west of Salt Lake

City), a rush ensued, and the rich placers were worked until the 1890's; then in 1896 the mining of copper came to predominate, with the Utah Copper Company, largely owned by John D. Rockefeller, holding the best claims and producing the largest amount of copper.

Thus during the years before the turn of the twentieth century, gold and silver no longer predominated as the metals of most value. Copper had become the giant. Arizona was producing more than 50 per cent of the nation's total output and Utah another 20 per cent. These were the years in which the electrical revolution was taking place, creating the demand for more and ever more copper. Thus the mineral riches which had first caused sizable numbers of Americans to emigrate to the Southwest continued to lure men to the region. Only West Texas and southern California failed to be enriched by mining. But because almost all Southwestern mining was hard-rock, not placer, only corporations with large resources could pay the cost of developing such operations. Little room was left for the individual prospector; he was forced to take a job as a mucker—working an eight- or ten-hour shift and bemoaning the low wages he received. The drive for unionism would disrupt the first two decades of the twentieth century, and the forces that led to unionism would produce a class of laborers ready to embrace the Progressive party's platform.

RANCHING AND FARMING

While the miners could disregard the question of land ownership and form their own codes to regulate the size of a mining claim, the ranchers and farmers were more concerned with valid titles to the acres they developed. But the question of land ownership in the Southwest was more complex than in any other part of the United States because of the Spanish and Mexican practice of granting land in large blocks. Some Spanish and Mexican grants were as large as eleven square leagues (approximately fifty thousand acres), for both these governments recognized that ranching in this arid area necessitated the holding of thousands of acres. Both the Treaty of Guadalupe Hidalgo and the Gadsden Purchase agreement obligated the United States to recognize existing land holdings—but to the American frontiersman who came West and found the best land held by a few people such holdings seemed immoral and illegal. Squatters settled on land held by Mexican grandees, while miners ripped out the mineral wealth without permission. The question of Spanish-Mexican land grant ownership in the Southwest (except for Texas, which had settled this question while a republic and which had entered the Union with full ownership of all its public lands) was not settled until near the end of the nineteenth century.

In January of 1852 a United States commission met in San Francisco to settle the California titles. Bowing to the wishes of the American squatters, this commission presupposed all titles fraudulent unless complete proof of ownership was presented. Of the 813 claims presented to it, the commission confirmed 521, rejected 273, and discontinued 19. Of those rejected, 132 appealed and 98 won a reversal. After winning approval of a grant, the owner then applied for a patent; often this was not issued until after another legal battle that might lead to the Supreme Court of the United States. Many claimants finally won, only to discover that they had lost almost everything they owned in legal fees, and the land had to be sold to cover these.

The same system prevailed in New Mexico. The Spanish-Mexican policy of granting land there had been even more lax, with the result that many titles could not be proved even though legitimate without a doubt. A great amount of fraud ensued with manufacturers of "valid titles" reaping a fortune. The most noteworthy case in New Mexico was the Maxwell Land Grant, covering 1,700,000 acres and finally approved by the United States Supreme Court. Lucien Maxwell sold the grant, which had made him the largest land owner in the history of the United States, to an English concern in 1869 for $650,000; the English syndicate resold the land, it passed through the hands of several corporate owners, and finally the litigation ended in the 1890's after the grant was broken up.

Arizona, which did not get a Surveyor-General until 1870, also had its problems. A total of 11,326,108 acres in Arizona were claimed under Spanish or Mexican titles, but only 121,187 acres were confirmed and patents issued. The largest claim, the Peralta Grant, totaled 10,467,456 acres, claimed by James Addison Reavis, the so-called "Baron of Arizona," whose claim ultimately was rejected as fraudulent and who was sentenced to jail for six years for conspiracy to defraud. Other notorious would-be swindlers included José Limantour, who in 1853 laid claim to four leagues of land that included most of San Francisco; he saw his claim approved in 1856, but two years later he was exposed as a fraud and fled the country.

Once the Spanish-Mexican grants were settled, the rest of the land in the Southwest, with the exception of Texas, was in the public domain and open to settlement according to the land laws of the United States. The Homestead Act of 1862 allowed every adult male the privilege of acquiring 160 acres if he lived on them five years and made improvements valued at one hundred dollars each year. Because so much of the West was arid, had no trees, and suffered from hot winds—and because a popular scientific theory of the time held that trees tempered the climate, increased the humidity, and perhaps increased the rainfall of the area—Congress in 1873 passed the Timber Culture Act, which provided that settlers could get an additional 160 acres by planting 40 acres of trees.

Four years later Congress again sought to remedy the aridity by passing the Desert Land Act, which provided that a settler could obtain title to 640 acres provided that within three years he irrigated the land (and paid a small sum). Finally, in 1894, Congress passed the Carey Act, which provided that each state or territory in the West could get up to one million acres if the land was "irrigated, claimed, occupied, and not less than 20 acres of each 160-acre tract cultivated by actual settlers, within ten years after the passage of this act." Not more than 160 acres could be allowed to any one settler, however. It was under these various acts that all non-Spanish and non-Mexican titles were granted and land passed from public to private ownership. Yet because of the aridity of much of the Southwest and the fact that the technology was insufficiently advanced to permit its irrigation, much of the land was left in the public domain. Only Texas, which proved very generous with its millions of acres, passed almost completely into private ownership; the Lone Star State sold its land for as little as fifty cent an acre, much to the detriment of its future citizens.

The economy of the Southwest, if mining is excluded, consisted principally of ranching and farming. The modern cattle industry was born in the triangular area between the South Texas cities of San Antonio, Laredo, and Corpus Christi. Cattle had been brought to this area by the first Spanish expeditions, had escaped, and had proliferated tremendously. These were longhorns, whose horns had actually grown longer in this brush country. When the Texans successfully gained their independence, in 1836, many Mexican ranchers who had captured the longhorns fled from the Lone Star Republic, fearing reprisals from the angry Texans, and they left their cattle to run wild. During the decade of the Texas Republic, hunters from Europe and the eastern part of the United States journeyed to South Texas to hunt these longhorns as big game, which indeed they were. Mavericks (unbranded cattle) abounded, free to anyone brave enough to flush them out of the brush and brand them. There were a few wild cattle in southern Arizona along the Chihuahua border, but only in small numbers. In California ranching was widespread in the Mexican period, but in the first days of the gold rush practically all the cattle were slaughtered for food.

Feeding the forty-niners—the population of California numbered slightly more than 100,000 in 1849, jumped to 224,435 in 1852, and reached 380,015 by the census of 1860—was a monumental task. The price of beef jumped almost immediately from five or six dollars a head to as much as five hundred dollars a head. When the California herds were exhausted, drovers from Texas and the Midwest, even from the Mexican state of Sonora, hurried to take advantage of the high prices. The first herd, driven from Texas to California by T. J. Trimmer, five hundred head, left Washington County in 1848; they were sold for one hundred dollars a head and started a stampede of Texans trying to cash in while the prices held. Sheep came from Chihuahua and New Mexico by way of the Gila Trail, and from the Midwest by way of the Humboldt Trail. Not all these cattle and sheep were slaughtered in California; many were used to stock the ranges. By 1860 there were more than three million head of cattle and more than one million sheep in California. But again, there was a divergence between the northern and southern parts of the state; sheep were centered in the north, while cattle predominated in the south. Both areas suffered greatly during the drought of 1863–64, however, and by 1870 the number of sheep and cattle had declined sharply, leaving Texas to dominate the post-Civil War ranching era.

At the end of the War Between the States there were an estimated five to six millions wild cattle in the brush country of South Texas; in the North, where industrialization had started, the workers in the cities wanted beef. The North had money; Texas was destitute following the collapse of the Confederacy. The problem was getting seller and buyer together—but no rails linked the two areas together. The problem was solved by walking the cattle to market. In the year 1866 an estimated 260,000 Texas cattle were driven northeast to the railhead at Sedalia, Missouri. Between the two points were thousands of farmers, many of whom attempted to stop or turn back the Texas cattle, claiming that the animals destroyed crops and transmitted to their own cattle the dreaded Texas fever. Yet the profits were so high that Texans continued to push northward; cattle worth six or seven dollars in Texas brought forty to fifty dollars at railhead.

In 1867 the railhead was extended westward and the town of Abilene, Kansas, established, largely through the perseverance of Joseph G. McCoy. This gave birth to the famous Chisholm Trail. Later, when the farmer's frontier pushed farther out on the plains, a new railhead was established at Dodge City, and the Great Western Trail came into being. Between 1865 and 1886—the era of the unfenced West—an estimated six million cattle were driven north or west from Texas to feed a hungry nation or to establish ranches in other states and territories. With these cattle went an estimated forty to fifty thousand Texas cowboys, taking with them their Spanish methods of handling cattle as well as the tools of their trade, likewise of Spanish origin.

The lot of a cowboy who went up the trail from Texas with cattle was not an easy one, but it was a break from the monotony of riding herd, branding and cutting, and the fall and spring round-ups of the cow-waddie who stayed at home. The typical trail herd consisted of approximately two thousand five hundred animals,

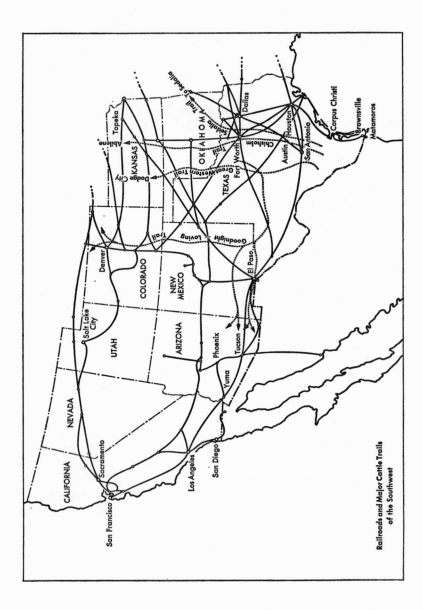

Railroads and Major Cattle Trails
of the Southwest

fifty or so horses, ten cowboys, a chuck-wagon, and cook. The cowboys' work began before sunup when they gulped down a hasty breakfast, and they worked straight through the day without lunch until the cattle were bedded down for the night, after walking twenty to thirty miles; then they had a supper of beef, beans, biscuits, and coffee. Many of these hard-working Texans were killed crossing swollen streams or lost in stampedes. For those who survived there were three months of uninterrupted work, often with only four hours' sleep at night, finished only when the cattle were sold to a buyer at Abilene or Dodge City. There they received their pay, which more often than not was squandered on whiskey, women, and gambling in the wide open, end-of-trail towns. Then it was back down the trail to Texas to work on a spread until spring, when another trail herd was gathered and the cycle started again.

When the Indians were removed, the center of ranching in Texas moved from the brush country of South Texas westward to the plains and Panhandle. Charles Goodnight and his partner, Oliver Loving, pioneered in the driving of cattle to this region; the Goodnight-Loving Trail ran to New Mexico and Colorado by way of the Concho and Pecos rivers, supplying Indian reservations and military posts through lucrative contracts. In 1876 Goodnight moved to the Palo Duro Canyon area of the Panhandle to establish, with English financing, his famous JA Ranch. By the 1880's the entire Panhandle and plains country of the Lone Star State formed one vast, unfenced range, a bovine heaven of water and lush grass that stretched from the fabled King Ranch near Corpus Christi to the XIT across the top of the Panhandle. In between were the Spade, the Spur, the Matador, the Taft, and literally thousands of other outfits.

New Mexico, with 98 per cent of its land unfit for farming, would also lean heavily on a grazing economy. Cattle had been brought to the area in 1598 by Juan de Oñate, but these animals played a minor role in the economy until after the 1860's. The Goodnight-Loving Trail proved a highway for Texas cattle after the Civil War, and the high prices paid by quartermaster officers and Indian agents, as well as by miners, soon caused the establishment of hundreds of ranches. The drives to stock New Mexico's ranges continued until about 1880, by which time almost all of eastern New Mexico was devoted to ranching. The greatest of these cattlemen was John Chisum. His range extended some 150 miles up the Pecos River, from the Texas border to Fort Sumner, and his herd was estimated at sixty thousand animals. In one year alone he marketed thirty thousand head at Kansas City.

Some of the cattlemen from Texas did not stop in New Mexico. A few, such as John Hittson, the cattle baron noted for his raid into New Mexico, moved on to Colorado, which was considered north of the tick fever line, to establish large spreads. Others continued west to Arizona, where reservations, army posts, and miners made ranching profitable. The river valleys of southern Arizona, the San Pedro and the Santa Cruz, proved a fine home for many large spreads, while in Yavapai County in the northern part of the Territory, ranching stayed after the placers played out. Among the famous outfits was the Sierra Bonita Ranch of Henry Clay Hooker, a refugee from the California gold rush who got enough money to start his spread by driving a flock of turkeys from California to the Nevada mines in 1866. On the San Bernardino land grant of forty thousand acres a former Texan, John H. Slaughter, located a ranch in 1884; only about one-fourth of it was north of the border. Slaughter would win more fame as the sheriff of Cochise County who tamed the town of Tombstone, but his ranch was one of the finest in the Southwest. The Aztec Land and Cattle Company, better known as the Hashknife, had sixty thousand cattle on its ranges in northern Arizona by 1880; lesser-known spreads included the Chiricahua Cattle Company, the Babacomari, the San Simon, the Empire, and the Redondo.

These cattle barons of the Southwest had to contend both with thieving Indians and with rustlers. Each rancher learned to fight or go broke, and lawlessness was rife for a time. The nearness of many of these spreads to the international boundary proved a source of profit and of suffering, for while cattle could be bought cheaply in Mexico the same animals could be stolen and quickly moved south of the border. "Hemp Justice" was one answer to rustling, but the founding of cattlemen's associations, both statewide and regional, did more in the long run to end the thievery through lobbying for effective legislation. And these ranchers had to contend with nature. Drought was a natural hazard in the thirsty

Southwest, and a prolonged spell without rain would ruin thousands of cattlemen; one drought in Arizona lasted from 1892 to 1895. Another threat was an unusually cold winter; the blizzards of 1886 left frozen cattle in their wake from Montana to Central Texas and contributed greatly to the ending of the open-range cattle industry.

While this phase of ranching existed, however, huge profits could be made. The open-range stockman usually owned very little land; instead he sought to control the water. The grass his cattle ate was on public land, and thus he had very little investment. With the price of beef at forty to fifty dollars a head, the profits to be made were fantastic, and legendary tales of the wealth to be had in ranching spread across the nation and around the world. In 1880 a British parliamentary committee investigated why the English market was almost dominated by beef from the American Southwest; it found that the open-range system, with its small overhead, allowed these ranchers to undersell the British stock-raisers and still make large profits. The result was a rush of investment from the British Isles in American ranching, especially from Scotland. By 1884 the foreign investors in American ranching controlled more than twenty million acres. The severe winter of 1886 brought ruin to thousands of such investors, but already the range was overcrowded and the free land was almost gone. By 1880 there was little free grass left in Texas, and by 1890 very little anywhere else.

The end of the open-range days was hastened by two inventions: barbed wire and the windmill. These two innovations brought an end to the romantic era of ranching, and ushered in the era of scientific cattle-raising. J. F. Glidden is generally credited with the invention of barbed wire in 1873, and within a decade its use had become widespread despite bitter opposition from some open-range enthusiasts that amounted to fence-cutting wars. Barbed wire allowed the fencing off not only of water but also of the best grazing lands, and it led ranchers to acquire title to the range they used. Enclosed pastures made possible the selective breeding of cattle, leading to improved breeds such as the Angus, the Hereford, and other strains. However, such breeds of cattle were not as hardy as the longhorn, which could walk sixty miles without a drink of

water. Windmills helped. Underground water was available at reasonable depths over most of the Southwest, and the wind-driven
pump brought it to the surface at a reasonable cost. The better
breeds of cattle were not capable of walking to market, but by the
time both windmills and barbed wire fences allowed the raising of
such stock the railroads had penetrated the region, providing easy
transportation to the slaughterhouses at Chicago, Kansas City, and
Fort Worth.

The sheep industry also had Spanish antecedents. The *Chaurros*
brought by the *conquistadores,* like the longhorn, was a poor-quality
animal—but hardy. Sheep were present in South Texas and in the
missions of California, but they found their best home in New Mexico. During the Spanish and Mexican periods of its history, the
Territory often exported as many as 200,000 head a year to the
interior of Mexico, this in addition to what the Navajos stole. During the California gold rush, sheep were driven westward to supply
the demand for meat. However, the Westerner never developed a
taste for mutton to any extent, and so the sheep-raisers concentrated on wool. In 1859 the purebred Merino sheep was imported
and crossbred with the *Chaurro,* producing a hardy animal that
averaged five to six pounds of wool a year. The annual wool clip in
New Mexico rose from 32,000 pounds in 1850 to 493,000 pounds
in 1860, to 685,000 pounds in 1870, and to 4,000,000 pounds in
1880. In seeking better grazing for their animals, these New Mexican sheep ranchers drove their animals into Las Animas, Huer-
fano, and Conejos counties of southern Colorado; by 1876, when
Colorado became a state, there were an estimated 2,500,000 sheep
there with an annual sale of 7,000,000 pounds of wool.

From New Mexico the sheep industry spread westward to Arizona and California. The first flock to arrive in Arizona after the
Civil War came from Cubero, New Mexico, to Apache County in
northeastern Arizona, driven by Juan Candelaria. Other sheep
ranchers joined them there, until the area north of the Mogollon
Rim was known as sheep country. The sheep industry in California
centered in the north, in Fresno, San Joaquin, Colusa, Merced, and
Sonoma counties, and the wool found a ready market in San Francisco. Soon they had spilled across the Sierra in their search for
grass, and Utah became another center of sheep-raising. By 1882

Utah had ten woolen mills, one of which was equipped with three thousand spindles. A drought in the early 1870's forced many California ranchers to send their sheep eastward into Arizona, and the arrival of Mormon settlers with their own flocks about the same time further increased the number of sheep in Arizona. These Mormons erected woolen mills at Tuba City and Sunset City. The arrival of the railroad in the Southwest proved a real stimulus to sheep ranching, for thereafter the animals could be shipped east where people liked the taste of mutton.

And in Texas the sheep industry rapidly came of age after the Civil War. In 1870 there were only 1,223,000 sheep in the Lone Star State, but ten years later the number had risen to 6,024,000. Like the cattle industry, it started in the area south of San Antonio, but it soon spread to the Edwards Plateau country of West Texas (the area around San Angelo).

The major problem of the sheepmen was their conflict with the cattlemen for grass. Almost without exception the sheepmen came into an area after it had been opened by cattlemen; this, coupled with the disposition of the sheep to eat the grass so short that a cow could not subsist on it, led to clashes, even open warfare, in places. New Mexican shepherds drove their flock onto Goodnight's JA Ranch on one occasion, whereupon the cowboys drowned four hundred of the "woolies" in the Canadian River. In Arizona the Graham-Tewksbury Feud erupted when sheep men attempted to drive their animals south of the Mogollon Rim, and twenty-nine men were killed. Gradually, however, the enmity subsided, partly because the claims that sheep were killing the range were proven false and partly because the price of wool proved more stable than that of beef and some ranchers began running both cattle and sheep, despite the ridicule of their neighbors. Also, the sheepmen banded together to form Sheep and Wool Growers Associations, which lobbied for favorable legislation.

Because of the cheapness of the land there, Texas became a mecca for many frontier farmers in the immediate post-Civil War period. The number of farms in the Lone Star State increased from 61,125 to 174,184 during the 1870's, but almost all of them were east of the line of semi-aridity that divides East and West Texas. Only in the lower and upper Rio Grande Valley was there farming on any scale; the technique of dry-land farming did not evolve until the twentieth century, and thus West Texas remained a cattleman's exclusive domain. Almost the same situation prevailed in New Mexico; the more arid portions of the Territory were devoted to grazing, while farming was consigned to a lesser role in the economy. In fact, the Spanish-Mexican developments in the field of agriculture were retarded by the arrival of the Americans, who quickly acquired possession of the available water, disregarding the Spanish water law of prior appropriation even though they enacted it into the civil code of the Territory. However, the Americans did stimulate agriculture in New Mexico in the long run, for they brought with them the iron plow and other tools, new strains of seed, and, perhaps most important of all, a different attitude toward farming, one which held the tilling of the soil to be an honorable way of life instead of labor reserved for *peones*. Then the arrival of the railroad opened outside markets, and New Mexico was overrun with immigrants seeking acres to farm. The sod-house frontier reached the Territory, along with the windmill and the small farming towns. The cattlemen fought this encroachment on their grazing acres (to which they usually did not hold title), but it was a losing battle. Yet these hopeful immigrants reckoned without nature. In wet years they swarmed across the land homesteading farms; when the droughts hit—as they always did—the land was dotted with abandoned homes and fields. Only irrigation from a permanent source of water would permit widespread farming in New Mexico.

Like its neighbor to the east, Arizona was largely a cattleman's domain during the territorial years. But in Arizona the farmers almost from the beginning did not depend on the scant rainfall but sought to irrigate from permanent sources of water. The first Americans imitated the Mexicans by digging *acequias* (water ditches) from the Santa Cruz and San Pedro rivers to the acres they put under cultivation. Also, they held scrupulously to the theory of prior appropriation, ensuring water for the farms first developed. But the widespread use of irrigation in this Territory came in an area not already settled by Indians and Mexicans. In the Salt River Valley of central Arizona an ex-Confederate adventurer named Jack Swilling noted the Ho-ho-kam Indian culture's ancient irrigation complex, which long since had been filled by dust. Forming the Swilling Irrigation Canal Company in 1867, he excavated these ditches the following year and opened the area to farmers. In the vicinity was born the village of Phoenix, and large profits were made from farming the rich alluvial soil in that hospitable climate. Crops included wheat, beans, corn, barley, garden vegetables, and many varieties of fruit, including citrus, which was introduced at an early date and which grew well in the Salt River Valley. A profitable haying industry sprang up to supply the ranchers and the army posts, while cotton was re-introduced (it had been grown and woven by the Indians long before the coming of the whites) and produced great wealth for many farmers.

Southern California proved the most productive farming region of the Southwest, however. There a mild climate, sufficient rainfall, and a rich soil joined to create a farmer's paradise. Stimulated by the high prices of the gold rush era, many of the first settlers of that region had turned to farming as a more certain road to wealth than working in the diggings. California's wheat production became legendary, and the introduction of newly invented farm machinery enabled the state not only to feed itself but also to have a surplus for export. Production of this staple jumped from 17,000 bushels in 1850 to 5,900,000 in 1860 and to 16,000,000 in 1870. Almost as spectacular was the increase in grape culture. Some vines had survived from the mission days; these were improved by the importation of foreign cuttings, and by 1863 more than two hundred varieties were under cultivation. By 1859 the yield in wine was half a million gallons, and was gaining a wide reputation for its quality. The state sought to stimulate a silk industry through a bounty system, but the brief boom ended ingloriously. Cotton likewise was in style for a brief season.

The other mainstay of the California agricultural economy developed in this period—the citrus industry. In 1857 William Wolfskill, one of the early American settlers of Los Angeles, planted several thousand trees, while Dr. Joseph Shaw, a pioneer horticulturist, was credited in 1874 with growing 75,000 young trees in his nursery. Gradually the citrus industry spread inland to poor grazing land, and with it came the introduction of the Washington navel orange, a seedless variety. By 1886 more than 2250 railroad cars of oranges were being shipped each year. Perhaps the best example of the opportunity in the citrus industry was that of George Chaffey, an engineer from Canada. Arriving in California in 1880, he and his brother acquired one thousand acres of land east of Los Angeles along with water rights in the mountains, subsequently adding another fifteen hundred acres. Concrete pipes were laid to bring water to the land, which had been considered unfit for agriculture, and by the end of 1882 they had sold fourteen hundred acres of citrus growing and had made a handsome profit. The towns developed were named Etiwanda and Ontario, and became famous for their agricultural productivity.

Chaffey left California in 1886 to undertake an irrigation project in Australia. He returned in 1898 and soon became involved in an almost fantastic project—diverting water from the Colorado River to irrigate what would be named the Imperial Valley. As engineer for the California Development Company, he completed a canal within twelve months, and by 1905 more than 120,000 acres were under cultivation. That year Chaffey sold his interests in the company for $100,000. His successors opened a new intake from the river because of silt at one of their headings, but this proved disastrous; when the Colorado next flooded, water poured loose in the valley—which in places was two hundred feet below sea level. The result was the conversion of the Salton Sink into the Salton Sea. In trying to halt the flooding, the California Development Company was bankrupted, and its assets were acquired by the Southern Pacific; at a cost of $1,600,000 the Southern Pacific managed to close the break during the winter of 1906–7 with six thousand carloads of rock and gravel. Chaffey's last project (1905–7) was irrigated farming through artesian wells; it resulted in the town of Whittier, California, just south of Los Angeles.

Everywhere in the Southwest the cry, both from farmers and from ranchers, was for water, more water. With a sufficient supply of water the desert would grow anything; without it it would remain desert. Southwestern irrigation gradually passed through three distinct stages: (1) by private individuals (by *acequias,* windmills, or other forms of pumping), (2) by canal companies (such as the one operated by Jack Swilling), and (3) by the federal government. Until the end of the nineteenth century most Southwestern irrigation was in the first two categories. Gradually, however, farmers in the Southwest realized that a permanent water supply demanded huge dams so expensive that private individuals or even companies could not afford to erect them. The Slough Reservoir, built by Mormon immigrants to the Little Colorado River area in 1886 at a cost of $200,000, was an excellent example; when floods came, as they did in 1903 and 1915, the structure washed away.

The third phase of Southwestern irrigation, that by the federal government, actually began in Phoenix in 1896. That year the National Irrigation Congress met in the Arizona capital, and during the course of the debate Buckey O'Neill made a speech favoring a national irrigation policy. Nevada's representative Francis G. Newlands favored the idea, and in 1902, after Teddy Roosevelt became president and bespoke his support, the Newlands Reclamation Act was passed; this legislation provided that the proceeds from land sales in the several states would be used to finance the construction of reclamation works. It was widely assumed that the act meant that each state of territory would receive the funds from the sale of land within its borders; in actual fact, the Southwest has received far more than its share.

Because of the report of Arthur Powell Davis, a field engineer for the federal government, the site of the first reclamation project in the West was the Tonto Basin site in Arizona (where Tonto Creek joins the Salt River). The site was chosen because Davis declared it had sufficient potential to prove a success, and thus to show what could be achieved in the West through reclamation projects. A contract for the building of a dam at the site was let on April 8, 1905. When the dam was completed in 1911, government auditors found that the cost had risen from the original estimate of three million dollars to more than ten million; however, this figure included a hydroelectric development, transmission lines to Phoenix, some seventy-six miles away, canals to carry the water to the Salt River Valley farmers, and roads to the dam site. The formal dedication of the project was held on March 18, 1911, with Teddy Roosevelt appropriately on hand to speak at the opening of Roosevelt Dam. Not until 1915 did the reservoir completely fill (the first water over the spillway was saved and used to christen the battleship *Arizona*). And in 1917 the Salt River Valley Water

Users Association was given formal charge of the operation of the dam and its canals. The 245,940 acres irrigated by the water in the reservoir was sold at $49.50 an acre, and this money, together with that brought in by the annual sale of water, has now repaid the federal government for the cost of building the project. The opening of this reclamation and flood control project inaugurated a federal program of dam building throughout the Southwest that would bring millions of acres under successful cultivation and which would reclaim those acres from the desert. More than this, the dam showed that man could overcome the harsh reality of nature in the Southwest to produce more than enough to feed the people living there; they could raise enough to export beef, mutton, wheat, fruit, and vegetables to other parts of the nation.

Coupled with the reclamation movement of constructing dams to store water and irrigate the desert was a drive for conservation of other natural resources and historic monuments. John Wesley Powell, explorer of the Colorado River during 1869–72, from his position as head of the Bureau of Ethnology and director of the United States Geological Survey did much to awaken the conscience of the nation about the wasteful policies being pursued. As a result the Forestry Bureau was created within the Department of Agriculture in 1890. Subsequently, Gifford Pinchot, a director of this bureau appointed by President Teddy Roosevelt, took the lead in establishing a National Conservation Commission; as the first head of this commission, Pinchot inventoried the nation's natural resources still in the public domain, an inventory that resulted in the withdrawal of 148,000,000 acres of forest land from possible alienation, along with 80,000,000 acres of coal lands, 4,700,000 acres of phosphate lands, and 1,500,000 acres of waterpower sites. By 1939 some 217 national forests had been designated, totaling 175,000,000 acres and located in 43 states and the Territory of Alaska. Much of this conservation movement met with violent opposition in the Southwest (along with other parts of the West), but the net result has been of great benefit to the region.

At the same time that the conservationists were working to preserve natural resources, a few anthropologist-writers were calling the attenion of the nation to the priceless historical treasures of the Southwest. Adolph F. A. Bandelier, Frank Hamilton Cushing,

A. L. Kroeber, Charles F. Lummis, and Dr. Frederick Webb Hodge, to name but a few of the giants in this movement, through their explorations and subsequent publications made the nation aware of irreplaceable ethnological treasures; the result was the creation of a system of national parks and historical monuments that included Grand Canyon, the Petrified Forest, the Mesa Verde Ruins, Montezuma's Castle, the ruins at Casa Grande, the Spanish mission of Tumacácori, and a host of others. In Texas, where the federal government owned no land, the citizens of the state purchased and gave to the nation Big Bend National Park and Padre Island National Park. Today these monuments and parks are administered by the Department of the Interior, which is also striving to create national wilderness areas, so that the people of today and tomorrow can see and enjoy both natural and man-made wonders.

POLITICOS IN THE STATEHOUSE

In his *History of Arizona,* published in 1905, Sidney R. DeLong declared that the deadliest enemy of prosperity in the Territory was the politician, who regarded the people as "game to be plucked." He warned, "Citizens of Arizona, look out for the politician! Politicians are insatiable and will absorb your life-blood." DeLong had accurately assessed the feeling of Southwesterners regarding the constituted authorities—but not their attitude toward law and order itself. A distrust of politicians was prevalent, and everywhere the frontiersmen believed that conniving lawyers and judges were conspiring to free criminals on technicalities. Yet these same frontiersmen believed the American system of government to be superior to anything else in the world, and they strongly desired the protection of life and property.

Traditionally, Americans have been distrustful of their officials. They revolted against England out of such distrust, and they carried this attitude into the national period, especially in the frontier regions of the original thirteen states. Under-represented in the state legislatures, suffering from legislation passed by "Easterners," and forced to pay taxes they felt to be disproportionately high, besides being subject to officials not of their own choosing (when living in an area not yet admitted to statehood), they had no love for authority—and this attitude became a hallmark of the West.

After the Civil War the distrust of government and of official-dom was strengthened by economic factors—big business was con-spiring with corrupt politicians to reap a fortune from the "little people." In California the villain was the railroad combine headed by Stanford, Huntington, Crocker, and Hopkins—the Southern Pa-cific. It was the biggest owner of land, the largest employer, and its influence over the government of the state complete. And it was the land policies of the Southern Pacific that led to public outcries and tragedy. The Southern Pacific advertised for immigrant farmers to fill up its land, and it brought them to California at reduced rates. After they arrived, the farmers found that promised land titles were not always supplied, that the freight rates charged made it almost impossible for a farmer to make a profit, and that the company was quick to evict tenants even though the tenants had made extensive improvements. A settlers' league was formed at Hanford in 1878 to protest the railroad's claiming land in San Benito and Tulare coun-ties which squatters had developed, and whose title the company had then claimed and secured from a compliant state legislature. The upshot was the "Battle of Mussel Slough" in which the squat-ters defended their land against eviction orders being served by a United States marshal; seven men died that day, and a panel of local men serving on the coroner's jury ruled: "the responsibility of the shedding of innocent blood rests upon the Southern Pacific rail-road company." Frank Norris later captured the spirit of this inci-dent in his novel, *The Octopus,* which defended the farmers in their struggle with the greed of the railroad trust; the Southern Pacific, implied Norris, was like an octopus in that it had many arms, each strangling some segment of the economy.

In Nevada the villain was the Bank of California. In 1864 this financial concern sent William Sharon to Virginia City to open a branch. By the early 1870's he was the virtual financial dictator of Nevada mining. Opposing Sharon were Adolph Sutro, who planned to tunnel through mountains to drain off the underground water that threatened the Comstock mines, and John Mackay, whose Consolidated Virginia company found the Big Bonanza. After Sharon recklessly gambled his bank's assets on the stock market, and lost, Mackay founded the Nevada Bank of San Francisco, which in turn dominated the Nevada mining fields. Although by 1881 the Comstock mines had virtually ceased production, the "Bank Crowd," as the financiers were known, continued to control almost every facet of Nevada's economy.

In Arizona it was the mining companies themselves, not the banks, which led to a rising demand for liberal reforms. By the end of the ninteenth century the day of the individual prospector had largely passed, and the mining industry was largely dominated by the copper companies. In Colorado the same situation prevailed, but there the mining of precious metals still predominated. Yet in both Arizona and Colorado there was widespread feeling that the giant corporations were exploiting the workers, paying them only a pittance while reaping huge profits. The practice of paying in scrip money good only at company stores, low wages, company housing, and hazardous working conditions led to a move for unionization; when the mining corporations opposed union organization, the trend was toward more and more radical unions, and the miners themselves tended to become more and more liberal in their political attitudes. The most radical labor union was the Western Federation of Miners. Later its members joined the International Workers of the World (the IWW, as it was called). Both organizations believed in direct action to achieve their ends.

In Texas the discontent focused more on the desperate plight of the farmer than on any particular business. The price of cotton, the principal money crop in the Lone Star State, fell from thirty-one cents a pound in 1865 to less than five cents a pound in 1898. While total production in number of bales was increasing, total income from this source was decreasing; it seemed that the more the farmers produced, the less money they received. The price of corn likewise dropped; a bushel worth forty-three cents in 1870 brought less than thirty cents in 1894. And a bushel of wheat worth $1.07 in 1870 brought only sixty-three cents by the mid-1890's. As a result, tenant farming, as opposed to private ownership, was on the increase in both Texas and California. The farmers blamed the railroads for their high freight rates, the elevator operators for their high charges, and the flour trust for its low payments. Even "Wall Street" came in for a share of the criticism.

And everywhere there was the money problem. In 1865, in the United States as a whole, there had been two billion dollars in circulation to serve the needs of the nation. In 1890, although the population had doubled and business activity had tripled, there were still only two billion dollars in circulation. This had led to an appreciation in the value of the dollar which severely pinched the debtor class—and most of the Southwest was in this category. For example, a man who borrowed money in 1880 found that by 1890 the dollar he repaid was worth some 25 per cent more in purchasing power than the dollar he had borrowed. Everywhere in the country among the debtor class there was a cry for "cheap" money. Southwesterners in general joined their voices to this chorus gladly, calling for the "free and unlimited coinage of silver" at a ratio of sixteen to one with gold. Such a move would have stimulated the production of silver and thus would have brought a measure of prosperity to the region.

There were also social factors causing political discontent in the Southwest during the post-Civil War period. In California a hatred of "foreigners" had led to the passage of a Foreign Miners' Tax in 1850, a tax applied most vigorously against the Chinese. The builders of the Central Pacific and Southern Pacific imported thousands of Chinese to lay their track. Then when this job was completed, the workers were laid off; they moved into town and began competing for what jobs were available. Violence and repressive measures were the result. In Los Angeles in 1871, more than a thousand whites moved into Chinatown, killed at least twenty-two Chinese and wrecked the entire quarter.

The reformers in the Southwest, as well as across the nation also wanted such progressive measures as women's rights, temperance, and a host of lesser changes. But the reformers were up against an entrenched power structure which controlled both economic and political machinery. And those in control of this machinery were rife with dishonesty, reflecting the national trend of corruption (New York's Tweed Ring, the Crédit Mobilier, the Star Route Frauds, Jay Gould's Black Friday, the Whiskey Ring, and the Indian Frauds). In Sacramento both the statehouse and the legislature were under the control of the Southern Pacific, and votes were bought and sold. In Arizona, according to one account, the Southern Pacific in 1877 sent $25,000 to Governor A. P. K. Safford to be used to get a bill allowing the railroad right-of-way across the territory; after the act passed, the governor reportedly returned $20,000 to the railroad officials, stating that only $5,000 was needed to buy the Arizona legislature.

But doubtless the greatest corruption, the most flagrant abuse of power, in the Southwest occurred in Texas during the Reconstruction era. Installed by federal bayonets, a carpetbag-scalawag administration headed by Governor Edmund J. Davis nullified the constitution drafted in 1866 by the Texans and wrote its own document in 1869. That constitutional convention even discussed the division of the state into two new states so there would be twice as many offices to be filled. Salaries for all state officials were raised to astronomical heights and the disfranchised Confederates saw their taxes raised and raised again; the state's credit was used to pay for these extravagances. Governor Davis and his cronies employed a secret police force of hundreds to enforce their profiteering schemes. In the election held in December 1873, after the U. S. Congress had repealed some of the acts disfranchising ex-Confederates, the Radical Republicans were defeated. Governor Davis would not recognize the election until both the courts and President Grant had refused to invalidate it.

Under Governor Richard Coke the Texans proceeded to undo the work of the Radicals, including even those measures which were beneficial. Laws were repealed, new legislation was enacted, and in 1876 a new constitution was drafted. Compulsory education, adopted by Davis's convention, was abandoned, salaries were cut to ridiculous levels (the governor's salary was reduced to four thousand dollars), and the powers of the government were severely restricted. The constitution of 1876 (which still prevails in Texas) spelled out in extreme detail the powers of all branches of government. The legislature was to meet only every other year, on the theory that the less often it met the less damage it could do. Almost any act of the government required a constitutional amendment, thus giving the people the final say in any change. The most lasting legacy of the Reconstruction era, however, was the virtual death of the Republican party in Texas, fastening a one-party government on the state.

In the years that followed the end of Reconstruction, governors came and went, but the face of politics changed little in the next decade and a half. Terms of office were only two years, but generally ex-Confederate veterans succeeded ex-Confederate veterans every four years, doing little because constitutionally they were incapable of doing more. As the election of 1890 approached, however, a demand for progress became evident. The Progressive movement was sweeping Texas under various names. First came the Greenback party, demanding a liberalization of national money policies. The United Friends of Temperance and the Bands of Hope were agitating for prohibition. The Farmers' Alliance, founded in Texas in 1875 and spreading across the South and Midwest, finally moved into the political arena under the banner of the Populist party. A growing hatred of the railroads and big business in general was causing political and social unrest. Championing this movement for reform, but under the banner of the Democratic party, was a thirty-nine-year-old native Texan, James Stephen Hogg.

Elected on a platform that included planks opposing the abuses of big business, Hogg persuaded the legislature to enact the legislation he wanted. These reforms included the establishment of a Railroad Commission with the power to set rates and fares (it did get freight rates reduced), a law forcing land corporations to sell their holdings within fifteen years, an Alien Land Law which checked further grants of the public domain to foreign corporations (in order to get the land into the hands of actual settlers), and an act restricting the amount of bonded indebtedness a county or municipality could undertake (the state was forbidden to go into debt by the constitution of 1876). In addition, and perhaps most important, Hogg secured the passage of antitrust legislation carrying heavy penalties against combinations that conspired to restrict trade, fix prices, or limit production.

Hogg was succeeded by Charles A. Culberson, the out-going governor's personal choice. Culberson's administration saw the strengthening of the antitrust laws and lawsuits which ultimately forced a Standard Oil affiliate, the Waters-Pierce Oil Company, from the state. Although Culberson was succeeded by two ex-Confederate conservatives, Joseph D. Sayers and S. W. T. Lanham, the tone of Texas politics had been changed irrevocably by the

"Progressives." During these eight years of comparative political calm and conservative administration the Terrell Election Law was passed (1903), which provided for the nomination of political parties' candidates by a statewide primary election, and more than a dozen antitrust suits were filed, including one against the Waters-Pierce Oil Company (1906) in which that firm was ousted from the state and fined $1,623,900. By 1915 one hundred and nineteen prosecutions had been made under the antitrust laws, of which eighty-four were settled by compromise; $3,324,766 in fines were collected.

The last gasp of the Progressive movement in Texas came just prior to World War I. In the election of 1914 there emerged a remarkable character, James E. Ferguson, a native Texan who had never run for elective office. A farm boy who educated himself for the law and then became a banker, Ferguson noted that 55 per cent of the state's qualified voters were members of tenant farm families; his fact led him to enter the governor's race that year on a platform advocating a law setting the rental of tenant farms at not more than one-third of the grain and one-fourth of the cotton they produced. He also advocated better educational facilities, penitentiary reform, a system of state-controlled bonded warehouses for the storage of surplus crops, and the building of improved highways. "Farmer Jim," as Ferguson became known in the campaign, won the Democratic primary, and so was elected in the general election as a matter of course. Once in office, Ferguson redeemed his campaign pledges from a harmonious legislative session: a farm tenant bill was passed along with a rural school aid bill and a compulsory school attendance law. Re-elected in 1916 without serious opposition, Farmer Jim in the legislative session of 1917 also secured a free textbook law and an act establishing a state highway commission (to take advantage of the federal matching-aid program to build or improve roads). However, Ferguson had become embroiled in a controversy with the regents of the University of Texas, and after the legislature had adjourned he vetoed the entire appropriation for the University. Primarily because of this veto, the legislative leaders called a special session and impeached the governor, using as an excuse the charge that Ferguson had deposited state funds in his bank in Temple without paying interest to the state. Farmer Jim was declared ineligible ever to hold any office of honor, trust, or profit under the state of Texas. But the reforms he had secured were on the law books—tenant farmers were protected, schooling was compulsory and free, and good roads were being built.

In California the first Progressive movement took longer to get under way, but the same results were achieved very rapidly once the voters were aroused. There the forces opposed to Chinese immigration, the railroad and its land monopoly, and the corrupt state government were fused together by the Panic of 1873, which did not make itself fully felt on the Pacific Coast until the summer of 1877. After rioting against the Chinese in July in San Francisco, the labor groups turned to political action, forming the Workingmen's party in October. Led by Denis Kearney, and inflammatory Irish orator from the docks who recommended "a little judicious hanging" for the capitalists and monopolists, this party soon showed considerable strength. In fact, it might have dominated the constitutional convention that met in Sacramento in September 1878 had not quarrels erupted between its leaders. As it was this party held one-third of the seats in the convention. The document completed on March 3, 1879, proved to be a bundle of compromises which did not please the reformers, however. It established a railroad commission and a State Board of Equalization (to eliminate tax inequities), and it attempted to halt the inflow of Chinese, but the sum total was bitterly disappointing to the Workingmen. In the election of May 7, the constitution was opposed not only by the banks, the railroads, and other business interests, but also by the Workingmen's party. However, the rural vote carried the bill by 11,000 votes out of a total of 145,000 cast; the Granger movement (a farmers' organization) was optimistic about the railroad commission and the tax equalization features and supported the document. This constitution remains the framework of California government, though it has been altered by hundreds of amendments.

Returning prosperity in the 1880's brought the death of the Workingmen's party, along with a lessening of Granger political activity. Southern Californians remained somewhat indifferent to their state government, and periodically they revived the dream of separation from their northern cousins. In 1889 petitions were circulated and forwarded to Washington to secure the joining of Arizona with southern California to form a new state, a movement that found little favor in Arizona. California had been dominated by the Democratic party from statehood to 1861 when the coming of the Civil War brought the Republicans to power under the governorship of Leland Stanford. The Grand Old Party retained its influence until 1881, after which the Democrats and Republicans were about evenly matched, the Democrats winning slightly more often. But whoever was in office usually found a supple conscience financially advantageous and kept a hand outstretched to the Southern Pacific.

The Federal Exclusion Act of 1882 largely settled the Chinese question as a factor in California politics, and afterward there was a growing tendency to blame all the state's ills on the railroad. Even the traditional corruption in government at all levels was laid at the Southern Pacific's door. The railroad commission established by the constitution of 1879 proved ineffective—in fact, it became nothing more than another tool of the Southern Pacific, which could refer all complaints to this branch of the government. At the turn of the century there was a rebirth of the progressive movement, primarily in the major cities of the state. A Progressive party captured San Francisco's government in 1901, and the following year a "Good Government" alliance secured the adoption of the initiative, referendum, and recall in Los Angeles, finally sweeping city offices into their camp in 1909. The next step naturally was to the statehouse, but the reformers chose to make this move not through a new party but through the Republican organization.

The candidate of the reformers in the election of 1910 for the governorship was Hiram Johnson, a San Francisco lawyer who had won fame for his role in cleansing the local government there. Under the auspices of the Lincoln-Roosevelt League, a formally organized Progressive organization, the reformers had won sufficient seats in the legislative election of 1908 to secure the passage of a direct primary law. Then under this act Johnson sought the Republican nomination in 1910. Traveling twenty thousand miles by automobile, he campaigned on a promise to "kick the Southern Pacific Railroad out of the Republican party and out of the state government." Not only did he win the nomination, but he also defeated an equally liberal Democratic nominee in the November general election, carrying with him a solid majority in the legislature. The stage was now set for further reform.

Under Johnson's leadership, the legislative session of 1911 passed a host of laws. The initiative, referendum, and recall became statewide, and women's suffrage likewise was added to the constitution. The railroad commission was given sufficient teeth to make its bite felt, and to its powers was added the right to regulate other public utilities. Child labor was restricted, the eight-hour day for women became law, compensation was provided for injured workingmen, and a state system of weights and measures was established. Because of this plethora of legislation, the Southern Pacific saw the handwriting on the wall and announced publicly its retirement from the political arena. But Johnson and the Progressives were still not satisfied, and in the legislative session of 1913, after the election of 1912 had shown the public to be in favor of their program, they enacted a civil service system, created new commissions to regulate the issuance of securities, provided for water and power development along with industrial safety measures, and set standards for the living conditions of migrant workers. Johnson was rewarded for his efforts by election to the United States Senate in 1917, a post he held until his death in 1945. He left the Progressives solidly in control of the Republican party of California and of the state government, although some of the later governors were not as enthusiastic about reform as was Johnson.

From 1864, when it achieved statehood, until 1881 Nevada was dominated by the mining and banking interests. So unsavory were politics in the state that many articles were published nationally describing the scandals attending the election of United States Senators from the Silver State. Even state offices were generally filled by mining men. Because Nevada owed its statehood to the Republican party, it tended to be dominated by that party during its first years. The first governor, Henry G. Blasdel, was honest and religious, and twice (1865 and 1867) vetoed acts legalizing gambling, but in 1867 the legislature overrode his veto on this issue. The second governor, L. R. "Longhorns" Bradley, was a cattleman who survived two terms but was defeated for a third term because in 1877 he vetoed a bill reducing taxes on the mines.

Beginning in 1881 the state suffered a two-decade depression because of the passing of the Comstock Bonanza and the declining price of silver. Farmers and ranchers suffered because their local market shrank. Because of this economic squeeze, Nevadans embraced the tenets of the Greenback party, and were even in sympathy with the Populists; in 1892 the state supported the presidential aspirations of James B. Weaver of Iowa, the Populist candidate. Locally, a Silver party rose to dominate Nevada politics, their candidates sweeping every election in 1894. The rise of William Jennings Bryan and the merger of the Populists with the Democrats led to a domination of the state by Democrats for a few years after 1896, but the discovery of gold at Tonopah and Goldfield returned the Republicans to the statehouse and the legislature. Control of Nevada had merely passed from the mining men of the Comstock to the mining men of southern Nevada—with the result that very little Progressive legislation was passed in the state.

Nevada in the twentieth century has completely turned its back on almost all parts of the Southwestern heritage. When the mineral base of its economy began to falter, it chose not to seek ways of overcoming the problem of aridity. Gambling and quick divorce were approved by the legislature, and the state has become widely known for both. To secure a divorce in Nevada is ridiculously easy once one party to it becomes a Nevada citizen—which requires only six weeks' residence. A large number of hotels, motels, and guest ranches have flourished on this trade alone. Gambling casinos provide the other major source of income. Reno and Las Vegas have become neon jungles where night and day have little meaning, for the click of chips and the whir of slot machines continues twenty-four hours a day, attracting get-rich-quick hopefuls from around the world.

Utah had a unique political history among Southwestern states in that the major force there from its inception was the Mormon Church. When Utah became a territory in 1850, Brigham Young, president of the Church, became the governor. Then in 1857 came the so-called Mormon War, settled peacefully by compromise the following year. The settlement called for the resignation of Young and the appointment of a "gentile" governor, which actually took place, but for all practical purposes Young continued to govern

Utah until his death in 1877. He practiced polygamy (he had an estimated twenty-seven wives and fifty-six children), and this tenet of the Mormon Church did much to prevent Utah from achieving the statehood its Church elders desired so they could have complete self-government. Under Young and his successors to the mantle of prophet, the Mormon Church continued to colonize, not only in Utah but also in California, Arizona, New Mexico, Nevada, and even northern Mexico. Young's policies were not changed by his successor, John Taylor, but Wilford Woodruff, who became president of the Mormons in 1889, was more progressive. Woodruff noted that the prosecution of Mormons for polygamy under the provisions of the Edmunds-Tucker law of 1882 was becoming effective and having a demoralizing effect on his followers, and in September of 1890 issued a "Manifesto" officially abandoning the practice. Statehood followed in January of 1896. The voters of Utah in the first years after statehood tended to associate with the Progressive branch of the Republican party, although William Jennings Bryan and the Democrats carried it in 1896. Utah was one of the first states to adopt the initiative, referendum, and recall, making this a part of their constitution in 1900. Otherwise the Mormons tended to keep their social change within the framework of their church.

Colorado, like Nevada, tended to be counted in the Republican party, partly because the party had secured its admission as a state in 1876, partly because its historic roots were in the Republican Midwest, and partly because it was dominated politically by the mining interests. However, the demonetization of silver and the Panic of 1893 brought hardships and distress that resulted in William Jennings Bryan sweeping the state for the Democrats in 1896. Then came the Cripple Creek boom, with production reaching fifty million dollars in 1900. The return of prosperity saw the state resume its pattern of voting Republican. However, it was the Progressives who gained control of the Republican party machinery. Begining with the election of a reform slate of candidates in Denver in 1906, the Progressives sought to curb the power of the public utilities and to extend the commission form of city government to the municipalities of the state. Later the Progressives shifted to Democratic candidates when the Republican party fell back into the hands of the bosses. The Progressive momentum would carry forward until the International Workers of the World, a labor union that had its start in Colorado's mines, gave the entire movement a black eye through its reliance on direct action (translated, dynamite and other forms of violence) to achieve its ends.

Writing in 1884, probably tongue-in-cheek, about the means whereby Arizona became a separate territory, Charles D. Poston declared that the necessary votes were secured by lame-duck congressmen: ". . . there were a number of members of the expiring Congress who had been defeated in their own districts for the next term, who wanted to go west and offer their political services to the 'galoots.' . . ." He concluded by stating that "Arizona was launched upon the political sea under command of as 'Mild mannered men as ever cut a throat or scuttled a ship.' " Upon close investigation it can readily be proved that this story has little validity. Nevertheless, the impression has persisted that the Southwestern territories were governed by nothing more than carpetbaggers, defeated Eastern politicians who were given office in the West as a reward for party service and loyalty rather than ability, and who intended only to get rich and leave. Actually these appointees proved about the same as the elected officials of that part of the Southwest which had already achieved statehood—some were honest, some dishonest; some were interested in progress, some in personal profit; some were statesmen, some scoundrels. In the immediate post-Civil War years the trend was toward appointing political hacks to office in Arizona and New Mexico, but by the administration of Benjamin Harrison, and thereafter, it was to appoint only residents of a territory to office in it.

The best example of a carpetbagger in Arizona was John Charles Frémont. Almost destitute by 1878, the aging "Pathfinder" reminded the Grand Old Party of a debt it owed him from 1864, and requested office in one of the territories. The Hayes administration complied by requesting the resignation of Governor John Philo Hoyt of Arizona and appointing Frémont to the post. Frémont used his office to involve himself in numerous mining ventures, but they never paid off. He was outside the Territory more than he was in it, and he promoted several schemes to restore his fortune. The resulted howl from Arizonans brought about his recall (he said he resigned) in 1881. On the other hand, during this same period of political carpetbaggers, one of Arizona's best territorial governors, A.P.K. Safford, was in office. Appointed in 1869, this native of Vermont and veteran of the California and Nevada mineral rushes pushed through a public school law and served as ex officio superintendent of public instruction without pay, he pressed for the completion of a rail link with the outside world, and he worked for the removal of the Indian menace. When he retired from office in 1877 it was with the best wishes and the genuine regret of most residents of the Territory. Of the seventeen men who governed Arizona Territory, all but three were Republicans: between 1863 and 1912 the Democrats were in office only for the eight years of the Cleveland administrations. Most of these men were figureheads, for the governor had little real power beyond the patronage at his disposal. Those chief executives who exercised any power did so by force of personality, and generally with good results. For example, Alexander O. Brodie, who governed from 1902 to 1905 as a result of his friendship with Teddy Roosevelt, secured the passage of the Cowan Bill, which forced the secretary of the Territory (also a federal appointee) to turn over to the territorial treasury the fees he collected through his office; this amounted to approximately fifty thousand dollars annually.

During the forty-nine years Arizona was a Territory, there were twenty-five sessions of the legistature—men elected locally. Most of these legislators were content to draw their federal compensation of four dollars a day for the sixty-day session, and were more concerned with placating and satisfying Washington than in accomplishing anything solid. Before the close of the Indian wars, the military officers and their families acted as a fluid aristocracy for the Territory, and were not without influence. By 1890, however, the military had been supplanted by railroad officials and mining company officers as the most effective lobbyists, along with cattlemen and farmers. These interest groups fought each other in seeking legislative advantage. Yet the American custom has been government by compromise, of "the art of the possible," and in the long run Arizona had little to regret as a result of the interplay of these groups and interests in its territorial legislature. Nevertheless, there was a growing spirit of reform, of Progressivism, by the turn of the twentieth century, a spirit that would seek a voice in drafting a constitution for the proposed state of Arizona, rather than in legislative action as it did in California and Texas.

New Mexico alone seemed above the growing Progressive spirit. Although the Territory officially became a part of the United States as a result of the Mexican War, the *patrón-peon* system continued. The Americans who acquired *haciendas* themselves became *patróns,* dominating their workers and using the debt-slavery system inherited from Spanish-Mexican days. In each county the wealthy Latin-American families joined with a few wealthy Americans to control elections and distribute political patronage. The poverty-stricken and illiterate *peon* voted for whomever his master told him to vote. The registration of voters was unknown during most of the territorial years, and stories were rife—not always without foundation—of large landowners voting their sheep at every election. After voter registration laws were enacted, they were only lightly observed and enforced. Such a practice was not New Mexican alone; in fact, it became almost a hallmark of the Southwest: the *patrón* system carried forward in the Rio Grande Valley of Texas; in Arizona crowds of Mexican citizens were brought north of the boundary and voted in every election; and in California the same chicanery was commonplace.

As in Arizona and in other territories, the governor of New Mexico Territory was appointed in Washington. Thus most offices were filled with Republicans between 1850 and 1912, for the patronage system prevailed in New Mexico to a degree almost unknown elsewhere. Contending first with the Indian menace, then with the lawlessness that gave rise to the infamy of Billy the Kid and a host of other thugs, and finally with securing statehood for an area more Latin than American, the eighteen territorial governors of New Mexico performed, for the most part, with competence if not brilliance.

Best known of New Mexico's territorial governors were L. Bradford Prince (1889–93) and Miguel A. Otero (1897–1906). Prince, a native of New York and veteran politician there, had settled in New Mexico in 1878 when he was appointed chief justice of the Territorial Supreme Court. He compiled the laws of the Territory; he was responsible for a bureau of immigration, and served as president of the Historical Society of the Territory. As governor he backed a move for statehood in 1889 that failed, and it was during his term of office that the legislature enacted the first public school law. Otero was the offspring of an old New Mexican family, although born in St. Louis. Under his leadership the Republician party was so firmly organized in New Mexico that even the appointment of a notary public in an obscure county was a matter of party patronage. A financier himself, Otero instituted fiscal reforms in the territorial government that saved large sums of money, making the territory's credit secure for the first time in its history. He supported the Spanish-American War strongly, and New Mexicans, along with Arizonans and Texans, served with distinction in Teddy Roosevelt's Rough Riders. And he worked tirelessly to end his own job by getting New Mexico admitted as a state. Finally among New Mexico's territorial chief executives might be noted General Lewis Wallace, who wrote the famous novel *Ben-Hur* while living in the governor's palace in Santa Fe, and who rode alone and unarmed to meet Billy the Kid in the hope of persuading the outlaw to end his career of murder.

Almost immediately after the final Indian campaign—the surrender of Geronimo in 1886—both New Mexicans and Arizonans were free to turn their energies in another direction, the seeking of total self-government through statehood. New Mexico called a constitutional convention in 1889, but the document produced was rejected by the voters in October of the following year. The negative reaction did not reflect a lack of desire for statehood; the document was rejected partly because it threw the weight of taxation on the small landowner, partly because the Democrats felt that they had been discriminated against in the apportionment of seats to the convention, and partly because the Catholic Church was opposed to the clause establishing non-sectarian public schools. Also, many Anglo-Americans feared the proposed constitution would allow the Latin-Americans to dominate the new state. Arizona called a constitutional convention for September of 1891. The seventeen Democrats and five Republicans who gathered in Phoenix drafted a document that was mildly liberal, and it was voted in by a majority of two to one. However, neither New Mexico nor Arizona secured its wishes in Washington in 1891. Nationally the Democrats and

Republicans were almost evenly balanced—the six electoral ballots Arizona and New Mexico would hold together might tip the balance of any election; the *Washington Post* succinctly summarized the situation with the statement, "The Times are not just now propitious for adding Democratic stars to the old flag." In addition, there was the money question then raging in the nation, and Eastern financiers feared that delegates from New Mexico and Arizona would favor the free and unlimited coinage of silver. In short, New Mexicans and Arizonans seemed a little too radical to Eastern conservatives.

By 1903 more than twenty bills had been introduced in Congress to admit New Mexico as a state, along with a similar number for Arizona. The Spanish-American War and the subsequent elevation of Teddy Roosevelt to the presidency, however, seemed to presage the admission of the two territories, for most of the Rough Riders had come from the Southwest. Yet just when success seemed within their grasp, Arizonans and New Mexicans were stunned by the strong opposition of Senator Albert J. Beveridge of Indiana, chairman of the powerful Senate Committee on Territories. After a whirlwind tour of Oklahoma, New Mexico, and Arizona, Beveridge announced that so few people in New Mexico spoke English that it did not merit statehood, that Arizona would be dominated by a few monied people. Of Arizona he said, "Arizona is a mining camp, and the bill admitting her is gerrymandered so shamefully that if the Republicans were to carry the State by 10,-000, she would still send two Democratic senators to Washington"; New Mexico, he declared, was "in a much worse state educationally, and her senators would be dictated to by certain interests." His report stated that the two territories did not deserve separate statehood—but might be joined together and admitted as one state. This prospect was horrifying, especially to Arizonans who feared domination by the more populous and agrarian New Mexico. Railroading and mining interests feared the burden of taxation would fall most heavily on them, and worked to defeat the measure.

Beveridge used his considerable powers as an orator to sell this idea, and a bill to this effect was introduced and passed the House. But in the Senate the measure was protested so loudly that it seemed dead. Then Senator Joseph B. Foraker of Ohio proposed a compromise to the effect that both territories would vote separately on the proposal and that if either rejected the measure it would be dropped. Both houses of Congress accepted the "Foraker amendment," and in November 1906 the election was held. New Mexicans voted for the measure by 26,195 to 14,735, a majority smaller than expected; Arizonans rejected it by a vote of 16,265 against to 3,141 in favor. Joint statehood was dead—but seemingly, so was statehood itself.

Enabling acts for the two territories did not clear Congress until June 1910. To the jubilation of the public in both territories, elections were held and constitutional conventions assembled. In New Mexico the election sent sixty-seven Republicans (of whom thirty-three were Latin-Americans, reflecting the old alliance between the wealthy members of both races) and twenty-nine Democrats (all Anglos); they produced a very conservative document which reflected little of the Progressive movement then strong in the United States, but which showed the truth of Beveridge's charge that a few wealthy people would dominate the state. In Arizona the story was different, however, for there a new element had been added to the pressure groups of the Territory—organized labor. Of the fifty-two delegates to the convention, forty-one were Democrats. The president of the convention was George W.P. Hunt, a banker-merchant from Globe whose principal boast was that he did not "wear a copper collar" (meaning that he was not a tool of the big mining interests). The document produced in Arizona was extremely liberal, including the initiative and referendum and the recall of *all* elected officials. The latter provision caused some apprehension, for President Taft's opposition to the recall of judges (and judges were to be elected in Arizona) was well known; the Reverend Seaborn Crutchfield, chaplain of the convention, reflected this fear in his opening prayer on the morning following the acceptance of the recall provision: "Lord, we hope that President Taft will not turn down the Constitution for a little thing like the . . . [recall]. Lord, don't let him be so narrow and partisan as to refuse us self-government."

The voters of both New Mexico and Arizona accepted the work of their constitutional conventions, and the work was forwarded to Washington. Early in August of 1911, Congress passed a joint resolution admitting the two as states, but, as expected by many, Taft vetoed the measure, stating that the recall provision of the Arizona constitution threatened the integrity and independence of the judiciary. Within a week Congress passed another joint resolution which excluded judges from the recall provision and on August 21, 1911, Taft signed it into law. The New Mexicans moved faster than the Arizonans; their elections for state offices were quickly held, Republicans winning most of them, and Taft signed their statehood proclamation on January 6, 1912. Election for state offices did not take place in Arizona until December 12, 1911, at which time the voters were asked also to approve the exclusion of the recall amendment to their constitution. This they did, and the Democrats had a landslide victory. Statehood came for "The Baby State" on February 14, 1912. After more than six decades of struggle, complete self-government had come to the entire Southwest.

6

THE TWENTIETH CENTURY

1912–1967

OIL: THE LAST BOOM

Economically the twentieth century dawned in the American Southwest not on January 1, 1901, but eleven days later. At Beaumont, Texas, on January 12, the Spindletop Oil Field blew in with a roar heard round the world. Fabulous Lucas No. 1 spurted "black gold" more than a hundred feet into the air, starting a gusher that spilled more than half a million barrels of oil onto the ground before it could be capped six days later. All previous oil wells dwindled in comparison to this phenomenon; the largest wells in existence were mere trickles compared to the dizzying spectacle at Beaumont which quickly was labeled the "Eighth Wonder of the World." Special trains were employed to bring hundreds, even thousands, of speculators who rushed to the area in the hope of acquiring leases. A feverish trading and selling of land and leases

268

ensued, spreading out around Beaumont for a radius of nearly 150 miles. Fortunes were made—and lost—overnight in the orgy of speculation that followed: one man, flipping through a roll of one hundred dollar bills, came across a ten spot, which he tore up with the comment, "Small change, what are you doing here?" Soon more than a hundred other wells were spudded in near by, and before the end of the year the Spindletop field had produced more than 3,500,000 barrels—with the result that the price of oil dropped to three cents a barrel.

The following year came the opening of the Sour Lake and Batson fields (near Houston), and production soared to more than seventeen million barrels in Texas alone. Additional uses for oil had to be found other than lubrication and illumination, the chief uses of petroleum at that time. Because oil suddenly had become so cheap, railroad executives were persuaded to convert locomotives to oil for power; by July 31, 1901, the Southern Pacific had begun converting all locomotives in its Atlantic Division to this source of power. Next came steamships, which also could easily be converted. Indeed, in almost every way that coal had been used, it was found that oil likewise would serve—and on the Gulf Coast oil was much cheaper. The American Brewery Company of Houston converted its coal-burning boilers to oil; the Star Flour Milling Company of Galveston began operating its fifty-horsepower milling machine with oil in 1901. Tankers began carrying Texas crude oil to other parts of the world, and by 1902 a Texas geologist, Robert T. Hill, could write that oil from the Lone Star State was "burning in Germany, England, Cuba, Mexico, New York, and Philadelphia. By its energy steamers are being propelled across the ocean, trains are hastening across the continent, electricity generated and artificial ice frozen in New York, ores ground and stamped in Mexico, Portland cement manufactured in Havana, and gas enriched in Philadelphia." Markets had been found. To capitalize on the boom giant petroleum corporations were formed: the Texas Company (Texaco), the Gulf Refining Company of Texas, the Magnolia Petroleum Company (Mobil), and, after the opening of the Humble field near Houston, the Humble Oil and Refining Company (Enco). Refineries were built along the Gulf Coast from Beaumont to Houston and inland at Fort Worth, Dallas, and San Antonio.

The techniques and knowledge growing out of the initial discoveries led to drilling in other parts of Texas, Louisiana, and Oklahoma. In the Lone Star State came discovery after discovery. The Petrolia field was opened in 1904. That same year came the Electra field near Wichita Falls; cattleman W. T. Waggoner, while drilling a water well, hit oil that would make him wealthy almost beyond measure, but all the rest of his life he deplored the discovery as "unfortunate," claiming that it had ruined his ranch. In the second decade of the twentieth century the Ranger field (1917), the Burkburnett field (1919), and the Mexia field (1920) were opened, and still the pace continued. In 1923 the Big Lake field in West Texas was opened, in 1924–25 the Wortham field, and in 1926 the Borger field, in the Panhandle. Natural gas was found in abundance in the Panhandle in 1918, one well alone producing 107,000,000 cubic feet per day. Soon the Permian Basin of West Texas was covered with wells, the existing towns were transformed into cities, and new settlements numbered thousands of residents almost overnight. Colorado City, Big Spring, Midland, Odessa, Pecos, Amarillo, Borger, and dozens of other towns became known throughout the nation as oil boomtowns. In 1928 Texas for the first time led all other states in the volume of oil pumped from the earth—256,888,000 barrels.

But the greatest discovery was still ahead. C. M. "Dad" Joiner, a wildcatter who had moved to Texas in 1927 and had secured leases in the eastern portion of the state, drilled two dry holes before striking it rich on his third try, a venture he had financed by selling shares of stock to anyone who would buy and at almost any price. The boom he started in 1930 resulted in more than nine thousand wells being drilled, wells that by 1938 had produced almost a billion and a quarter barrels of oil. This output reduced the price of oil nationally to eight cents a barrel and led a special session of the legislature to give the Texas Railroad Commission the authority to enforce production restrictions. This field, added to the ones already in production, enabled Texas to produce 36 per cent of the nation's oil in 1940, an output of 493,126,000 barrels that represented 23 per cent of the world production.

Petroleum had also been discovered in California before the twentieth century, but only in limited quantities. Whale oil was a big factor in California in the immediate post-Civil War period, large fleets of whaling ships sailing annually from San Francisco, Monterey, Palos Verdes, and San Diego. Some oil was discovered in the 1860's, and two decades later small quantities of oil were found in the Puente Hills, at Whittier, and at Summerland. In the 1890's fields north of the Tehachapi Range were opened, and by 1900 production was estimated at four million barrels. This early period saw the founding of what would become the Union Oil Company; the Pacific Coast Oil Company, which would become a Standard Oil affiliate; and the California Petroleum Company, later a subsidiary of the Texas Company. It was also during that period that E. L. Doheny, who was to become the giant of the California industry, induced the Santa Fe Railroad to experiment with oil to power its locomotives, leading to additional companies to find uses for petroleum.

By 1914, through extended drilling in the proven fields, oil production in California, had jumped to an annual output of 104,-000,000 barrels. Then in the aftermath of World War I strikes were made that pushed California near the top of oil-producing states. In 1920 the Huntington Beach field was opened, followed by discoveries the next year at Santa Fe Springs and Signal Hill. By 1923 these three fields, all in the vicinity of Los Angeles, had brought the state's total production to 264,000,000 barrels. Refining and storage facilities were constructed in the vicinity, and the city of Long Beach boomed. In 1924 tanker ships made 1704 runs to the East Coast of the United States carrying California petroleum. California was second only to Texas in the production of oil, and natural gas was heating its homes and fueling its industries.

New Mexico has also received a large income from petroleum. The first discoveries there came as a result of the opening of the Permian Basin area in Texas; it was discovered that this geologic region extended across the state line, and drilling was begun. The first well was completed in 1922 in southeastern New Mexico, but it was natural gas that came to the surface, not oil. Oil was soon found, however, and the Permian area came to be a major producer. Since many of these discoveries were on public land, the state benefited from royalty payments; by 1938 approximately 82 per cent of the income of the Land Office was from oil and gas leases of public land. A subsequent discovery of oil and gas was made in the San Juan Basin of northeastern New Mexico, some wells producing dry natural gas alone, with the result that the town of Farmington boomed. The influx of oilmen, principally from Texas, did much to change the social character of this region of New Mexico which till then had been the domain principally of Indians and Latin Americans. Today mining is the leading economic activity in New Mexico, and the petroleum industry accounts for about 53 per cent of this activity. Production in 1958 was valued at $293,783,000.

The rapid rise in the value of New Mexico's petroleum output that took place shortly after World War II came largely because its natural gas was piped to the Pacific Coast and the Rocky Mountain West. The startling rise in California's population led to such demands for natural gas that only about 10 per cent of the demand could be met by that state's petroleum industry; so natural gas was piped from New Mexico.

New Mexico was not alone in profiting from pipelines. The flow of oil from beneath the soil of Texas also had to be transported to refineries and markets, and pipelines were a less expensive method than any other. By 1918 there were 3116 miles of trunk pipelines in Texas, yet this was inadequate. In 1927–28 alone more than 5500 miles of pipelines were laid in West Texas under the most difficult circumstances; for example, the Pasotex Petroleum Company laid an eight-inch line the 195 miles from Winkler County to its refinery at El Paso, at one point spanning a canyon on an eight-thousand-foot-long trestle. By the end of World War II, pipelines from the Lone Star State stretched eastward to the Atlantic, westward to the Pacific, and northward to the Great Lakes; Texas was supplying more than half the nation with natural gas.

The oil and gas industry had become the largest single employer in Texas by 1958. A census that year showed that the one hundred and thirty-four refineries in the state employed almost fifty thousand people and produced goods worth $626,596,000 in net value. Closely allied to petroleum was the chemical industry, which had come of age in Texas during World War II. Using the hydrocarbons of natural gas and petroleum, these plants made an almost infinite number of compounds which in turn were used to produce plastic articles, synthetic rubber, and synthetic fibers. In 1958 this segment of the economy brought $1,063,136,000 to Texas—the only branch of industry to net more than a billion dollars that year. In fact, when everyone working in the oil and gas industry was counted, from oil field driller to salesman, it was found that one in five in the Lone Star State was connected with this endeavor. California similarly has profited hugely from the growing petrochemical industry. In recent years this branch of industry has yielded an annual income of approximately one-third that of all the state's agricultural products combined.

Considering its total importance to the economy of the Southwest, it is little wonder that politicians from the region have fought so hard in Washington to preserve the depletion allowance (which amounts to a federal subsidy through a tax break). And since large amounts of money are made by the owner of land under which oil is found, it is not surprising that Texas in the national election of 1952 voted for Dwight D. Eisenhower, the Republican who promised to help Texas retain title to its tidelands (oil was discovered offshore along the coast of the Lone Star State, which claimed that by right of its Spanish heritage it owned more than ten miles out from the beach rather than the three which the United States government would have allowed it). Arizona alone has not shared in this bonanza of black gold; not until the spring of 1967, when a substantial strike was made in the northeastern corner of the state, were there any known deposits in the Grand Canyon State. The huge deposits of oil and natural gas found in the Southwest have contributed more to the economy and development of the region than any other single factor, for intimately connected with the industry was the automobile and the "good roads" movement.

In the pre-twentieth-century refining of petroleum, gasoline was considered a dangerous by-product because of its high volatility. The major product extracted in refining was kerosene, which was used principally for illumination; lubricants constituted the other major use. However, just as the great discoveries were being made in the Southwest, the "horseless carriage" was coming of age, and as an increasing number of people bought cars there was a corresponding increase in the market for gasoline. In addition, the sale of more cars brought a growing demand for paved roads—and one of the major paving substances was asphalt, also a product of petroleum. Because of the immense distances to be traveled in the Southwest, residents of the region took to the automobile rapidly, and they demanded good roads on which to travel.

California led the way in planning and constructing hard-surfaced roads. The State Highways Act of 1909 authorized the Department of Engineering to map a projected highway system running "north and south through the State, traversing the Sacramento and San Joaquin Valleys and along the Pacific Coast, by the most direct and practicable routes, connecting the county seats of the several counties . . . and joining the centers of population. . . ." The following year a bond issue of $18,000,000 was voted for the purpose; this, along with the $55,000,000 voted in 1916 and 1919, provided operating funds and the start of an excellent system of roads. By 1920 there were 604,000 automobiles registered in California, which had become a state on wheels.

Texas too sought to provide good roads for the large number of automobiles purchased by its citizens. But because the state was so large and the cost of building highways so expensive, new taxes had to be imposed. At first the roads were constructed out of existing state funds, supplemented by sums provided by the federal government on a matching basis, but great scandals attended this building during the 1920's. Then, in 1933, the legislature, working on the theory that the users of the highways should pay for their construction, voted a tax on gasoline that would rise quickly to four cents a gallon. New Mexico and Arizona were slower to build good roads —as late as 1929 Arizona had only 281 miles of hard-surfaced highways—but during the 1930's as an anti-depression measure both states joined in the "good roads" movement. Governor George W. P. Hunt of Arizona, who held office fourteen of the twenty years between 1912 and 1932, incurred great hostility from labor unions by using convict labor to construct highways, but he used the "good roads" theme very effectively in his campaigns. By World War II an excellent system of highways crisscrossed the Southwest. Principal among these were the two major east-west roads, U.S. 66 and U.S. 80. The first ran from Los Angeles east across northern Arizona to Albuquerque, and on through the Texas Panhandle to Oklahoma City and St. Louis; the second ran from

San Diego to Tucson, Las Cruces, El Paso, Fort Worth, Dallas, and east to the Atlantic Ocean in Georgia. Since World War II, highway construction has continued to be one of the three chief items in Southwestern state budgets, and automobile ownership in the Southwest has held steadily at almost one car for each two citizens (well above the national average).

WORLD WAR I

On July 1, 1917, the copper miners at Bisbee, Arizona, were led on strike by the radical labor union, the International Workers of the World. The IWW, or "Wobblies" (the union was known by both names), persuaded the workers to present demands that were extravagant—at a time when any threat to curtail production seemed to the public nothing less than treason because of the global conflict then raging. Inflamed with the apparent success of their strike, as well as by the heated oratory of the IWW organizers from outside the state, the workers were insensitive to patriotic appeals and refused all efforts to end the strike. Public-spirited citizens of the Bisbee area decided that the only solution to the problem was the expulsion of all outside agitators, along with the local workers most outspoken in favor of the strike. During the night of July 11–12, with the connivance and help of local law-enforcement officials, some 1200 citizens rounded up IWW suspects and labor leaders, as well as vagrants and other undesirables, and on July 13 a train left the town carrying 1286 deportees. These people were unloaded from the train in the desert of New Mexico near the town of Hermanas. After this drastic action the strike collapsed and the miners went back to work with no further threat of a strike.

In Brenham, Texas, a membership drive for the American Red Cross was moving slowly in December of 1917, whereupon the wealthier citizens of the community gathered in the local opera house and donated funds to purchase memberships for those unable to pay the fees. For those who had the money but refused to join, the same gathering voted to purchase an "armload of buggy-whips." Shortly after this patriotic meeting adjourned, it was reported that one resident of the town had refused to join, commenting, "To Hell with the Red Cross." The next day a number of "influential and esteemed" citizens of Brenham caught the man, along with five other non-joiners; unmasked and in broad daylight the esteemed citizens proceeded to give the six dissenters "a touch of the hot time they wished for the noble international organization" (in the words of a local newspaper account of the incident). The end of the membership drive found the county exceeding its quota by one thousand. Southwesterners believed in the war to make the world "safe for democracy." In fact, war had already been raging in the region and near it.

The outbreak of the Mexican Revolution of 1910 had brought much excitement and some bloodshed to the Southwest. One of the losers in this revolution, Francisco "Pancho" Villa, decided to show his hatred of the United States by creating border incidents. At first there was a shadowy conspiracy known as the Plan of San Diego whereby an invasion force was to cross the border and re-conquer Mexico's lost provinces, the area that had become the American Southwest; this area was then to be given to the Indians and Latin Americans to form a buffer republic between the United States and Mexico. When this plot failed, Villa, on the night of March 8–9, 1916, with a force estimated at between five hundred and one thousand men, struck at Colombus, New Mexico. Units of the 13th U. S. Cavalry stationed there quickly rallied and drove the Mexicans away after fifteen Americans had been killed and seven wounded. President Woodrow Wilson ordered General John J. Pershing and an expeditionary force into Mexico to capture Villa and to prevent further raids. Pershing crossed the border on March 15 and did not return until February 5, 1917. During this extended campaign the troops fought two engagements, one at Parral and another at Carrizal, but never captured Villa; however, Pershing's force so harassed the Mexican bandit that his followers were scat-tered. Also, the engagement allowed the American army for the first time to use modern weapons of war, including the airplane, and gave it practical field experience that was helpful in World War I. Scattered border incidents continued to plague Arizona es-pecially, and gun-running, smuggling, and illegal immigration con-tinued to be a problem until the late 1920's. It has been estimated that between 1910 and 1928 more than a million Mexicans fled to the United States, some of them to remain permanently and swell the Latin population already here.

The entry of the United States into World War I in April 1917 touched off a wave of enlistments which, coupled with the draft, saw almost four hundred thousand men from the Southwest entering the various branches of military service. More than 197,000 came from Texas and served in such commands as the Thirty-sixth and Ninetieth divisions. California contributed more than 150,000 men, especially to the Ninety-first Division. About twelve thousand Arizonans and seventeen thousand New Mexicans marched off to war. One of the most famous Southwesterners in the war was Lieutenant Frank Luke, Jr., the "Arizona Balloon Buster." This twenty-one-year-old pilot shot down twenty-one enemy aircraft during his thirty-nine days of actual combat before he was forced down behind German lines; rather than surrender he died blazing away at the German soldiers who came to capture him. For his exploits he received the Congressional Medal of Honor.

Because of its mild climate and relative dryness, Texas was the site of many military bases. Camp Travis at San Antonio was the nation's largest training base, and near by was Kelly Field. In fact, the many flying fields established in Texas provided many people with their first glimpse of an airplane; at these bases young men were trained as pilots, navigators, bombardiers, gunners, observers, and aerial photographers. California also had several military bases. The regents of the University of California voted to place the institution, its equipment, and its resources at the disposal of the federal government; subsequently some 3500 men were trained there, approximately half becoming commissioned officers. Stanford University and the University of Southern California made the same offer.

For those who did not enter the military service, there was much work to do at home in the Southwest, providing the artifacts of war and the food on which the army marched. Industry was not yet a major factor in the region, but patriotic feelings could be expressed in other ways. Each state had its Council of Defense, a branch of the National Council of Defense. These state agencies co-ordinated the selling of Liberty Bonds, secured support for the Red Cross, promoted recreational facilities for servicemen, distributed patriotic pamphlets, encouraged the conservation of food, and watched for disloyal words and deeds. And when the conflict ended, these councils helped the returning veterans to find employment.

Each state had its branch of the Food Administration, a national organization headed by Herbert Hoover, who popularized the slogan, "Food Will Win the War." Campaigns were conducted to get housewives to conserve food through such devices as "Wheatless" and "Meatless" days and by growing vegetables at home; and the state organizations requested merchants to conform to definite rules to ensure both fair distribution and conservation. Farmers and ranchers throughout the Southwest benefited from the rising prices that accompanied the conflict, and their record of production reflected their desire both to aid in winning the war and to cash in on the prosperity that accompanied it. Because of the demand for uniforms cotton prices boomed, and California and Arizona farmers hastily plowed and planted this staple; in fact, so much grazing land in Arizona was converted to cotton during the conflict that the dairy industry suffered. The price of beef boomed, and the ranchers of Texas, New Mexico, and Arizona enjoyed a prosperity they had not known since the early 1880's; in addition, there was a strong market for horses and mules, for World War I was still fought largely with genuine horsepower. Grape and raisin prices were inflated by the war, and thousands of acres in California were planted to vineyards as a result; when the war ended, the production was so high and the prices so low that many lost their ranches and homes through foreclosure (between 1919 and 1923 the price of raisins dropped from $235 to $45 a ton).

In Arizona the greatest economic benefit from the war came from rising copper prices. In 1914 the average price of copper was 13.6 cents per pound; by 1916 the price had stabilized at 27.2 cents per pound; and in 1918 the price stood at 24.6 cents per pound. Production rose accordingly. In 1915 the state produced 432,000,000 pounds; in 1920, it turned out 559,000,000 pounds. But production figures alone do not tell the full story, for the huge profits that were made were used to modernize the mines and smelters and to open new ore bodies. Thus after the war's end the mining corporations were in an excellent position to capitalize on the boom of the 1920's. But this prosperity for the companies was not filtering down to the workers, and labor discontent and turmoil was the result. The miners lived in company houses or houses built on company property; their electricity was furnished by company power plants; merchandise came into the communities on company railroads, and was sold in company stores; water came from company reservoirs. Prices at the company stores averaged 25 per cent higher than in towns not so dominated. And yet during this period when the price of copper was rising rapidly, along with mild inflation in most facets of the economy, the wages of the miners generally rose not at all. This created fertile ground for union activity, and several bitter strikes, such as the one at Bisbee, resulted. The national guard had to be called out and martial law declared in some places to restore order. Finally in late 1917 a federal presidential commission came to Arizona to study and settle the strikes, and agreements were made for a United States administrator to reside in each district to hear and adjust complaints. In the long run the mining unions lost more than they gained by their agitation during this period; most unions had pledged no strikes during the war and held to their promises. Radical unions, such as the IWW, which urged its members to have nothing to do with a "capitalists' war," were stigmatized as unpatriotic and lost public respect. The benefits of unionization would not come to Arizona's copper workers until the days of the New Deal.

In California the IWW tried even more drastic measures. Governor William D. Stephens, who had become chief executive after Hiram Johnson's election to the national Senate, became widely known for his patriotic efforts. On December 17, 1917, a bomb destroyed part of the governor's mansion in Sacramento; fortunately no one was hurt. Then while the search was on for the bombers, Governor Stephens received a note demanding fifty thousand dollars. If it was not paid, bombs would destroy the mansion, the capital building, and several other public edifices. And on January 17, 1918, postal authorities in San Francisco discovered a bomb in the mails addressed to the governor. At first Stephens laid the blame for these events at the door of pro-German elements, but later he came to accept the commonly held belief that the IWW was responsible for the violence. As a result of the Sacramento Police Department's investigation of the bombing of the governor's mansion, fifty-five members of the IWW were arrested and convicted. The governor proceeded then to suppress the organization in California.

The Southwest treated racial minorities very badly during the conflict, particularly the second and third generation German settlers of Texas. "Once lead these people into war," said Woodrow Wilson just before the United States entered the conflict, "and they'll forget there ever was such a thing as tolerance. To fight you must be brutal and ruthless, and the spirit of ruthless brutality will enter into every fiber of our national life. . . ." The persecution of German-Americans bore out Wilson's prediction, going to such ridiculous lengths as the renaming of the frankfurter as "liberty pups" and sauerkraut as "liberty cabbage." Slogans such as "America for Americans" and "100% Americanism" became current. The Texas legislature responded by passing an act forbidding instruction in the public schools in any language but English. Nor did this hostility end with the war; in 1919, for example, Governor Will Hobby vetoed the appropriation for the German Department at the University of Texas, stating that an end to the offerings of this department would lead to purer Americanism. There were laws passed in most Southwestern states providing that only American citizens could vote in local elections. Yet in California the anti-foreign feeling worked exactly in reverse. Prior to the war there had been a tide of hatred directed at the Japanese, with many oppressive—even unconstitutional—legislative measures aimed at them. During the war, however, there was less discrimination because Japan was an ally of the United States.

One other notable social change occurred during the Great War —prohibition at last became nationwide through the Eighteenth Amendment. For years the Progressives had been agitating to achieve a restriction on the manufacture or sale of alcoholic beverages, and under the guise of patriotism they achieved their goal. Wheat, barley, and other grains used in the manufacture of whiskey and beer were in short supply because of the global conflict, and a prohibition on the manufacture of alcoholic beverages would conserve these grains. In the Southwest the "drys" had their strongest camp in Texas. Even before national Prohibition the state had passed a law forbidding the sale of liquor within ten miles of any army post (and there were so many military bases in Texas that this measure virtually dried up all sources of liquor). And it was a Texan, Senator Morris Sheppard, who authored the Eighteenth Amendment. Most of the Southwest was so close to the Mexican border, however, that its citizens did not find it difficult to obtain liquor.

When the fighting came to an end, the Southwest emerged much stronger than it had been before the conflict. Its men had served with honor on the battlefields, and the people at home had worked on the farms and in the growing number of factories with equal diligence. The Southwest was prosperous, but it was a prosperity still based largely on an extractive economy of farming, ranching, and mining. Many Southwesterners were now hoping to use the technology of the Industrial Revolution to harness the rivers and provide enough water for both the growing cities and the expanding agricultural endeavors.

AGRICULTURE AND IRRIGATION

The success of Roosevelt Dam in Arizona, which made possible more extensive farming of the Salt River Valley and the growth of Phoenix, led to increased demands for more and still more reclamation projects in the Southwest. The Colorado and the Rio Grande, the two major rivers of the region, were the main targets. But before any dams were built, agreements had to be reached between the various states and between the United States and Mexico on the distribution of the water. First to be tackled was the Colorado, and an agreement concerning distribution of the water was hammered out prior to the building of the dams. Meeting in Santa Fe in the fall of 1922, representatives of the seven states drained by this mighty river drew up an agreement called the Santa Fe Compact. Signed by all seven state delegates and by Secretary of Commerce Herbert Hoover, the representative of the federal government, this agreement called for an allocation of the water based on prior appropriation. However, Arizona refused to ratify the agreement; Governor George W. P. Hunt declared that (1) water from the Colorado should not be used to irrigate land in Mexico (that nation was allotted 1,500,000 acre-feet of water from the Colorado on the theory of prior appropriation), (2) that California would try to usurp water that belonged to Arizona, and (3) the program should be undertaken not on credit, but only as money was in hand with which to do the work.

Despite Arizona's failure to ratify the compact, the federal government proceeded with the project of taming the Colorado. On December 21, 1928, President Calvin Coolidge signed the Swing-Johnson Act which provided for the construction of Boulder Dam, and for the All-American Canal which would take water to the Imperial and Coachella valleys of California. Arizona fought this act before the U. S. Supreme Court, but lost, and a contract for constructing the dam was let in March of 1931. Supervised by Dr. Elwood Mead, United States Commissioner of Reclamation, the work was completed almost exactly five years later. Lake Mead, the crooked 115-mile-long reservoir behind the dam, proved capable of holding 31,000,000 acre-feet of water, enough to irrigate some one million acres of land. Because so much of the water was allotted to California, while the location was entirely in Arizona and Nevada, a common saying arose in Arizona that although California profited most from the project "she didn't give a dam site for it."

Other dams on the Colorado were soon built or projected as soon as the first dam, finally named Hoover Dam, was under construction. The Imperial Dam and reservoir, twenty miles upstream from Yuma, was completed, it diverted water into the All-American Canal. Next came Parker Dam, which was started in 1934; the water from this project was to be piped through an aqueduct across deserts and mountains to supply Los Angeles and other coastal cities. By this time the state of Arizona was growing desperate, and Governor Benjamin B. Moeur took desperate measures. He called out the state militia and sent it to the Parker Dam site with orders to halt the construction. The federal government went to court, but, in the case of United States *v.* Arizona, decided in April 1935, the government's suit was dismissed on the grounds that no specific statutory authorization for the dam was on record. Congress quickly authorized the dam, and Governor Moeur was forced to give way. Arizona still was not satisfied, and for the third time it appealed to the U. S. Supreme Court. In 1936 the state brought suit calling for an equitable appropriation of the waters of the Colorado between Arizona and the other basin states and a judicial limitation to the amount California could receive. Prior to the enactment of the Boulder Canyon Project Act, California had agreed to a self-limiting clause which would restrict its total share of Colorado River water to 4,400,000 acre-feet of water. Arizona wanted this limitation reinforced by the Supreme Court. But again it lost; the Supreme Court threw the case out because the federal government had not agreed to be sued. The last dam to be completed on the Colorado was Glen Canyon Dam, dedicated in the fall of 1966. It holds back the waters of Lake Powell. All of these dams contain hydroelectric facilities, and the power from them turns the wheels of industry and lights the homes of much of the Southwest.

During World War II, when a growing industrialization in Arizona created an increased demand for both electricity and water, the state bowed to the inevitable. In February 1944 the legislature ratified the Colorado River Compact, and the state negotiated with the Secretary of the Interior to receive its 2,800,000 acre-feet of water from the Colorado. Yet canals were available only in the vicinity of Yuma, Arizona, where shortly after World War II there was a boom in land, allotted to veterans on a preferential basis. The central portion of the state, where agricultural water was desperately needed, was not receiving water. To enable Arizona to get its full 2,800,000 acre-feet, as well as to transport the water to that part of the state most needing it, the Central Arizona Project was conceived. This project, which is still awaiting congressional action, would see the construction of two dams near the Grand Canyon, with canals and pumping stations. The cost of this project is so high and the protests of conservationists so loud that to date nothing has been done.

While the Central Arizona Project has been debated, the feud between Arizona and California over Colorado River water has continued. In 1953 California made diversions from the Colorado in excess of its 4,400,000 acre-feet self-imposed limitation. Arizona once again went before the U. S. Supreme Court, suing to restrict California to 4,400,000 acre-feet. It also sought to get uncontested title to an additional one million acre-feet of water in the Colorado, contending that this amount belonged to it as compensation for the inclusion of the Gila in the Colorado River Compact of 1922. California contended that what it had taken was surplus water subject to appropriation. The case of Arizona *v.* California came to trial on June 14, 1956, and ended more than two years later. Judge Simon Rifkind characterized this trial as "the greatest struggle over water rights in the latter day history of the West," and indeed it was. On June 3, 1963, the Supreme Court announced its opinion in the case in a decision that split five to three. The court upheld, in its main outlines, the position taken by Arizona, declaring that the waters of the Gila were reserved to Arizona. But to the consternation of all those who believed the law of prior appropriation was inviolable, the court declared that the allocation of water depended entirely on valid contracts with the Secretary of the Interior. Thus the long-cherished and upheld doctrine of prior appropriation was replaced by the discretion of the Secretary of the Interior. The final outcome of this struggle for water is yet to be determined. In 1966 a tentative agreement was reached between all the basin states that would allow the Central Arizona Project to be constructed, but as yet Congress has not acted and Arizona alone cannot finance it.

There has also been a struggle for the water carried to the Gulf of Mexico by the Rio Grande. Colorado, New Mexico, Texas, and Mexico have quarreled over the distribution. In the decade following the end of World War I the lower Rio Grande Valley boomed through private irrigation. As the life-giving canals spread, real estate agents ran excursion trains filled with prospective buyers to this valley without charge for transportation or meals; at times the land sales from a single trainload totaled more than a million dollars. This success stimulated the federal government to plan dams on the Rio Grande, both in the interest of reclamation and of flood control. However, the Rio Grande is an international stream, and any efforts to tame and use it had to be done with the approval of Mexico.

In 1906 the United States and Mexico signed a treaty providing for the construction of Elephant Butte Reservoir in New Mexico primarily as a flood control measure, although the water thus impounded did irrigate thousands of acres. Then in 1933 came the

Rio Grande Rectification Project, which helped relieve the El Paso-Juarez valley of flood danger. Next Congress passed an act in June 1936 for a canal project between El Paso and Caballo, the American Dam, which was completed before 1947. The threat of flooding in the Lower Rio Grande Valley was lessened by an agreement made by the United States and Mexico in 1932 which provided for the construction of floodways on each side of the river. The United States subsequently constructed more than three hundred miles of floodway levees by the 1950's.

Use of Rio Grande water for irrigation started with the Rio Grande Compact, signed by delegates from Colorado, New Mexico, Texas, and the federal government at Santa Fe on March 18, 1938. However, all dams constructed below El Paso required the consent of the Mexican government. A treaty to this effect was signed in 1945, providing for a distribution of water between the two nations. The first project completed under the terms of this agreement was Falcon Dam, finished in 1953 and dedicated by the presidents of the two republics. This reservoir impounds 3,300,000 acre-feet of water which is used to irrigate both on the Texas side of the river and in the area around Reynosa and Matamoros in the Mexican state of Tamaulipas. Two other dams are under construction, and the water from the three dams should irrigate more than a million acres on both sides of the boundary.

Although not as spectacular, the drilling of wells to tap underground water for irrigation purposes has opened as much, if not more, land to farming in the Southwest as have the dams. A few hardy farmers had penetrated the High Plains of West Texas even before this phenomenon, taking advantage of the seasonal rains to raise small crops through a technique known as "dry-land farming." Department of Agriculture figures reveal that only 50,588 bales of cotton were grown in West Texas in 1918. Then came the wells, and land worth only ten dollars an acre soared to seven and eight hundred dollars an acre by the mid-1960's. Mechanical farming could profitaby be conducted because machinery could be used efficiently on the level, treeless plains. Soon most of the great ranches were broken up, to be replaced by fields of cotton, sorghum, and wheat. In 1920 West Texas supported 2,068,768 head of cattle; by 1925 the number had declined to 1,739,476, while the number of bales of cotton had risen to 1,130,713 by that same year. The number of acres under cultivation jumped from 45,101 in 1909 to 2,334,393 in 1924. The ranchers began shifting their activity to the Edwards Plateau, to the Trans-Pecos region, to the coastal plains south and southwest of San Antonio, and even into East Texas, traditional homeland of cotton farmers.

This same technique of drilling irrigation wells, often using natural gas to power the pumps, spread to northeastern New Mexico in the vicinity of Clayton, to the Rio Grande Valley near Socorro, and to arid area near Deming in the south-central part of the state. In Arizona the drilling of wells opened farmlands near Willcox in the southeastern portion of the state, as well as in areas where insufficient canal water was available. However, in Arizona and New Mexico the drilling of too many wells in some areas resulted in an alarming lowering of the water table, and led the two states to restrict the number of wells that could be drilled in any water area. Texas as yet has not taken this step, although it may be necessary in the future; to prevent such a law being passed, as well as to aid the farmers in other parts of the Southwest, scientists are experimenting with a variety of ways to recharge the water table. Hopefully they will find a way; should they fail, the pumps eventually will bring no moisture to the surface, and the desert will reclaim land which is now productive.

Scientists are also now working on another measure which holds promise of water for the Southwest, as well as all arid portions of the world—desalting ocean water. For the past several years experiments have beeen conducted to find a cheap way of converting salt and brackish water to make it fit for human, animal, and agricultural purposes. Atomic power and other methods are being tried in the hope of reducing the cost to less than fifty cents per thousand gallons, which would be competitive with the cost of water for human consumption; for agriculture the cost must be cheaper by far, for after desalting it would have to be transported by canal and pumped to the fields. Contracts were recently signed by the Department of the Interior, the Metropolitan Water District of Southern California, and the Atomic Energy Commission to build a pilot plant in southern California; with the full resources of mid-twentieth century technology focused on the problem, a solution ought to be found.

Using what water is available to them, Southwesterners have been growing an increasing percentage of the nation's agricultural produce despite a labor problem of growing proportions. Traditionally the farmers of the Southwest had used migratory American workers and imported Mexican labor to perform the difficult work of stooping and bending to harvest garden vegetables, pick fruit, and feed livestock. During the early years of the twentieth century there was no shortage of such "field hands" despite the abysmal conditions under which these workers were forced to live and the low wages they received. From 1929, when the Depression began, until 1941, tens of thousands of Southerners fled their homes, moving to California where they collectively were known as "Okies," a diminutive for Oklahomans. These poorly educated, unskilled migrants poured into the fields for wages that would attract no one other than themselves and illegal immigrants from Mexico called "wetbacks," a term applied first in Texas to those who swam the Rio Grande to avoid border patrol agents. When World War II started and the unskilled Americans either were drafted or found work in defense plants, the farmers came more and more to rely on Mexican labor, legalized under Public Law 28 which provided for an annual supply of workers from Mexico; as many as 750,000 such workers came to the United States annually after the war, happy to receive wages low by American standards but high by their own.

Attempts to unionize the farm workers of the Southwest failed time after time because of the unskilled nature of the labor performed and the competition of Mexican labor. In the early 1960's, however, the United States government, under pressure from organized labor, terminated its agreement with Mexico to allow an annual influx of Mexican workers. This, coupled with a growing reluctance on the part of Americans to perform the hot, dirty, hard work of harvesting crops, has led to a shortage of field hands. Some farmers have turned to increased mechanization to solve the problem; others have increased wages somewhat in an attempt to interest high school and college boys in the work; still other farmers have relied on "wetbacks," knowing that the penalty for hiring such illegal immigrants is slight. In 1965 the farmers of the lower Rio Grande Valley, Arizona, and California saw crops rotting in the fields for want of crews to harvest them, and have applied political pressures on Washington officials to reinstate the quota system of workers from Mexico. Labor officials have exploited the situation to gain their first significant victories in organizing farm workers in California and Texas.

The increased use of machinery has enabled the farmers to operate larger and still larger farms, with the result that the total number of farms in the Southwest has declined. But the acreage under cultivation continues to increase. The average farm in California in 1954, for example, was 307.1 acres. The average New Mexico, Arizona, and West Texas farm was even larger. California has led the nation consistently in total farm income, reaching three billion dollars in 1959 and increasing since. More than two hundred crops are grown there, including more than a third of all the nation's fruits and a fourth of its vegetables. Only about 2 per cent of New Mexico is under cultivation and just slightly more in Arizona, with cotton the most valuable crop in both; 58 per cent of New Mexico's total crop value in 1958 was cotton. In Texas more than two million bales of cotton have been shipped from Lubbock every year for the past several years, about one-sixth of the nation's total output. Sorghum has been a close second, with wheat and other grains following. In 1966, out of a total national cotton production of some eleven million bales, Texas produced almost three and three-quarter million bales, California one and one-half million, Arizona 600,000 bales, and New Mexico 200,000 bales. California is the leading producer of citrus, with Texas third and Arizona fourth.

Such production has brought high income to the Southwest's farmers. In 1965, for the seventeenth consecutive year, Arizona's farms led the nation as earners of the highest realized net income; their average was $21,423 per farm, compared with a national average of $4,604. California and New Mexico were not far behind this figure, well above the national average. The figure for West Texas alone is impossible to determine, for U. S. Department of Agriculture statistics for the state include the eastern portion, where farms and incomes are small. However, residents of Castro

County in West Texas had the highest income per family of any county in the United States; and in Lubbock County more than five hundred farmers paid taxes on incomes of more than $100,000 in 1962.

Southwesterners did not confine their use of water to irrigation alone during the period between the two world wars. They also discovered a means of irrigating the air to make their homes and businesses more pleasant during the summer months. Because of the extreme heat of summer in most parts of the Southwest, it was a custom for wealthier residents to send their families to the Pacific Coast or to the mountains during the months of June, July, and August. Electric fans, introduced shortly after the turn of the twentieth century, did little but stir the hot air. Then in 1934 came the evaporative cooler, known for years as the "Arizona Cooler." This device consisted of a low-speed electric exhaust fan mounted inside a cabinet, the sides of which were pads of excelsior; water was kept running through the excelsior, and the moist air blown out by the fan cooled through evaporation. A. J. Eddy of Yuma is generally credited with the invention of this device, while Norman Hindle, manager of the Imperial Hardward Company store in Yuma, was the one who popularized the idea. In 1934 Hindle almost cornered the market on low-speed electric exhaust motors, hired carpenters to manufacture cooler boxes and pads, and sold the finished product for approximately sixty dollars. His business was so good that every morning people stood in line to buy, and Hindle sold more than one thousand coolers in the first month of his operation. Naturally the idea spread rapidly, causing many cities to have to expand their electrical distribution facilities to take care of the increased load. The Wagoner Manufacturing Company, which made one of the best motors for coolers, had ordinarily carried six of them in stock in their Los Angeles warehouse, but the idea grew so rapidly that by 1937 they had ten thousand fans in stock in that same warehouse. The evaporative cooler changed the pattern of life in the Southwest. After its invention very few people found it necessary to leave during the summer months; business houses, which previously had expected to lose money during the summer and which remained open hoping to lose as little as possible, suddenly found themselves making an unexpected profit. Finally, the boom

in evaporative coolers doubtless stimulated the development of re-
frigerated cooling devices, for it showed that something could be
done to mitigate the rigors of the desert. In fact, the invention of air-
conditioning devices made life so bearable that it stimulated the
population boom which is still under way in the Southwest.

WORLD WAR II

Californians and other Pacific Coast residents had good reason to
be uneasy in World War II, for they feared that a Japanese attack
might come on the mainland. Early in 1942 a Japanese sub-
marine did in fact surface at Goleta, near Santa Barbara, and
fire a shell which damaged a wooden jetty. Some frightened
residents put their homes up for sale and fled away from the coast.
The tension reached such heights that, when practice anti-aircraft
guns were fired in Los Angeles on the evening of February 24,
1942, the newspapers erroneously reported that Japanese planes
had bombed the city. Soon, however, this initial fear was turned to
a fierce determination to revenge the "day that will live in infamy," as President Franklin D. Roosevelt called Sunday, December 7, the day the Japanese made a surprise attack on Pearl Harbor.

In California there was a long history of hatred and distrust of
the Japanese-Americans living in the state. In 1940 there were
120,000 of these Nisei in California. Although there was no evidence to indicate disloyalty on their part, by order of General John
L. DeWitt, commander of the Western Defense Command, the
Nisei were relocated away from the Pacific Coast. Many had to sell
their homes, businesses, and farms at a fraction of their value (estimates of their property loss ran as high as $365,000,000), and
their radios, guns, and any suspicious personal effects were confiscated. They were herded into barbed-wire enclosures in southeastern California and in western Arizona and kept under military
guard, yet charged with no crime. For a time the town of Poston,
Arizona (north of Yuma), became the third largest city in the
state because of the Japanese interned there. Only about 65,000 of
these internees returned to the West Coast after the war, and the

property confiscated from them is yet to be returned. Yet during the war no acts of treason or espionage were ever traced to them, and many of the young men enlisted in all-Nisei regiments and fought gallantly in the European theater.

The shipbuilding industry boomed in California during the war. At Richmond, Oakland, and San Pedro the shipyards had already shifted to wartime production before the outbreak of hostilities; after the start of the war Henry J. Kaiser enterprises took control of Calship at Los Angeles, shipyards were opened at Sausalito and Vallejo, and from these establishments came cruisers, destroyers, cargo carriers, and auxiliary vessels. To supply these yards with the necessary metal, Kaiser Industries built the largest steel mill in the West at Fontana. Aircraft were already being manufactured in southern California before the war—at Ryan Aeronautical Corporation in San Diego and Lockheed Aircraft Company in Los Angeles; during the war Consolidated Vultee, Douglas, North American, Northrop, and Hughes aircraft companies likewise became California giants. Such expansion caused hundreds of thousands of workers to move to the state, creating housing and school shortages. The population of Vallejo jumped from 20,000 in 1941 to 100,000 in 1943. Housing projects were financed by the government, but thousands of workers had to content themselves with substandard housing and commute to work, straining the capacity of train and bus facilities because of the gasoline rationing in effect.

The petroleum industry also grew rapidly in California during the war. Between 1939 and 1945 it increased its production by 50 per cent, and the refineries grew correspondingly. Allied to the oil industry was the petrochemical industry; because of Japanese conquests in Malaya and the Dutch East Indies, which cut off supplies of natural rubber, plants in California and Texas started to manufacture synthetic rubber from crude oil. The electronics industry received a strong impetus from the war, and so did munitions, machinery, and metal fabrication. The industrial output jumped from a value of $2,798,180,000 in 1939 to an astounding $10,141,496,-000 in 1944. And almost two-thirds of this industry was clustered in the area around Los Angeles and San Diego.

Because California is a coastal state, it became a major training and staging point for troops of the army, navy, and marines. The army developed large camps at Monterey, Paso Robles, San Luis Obispo, and Santa Maria. The marines developed a huge complex, including facilities to practice amphibious operations, at Camp Pendleton (near Oceanside), and enlarged the recruit training depot at San Diego. The navy expanded its facilities at San Diego, both for recruit training and for shipping, while the Army Air Corps established flying fields at Victorville, Merced, and Santa Ana. To ship these troops overseas, the navy acquired Treasure Island at San Francisco and converted it into a huge naval installation; the navy also acquired Terminal Island in Los Angeles harbor and at a cost of $78,000,000 converted it into a suitable base. The factory workers brought their families with them, and the servicemen brought theirs—the population of the state jumped an incredible 1,916,000 between 1940 and 1945.

Arizona also saw boom years during the war. Because of the fear of a Japanese bombardment of the Pacific Coast, or even an actual invasion, the war planners in Washington deliberately encouraged the establishment of some industries in Arizona because of its nearness to the Pacific ports; in addition, Arizona enjoyed fair weather all year, and it was near an almost unlimited supply of Mexican labor. As a result, the state saw an industrial boom for the first time in its history. Consolidated Vultee established a plant at Tucson, the Garrett Corporation built its AiResearch plant at Phoenix Sky Harbor airport, and Goodyear Aircraft manufactured plane parts and balloons at Litchfield Park, adjacent to a naval air facility. The Allison Steel Company built portable bridges in Phoenix, while parts for tanks and airplanes were fabricated by subcontractors in a dozen towns and cities, and the Aluminum Company of America built a huge aluminum extrusion plant at Phoenix. Federal government statistics show the result; in 1940 the gross return from manufacturing in Arizona had stood about $17,000,000, but by 1945 this figure had jumped to $85,000,000 for the one year.

Tens of thousands of troops came to Arizona to train at its military establishments. Air bases were quickly operating at Luke Field near Phoenix, Williams Field near Chandler, and Davis-Monthan Field at Tucson, while training facilities were constructed at Marana and Ryan Fields near Tucson, Thunderbird Field near Phoenix, and Falcon Field at Mesa. Gunnery training was conducted at

Kingman; historic Fort Huachuca was used to train Negro soldiers, while Camp Horn near Wickenburg and Camp Hyder near Yuma were centers for training two hundred thousand soldiers in desert warfare. In addition, there were several prisoner-of-war camps for Germans and Italians in the state. As in California, the influx of residents to man Arizona's factories, many of which ran on a twenty-four-hour-a-day basis, resulted in severe housing shortages, inadequate schooling, and overstrained service facilities.

In New Mexico the war brought the first real industry the state had ever known. The only manufacturing activity of any importance before 1941 was in the processing of forest products, but even this was very minor. In 1933 there were less than three thousand people employed in manufacturing establishments. During the war the ordinance industry rose to become the dominant industrial activity, for which few statistics as yet are available. Perhaps the most dramatic single incident of World War II anywhere in the world occurred in New Mexico, and was connected with the ordinance industry—the explosion of the first atomic bomb. Working secretly at Los Alamos, government scientists constructed the first nuclear device. It was exploded on July 16, 1945, at the Trinity Site, showering the area with radioactive material. The town of Los Alamos grew as a result of the need for further developments in this field, and Los Alamos County was created in 1949. New Mexico's chemical industry, closely connected with its petroleum production, also started during the war. Because of its dry, warm climate, New Mexico was the site of several air fields and Army training bases: flight training, aerial gunnery, and bombardier instruction were carried on at Albuquerque, Roswell, Carlsbad, and Deming. Ordinance depots were located at several sites remote from population centers, while prisoners of war were kept at Roswell.

As in World War I, Texas was again the center of training activities, no less than fifteen posts being located in the state. The Third Army, which controlled basic training camps from Arizona to Florida, was headquartered at San Antonio, as was the Fourth Army, which prepared men for overseas combat through advanced training bases in nine states. And as the tide of battle turned in favor of the allies, twenty-one prisoner-of-war camps were constructed in

Texas. Texas was also the site of many air training bases. Randolph Field at San Antonio, often called the "West Point of the Air," had been completed at the Alamo City in 1930 at a cost of $11,-000,000; along with Kelly and Brooks fields, it made San Antonio a hub of flying activity during the war. Other fields were constructed at Lubbock, Midland, Wichita Falls, San Angelo, San Marcos, and elsewhere, and the national headquarters of the Air Force Training Command was in Fort Worth at Carswell Field. In addition, the navy had a vast aerial complex at Corpus Christi and a primary training base at Grand Prairie.

Because of this flying activity, it was natural for aircraft factories to be constructed in the state. These included the Southern Aircraft plant at Garland, the North American Aviation factory at Grand Prairie, and the enormous Consolidated Aircraft Corporation complex at Fort Worth. To fuel these aircraft, as well as tanks and warships, the oil industry expanded rapidly. The petrochemical industry, located primarily in the area between Houston and Galveston, also came of age between 1941 and 1945. Synthetic rubber plants were constructed, and munitions factories mushroomed; along the Gulf Coast shipyards were enlarged and new ones started. The world's largest tin smelter was built at Texas City, and steel mills were erected at Daingerfield and Houston. There was full employment, and many women for the first time in the state's history went into the factories to become riveters, punch press operators, and assembly line workers.

Everywhere in the Southwest the agricultural complex turned to the staggering problem of producing sufficient food for a nation—and a world—at war. Because of the manpower shortage there was a decrease in the total number of farms but an increase in the acreage under cultivation, and the total valuation of farm implements and machinery went up almost a quarter of a billion dollars for the states of Texas, New Mexico, Arizona, and California. The war also brought an increased production from Southwestern mines, particularly in the copper industry; existing mines, such as the one at Santa Rita del Cobre in New Mexico, were expanded, while marginal claims never before worked were put into production.

At home Southwesterners, along with other Americans, became familiar with rationing stamps for the purchase of gasoline, meat, sugar, coffee, shoes, automobile parts, tires, and other items. They participated in scrap iron drives, and scoured junk heaps and trash dumps. They grew "victory gardens" to conserve food, and they took part in numerous war bond drives. Apart from the unwarranted mistreatment of the Nisei, there was little persecution of the so-called "hyphenated Americans" during this conflict; few doubted that the German element in Texas consisted of true citizens, and no whips were used on recalcitrant civilians. "Remember Pearl Harbor," like "Remember the Alamo," was so effective a slogan that loyalty was taken for granted.

Even before Congress voted a declaration of war against Japan, Germany, and Italy shortly after the bombing of Pearl Harbor, Southwesterners were crowding into recruiting offices. There was a national draft system, but few waited for "Greetings" from the President. Out of a total population of six and a quarter million, Texas sent some 750,000 men to the army, navy, marines, coast guard, and merchant marine, along with 12,000 women to the auxiliary forces. The 36th Division and 56th Cavalry were all-Texan units, while a high percentage of the members of the 19th Division, 1st Cavalry Division, and 103rd Infantry Regiment were Texans. Twelve admirals and 155 generals had been born in Texas, including Chester W. Nimitz, Commander in Chief of the Pacific Fleet, and Dwight D. Eisenhower, Supreme Allied Commander in Europe. The director of the Women's Army Corps (WACS) Colonel Oveta Culp Hobby, was a Texan. Thirty Texans won the Congressional Medal of Honor and six the Navy Medal of Honor, among whom were Lieutenant Audie Murphy, the "most decorated" soldier of World War II, and Commander Samuel D. Dealey, the "most decorated man in the Navy."

New Mexicans had an early interest in operations in the Pacific. The 200th Coast Artillery, an anti-aircraft unit, was entirely from New Mexico; as a national guard unit it had been called to active duty in August of 1941 and sent to Clark Field in the Philippines. Surrendering in April of 1942 to a superior Japanese force, this unit was subjected to the infamous "Bataan March" en route to imprisonment. More than 25,000 New Mexicans saw service in the conflict, three of them receiving the nation's highest military decoration. Arizona contributed some 30,000 men to the various branches of the service; among them the famed "Bushmasters" of the Arizona national guard. One Arizonan, Silvestre S. Herrera, received the Medal of Honor. California sent some 700,000 men to the various theaters of combat in one branch or another of the armed forces, of whom twenty-one were awarded the Medal of Honor; perhaps most noteworthy of these men was General James H. Doolittle who in 1942 led a daring and unexpected bombing raid over Tokyo, Japan.

The end of World War II, with the unconditional surrender first of Germany and then of Japan in the spring and summer of 1945, found the Southwest far more prosperous than at any time in its history. Personal income in California had jumped from just over five billion dollars in 1941 to almost thirteen billion in 1945. Even when a 30 per cent inflation is recognized, this was still a great gain. In more personal terms, the prosperity generated by the war can be seen in Yuma, Arizona, where John Huber had opened a jewelry store in the early 1930's. His business was very slow until the start of the war, when suddenly some fifty thousand soldiers were stationed nearby. Overnight his business became spectacular. Anything on the shelves would sell; unsalable merchandise which for years had been molding in the basement was resurrected, for Huber, selling watches, rings, and silverware, was in a business that attracted the soldiers. Business became so fantastic, in fact, that he had to post a guard at the front door and let in only a few customers at a time. By the end of the war, Huber was a wealthy man.

And yet the greatest boom was still to come for the Southwest. Tens of thousands of soldiers, airmen, and sailors who had received their first glimpse of the Southwest courtesy of the military service would return as civilians, bringing their families, to settle permanently. Some of the factories which had been built in the region during the war would close, but others would stay and would attract still other industries to the region. Servicemen who had been sent to Southwestern universities and colleges to study during the war would return to study on the G.I. Bill, and educational facilities would grow to keep pace with their demands. The Southwest was no longer the home of prospectors, cowboys, and plowmen, but of factory workers, agricultural workers, and tourists.

THE POSTWAR YEARS

The end of World War II brought widespread rejoicing to the Southwest along with the rest of the nation, even though there was fear in the industrialized parts of the region that the end of hostilities would mean a depression. However, some displaced war workers returned to their prewar homes, and nonmilitary construction projects, homes and highways, provided full employment for the rest. And there was a boom in industries providing consumer items; with a large backlog of savings, people wanted the goods and services which had been denied them during the war: new cars, new homes, new furniture, and new clothes. The feared depression turned into a three-year boom.

In California, highway construction, public housing, and industrial expansion got underway. No new roads had been constructed during the war, and there was a considerable amount of repair work to be done on existing ones. Towns and cities had to be bypassed and major routes widened. A term that came into general use was "freeways"—superhighways that eliminated grade intersections. There was a $65,000,000 addition to the Kaiser steel mill at Fontana and such large building projects as a Statler Hotel in Los Angeles and the Crenshaw and Westchester shopping centers in the same city. To ease the critical housing shortage in southern California, numerous multistory apartments and housing projects were built. The railroads contributed to the boom by replacing their pre-war equipment with lightweight streamliners. Automobile assembly plants for all major makes were constructed in California to satisfy the increasing demand for cars. And television created an electronics boom. Perhaps most spectacular of California's postwar industries has been the electronics industry.

California and Texas have received a disproportionately large share of the money spent by the federal government in the field of defense and aerospace. North American at its El Segundo plant is responsible for the two prototypes of the B-70, the largest, fastest super-bomber yet built, and it produces the X-15 supersonic rocket plane that has set many speed and altitude records. North American's Rocketdyne Division has developed the power plants for most of America's space probes, as well as the Saturn engine that may launch a man toward the moon, and it has helped to design the Tiros weather satellites. The Lockheed Corporation at Burbank and Sunnyvale has worked closely with the government in missile and aircraft production, in producing Polaris submarines, and in developing the Samos (spy-in-the-sky) satellite. The Douglas Corporation at Santa Monica manufactured the Thor-Able booster rocket, worked on the Nike-Zeus missile, designed the Atlas Inter-Continental Ballistics Missile (ICBM), and is building several standard fighter planes for the air force and navy.

The entertainment industry, whose capital is Hollywood, has contributed much to the California economy. From small beginnings in the early years of the twentieth century, the motion picture industry has grown steadily, and it now provides employment for tens of thousands of people. When the television industry was in its infancy, it also came to Hollywood which was the only source of actors, technicians, and administrators capable of satisfying its voracious appetite. As television grew, attendance at movies declined across the nation. But the entertainment industry survived in California, and now is bigger than ever.

Agriculture continued to contribute to the heated economy. The Marshall Plan of aiding allies in the growing struggle with Russia, dubbed the Cold War, called for thousands of tons of foodstuffs, and the farmers struggled to keep pace. The result of this activity can be seen in California's population figures: 10,586,223 in 1950, a 53 per cent increase over 1940. And this was just the beginning; by 1960 it had grown to 15,717,204, a 48.5 per cent increase over 1950. Census experts have estimated that more than two thousand persons a day immigrate to California. By the mid-1960's California had surpassed New York as the nation's most populous state. It is notable that 70 per cent of this growth in California has been in the southern part of the state.

In Arizona the end of hostilities did mean the loss of many industrial jobs and a substantial loss of wartime population. Industrial output fell from $85,000,000 in 1945 to $53,000,000 in 1946. Yet for every war worker who left there were more who stayed, and many veterans of the armed forces who had received their first glimpse of the Southwest at Arizona camps returned to the state either to recuperate from war wounds, to go to school on the G.I. Bill, or to start businesses. This influx of population led to a booming construction industry, the growth of retail trade establishments, and a healthy economy in general. Some war plants were closed, but only temporarily, and industries that remained helped to attract other industries to the state. The Aluminum Company of America (Alcoa) plant at Phoenix was acquired by Reynolds Aluminum Corporation. AiResearch, which closed in 1946, was reopened in 1951. Motorola, a major manufacturer of radio, television, and electronic parts, established a plant in Phoenix soon after the war ended; and the copper mining corporations found that the end of the war brought more, not less, demand for their product. In 1950 the population stood at 749,587, a gain of more than 50 per cent. Then the Korean War broke out, and hundreds of manufacturing firms chose Arizona locations. Electronics and aircraft component industries predominated in this growth, which by 1964 saw the total value of manufacturing in the state top one billion dollars, the largest factor in the economy for more than a decade. By 1960 the population stood at 1,302,161. Arizona thus led the nation in per cent of population increase from the end of World War II to 1960, 111 per cent; income growth was up 296 per cent; life insurance in force jumped 765 per cent; in fact, by almost every index of measuring growth Arizona either led the nation or was close behind the leaders. Although federal crop restrictions, thought necessary by Department of Agriculture functionaries, had reduced total cotton acreage, agricultural income was up 167 per cent. Nor is the end in sight; the U. S. Bureau of the Census predicts the state population will be almost two million by 1970.

New Mexico's postwar growth has not been as spectacular as that of other parts of the Southwest, but still it has been substantial. The population of the state stood at 532,000 in 1940, reached 681,000 by 1950, and 951,000 in 1960. Agriculture, including ranching, accounts for less than 6 per cent of the total income, while manufacturing has accounted for only a little more. Recent figures show approximately twenty thousand people working in some type of manufacturing. Twenty-four per cent of the state's gross production in terms of dollars comes from mining: copper, gold, silver, lead, zinc, coal, potash, uranium, and petroleum. Approximately 85 per cent of the nation's potash comes from a small area near Carlsbad, but the cost of transportation is so high (because of the low value per unit weight) that New Mexican congressmen have fought strongly for a high tariff on imports of the substance. In the spring of 1950 a Navajo accidentally discovered uranium in northwestern New Mexico, leading to a rush that rivaled gold booms. The uranium rush is probably the last mineral boom for the Southwest. A geiger counter, a pick, and shovel were all a prospector needed to hunt the element; but the newer and more glamorous metals now being sought require such elaborate and expensive tools to discover that few individual prospectors take the field in search of them. It has been estimated that the deposits near Grants and Gallup total 72 per cent of the known uranium ore reserves and 52 per cent of the total milling capacity in the United States.

The major factor in New Mexico's economy has been tourism. Beginning with the quadricentennial celebration of Coronado's visit to New Mexico, the state has promoted tourism to the point where it brings more money to the area than any other single industry. Highway signs and roadside markers point out sites of historic interest, while the state bureau of tourism places advertisements in leading Eastern magazines touting New Mexico's many attractions. Many of the towns along U. S. Highways 80 and 66 would have no reason for existence were it not for the annual crop of tourists bringing millions of dollars for food, gasoline, lodging, curios, and souvenirs. Dude ranches by the thousands cater to the needs of Easterners who wish to see the "Old West" in superb comfort. Finally, it should be noted that New Mexico's biggest employer is the federal government. Estimates for the year 1956 indicate that 21.6 per cent of the total income of the state came from the federal government, and one in five workers were employed by it. Since that time the percentage has risen slightly.

The postwar boom in Texas, like that in California, has been of such proportions as almost to defy description. Dry statistics from the Federal Bureau of the Census give an indication of this growth: in 1949 the net value of industrial products in the state was $1,813,914,000; in 1958 it was $5,059,438,000, a gain of more than 200 per cent in less than a decade. Industrial wages kept pace with this growth: from $922,269,000 in 1949 to $2,294,982,000 in

1958. Twenty per cent of all jobs in the Lone Star State are connected with the oil industry in one way or another, making the
petroleum business the largest state employer; the petrochemical
industry alone brought $1,063,136,000 to Texas in 1958. Plants
manufacturing scientific and technical instruments and components
have centered in Dallas and in Houston, near the Manned Space
Center of the National Aeronautics and Space Authority (NASA).
In addition, there are factories producing heavy equipment, cotton
gins, oil field and construction machinery, farm implements, and
general industrial equipment; Ford and General Motors have assembly plants in the state; and several aircraft factories, Chance
Vought, Convair, Consolidated, Temco, and Bell Helicopter, are in
the state. Also, there are a growing number of textile mills, shoe and
boot factories, clothing manufacturers, furniture makers, and proc-
essors of farm and ranch products. In 1955 Texas led every state in
the production of oil, petrochemicals, natural gas, carbon black,
helium, sulfur, cotton, rice, beef cattle, wool, and mohair. During
the war Texas started down the road to industrialization, a trend
that gained momentum during the Fabulous Fifties, and which in
the Soaring Sixties has made the state predominantly urban; more
citizens work in factories than anywhere else.

Another startling feature about the Southwest which started during the war and which has continued during the 1950's and 1960's
is the rapid growth of major cities. Los Angeles leads the Southwest as a major urban center with a metropolitan population of
6,742,696 in 1960 and now close to 7,500,000. This includes the
suburbs of Beverly Hills, San Fernando, Culver City, Santa Monica, Burbank, Glendale, Pasadena, Alhambra, South Pasadena,
Vernon, Huntington Park, Torrance, Inglewood, Gardena, Hawthorne, El Segundo, and Long Beach. It is California's leading city
not only in terms of population but also in weath, manufacturing,
commerce, aviation transport, and ocean shipping; in addition, it is
the nation's center of the movie, television, and entertainment industry. It boasts a major league baseball and professional football
teams, zoos, parks, symphony orchestra, and museums, as well
as slums, such as Watts, where the people rioted in the summer of
1965, and an air pollution problem—commonly called smog—
worse than any major city in the United States. It is a sprawling,

bustling giant with all the problems of a great metropolitan area: governed by a mayor and council hampered by autonomous departments with the right to separate revenues, with teen-age demonstrations along Sunset Boulevard, racial troubles, scenic beauty, and a population that grows alarmingly each year.

Down the coast from Los Angeles—with almost no open spaces in between—is San Diego, the oldest city in California. Like San Francisco, it boasts a great natural harbor (the Los Angeles harbor was created, with federal subsidies). The population of San Diego jumped from 17,700 in 1900 to 628,200 in 1963; its metropolitan area in 1963 totaled 1,164,100, a figure that includes almost a dozen suburban communities. Its economy is based on aircraft manufacture, missile production, electronics, shipbuilding, shipping, fishing, military installations, and tourism. Charles Lindberg's *Spirit of St. Louis* was built there in 1927, and today the most modern jet fighters roll from its assembly lines. San Diego's zoo is famous, and so are its parks, art galleries, and museums; in addition, Sea World is a tourist attraction and so is Presidio Park which recalls the days when the Dons of Spain walked its street. The city is one of California's loveliest, and its dealings with racial minorities and their problems reflect a civic pride.

To the east, almost in the center of Arizona, stands Phoenix, the fastest growing city in the nation. From a population of 11,134 in 1910, it grew to 439,170 by 1960, and now is approaching 600,-000; when its suburbs of Mesa, Tempe, Scottsdale, Glendale, Chandler, Apache Junction, and Sun City (a retirement community) are included, metropolitan Phoenix has a total population of approximately 900,000. Its economy consists of diversified manufacturing, particularly electronics, irrigated farming that includes large annual shipments of citrus fruit, cotton, and garden vegetables, and the nearby air force and naval installations. The architecture of Phoenix, once almost exclusively Spanish, has changed rapidly to modern American, but the landscapes and parks are still dominated by desert vegetation.

Arizona's other major city is Tucson, a metropolitan area that contains some 325,000 people. The Old Pueblo, as it is known, has little manufacturing despite the fact that copper mines in the vicinity are responsible for a large percentage of the state's output.

There is an air force base within the city limits, but Tucson's principal income is derived from its climate: tourists, winter visitors, health seekers, and retired people accounted for some ninety million dollars in income in 1966.

New Mexico boasts only one real metropolitan area, Albuquerque. It is the commercial and financial center of the state and has an economy based on agriculture, timber, minerals, military bases, and tourism. Albuquerque is noted as a winter sports area; skiing in the nearby Sandia Mountains is now easily accessible via the longest tramway in the United States. In the center of the city is Old Town Plaza, an area of shops and amusements that brings its Spanish heritage strongly to mind. However, in its commercial district modern architecture is very much in evidence.

Even more Hispanic in flavor is El Paso, down the Rio Grande from Albuquerque. "The Pass of the North" had a population of 276,687 in 1960, and now contains almost 400,000 people; in addition, just across the Rio Grande in the Mexican state of Chihuahua is Ciudad Juárez with a population of 350,000. El Paso is a noted health and tourist resort, and derives a large income from this source every year. The large military installation of Fort Bliss is there also. But manufacturing is growing constantly in importance, and this includes the smelting of ore, oil refining, and meat packing, while agriculture through irrigated farming continues as a healthy segment of the economy. The buildings and residences of this city are more typically Spanish than in any other Southwestern city, and the street signs are bi-lingual.

On the high plains of West Texas and in the heart of the Panhandle are two growing cities, Lubbock and Amarillo. Each contains approximately 160,000 people and each is the hub of huge agricultural enterprises. In addition, each receives a large income from the oil and gas industry and from cattle.

Just on the fringe of the Southwest are two cities more and more often linked by a hyphen, Dallas and Fort Worth. Dallas has proved the most aggressive in pursuing industry, including aircraft and electronics manufacturing, automobile assembly, food processing, a rapidly expanding clothing industry, and petroleum processing. In addition, it is a center of finance and insurance companies and a major distribution point for the Lone Star State. This metro-

politan area (population 1,083,601, according to the census of
1960) is now seeking financial aid from the federal government to
dredge the Trinity River to the Gulf Coast, giving it a deep-sea
port. Fort Worth on the other hand, has retained far more of the
Southwestern architecture, attitudes, and approach to life. Some
650,000 people live in its metropolitan area. Its economy is based
on agriculture, ranching, meat packing, flour milling, oil refining,
the manufacture of food and clothing, and an Air Force base.

San Antonio, the third largest city in Texas in population, is a
progressive and modern city which has retained almost as much of
its Spanish charm as El Paso. The San Antonio River flows through
the city, providing a setting for a long Hispanic plaza and park,
while near by are four of the early missions, including the chapel of
San Antonio de Valero (best known as the Alamo), and the Spanish governor's palace. Its people—half a million—derived their income from agriculture, ranching, some manufacturing (principally
the processing of food), tourism, and the huge military complex of
army and air force bases which surround it.

On the Gulf Coast is Corpus Christi, almost a duplicate of San
Diego in many ways. Wide boulevards lined with palms, white-
washed homes topped with red tile, and a large Latin-American
population give this city an air of having a long Spanish heritage,
although it was not established until 1846. It has a population of
almost a quarter of a million. Corpus, as its residents usually call it,
has an excellent harbor developed by subsidies from the federal
government, a huge naval air station, and tens of thousands of tourists who come to enjoy its sub-tropical climate, its natural beauty,
and nearby Padre Island National Park.

If Los Angeles, more national in outlook than regional, stands at
one end of the Southwest, Houston stands at the other. Houston
has grown from 44,633 in 1900 to a metropolitan complex of
1,243,158 residents in 1960, and an estimated 1,500,000 at the
present time. The Chamber of Commerce likes to label Houston
"the largest city in the South"; but it is neither Southwestern nor
Southern. High-rise buildings produce a skyline not unlike that of
Eastern cities, while the Astrodome, a roofed sports stadium
capable of seating more than 50,000 in air-conditioned comfort,
certainly defies a regional label. Like Los Angeles, Houston boasts

major league football and baseball teams, is a center of commerce and manufacturing, and is a huge seaport, linked to the Gulf by a fifty-mile waterway developed with federal funds. An electronics industry is growing in the city to supply the National Aeronautics and Space Administration (NASA), headquartered just outside the city limits and providing thousands of jobs. A convention city, Houston also contains a symphony orchestra, an opera association, museums, and art galleries.

These cities of the Southwest have several features in common. They have grown in size faster than most other cities in the country. Almost without exception, their economies are based on manufacturing, which started during and after World War II; on agriculture and ranching; on exploitation of natural resources, principally copper and petroleum; on nearby military installations; and on their climate, which has provided an unexpected bonanza of tourism. As roads were paved, as fast passenger trains were put into service, and as air travel came of age, Easterners and Northerners came in ever-increasing numbers, either as summer visitors, retired people, or health seekers. "The Sunshine Boom" this phenomenon has been called. Whole cities have sprung into existence solely as retirement centers, with town restrictions preventing anyone younger than a certain age living there. It has been estimated that one in every four non-native-born residents of Arizona moved to the state for his health or because of a health problem in the family, and other parts of the Southwest have received an influx of residents for the same reasons. This is no recent phenomenon; health-seekers started coming to the Southwest in the late nineteenth century when climate was thought to be a cure for tuberculosis and other respiratory diseases.

New Mexico early began a program of attracting tourists through highway markers, historic markers, maps, and tour trails, and thus for a time it received the most income from this source. Other Southwestern states quickly followed where New Mexico led, however, and now all derive a large percentage of their total revenue from tourism. Arizona, for example, reaped an estimated $490,000,000 in 1966 from tourism, and southern California easily topped this figure. A recent poll of foreign visitors to the United States showed the Grand Canyon to be the outstanding natural attraction in the West, and Disneyland near Los Angeles is probably the most famous amusement park in the world. The Southwest also attracts tourists because here the visitor can see—and almost feel —the blending of divergent cultures; here he can see Indians perform their own rituals, he can visit buildings dating from the Spanish period, and he can live at a genuine ranch and see cowboys at their daily tasks. In short, he can glimpse a way of life unknown elsewhere in the United States.

In the rapid urbanization of the Southwest, agriculture and ranching have not been forgotten. Thousands of acres have been taken out of production under federal programs which have subsidized the retirement of farm land, through such means as the soil bank, but each year more and more has been grown on less and less land. Ranching has continued to be a major factor in bringing income to the region, with total beef production climbing each year that drought does not curtail the effort. And as the total population of the United States—and the world—climbs, an ever-increasing percentage of the nation's food supply will be produced on what once was considered "the Great American Desert." The Southwest is a borderland between the Latin-American world of *"mañana"* and the Anglo-American world of "get it done yesterday." It is an awakening giant.

POLITICS IN THE TWENTIETH CENTURY

Building on the earlier economic base of mining, ranching, and farming, the Southwest has come of age in the twentieth century. Today, although the national image of the region may still include lonely prospectors, tough cowboys, and chivalrous outlaws, the Southwest is an industrial area of big business with an aggressive outlook. Yet in no area of its existence is the Southwest so tied to its past as in politics. On the one hand, the residents are firmly committed to the concept of rugged individualism, ready on any occasion to declaim against encroaching paternalism in government and to bemoan the high taxes that federal services require. On the other, Southwesterners are firmly committed to the necessity of federal funds for conquering the harsh realities of geography and the resulting difficulties of wresting a livelihood from an inhospitable land. The Southwest was acquired from Mexico through federal expenditures for a war and for purchase; the Indian menace was removed at federal expense; transportation with the outside world was made possible by funds from the national treasury, as was the building of giant dams and aqueducts to reclaim an arid land; the mines were protected by import duties and their output guaranteed a good price through federal subsidies and purchasing programs; and the produce of its fields, animal and vegetable, have been subsidized in many ways. In effect, the Southwest has posed as a land devoted to individualism, yet it has elected representatives to Washington who talk individualism while voting for the expenditure of more and yet more federal funds for Southwestern projects. The best description for this phenomenon is "political schizophrenia."

In the selection of its governors and representatives in Washington, the Southwest has been true to its self-claimed devotion to individualism. Its political leaders have been outstanding—but not always outstanding in the sense of seeking state and regional improvements. Each state has been dominated by a few political figures, but not political bosses in the traditional Eastern or Midwestern concept. The voters of the region have been overwhelmingly Democratic in their registration, but have elected Republicans with surprising frequency. In fact, it can be said that the Southwest has as unique a political heritage as a historic heritage.

In Texas the Progressive governorship of James E. "Pa" Ferguson came to an end with his impeachment in 1917. However, Fergusonism would dominate Texas politics for almost a quarter of a century. In 1918 Pa contested the governorship with his successor, William P. Hobby, but lost. Two years later, because the courts had ruled that his impeachment prevented him ever from holding a state office, he formed the American political party and ran for the presidency of the United States, getting about sixty thousand votes. Two years later he ran for a U. S. Senate seat, contending that this was not a state office, and received 265,233 votes, some 52,000 less than his opponent. In 1924 Governor Pat Neff, a Baptist who refused to hold an innaugural ball because he did not believe in dancing, chose not to run for a third term. That year Pa Ferguson hit upon the expedient of running his wife for governor; "Ma" (her initials were M.A.) surprised the state's political experts by finishing a surprising second in the Democratic primary and thus gaining a berth in the runoff. "A vote for me is a vote of confidence for my husband," she would say to her audiences; then Pa would speak. To the charges that his wife was merely a front, Pa would reply that the state could get "two governors for the price of one" by electing his spouse. His major platform plank was ending the power of the Ku Klux Klan in Texas, an organization that was anti-Catholic, anti-Negro, and anti-Jewish, and which had grown up in the postwar era to enforce morality through swamp justice. Ma won a surprising victory in the runoff, carrying the state by almost one hundred thousand votes. One of her first acts as governor was to request the legislature to pass a law making it a criminal offense to wear a mask in public; the legislature complied, and the Klan was broken as a social-political force in Texas. Mrs. Ferguson could say of the family fortunes, as their car came to a halt in front of the governor's mansion, "We departed in disgrace; we now return in glory."

The glory lasted only two years, however. In the election of 1926 the Fergusons went down to defeat because of charges of fraud in the state highway construction projects and in Ma's liberal use of the pardoning power. Attorney General Dan Moody was swept into office for the following four years—a quiet, conservative period in the statehouse. In 1930 Ma emerged from retirement to contest for the governor's seat, only to lose to oil-millionaire Ross Sterling in the runoff. Two years later, with the national depression affecting every pocketbook in the state, Ma defeated Sterling to become governor a second time. However, she seemed to have mellowed with age, for her second term was quiet and relatively uneventful. She kept her campaign pledge to get a $20,000,000 bond issue passed for relief measures. In the election of 1934, the Fergusons were defeated by the conservative James V. Allred, the attorney general who had attracted widespread attention because of his determined fight against monopolies and his enforcement of the anti-trust laws. In 1936 he was returned to office overwhelmingly, and it seemed that the Fergusons were through, but they would return for one last try; in 1940 Ma again made the race for governor, but the people had a new champion.

In 1938 a Fort Worth radio announcer and flour salesman, who admittedly had never paid a poll tax or voted, declared his candidacy for governor, to be answered by an amused chuckle from editors, businessmen, and politicians. W. Lee O'Daniel was president of a flour firm marketing "Hillbilly Flour" and was master of ceremonies of a weekday radio program devoted to the hillbilly music of a group called the "Light Crust Doughboys." On the air he told housewives how to mend broken dishes and broken hearts, sang hillbilly and religious music, recited such poems as "The Boy Who Never Got Too Old to Comb His Mother's Hair," told stories of national and state heroes, gave advice on morals, safety, and thrift —and sold flour. For his campaign "Pappy," as he was called, used a bus fitted with a loudspeaker and took his Light Crust Doughboys with him. His platform, he declared, was the Ten Commandments and his motto the Golden Rule. When asked to translate these generalities into specifics, he replied by promising higher old-age pensions and deriding "professional politicians." Just before the election a reporter asked Pappy what he thought of his chances; O'Daniel replied, "I don't know whether or not I'll get elected, but, boy! it sure is good for the flour business." He won without a runoff, both then and two years later. In 1941, following the death of U. S. Senator Morris Sheppard, Pappy entered the lists for this seat, contesting with twenty-eight other candidates, among them Texas congressman Lyndon Johnson. O'Daniel told his audiences that he was going to Washington to help "that boy" (Franklin D. Roosevelt), and said he would place Texas politicians on the national scene "on probation." By a scant margin Pappy was elected to fill the vacant seat, and in 1942 he won re-election despite opposition by two former governors, Allred and Moody. In 1948 Pappy chose to retire, his seat going to Lyndon Johnson in an election long remembered in the Lone Star State for the irregularities that saw Lyndon Johnson winning by a scant eighty-seven votes.

Texas politics since World War II have been a little more dignified, with showmanship considered of less importance than ability. However, the contests have lost none of their heat. Coke Stevenson succeeded O'Daniel as chief executive and governed during the war. In the election of 1946 Railroad Commissioner Beauford Jester defeated Dr. Frank Rainey, ex-chancellor of the University of Texas who had been fired because "dirty" books were used in sophomore literature classes. When Jester died in 1949 Lieutenant-Governor Allan Shivers succeeded him, then won three consecutive victories on his own to govern until 1956. There was a scandal in the state system which helped veterans to acquire farms, and Shivers was discredited somewhat, though his involvement in the fraud was never proved, and U. S. Senator Price Daniel returned to win the race for governor. After three terms in office, Daniel was defeated in 1962 by John Connally, who had served the federal government as Secretary of the Navy. Connally easily won re-election in 1964 and 1966, as the three-term precedent became more firmly entrenched.

Texans serving with note on the national scene during the twentieth century include such famous persons as Colonel E. M. House, unofficial adviser to President Woodrow Wilson; Senator Morris Sheppard, author of the Eighteenth Amendment (Prohibition); Albert Sidney Burleson, Postmaster General in Wilson's cabinet; David Franklin Houston, Secretary of Agriculture in Wilson's cabinet; John Nance Garner, Vice-President during Franklin D. Roosevelt's first two terms as President; and Sam Rayburn, an East Texas congressman who through long years of service and distinguished contributions became Speaker of the House of Representatives and a strong voice at the national level. Finally there is Lyndon B. Johnson, who went to Washington in 1933 as an assistant to a South Texas congressman, then was elected to Congress himself in 1936. In the election of 1948 he narrowly won a seat in the United States Senate, where as Majority Leader he gained a reputation for "getting things done." An ardent supporter of the New Deal of Franklin D. Roosevelt, Johnson began changing his image to that of conservative in the postwar period to match that of his home state; however, the narrowness of his election both in 1948 and 1954 showed that his home state was not overwhelmingly convinced that he reflected the viewpoint of his "fellow Texans," as he was wont to address them.

In the national election of 1960 Senator Johnson went to San

Francisco determined to secure the Democratic nomination, only to lose to the junior Senator from Massachusetts, John F. Kennedy. In a bid for Southern support, Kennedy asked Johnson to join him on the ticket as the vice-presidential nominee. Some serious political observers have suggested that the proud Texan accepted the invitation because he feared his home base was not sufficiently secure; he could never project a national image as a liberal and at the same time win re-election at home. The Kennedy-Johnson ticket did carry the South and Texas, although there were many cries of fraud in the Lone Star State's election. Then when John F. Kennedy was assassinated in Dallas in 1963, Johnson became the leader of the nation.

In its over-all voting patterns, Texas has reflected more of the Old South than of the Southwest. This has been due to the fact that the constitution of 1876, under which the state is still governed, reflects the rural element that framed it. Texas has been almost exclusively Democratic in its balloting, the winning of the nomination of that party usually sufficing to ensure victory in the November general elections. The Republicans have carried the state in only three presidential elections since Reconstruction—1928, 1952, and 1956; in each instance the Republican was more conservative than his opponent. And the Republicans have managed to elect one senator, John Tower, in 1961 and 1966, and a few representatives. Generally it has been the votes in the Southwestern portion of the state—i.e. West Texas—which have enabled the Republicans to win these few victories. One other fact stands out; although every governor since Reconstruction has been a Democrat, in recent years these men have been conservatives at odds with the national philosophy of their party.

New Mexico, by contrast, has remained a political frontier, a throwback to the Jacksonian era when "to the victor belongs the spoils" was a way of life, not just a motto. The arrival of statehood in 1912 did not alter the existing alliance between the influential Spanish-Mexican families and the handful of American families who emulated them, an alliance that allowed them to dominate territorial politics. The absence of a merit system enabled the winning faction to hand out territorial jobs from the top to the bottom, bringing state business to a complete standstill when a new administration took office. Because the national administrations tended to be Republican from 1860 to 1912, New Mexico was Republican too, the Washington political appointees conspiring with local *patrónes* to dominate the Territory. Thus when New Mexico became a state the Republicans had such an edge that they were able to dominate the legislature from 1912 to 1921 and from 1927 to 1931. However, from 1931 to the present day both houses have been Democratic with only one exception, and in that instance the Republicans dominated the house by only one vote.

In its gubernatorial contests, New Mexico proved evenly balanced during its first eighteen years as a state, the Democrats winning four times and the Republicans four times. William C. McDonald, a Democrat, won the first election, followed by Ezequial Cabeza de Baca, a Democrat who died in office in 1917; Washington E. Lindsey, Republican and progressive, 1917–18; Octavian A. Larrazolo, Republican and liberal, 1918–20; Merritt C. Mechem, Republican, 1920–22; James Hinkle, a Democrat and liberal, 1922–24, who was not renominated because he was charged with discriminating against Latin-Americans in his appointments; Arthur T. Hannett, Democrat, 1924–26; and Richard C. Dillon, Republican, 1926–30, who was the first governor in New Mexico to serve two terms, and he did so by doing almost nothing. From 1930 to the present only two Republicans have been elected chief executive of New Mexico, Edwin L. Mecham whose victories in 1950, 1952, and 1956 reflect both his personal charm and the voters' disenchantment with Democratic leadership, and David F. Cargo whose victory in 1966 reflected a noteworthy shift in the Southwest toward Republicans and moderate conservatism. The Mexican-American voters of the state as a rule have allied themselves strongly with the Democratic party, but that party has not been in tune with its national leadership in the trend toward liberalism.

On the national scene the first New Mexican to win real stature was Albert Bacon Fall, who was sent to the U. S. Senate immediately after statehood. In 1921 his friendship with Warren G. Harding brought him an appointment as Secretary of the Interior. In that position he was involved in the Teapot Dome scandal; as Secretary of the Interior he signed leases allowing H. F. Sinclair to take oil from the naval oil reserves. Both were tried for conspiracy to defraud the government; the charges later were dismissed, but the scandal ruined Fall's career. Two other New Mexican senators rose to prominence: Dennis Chávez and Clinton P. Anderson. Chávez, after a long career in state politics, went to Congress in 1930, then became a senator in 1935; his base was the Latin-American population of the state, and he was a tireless supporter of the New Deal philosophy until his death in 1962. He is generally credited with securing for the state its many federal installations and jobs. Anderson, however, has made a reputation as a national statesman rather than as a representative of a Southwestern state. Formerly a newspaper editor, Anderson went to Congress in 1941, then became Secretary of Agriculture from 1945 to 1948, finally moving to the Senate in the election of 1948 where he has become a recognized authority for his work, particularly on the Atomic Energy Commission.

Arizona, like New Mexico, has been in the Democratic camp more than the Republican. Of its thirteen governors since statehood, eight have been Democrats and five Republicans. Of these men the most colorful was George W. P. Hunt, who won the chief executive's office seven times. His was a rags-to-riches story, for he came to the Grand Canyon State as a prospector in 1881, rose to become a merchant and banker, was seven times a legislator before statehood, and was president of the constitutional convention. Hunt pretended to be very liberal, declaring that he always kept the front door open to the laboring class; he failed to advertise, however, that his back door was always open to copper and railroading interests. In the dramatic shift to Republicans in the election of 1966, Arizona not only elected Jack Williams governor but also gave the Grand Old Party a majority in both houses of its legislature for the first time in its history.

First and foremost among Arizona's national leaders has stood Carl Hayden, who went to Congress in 1912, then rose to the Senate in 1926 and has remained there since. Also noteworthy are Earnest McFarland, who served in the Senate from 1941 to 1952, where he was Majority Leader for a time, and who then governed the state for four years; and Stewart Udall, who became Secretary of the Interior in 1961. But perhaps the most famous Arizonan of all on the national scene is Barry Goldwater, senator from Arizona from 1953 to 1964 and in the latter year the Republican nominee for president. Goldwater has become a symbol of conservative thinking in the United States, but even he has worked for federal financing of the Central Arizona project.

Since the departure of Hiram Johnson from the California governorship, for the U. S. Senate, the state has elected eight Republicans and two Democrats. Yet the Democrats have a majority of two to one in registered voters over their opponents. The overall tenor of California's politics has been toward liberalism, although there is a strongly entrenched element of the radical right in the state, especially in southern California. The John Birch Society has a higher percentage of membership in this part of the Southwest than in almost any other part of the nation. There was also a confusing law that allowed cross-filing in primaries, a holdover from the Progressive movement at the turn of the twentieth century that made party politics less meaningful than the choice of candidates. This law was recently repealed, but Californians still tend to vote for the candidate rather than the party.

William D. Stephens, who succeeded Johnson, was a strong wartime governor, and won his own four-year term as a result. The next governor of note was James Rolph, Jr., perhaps California's most picturesque chief executive. He rose to prominence as a reform mayor of San Francisco, then in 1930 won the Republican primary as an avowed "wet" in a contest that had Prohibition as its major issue. As a Depression governor, Rolph showed great concern for the plight of the "poor, the stricken and the unfortunate," as he termed the "wards of the state." He used the thirty-million-dollar surplus in the state treasury to aid the needy, which included literally tens of thousands of immigrants from the South and Midwest—the "Okies." Rolph died in office in June 1934 and was succeeded by Frank F. Merriam, another Republican; and contrary to the national trend during the Depression, he won the office in his own right in the election that year. He was followed by Culbert L. Olson, the first Democrat to hold the office in forty years; and he was in office when World War II broke out. But it was Earl Warren, a Republican, who gained fame as the wartime governor of California. He came to the office in 1943. Warren won re-election twice, and governed the state for almost eleven years, the longest of any California chief executive; he resigned on October 4, 1953, to become Chief Justice of the United States Supreme Court. A Democrat, Pat Brown, who first won the office in 1958, attempted to win a third term in 1966, but was defeated by Ronald Reagan, a movie actor and a Republican who ran as a moderate conservative.

Nationally, California has been represented not only by Earl Warren, but also by a president and a vice-president. Herbert Hoover was born in Iowa, but grew to manhood in California. Richard M. Nixon rose from congressman to senator to vice-president while a Californian, moving to New York only after losing the race for governor in 1962 to Pat Brown. Also prominent from California was Senator William F. Knowland, an Oakland publisher who served as Majority Leader before trying unsuccessfully to become governor in 1958.

In the Southwest as a whole the Democratic party has almost two registered voters for each registered Republican. Yet this ratio is changing rapidly as the Democratic party moves more and more to the political left and the Republican party to the right. Excluding northern California and East Texas from the count, the strength of the two parties is yet more evenly matched. Terms of office in the Southwestern states are short, the governors of Texas, New Mexico, and Arizona serving only two-year terms; the pay is low, the governor of New Mexico receiving $17,500, and Arizona's chief executive receiving $22,500 but no official residence; their power is severely limited by the terms of the state constitutions; and the extreme detail of the constitutions prevents the legislatures from acting effectively. The result of these factors has been an abdication of state action in most areas, leaving it to the federal government to act. The national election of 1964 reflects the prevailing Southwestern attitude: Lyndon Johnson won in Texas, New Mexico, and California, while Barry Goldwater, who personifies Southwestern virtues and philosophy far more than his opponent, carried only his home state of Arizona—and that was probably because he was a native son.

Yet coming from the Southwest no longer is an obstacle to high national office. In recent years both major national political parties have nominated natives of the region as candidates for the presidency, while cabinet members and other high-ranking government officials have been Southwesterners. But the Southwest must soon overhaul its state governments. It must soon act, accomplish, and change—or else accept the doctrine of federal control. It must end its tradition of electing men who talk conservative at home but who vote liberal in Washington. In short, the complexities of mid-twentieth century leave it little room for political schizophrenia.

SOCIAL AND CULTURAL CURRENTS IN THE SOUTHWEST

On March 20, 1880, at an event celebrating the arrival of the railroad at Tucson, Arizona Territory, William S. Oury spoke glowingly about the future, but he also noted with sadness the passing of an era. "Our mission is ended today," he declared, referring to the pioneer.

> Here then arises the question, what are you to do with us? The enterprise of such men as now surround me has penetrated every corner of our broad land, and we now have no frontier to which the pioneer may flee to avoid the tramp of civilized progress; moreover, the weight of years had fallen upon us, consequently the few remaining years which the Divine Master may have in store for us must be spent amongst you; and in the whirl of excitement incident to the race after the precious treasure embedded in our mountain ranges, our last request is that you kindly avoid trampling in the dust the few remaining monuments of the first American settlement of Arizona.

Oury knew the Southwest as few men did; he had been one of the last men sent from the Alamo before its fall, had fought at San Jacinto, and had moved westward with the tide of history. As a pioneer, he knew the rapidity of change—and the Souhwesterner's tendency to ignore the past in order to concentrate on the future. Yet a knowledge of that past, he perceived, was necessary to an understanding and appreciation of the present and future. In 1884 he helped to found the Society of Arizona Pioneers and served as its first president. And yet that Territory was a late-comer to this field, for the Society of California Pioneers had been established in

1850 and the Historical Society of New Mexico in 1859. Then in 1883 came the founding of the Historical Society of Southern California, headquartered at Los Angeles, the California Historical Society, at San Francisco, in 1886, and eleven years later the Texas State Historical Association.

These societies for the most part were little more than antiquarian clubs, their accomplishments miniscule in comparison with their opportunities. The Historical Society of New Mexico, for example, adjourned *sine die* in 1863 and did not meet again until a reorganization in 1880; then in 1926 it began publishing a historical quarterly, but in the early 1960's the quarterly had to be subsidized by the University of New Mexico in order to continue publication. The California Historical Society accomplished little until it was reorganized in 1922, when it began publishing a quarterly. The Society of Arizona Pioneers was given official status in 1897 by the legislature, which renamed it the Arizona Pioneers' Historical Society, but the organization remained a social club until the late 1950's when it began functioning as a proper state historical society; its quarterly journal dates from 1960. Of all these early organizations only the Texas State Historical Association has enjoyed a uniformly satisfactory existence; that society was organized by professional historians and has continued to be administered by professional historians.

Education in the Southwest began with the Jesuit and Franciscan padres who worked both inside and outside the missions to teach the young—and often the adults also. During the Mexican period of Southwestern history very little was accomplished in this field, and the few parents who could afford it sent their children elsewhere to acquire the fundamentals of knowledge. Texas, the first area to break away from Mexico, was the first to encourage a system of free public schools; in fact, one of the grievances listed as a reason for declaring independence from Mexico was that nation's failure to provide for education. After statehood and the Mexican War, the Texas legislature turned to making this dream a reality; in 1854 a public school law set aside $2,000,000 as a permanent endowment for schools (the money came from the funds paid by the federal government for the land claimed by Texas and given up by terms of the Compromise of 1850). Part of the public domain likewise was set aside for the schools. Reconstruction indirectly set back the cause of public education in Texas by many years, for although compulsory, *integrated* schooling was provided for by the carpetbag-scalawag government, it was dispensed with by the Texans who subsequently controlled the government. Not until 1915 was compulsory attendance again enacted.

California also provided early for a system of free public schools. Several such schools were in operation before statehood in 1850. And the first constitution obligated the legislature to provide for schools, to operate for at least three months each year, which was done in 1851. The school law of 1866 completed the task of providing statewide educational facilities. Arizona lagged considerably behind Texas and California in education, the first school law reaching the statute books in 1871 during the meeting of the sixth territorial legislature. Like its sister territory of New Mexico, Arizona had a severe language handicap—some of its citizens spoke only Spanish, some only English, and some only the various Indian dialects. As Miss Elizabeth Post later wrote of her experience at Ehrenberg, Arizona, in 1872, "I had fifteen pupils not one of whom knew any English; and I knew nothing of Spanish." Even that was not as bad as the difficulty faced by Miss Clara Stillman who came to Bisbee, Arizona, in 1881; she asserted that no one worried about fire drills: "The Indian drill was the real thing. Four blasts from the whistle at the hoisting works—two short, one long, one short—warned the villagers that there was danger, and women and little children, as well as school boys and girls, sought shelter in the [copper mine] tunnel."

New Mexico simply disregarded the problem of public education until the beginning of the twentieth century; the widespread poverty of the region was one excuse, but the principal reason for this failure was the opposition of the Catholic clergy, which wanted the parochial school system to have no competitor. In 1889 a law requiring teachers to be able to read and write either Spanish or English was passed, and in the 1890's there was a compulsory attendance law (that was more flouted than followed). Gradually Spanish has been eliminated as a language of instruction, and a statewide system of public schools has become a reality. But the feud continues about the role of the Church in this system, for in many public schools Catholic nuns, members of religious orders, and lay brothers are employed as teachers.

Similar progress has been made in the realm of higher education. The oldest institutions almost invariably are denominational. Baylor University in Texas, founded by Baptists, was chartered in 1845 by the Republic; the University of Santa Clara, California, a Catholic school for men, traces its origins to 1851, and St. Michael's College in Santa Fe, also Catholic, opened its doors in 1859. The University of Southern California was founded in 1879 at Los Angeles by the Methodists; three years later the City of the Angels developed a branch of the state normal school at San Jose, a branch that later would develop into the University of California at Los Angeles (U.C.L.A.). Finally, San Diego State College was founded in 1897. In the mid-twentieth century the legislature pulled the California state colleges and universities into a cohesive system.

In Texas the first public institution of higher learning was a Morrill Land Grant college: Texas Agricultural and Mechanical College, opened in 1876. The University of Texas was first authorized by the legislature in 1858, but did not open its doors until 1883. Arizona's first public university was approved in 1885, but six years elapsed before it admitted students. A normal school at Tempe was also authorized in 1885; opening its doors early in 1886, it grew and changed until it became Arizona State University. The New Mexican legislature in 1889 authorized its first public institutions of higher learning: a university at Albuquerque, an agricultural college at Las Cruces, and a school of mines at Socorro; the first two would grow into the University of New Mexico and New Mexico State University. Other Southwestern schools of note are: Texas Technological College, opened in Lubbock in 1925; Texas Western College at El Paso, a branch of the University of Texas intended as a school of mines, which opened in 1914, and which has recently been renamed The University of Texas at El Paso; and two private schools, Texas Christian University at Fort Worth, opened in 1873, and Southern Methodist University at Dallas, established in 1910.

Besides wanting excellent educational systems, Southwestern pioneers also wanted the trappings of culture they had left behind in the East. Traveling theater groups played to packed houses in almost every mining camp in the Southwest, each of which had an "opera house." Literature flowed from the pens of newcomers to the region, and literally thousands of books have been published dealing with the adventures of gold-seekers, ranchers, peace officers, pathfinders, and even businessmen.

Art, music, literature, and the theater are still an integral part of the Southwest. Every city of any size has its little theater group, its symphony orchestra, its artists, and its musicians. Traveling road companies, as well as local productions, bring Broadway hits and great plays of the past to every city of any size. There are plenty of writers and artists in the Southwest, and not only at the universities and colleges. The Taos art colony has several famous members, while Tucson has over four hundred artists making a living from their products.

The Southwest has a good record of race relations. The Indians are widely accepted as an asset to the region, an attraction for tourists and tourist dollars. When educated, they have little difficulty finding employment in the cities, and may leave the reservations to join the white man's society with minimum difficulty. The largest minority bloc in the Southwest is the Latin-American community, where again there is little discrimination. In Arizona and New Mexico the first Anglo-American settlers intermarried with the Spanish-Mexican element because there were so few women of their own race on the frontier. This easy mingling of races has continued to the present. In Texas, because of the history of the area, too many Anglo-Americans have remembered the Alamo and Goliad and have continued the racial hatreds of those days. In California the trend has followed that of Texas—for different reasons. There they have thought of the "Spaniards" as acceptable but the "Mexicans" as unacceptable; in effect, this has meant that a Latin American with money is considered a Spaniard and one without it a Mexican. The percentage of Negroes in the Southwest has been small; but in such large cities as Los Angeles Negroes have congregated in large numbers. The Watts Riot of 1965 in Los Angeles was very similar to the riots in Chicago, Detroit, San Francisco, New York, and other cities.

The Negroes and Latin Americans are more urban than rural.

As a group they are financially deprived, their annual incomes far below that of the Anglo-American majority. Fortunately their educational gap is closing, rapidly among the young, and with education will come a higher income and a better standard of living. Intermarriage between Latin Americans and Anglos is increasing in the Southwest; in the 1920's the intermarriage rate was 10 per cent, in 1963 it was 25 per cent. While Southwesterners can point with pride to the strides that have been made, much remains to be done, particularly for the Indian.

7

THE SOUTHWEST IN
PERSPECTIVE

"Changed unspeakably and utterly," Emerson Hough wrote with regret in *Century Magazine* in 1902, "the Old West lies in ruins." Today too the Southwest is changed—but it does not lie in ruins. Just as an elderly person looks in the face of a lifelong friend and sees in it many shadows of the young person he once knew despite the changes that time and experience have wrought, so the old-timer today can look at the Southwest and see echoes of the region that was—echoes in the vast, open spaces between the cities, and echoes in the architecture, place names, food, dress, even the patterns of speech and thought in the metropolitan areas.

But the face of the region has changed—the dynamic advances from without have combined with the restless energy and boundless resources from within to build a modern Southwest. Air conditioning has made the extreme heat of summer bearable; canals, dams, and irrigation wells have made extensive farming and ranching possible on what once was desert land; hydroelectric power, climate, and natural resources have brought industry; modern transportation has made the region accessible; and the influx of people has necessitated the building of skyscrapers, apartment houses, and tract homes, with the result that large cities have developed.

Yet these changes are nothing compared with what the future holds. When desalted ocean water is available, wild Saguaro cacti, Joshua and mesquite trees, and other desert vegetation will give way to still more orderly rows of cotton, sorghum, and corn. The cities will grow larger and—as invariably happens—lose much of their regional flavor. Houston and Los Angeles have already turned their backs on their Southwestern heritage and have become truly national cities, thereby forfeiting much of their charm. Even Phoenix, a true child of the desert Southwest, is becoming a carbon copy of Eastern cities. Other cities of the region, such as Corpus Christi, San Antonio, El Paso, Santa Fe, Albuquerque, Tucson, and San Diego, have made an effort (sometimes consciously, sometimes unconsciously) to retain their regional flavor. They have tried to combine the best of the old with the best of the new, keeping their charm yet staying abreast of the times.

The failure of many Southwesterners to appreciate their historical heritage has led to several disturbing trends besides the changes in the architecture of their cities. They are changing the names of their streets to "Elm" and "Maple." They are aping the manners, customs, and dress of Easterners. And in the process they are doing a disservice to their own ancestors and to the nation. The Southwest has much worthy of preservation, many contributions to make to the national heritage that should not be lost. Nor have Southwesterners learned that the changes they are making are losing them money. The tourist does not journey to the region to see a reflection of what he left at home. He comes to see something different.

Despite the many changes that time has wrought, and the many more innovations that the future holds, nature will always be waiting for the unwary in the region. The mountains will remain, the rains will not fall more often, nor will the lava beds give way to the plow. And just as these facts are immutable, so hopefully is the Southwestern heritage of courage and fortitude, of generosity and hospitality, of informality and openness. If these traits of a unique past remain, then the sacrifices of the pioneers will not have been in vain, and the regionalism of the Southwest will truly be making a contribution to the national heritage.

A BIBLIOGRAPHICAL NOTE

The writer of a general history must of necessity rely on hundreds of published works: books, monographs, articles. He cannot do all the original research himself, for such would be the task of several lifetimes. Nor can he, for reasons of space, include in the bibliography of a single volume all the materials he has consulted. Unfortunately there is no comprehensive bibliography of the Southwest now available to which the inquisitive reader can be referred. Such a work would fill many volumes—and still be incomplete. Therefore I have chosen to include only a short listing of works generally available. The first section lists some of the bibliographies of the region; section two contains a selected number of regional histories; section three includes histories of the states covered in this volume; section four is a listing of the scholarly journals which devote themselves to a study of the Southwest; and section five is a recommended reading list of firsthand accounts, general works, even novels, which I recommend.

BIBLIOGRAPHIES

Alliot, Hector. *Bibliography of Arizona.* Los Angeles, 1914.
Blumann, Ethel, and Mabel W. Thomas. *California Local History: A Centennial Bibliography.* 2 vols. Stanford, 1950.
Campbell, Walter. *The Book Lovers' Southwest.* Norman, 1955.
Cowan, Robert E., and Robert G. Cowan. *A Bibliography of the History of California, 1510–1930.* 3 vols. San Francisco, 1933.
Dobie, J. Frank. *Guide to Life and Literature in the Southwest.* Dallas, 1965.
Jenkins, John H. *Cracker Barrel Chronicles: A Bibliography of Texas Towns and County Histories.* Austin, 1965.
Powell, Lawrence C. *Southwestern Book Trails.* Albuquerque, 1963.
Rader, Jesse L. *South of Forty, from the Mississippi to the Rio Grande: A Bibliography.* Norman, 1947.
Raines, C. W. *A Bibliography of Texas.* Austin, 1896, and reprint.

Rittenhouse, Jack D. *New Mexico Civil War Bibliography.* Houston, 1961.

Saunders, Lyle. *A Guide to Materials Bearing on Cultural Relations in New Mexico.* Albuquerque, 1944.

Streeter, Thomas W. *Bibliography of Texas, 1795–1845.* Cambridge, 1955.

Wagner, Henry R. *The Spanish Southwest, 1542–1794.* 2 vols. Albuquerque, 1937, and reprint.

Wallace, Andrew. *Sources and Readings in Arizona History.* Tucson, 1965.

Winkler, Ernest W. *Check List of Texas Imprints.* 2 vols. Austin, 1963.

Winther, Oscar O. *A Classified Bibliography of the Periodical Literature of the Trans-Mississippi West, 1811–1957.* Bloomington, 1961.

REGIONAL HISTORIES

Billington, Ray A. *Westward Expansion.* New York, 1949, and subsequent revisions.

Hafen, LeRoy R., and Carl C. Rister. *Western America.* New York, 1941, and subsequent revisions.

Hollon, W. Eugene. *The Southwest: Old and New.* New York, 1961.

Perrigo, Lynn. *Our Spanish Southwest.* Dallas, 1960.

Peyton, Green. *America's Heartland: The Southwest.* Norman, 1948.

Richardson, Rupert N., and Carl C. Rister. *The Greater Southwest.* Glendale, 1934.

STATE HISTORIES

Bancroft, Hubert H. *History of Arizona and New Mexico.* San Francisco, 1889, and reprint.

———. *History of California.* 7 vols. San Francisco, 1886–90, and reprint.

———. *History of Nevada, Colorado, and Wyoming.* San Francisco, 1890.

———. *History of the North Mexican States and Texas.* 2 vols. San Francisco, 1884–89.

———. *History of Utah.* San Francisco, 1889.

Beck, Warren A. *New Mexico: A History of Four Centuries.* Norman, 1962.

Caughey, John W. *California.* Englewood Cliffs, 1953.

Cleland, Robert G. *From Wilderness to Empire: A History of California,* ed. by Glenn S. Dumke. New York, 1959.

Connor, Seymour V. *The Saga of Texas*. 6 vols. Austin, 1965.

Fehrenbacher, Don E. *A Basic History of California*. Princeton, 1964.

Hafen, LeRoy R., and James H. Baker. *History of Colorado*. 5 vols. Denver, 1927.

Hammond, George P., and C. Donnally Thomas. *The Story of New Mexico*. Albuquerque, 1947.

Hulse, James W. *The Nevada Adventure*. Reno, 1965.

Ostrander, Gilman M. *Nevada: The Great Rotten Burough, 1859–1964*. New York, 1966.

Paré, Madeline, and Bert Fireman. *Arizona Pageant*. Phoenix, 1965.

Reeve, Frank D. *New Mexico*. Denver, 1964.

Richardson, Rupert N. *Texas: The Lone Star State*. Englewood Cliffs, 1958.

Rolle, Andrew F. *California*. New York, 1963.

Sutton, Wain. *Utah: A Centennial History*. 3 vols. New York, 1949.

Wyllys, Rufus K. *Arizona: The History of a Frontier State*. Phoenix, 1950.

JOURNALS OF HISTORY

Arizona and the West. Tucson: The University of Arizona.

California Historical Society Quarterly. San Francisco: 2090 Jackson Street.

The Colorado Magazine. Denver: E. 14th Avenue at Sherman Street.

The Journal of Arizona History. Tucson: 949 East Second Street.

Nevada Historical Society Quarterly. Reno: P. O. Box 1129.

New Mexico Historical Review. Albuquerque: The University of New Mexico.

Panhandle-Plains Historical Review. Canyon (Texas): Panhandle-Plains Historical Society.

Password. El Paso: 1503 Hawthorne.

Southern California Quarterly. Los Angeles: 200 East Avenue 43.

Southwestern Historical Quarterly. Austin: Box 8059, University Station.

Texana. Waco (Texas): 1301 Jefferson Avenue.

Utah Historical Quarterly. Salt Lake City: 603 East South Temple Street.

West Texas Historical Association Year Book. Abilene: Hardin-Simmons University.

RECOMMENDED GENERAL READING

Abbott, E. C., and Helena H. Smith. *We Pointed Them North.* Norman, 1955.

Adams, Andy. *The Log of a Cowboy.* New York, 1903, and reprints.

Allen, Merritt P. *William Walker, Filibuster.* New York, 1932.

Arnold, Elliott. *Blood Brother.* New York, 1947, and reprint.

Arrowsmith, Rex. *Mines of the Old Southwest.* Santa Fe, 1963.

Athearn, Robert G. *Rebel of the Rockies: A History of the Denver and Rio Grande Railroad.* New Haven, 1962.

Atherton, Lewis E. *The Cattle Kings.* Bloomington, 1961.

Bailey, Jessie B. *Diego de Vargas and the Reconquest of New Mexico.* Albuquerque, 1940.

Baldwin, Gordon. *The Warrior Apaches.* Tucson, 1966.

Barker, Eugene C. *The Life of Stephen F. Austin.* Austin, 1949.

Bartlett, John R. *Personal Narrative of Explorations and Incidents.* . . . New York, 1854, and reprint.

Bartlett, Richard A. *Great Surveys of the American West.* Norman, 1962.

Bieber, Ralph P., and LeRoy R. Hafen (eds.). *The Southwest Historical Series.* 12 vols. Glendale, 1931–43.

Bolton, Herbert E. *Coronado: Knight of Pueblos and Plains.* Albuquerque, 1949, and reprint.

———— (ed.). *Kino's Historical Memoir of Pimería Alta.* 2 vols. Cleveland, 1919.

————. *The Spanish Borderlands.* New Haven, 1921.

———— (ed.). *Spanish Exploration in the Southwest, 1542–1706.* New York, 1908, and reprint.

————. *Texas in the Middle Eighteenth Century.* Berkeley, 1915, and reprint.

Bonsal, Stephen. *Edward Fitzgerald Beale.* New York, 1912.

Bourke, John G. *On the Border with Crook.* New York, 1891, and reprint.

Brinckerhoff, Sidney B., and O. B. Faulk. *Lancers for the King.* Phoenix, 1965.

Cabeza de Vaca, Alvar Nuñez. *Relation that Alvar Nuñez Cabeza de Vaca gave.* . . . Available in several editions.

Cather, Willa. *Death Comes for the Archbishop.* New York, 1927, and reprint.

Caughey, John W. *Gold is the Cornerstone.* Berkeley, 1948.

Clarke, Dwight L. *Stephen Watts Kearny: Soldier of the West.* Norman, 1961.

Cleland, Robert G. *A History of Phelps-Dodge, 1834–1950.* New York, 1952.

———. *Pathfinders.* San Francisco, 1929.

Colton, Ray C. *The Civil War in the Western Territories.* Norman, 1959.

Cooke, Philip St. George. *The Conquest of New Mexico and California.* New York, 1878, and reprint.

Crampton, C. Gregory. *Standing Up Country.* New York, 1964.

Dale, Edward E. *The Range Cattle Industry.* Norman, 1930.

Dobie, J. Frank. *Apache Gold and Yaqui Silver.* Boston, 1939.

———. *The Longhorns.* Boston, 1941.

———. *The Mustangs.* Boston, 1952.

Douglas, William O. *Farewell to Texas: A Vanishing Wilderness.* New York, 1967.

Duval, J. C. *Early Times in Texas.* Dallas, 1936.

Edwards, Everett. *Agriculture: The First Three Hundred Years.* Washington, 1940.

Elliott, Russell R. *Nevada's Twentieth Century Mining Boom: Tonopah —Goldfield—Ely.* Reno, 1966.

Faulk, Odie B. *The Last Years of Spanish Texas, 1778–1821.* The Hague, 1964.

———. *Too Far North—Too Far South.* Los Angeles, 1967.

Fenin, George N., and Everson, William K. *The Western, from Silents to Cinerama.* New York, 1962.

Forbes, Jack D. *Apache, Navajo, and Spaniard.* Norman, 1960.

———. *Warriors of the Colorado.* Norman, 1965.

Forrest, Earle R. *Arizona's Dark and Bloody Ground.* Caldwell, Idaho, 1936, and reprint.

Frantz, Joe B., and Duke, Cordia S. *6000 Miles of Fence.* Austin, 1961.

Friend, Llerena. *Sam Houston: The Great Designer.* Austin, 1954.

Furniss, Norman F. *The Mormon Conflict, 1850–1859.* New Haven, 1966.

Garber, Paul N. *The Gadsden Treaty.* Philadelphia, 1923, and reprint.

Gard, Wayne. *Rawhide Texas.* Norman, 1965.

Garrett, Julia K. *Green Flag Over Texas.* New York, 1939.

Geiger, Maynard J. *The Life and Times of Fray Junípero Serra, O.F.M.* 2 vols. Washington, 1959.

Goetzman, William H. *Army Exploration in the American West, 1803–1863.* New Haven, 1965.

——. *Exploration and Empire: The Explorer and Scientist in the Winning of the American West.* New York, 1966.

Green, Thomas J. *Journal of the Texian Expedition Against Mier.* New York, 1845, and reprint.

Greever, William S. *The Bonanza West.* Norman, 1963.

Gregg, Josiah. *Commerce on the Prairies.* Available in several editions.

Grivas, Theodore. *Military Governments in California, 1846–1850.* Glendale, 1963.

Hackett, Charles W. (trans. and ed.). *Pichardo's Treatise on the Limits of Louisiana and Texas.* 3 vols. Austin, 1931–41.

——. *Revolt of the Pueblo Indians of New Mexico and Otermín's Attempted Reconquest.* 2 vols. Albuquerque, 1942.

Hafen, LeRoy R. *The Overland Mail, 1849–1869.* Cleveland, 1926.

Hagan, William T. *Indian Police and Judges.* New Haven, 1966.

Haley, J. Evetts. *Charles Goodnight, Cowman and Plainsman.* Norman, 1949.

——. *Jeff Milton: Good Man with a Gun.* Norman, 1948.

——. *The XIT Ranch of Texas.* Norman, 1953.

Hall, Martin H. *Sibley's New Mexico Campaign.* Austin, 1960.

Hallenbeck, Cleve. *The Journey of Fray Marcos de Niza.* Dallas, 1949.

Hammond, George P., and Agapito Rey. *Don Juan de Oñate.* Albuquerque, 1953.

——. *Narratives of the Coronado Expedition, 1540–1542.* Albuquerque, 1940.

Harris, Benjamin B. *The Gila Trail,* ed. by Richard H. Dillon. Norman, 1960.

Heyman, Max L. *Prudent Soldier: A Biography of Major General E. R. S. Canby, 1817–1873.* Glendale, 1959.

Hine, Robert V. *California's Utopian Colonies.* New Haven, 1965.

Hogan, William R. *The Texas Republic: A Social and Economic History.* Norman, 1946.

Hollon, W. Eugene. *The Great American Desert.* New York, 1966.

Holmes, Jack E. *Politics in New Mexico.* Albuquerque, 1967.

Horgan, Paul. *A Distant Trumpet.* New York, 1963.

——. *Great River: The Rio Grande.* 2 vols. New York, 1952.

Horn, Calvin. *New Mexico's Troubled Years.* Albuquerque, 1963.

Hough, Emerson. *North of 36.* New York, 1923, and reprints.

Hunt, Aurora. *Major General James Henry Carleton. 1814–1873.* Glendale, 1958.

Hutchinson, W. H. *A Bar Cross Man.* Norman, 1956.

Inman, Henry. *The Old Santa Fe Trail.* Topeka, 1899.

Jackson, W. Turrentine. *Wagon Roads West*. Berkeley, 1952.

Jacobs, Lewis. *The Rise of the American Film*. New York, 1939.

Johnson, Virginia W. *The Unregimented General: A Biography of Nelson A. Miles*. Boston, 1962.

Jones, Billy Mac. *Health-Seekers in the Southwest, 1817–1900*. Norman, 1967.

Jones, Oakah L., Jr. *Pueblo Warriors and the Spanish Conquest*. Norman, 1966.

Joralemon, Ira B. *Romantic Copper: Its Lure and Lore*. New York, 1935.

Keleher, William A. *Turmoil in New Mexico, 1846–1868*. Santa Fe, 1952.

———. *Violence in Lincoln County, 1869–1881*. Albuquerque, 1957.

Kendall, George W. *Narrative of the Texan–Santa Fe Expedition*. New York, 1844, and reprint.

Kerby, Robert L. *The Confederate Invasion of New Mexico, 1861–1862*. Los Angeles, 1958.

La Frage, Oliver. *Laughing Boy*. Boston, 1929, and reprint.

Lamar, Howard R. *The Far Southwest, 1846–1912*. New Haven, 1966.

Lavender, David S. *Bent's Fort*. Garden City, 1954.

Leckie, William H. *The Buffalo Soldiers*. Norman, 1967.

———. *The Military Conquest of the Southern Plains*. Norman, 1963.

Lummis, Charles F. *The Land of Poco Tiempo*. New York, 1902, and reprint.

McCoy, Joseph G. *Historic Sketches of the Cattle Trade of the West and Southwest*, ed. by Ralph P. Bieber. Glendale, 1940.

Mann, Dean E. *The Politics of Water in Arizona*. Tucson, 1963.

Marcosson, Isaac F. *Anaconda*. New York, 1957.

Marshall, James. *Santa Fe: The Railroad that Built an Empire*. New York, 1945.

Melendy, H. Brett, and Benjamin F. Gilbert. *The Governors of California*. Georgetown, California, 1965.

Myers, John M. *The Last Chance: Tombstone's Early Years*. New York, 1950.

Nevins, Allan. *Frémont: Pathmarker of the West*. New York, 1955.

Nordhoff, Walter. *The Journey of the Flame*. Boston, 1933, and reprint.

Oates, Stephen B. *Confederate Cavalry West of the River*. Austin, 1961.

Ormsby, Waterman L. *The Butterfield Overland Mail*, ed. by Lyle H. Wright and Josephine M. Bynum. San Marino, California, 1942.

Oswalt, Wendell H. *This Land Was Theirs: A Study of the North American Indians.* New York, 1966.

Parkman, Francis. *La Salle and the Discovery of the Great West.* Boston, 1898.

Pattie, James O. *Personal Narrative.* . . . Available in several editions.

Paul, Rodman W. *Mining Frontiers of the Far West, 1848–1880.* New York, 1963.

Pearce, William M. *The Matador Land and Cattle Company.* Norman, 1964.

Pelzer, Louis. *The Cattleman's Frontier.* Glendale, 1936.

Pike, Zebulon M. *An Account of Expeditions.* . . . Available in several editions.

Pitt, Leonard. *The Decline of the Californios: A Social History of the Spanish-Speaking Californians, 1846–1890.* Berkeley, 1966.

Pomeroy, Earl. *The Pacific Slope.* New York, 1965.

Richardson, Rupert N. *Comanche Barrier to South Plains Settlement.* Glendale, 1943.

Richman, Irving B. *California Under Spain and Mexico.* Boston, 1911.

Rickey, Don. *Forty Miles a Day on Beans and Hay.* Norman, 1963.

Rister, Carl C. *Oil! Titan of the Southwest.* Norman, 1949.

———. *The Southwestern Frontier, 1865–1881.* Cleveland, 1928.

Sacks, B. *Be it Enacted: The Creation of the Territory of Arizona.* Phoenix, 1964.

Schmitt, Martin F. (ed.). *General George Crook: His Autobiography.* Norman, 1960.

Siegel, Stanley. *A Political History of the Republic of Texas.* Austin, 1956.

Singletary, Otis A. *The Mexican War.* Chicago, 1960.

Smith, Cornelius C., Jr. *William Saunders Oury.* Tucson, 1967.

Smith, Fay, John Kessell, and Francis Fox. *Father Kino in Arizona.* Phoenix, 1966.

Smith, Justin. *The War With Mexico.* 2 vols. New York, 1919.

Sonnichsen, C. L. *The Mescalero Apaches.* Norman, 1958.

———. *Roy Bean: Law West of the Pecos.* New York, 1943.

Spicer, Edward H. *Cycles of Conquest: The Impact of Spain, Mexico, and the United States on the Indians of the Southwest.* Tucson, 1962.

Spratt, John S. *The Road to Spindletop.* Dallas, 1955.

Steward, George R. *John Phoenix, Esq., the Veritable Squibob.* New York, 1935.

Taylor, Virginia (trans. and ed.). *The Letters of Antonio Martinez.* Austin, 1957.

Terrell, John U. *War for the Colorado River*. 2 vols. Glendale, 1966.

Thomas, Alfred B. *Teodoro de Croix and the Northern Frontier of New Spain, 1776–1783*. Norman, 1941.

Thrapp, Dan L. *The Conquest of Apachería*. Norman, 1967.

Thurman, Michael E. *The Naval Department of San Blas: New Spain's Bastion for Alta California and Nootka*. Glendale, 1967.

Tolbert, Frank X. *An Informal History of Texas*. New York, 1961.

Towne, Charles W., and Edward N. Wentworth. *Shepherd's Empire*. Norman, 1945.

Twitchell, Ralph E. *Leading Facts of New Mexican History*. 5 vols. Cedar Rapids, Iowa, 1911–17.

Utley, Robert M. *Frontiersmen in Blue: The United States Army and the Indian, 1848–1865*. New York, 1967.

Wallace, Edward S. *The Great Reconnaissance*. Boston, 1955.

———. *Destiny and Glory*. Boston, 1957.

Wallace, Ernest, and E. A. Hoebel. *The Comanches*. Norman, 1952.

Warren, Harris G. *The Sword Was Their Passport*. Baton Rouge, 1943.

Webb, Walter P. *The Great Plains*. Boston, 1931, and reprints.

——— (ed.). *The Handbook of Texas*. 2 vols. Austin, 1952.

———. *The Texas Rangers*. New York, 1935.

Wellman, Paul I. *Broncho Apache*. New York, 1936.

———. *A Dynasty of Western Outlaws*. Garden City, 1961.

———. *Glory, God, and Gold*. Garden City, 1954.

———. *The Indian Wars of the West*. New York, 1954.

Wentworth, Edward N. *America's Sheep Trails*. Ames, Iowa, 1948.

Wilson, Neill C. *Southern Pacific: The Roaring Story of a Fighting Railroad*. New York, 1952.

Winther, Oscar O. *The Transportation Frontier*. New York, 1964.

Woodward, Arthur. *Feud on the Colorado*. Los Angeles, 1955.

———. *Lances at San Pascual*. San Francisco, 1948.

——— (ed.). *The Republic of Lower California, 1853–1854*. Los Angeles, 1966.

Wyllys, Rufus K. *The French in Sonora, 1850–1854*. Berkeley, 1932.

Young, Otis E. *How They Dug the Gold*. Tucson, 1966.

———. *The West of Philip St. George Cooke, 1809–1895*. Glendale, 1955.

INDEX

335

Soto, Hernando de, expedition of, 9, 17
South Platte River, 166
Southern Methodist University, 319
Southern Overland U. S. Mail and Express, 219
Southern Pacific Railroad, 246, 269; building of, 221–5; and California politics, 250, 252, 257–8; and Arizona politics, 252–3
Sour Lake Oil Field (Texas), 269
Spain in the Southwest, 5–92
Spanish-American War, 265
Spanish Fort (Texas), battle at, 53
Spade Ranch (Texas), 239
Spindletop Oil Field (Texas), 268–9
Springfield (Missouri), 220
Spur Ranch (Texas), 239
Stage lines: in California, 177; transcontinental, 177–9
Staked Plains, Coronado on, 15
Standard Oil Company, 254–5, 271
Stanford, Leland, 220, 250, 257
Stanford University, 277
Stanton, Edwin, 195
Steamboats, on the Colorado River, 179–81
Stearns, Abel, 103
Steen, Enoch, 157
Stephens, William D., 279–80, 314
Sterling, Ross, 308
Steven (Estevanico): with Cabeza de Vaca, 8–9; guides Marcos de Niza, 9–10
Stevens, Alexander H., 141
Stevenson, Coke, 309–10
Stillman, Clara, 318
Stimler, Harry, 230
Stockton, Robert F., 133–4
Stoneman, George, 135, 171, 213
Strait of Anián, search for, 18–21
Stratton, Emerson O., 231
Stuart, Alexander H. H., and boundary survey, 152
Sublette, William L., 100
Sulphur Springs (Arizona), 215
Summerland (California), 271
Sumner, Edwin V., 155
Sunnyvale (California), 298
Sunset City (Arizona), 243

Superior (Arizona), 232
Sutro, Adolph, 250
Sutter, John A., 103, 157
Sutter's Fort, 128, 132
Swilling, Jack, discovers gold, 226; irrigation project, 244–5
Swing-Johnson Act, 282

Taft Ranch (Texas), 239
Taft, William H., 266, 267
Tampico (Mexico), 45
Tamaulipas (Mexico), 45, 285. See also Nuevo Santander
Tampa Bay (Florida), 6, 17
Taos (New Mexico), 20, 23, 25, 27, 107, 141, 319; revolt at, 24, 136–137; mountain men at, 99
Tatum, Lawrie, 210
Taylor, John, 260
Taylor, Zachary: in Mexican War, 129–30; and Compromise of 1850, 140–41
Teapot Dome scandal, 312
Tehachapi Range (California), 271
Tehuas Pueblo (New Mexico), 25
Tejas Indians, 29, 30; missions for, 34–5, 37
Tejo, and Seven Cities of Cíbola, 9
Television industry, 298
Terminal Island (California), 292
Terrell Election Law (Texas), 255
Terrenate (Sonora), 48
Terreros, Alonso Giraldo de, and San Sabá mission, 52–3
Texas: Spaniards explore, 6–8, 28–30; French settle, 30–33; Spaniards settle, 34–40; Comanche wars, 46, 50–54, 169–70, 207, 209–12; Louisiana boundary, 85, 90; Mexican Revolution of 1810, 87–91; colonized by Americans, 107–11; Revolution, 111–19; Republic, 119–25, map, 124; Mexican War, 125–6, 129–30, 137; and Compromise of 1850, 138–47; roads opened to, 168–71; camels in, 182; population, 183; Civil War, 183–6, 189, 200–202; railroads, 220–25; land titles, 233–6; ranching, 236–9, 242–3; farming, 243–

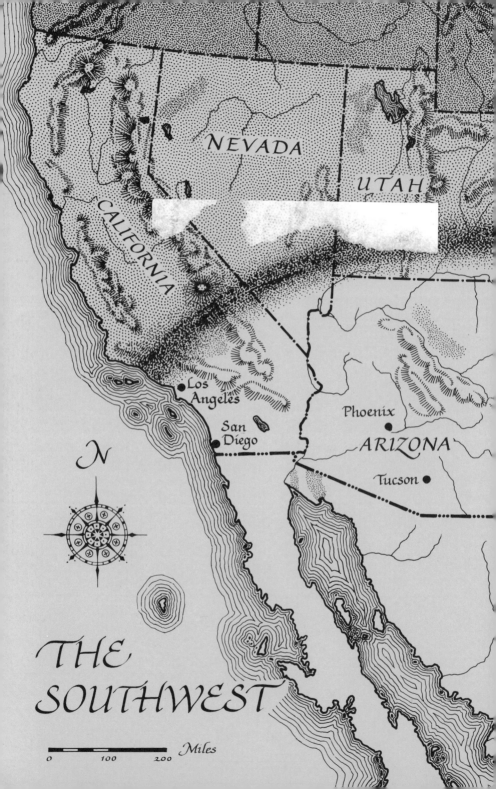

N

CALIFORNIA

NEVADA

UTAH

Los
Angeles

San
Diego

Phoenix

ARIZONA

Tucson

THE
SOUTHWEST

Miles

0   100   200